Basic Legal Research
for Paralegals

McGraw-Hill Business Careers Paralegal Titles

MCGRAW-HILL PARALEGAL TITLES: WHERE EDUCATIONAL SUPPORT GOES BEYOND EXPECTATIONS.

Building a solid foundation for a successful paralegal career is becoming more challenging as the needs of students and instructors continue to grow. The McGraw-Hill paralegal texts offer the solution to this ever-changing environment. Integrated real-world applications in each chapter teach students the practical skills needed for a thriving career in the field. A common vocabulary among all McGraw-Hill titles ensures consistency in learning. Up-to-date coverage of the available technology used in a legal setting and a purposefully designed set of pedagogical features with shared goals across the list provide the systems needed for students to fully grasp the material and apply it in a paralegal setting. With a thorough set of ancillaries and dedicated publisher support, these texts will facilitate active learning in the classroom and give students the skills sets desired by employers.

Introduction to Law & Paralegal Studies
Connie Farrell Scuderi
ISBN: 0073524638
© 2008

Introduction to Law for Paralegals
Deborah Benton
ISBN: 007351179X
© 2008

Basic Legal Research, Second Edition
Edward Nolfi
ISBN: 0073520519
© 2008

Basic Legal Writing, Second Edition
Pamela Tepper
ISBN: 0073403032
© 2008

Legal Research and Writing for Paralegals
Neal Bevans
ISBN: 007352462X
© 2008

Contract Law for Paralegals
Linda Spagnola
ISBN: 0073511765
© 2008

Civil Law and Litigation for Paralegals
Neal Bevans
ISBN: 0073524611
© 2008

Wills, Trusts, and Estates for Paralegals
George Kent
ISBN: 0073403067
© 2008

Legal Terminology Explained for Paralegals
Edward Nolfi
ISBN: 0073511846
© 2008

The Law Office Reference Manual
Jo Ann Lee
ISBN: 0073511838
© 2008

The Paralegal Reference Manual
Charles Nemeth
ISBN: 0073403075
© 2008

The Professional Paralegal
Allan Tow
ISBN: 0073403091
© 2009

Ethics for Paralegals
Linda Spagnola
ISBN: 0073376981
© 2009

Family Law for Paralegals
George Kent
ISBN: 0073376973
© 2009

Torts for Paralegals
ISBN: 0073376930
© 2009

Criminal Law for Paralegals
ISBN: 0073376965
© 2009

Real Estate Law for Paralegals
ISBN: 0073376957
© 2009

Law Office Management for Paralegals
ISBN: 0073376949
© 2009

Basic Legal Research for Paralegals

Second Edition

Edward A. Nolfi

Boston   Burr Ridge, IL   Dubuque, IA   Madison, WI   New York   San Francisco   St. Louis
Bangkok   Bogotá   Caracas   Kuala Lumpur   Lisbon   London   Madrid   Mexico City
Milan   Montreal   New Delhi   Santiago   Seoul   Singapore   Sydney   Taipei   Toronto

 **McGraw-Hill**
Irwin

BASIC LEGAL RESEARCH FOR PARALEGALS

Published by McGraw-Hill/Irwin, a business unit of The McGraw-Hill Companies, Inc., 1221 Avenue of the Americas, New York, NY, 10020. Copyright © 2008 by The McGraw-Hill Companies, Inc. All rights reserved. No part of this publication may be reproduced or distributed in any form or by any means, or stored in a database or retrieval system, without the prior written consent of The McGraw-Hill Companies, Inc., including, but not limited to, in any network or other electronic storage or transmission, or broadcast for distance learning.

Some ancillaries, including electronic and print components, may not be available to customers outside the United States.

This book is printed on acid-free paper.

1 2 3 4 5 6 7 8 9 0 VNH/VNH 0 9 8 7

ISBN   978-0-07-352051-3
MHID   0-07-352051-9

Editorial director: *John E. Biernat*
Publisher: *Linda Schreiber*
Associate sponsoring editor: *Natalie J. Ruffatto*
Developmental editor: *Tammy Higham*
Marketing manager: *Keari Bedford*
Project manager: *Bruce Gin*
Production supervisor: *Jason I. Huls*
Lead designer: *Matthew Baldwin*
Lead media project manager: *Cathy L. Tepper*
Cover design: *Studio Montage*
Cover image: *@Getty Images*
Typeface: *10/12 Times Roman*
Compositor: *Techbooks*
Printer: *Von Hoffmann Corporation*

Library of Congress Cataloging-in-Publication Data

Nolfi, Edward A., 1958-
    Basic legal research for paralegals / Edward A. Nolfi.—2nd ed.
        p. cm.—(McGraw-Hill business careers paralegal titles)
    Rev. ed. of: Basic legal research. c1993.
    Includes indexes.
    ISBN-13: 978-0-07-352051-3 (alk. paper)
    ISBN-10: 0-07-352051-9 (alk. paper)
    1.   Legal research—United States.   I. Nolfi, Edward A., 1958- Basic legal research.   II.   Title.
KF240.N65 2008
340.072'073—dc22

                                                                    2006035510

www.mhhe.com

Dedication

The first edition of this book was dedicated to my students. This edition is dedicated to my mentors and teachers, especially Alfred W. Gans and Earnest H. Schopler. Al said collect all the arguments and write your thesis. Earnest said let your writing be guided by your research.

About the Author

As an associate editor with the Lawyers Co-operative Publishing Company in the mid-1980s, Edward A. Nolfi learned legal research from the inside out. While preparing annotations for *American Law Reports, Federal,* and casenoting the Internal Revenue Code for the *United States Code Service,* he researched the knowledge, wisdom, tips, and tricks of current and former editors.

In 1988, Ed brought his wealth of knowledge to the paralegal classroom, leading the paralegal program at the Academy of Court Reporting in Akron, Ohio. In addition to engaging in the general practice of law, he later taught at several schools, including Kent State University in Kent, Ohio, and Mount Aloysius College in Cresson, Pennsylvania.

In 1999, Ed returned to law publishing as part of the $200 million Case Law Summaries Project at LexisNexis. He became the only case law editor promoted three times, to a position with both editorial and management duties, including project management and product development. After completing another look "behind the curtain" of law publishing, Ed shares more of his knowledge and insight in this second edition of *Basic Legal Research.*

Edward A. Nolfi's educational background includes receiving an A.B. with Honor Thesis (Religious Studies) from Brown University, and a J.D. (Law) from the University of Akron School of Law. He is admitted to the bar in New York and Ohio, and in several federal courts, including the United States Supreme Court. Ed is also the author of *Basic Wills, Trusts, and Estates,* and the *Ohio Supplement to Basic Civil Litigation,* each published by Glencoe/McGraw-Hill in the early 1990s.

Preface

Legal research is an art. It is a specialized knowledge blended with specialized skills. It is the knack of effectively using law books and other media. The key to its mastery is acquiring knowledge of the true nature of law books, accompanied by significant experience with their use and practical application.

In a candid speech to the Los Angeles Bar Association in 1932, William Mark McKinney, then Editor-in-Chief of the Bancroft-Whitney Company, spoke eloquently about the great value of law books, tempering his praise with an admission: "There is no such thing as a 100-percent perfect law book."

The law is embodied in words and contained in countless books and other media. But it is a serious mistake to believe that all legal resources are created equal. They are not. They must be carefully examined and questioned, and also used creatively, if their full value is to be obtained.

Most legal research books are sonorous legal bibliographies. They read like publishing house catalogs. The reader is introduced to one book after another and one feature after another, with little or no attempt to make sense of the books as a whole. The value of each book and each feature is never questioned. Thus, the reader is left with no sense of which books are good and which are bad; no sense of which ones are easy to use and which are difficult; no sense of which books are worth reading, and which ones should be left on the shelf.

The book in your hands is an "insider's guide" to the art of legal research. I have endeavored to rate fairly the principal books and features I discuss. In general, I have endeavored to describe how these books are actually written. Inside knowledge is invaluable. In the same way that a navigator's chart is a map of the sea, legal resources are a map of the law. If navigators fail to take into account the distortions inherent in their charts, they may go off course and not reach their desired destination. Similarly, if legal researchers fail to take into account the distortions inherent in the resource they are using, they may be deceived and not find the appropriate law they are looking for.

This book does not cover every legal resource. No one can claim an intimate knowledge of every legal resource. Yet, experienced legal researchers know that some resources are used repeatedly, or should be, while others are to be used rarely, if at all. This book, *Basic Legal Research,* covers the principal law books and other legal resources used by general practice lawyers and paralegals in the United States, with a decided emphasis on national sources. If, after reading this book, you want to know more, you can always consult a sonorous legal bibliography, local guide, or specialized text.

ORGANIZATION OF THE TEXT

The book's text is divided up into 13 chapters. Each includes a systematic approach that introduces legal research through a summary of the U.S. legal system, law publishing, law books, and law libraries, with a section on the purpose of legal research and strategies. The Appendix provides the text of the most fundamental document in U.S. legal research, the Constitution of the United States.

The principal sources of the law—such as cases, statutes, constitutions, court rules, and administrative regulations—are described and their use discussed. Secondary sources of law are explored and their value and use to the researcher are examined. Proper legal citations are described and analyzed. How to use *Shephard's Citators, The Bluebook: A Uniform System of Citation,* as well as *ALWD* are explained. Finally, an overview of how to use computer-assisted legal research is provided along with the most popular and recognized sources. All of the chapters build a systematic base for how to best navigate through the vast amount of legal resources available to the researcher.

Text Design

Each chapter begins with course objectives followed by an introduction. A "case fact pattern" opens the discussion in each chapter, presenting a sample situation in which the student is introduced to the information discussed in the chapter. A Day in the Life of a Real Paralegal concludes each chapter, wrapping up the key topics covered in the chapter.

This text is designed to be user-friendly. Key terms are boldfaced and defined in the margin, with an alphabetical list of these terms at the end of each chapter. This edition includes several new boxed features:

- **Research This** provides students with hands-on tasks, asking them to apply the legal research techniques discussed in the text.

- **CYBER TRIP** focuses on the important role the Internet plays in legal research and provides Web links and information about online resources.

- **Eye on Ethics** keeps ethics in the forefront, raising issues every paralegal will face in the profession.

Further, each chapter contains assessments, exercises, and a puzzle to amplify the legal research concepts presented, thus enhancing the learning process. Students are encouraged to complete all assessments and activities, and to keep this text at home or in the office as a handy desk reference.

Acknowledgments

The author wishes to acknowledge the contributions of the following reviewers, whose efforts, suggestions, ideas, and insights helped shape this text into the valuable tool it is.

Donna Bookin
Mercy College

Bob Diotalevi
Florida Gulf Coast University

Amy Feeney
Wilmington College

Angela Masciulli
MTI College

Broderick Nichols
University of Memphis

B. Arthur Swerine
DeVry University

Debbie Vinecour
SUNY-Rockland

The author also gives special thanks to his wife, Sheri, and his sons, Anthony and Brian, for enduring everything.

A Guided Tour

Basic Legal Research

This book is an "insider's guide" to the art of legal research. Using a hands-on approach, BLR provides students with an easy and approachable way to learn about the processes, materials, and background of legal research. It explains the many methods of legal research in a simple and straightforward manner and language. This text is essential for all law office personnel and paralegal professionals.

The pedagogy of the book applies three goals:

Learning Outcomes

- Critical thinking

- Vocabulary building

- Skill development

- Issues analysis

- Writing practices

Relevance of Topics without Sacrificing Theory

- Ethical challenges

- Current law practices

- Technology application

Practical Application

- Real-world exercises

- Portfolio creation

- Team exercises

Chapter Objectives

Chapter Objectives introduce the concepts students should understand after reading each chapter as well as provide brief summaries describing the material to be covered.

Chapter 1

Before Beginning Legal Research

CHAPTER OBJECTIVES

After reading this chapter, you should be able to:

- Understand the importance of legal research.
- Explain the purpose of legal research.
- Understand how legal research is used by the attorney.
- Understand the role of the paralegal or legal assistant as a research assistant.
- Identify the process of legal research.

The mastery of legal research is one of the most critical skills sought in people seeking employment in a legal environment. Most legal documents will require the locating, analyzing, and communicating of the law by legal professionals. This task is usually completed by paralegals and legal assistants. This chapter will demonstrate how to establish a starting point from which to launch your legal research.

Case Fact Patterns

Case Fact Patterns ask students to dig a little deeper and give more information on a research topic, something they will do on the job.

Eye on Ethics

Eye on Ethics raises legitimate ethical questions and situations attorneys and paralegals often face.

A Day in the Life

A Day in the Life gives the students a look at what the on-the-job experience will be, incorporating real-world research and procedural assignments.

Cyber Trip

Cyber Trip provides a list of relevant Web sites that students should visit in order to learn more about the topics presented in the chapter. Often, questions are posed to the students in order to help them determine how these Web sites could help in the everyday life of a paralegal.

Research This!

Research This! engages students to research cases in their jurisdiction that answer a hypothetical scenario, reinforcing the critical skills of independent research.

Chapter Summary

Chapter Summary provides a quick review of the key concepts presented in the chapter.

Summary

The legislative branch of government makes statutes. Federal law is made in the sense of being "dreamed up" by Congress. A proposed permanent law introduced in the House of Representatives or in the Senate is known as a bill. A bill that passes both houses is presented to the President and becomes law if the President signs it, if the President returns it within 10 days (Sunday excepted) and the veto is overridden by a two-thirds vote in each house, or if the President does not return it within 10 days (Sunday excepted) and the houses of Congress have not adjourned. Bills should be compared and contrasted with joint resolutions, concurrent resolutions, and simple resolutions. The laws enacted by the legislature are subject to interpretation by the courts. As a practical matter, the only time a legal researcher need research legislative history is if a court is deciding a case of first impression as to interpreting a statute. Legislative intent can be inferred from amendments, committee reports, debates, and hearings. While state legislative history theoretically exists, sources of state legislative history are usually nonexistent. Slip laws are collected and officially published in chronological order by the U.S. Government Printing Office in the *United States Statutes at Large* (Stat.).

Statutes come out chronologically, but they may be found topically with a specialized collection known as a code. The process of collecting permanent public statutes topically, adding amendments, and deleting expired, repealed, or superseded statutes is known as codification. The *United States Code* (U.S.C.) officially collects federal statutes topically in 50 titles. Titles may be divided into subtitles, chapters, subchapters, parts, and subparts. Under each title, statutes are organized into sections. Sections may be divided into subsections, paragraphs, subparagraphs, sentences, and words. Statutes are cited by title number, code abbreviation, and section number. The U.S.C. does not provide useful cross-references to other law books and it does not include summaries of court opinions that have interpreted particular statutes. Thomson/West and LexisN... ach publish a f... tated code. Each ... ltivolume se... ach title of

Key Terms

Key Terms used throughout the chapters are defined in the margin and provided as a list at the end of each chapter. A common set of definitions is used consistently across the McGraw-Hill paralegal titles.

Key Terms

administrative agencies	9	executive order	9
case law	9	*ex post facto*	9
case of first impression	8	FAQ	14
cases	9	federalism	8
common law	8	judicial	9
constitutional law	8	jurisprudence	7
executive	9	justices	13

Discussion Questions and Exercises

Discussion Questions and Exercises ask students to apply critical thinking skills to the concepts learned in each chapter. The Discussion Questions focus on more specific legal topics and promote dialogue among students. The Exercises introduce hypothetical situations, and students will determine the correct answers using their knowledge of topics presented in the chapter. Both sets of questions are found at the end of each chapter.

Exercises

1. Visit Web sites for LexisNexis, Westlaw, and www.findlaw.com. Look at the materials and describe the similarities and differences between them.
2. Go to www.uscourts.gov and find the information related to the United States Bankruptcy Courts. What is the difference between Chapter 7 and Chapter 13 bankruptcy?
3. Go to www.law.cornell.edu and find the Uniform Commercial Code. Describe what the Uniform Commercial Code covers.

Vocabulary Builders

Vocabulary Builders at the end of each chapter utilize the key terms to help students become more familiar using their legal vocabulary.

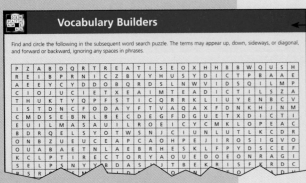

Vocabulary Builders

Find and circle the following in the subsequent word search puzzle. The terms may appear up, down, sideways, or diagonal, and forward or backward, ignoring any spaces in phrases.

Supplements

Instructor's Resource CD-ROM

An Instructor's Resource CD-ROM (IRCD) will be available for instructors. This CD provides a number of instructional tools, including PowerPoint presentations for each chapter in the text, an instructor's manual, and an electronic test bank. The instructor's manual assists with the creation and implementation of the course by supplying lecture notes, answers to all exercises, page references, additional discussion questions and class activities, a key to using the PowerPoint presentations, detailed lesson plans, instructor support features, and grading rubrics for assignments. A unique feature, an instructor matrix, also is included that links learning objectives with activities, grading rubrics, and classroom equipment needs. The activities consist of individual and group exercises, research projects, and scenarios with forms to fill out. The electronic test bank will offer a variety of multiple choice, fill-in-the-blank, true/false, and essay questions, with varying levels of difficulty and page references.

Online Learning Center

The Online Learning Center (OLC) is a Web site that follows the text chapter-by-chapter. OLC content is ancillary and supplementary and is germane to the textbook—as students read the book, they can go online to review material or link to relevant Web sites. Students and instructors can access the Web sites for each of the McGraw-Hill paralegal texts from the main page of the Paralegal Super Site. Each OLC has a similar organization. An Information Center features an overview of the text, background on the author, and the Preface and Table of Contents from the book. Instructors can access the instructor's manual and PowerPoint presentations from the IRCD. Students see the Key Terms list from the text as flashcards, as well as additional quizzes and exercises. The OLC can be delivered multiple ways—professors and students can access the site directly through the textbook Web site, through PageOut, or within a course management system (i.e., WebCT, Blackboard, TopClass, or eCollege).

PageOut: McGraw-Hill's Course Management System PageOut

is McGraw-Hill's unique point-and-click course Web site tool, enabling you to create a full-featured, professional-quality course Web site without knowing HTML coding. With PageOut, you can post your syllabus online, assign McGraw-Hill Online Learning Center or eBook content, add links to important offsite resources, and maintain student results in the online grade book. You can send class announcements, copy your course site to share with colleagues, and upload original files. PageOut is free for every McGraw-Hill/Irwin user and, if you're short on time, we even have a team ready to help you create your site! To learn more, please visit http://www.pageout.net.

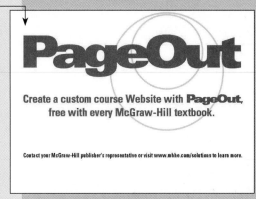

Create a custom course Website with **PageOut**, free with every McGraw-Hill textbook.

Contact your McGraw-Hill publisher's representative or visit www.mhhe.com/solutions to learn more.

Brief Table of Contents

Table of Contents

Chapter 1

Before Beginning Legal Research

CHAPTER OBJECTIVES

After reading this chapter, you should be able to:

- Understand the importance of legal research.

- Explain the purpose of legal research.

- Understand how legal research is used by the attorney.

- Understand the role of the paralegal or legal assistant as a research assistant.

- Identify the process of legal research.

The mastery of legal research is one of the most critical skills sought in people seeking employment in a legal environment. Most legal documents will require the locating, analyzing, and communicating of the law by legal professionals. This task is usually completed by paralegals and legal assistants. This chapter will demonstrate how to establish a starting point from which to launch your legal research.

THE PURPOSE OF LEGAL RESEARCH

Why do legal research at all? What is the big deal? Doesn't the judge know all the law? It can't be that complicated, can it?

Legal research is important because the law is important. The law is made up of rules and procedures that govern our daily lives. The law is complicated, but legal research will allow you to cut through it and make effective arguments to the judge. Ethical codes and rules require legal professionals be competent, and legal research ability is part of that competence.

THE COURT MAY NOT KNOW

One of the biggest misconceptions about the law is the notion that the courts know everything there is to know about the law. Courts are run by judges, who are human beings. No one has ever read all of the existing cases, statutes, regulations, and other sources of the law. Moreover, the law is always changing. It is so vast that no one person can ever know all of it. The best one can do is research the law, thoroughly.

Just because judges can't know everything, however, does not mean they don't know anything. In the same way that the average paralegal knows more law than the average layman, and the average lawyer knows more law than the average paralegal, so the average judge knows more law than the average lawyer, and thus is worthy of respect. However, because

Case Fact Pattern

A local accounting firm has come to the law firm where you work seeking representation in a lawsuit. It seems three former employees of the accounting firm are suing the firm for physical injuries and damages that they sustained as a result of exposure to second-hand smoke in the office. The employees do not have individual offices, but each has their own cubicle. The firm has designated a smoking area within the building that is separate and down the hallway from the employee cubicles. Employees of the firm are required to remain in the smoking area when smoking in the office. However, smoke travels throughout the office. The former employees claim they were exposed to second-hand smoke and developed physical ailments that they allege are a result of this exposure. The attorney assigned to the case has asked you to research the pertinent issues as they relate to current laws and to relay your findings in a legal memorandum.

judges don't know every law, they can be convinced by an effective argument. The wise advocate tactfully makes the judge aware of the law, to the advocate's—and the advocate's client's—advantage.

LEGAL KNOWLEDGE AND RESEARCH

Attorneys spend a great deal of time learning about the law. However, no matter how much time someone spends studying it, it is impossible for anyone to know all the law about every topic and from every jurisdiction. Hence, even the most experienced attorneys must be able to do legal research. In addition, the law changes constantly. Every year thousands and thousands of laws change all over the United States. These changes could be anything from a city ordinance to a U.S. Supreme Court ruling. In order for a lawyer to make proper representations to courts of the status of the law—as it relates to their clients' cases—it is imperative for them to be able to stay abreast of the continual changes in the law, especially in the jurisdiction in which they practice. The process of finding the law is called legal research.

Attorneys are required to prepare legal documents as well as appear in court. The legal research that they use in their craft must be appropriate, relevant, and up-to-date. Basing a client's case on bad legal research and analysis could lead to the following: losing the client's case; a loss of reputation; embarrassment; sanctions by the court; and, in some cases, malpractice suits, disbarment, or some other disciplinary action. Good legal research is extremely important to the attorney because their license to practice law could be on the line.

Attorneys are typically charged with handling numerous cases at the same time. Their time is valuable and limited. Therefore, many attorneys rely on paralegals and legal assistants to handle the time-consuming and often tedious job of conducting legal research. The research conducted by a paralegal or legal assistant is extremely important. The attorney will use the research gathered by staff members to advise clients, write legal documentation, and argue in court. Accuracy and thoroughness in this research is expected and valued.

Eye on Ethics

For lawyers in most states, Rule 1.1 of the Rules of Professional Conduct generally requires lawyers to provide competent representation to their clients, including the thoroughness and preparation reasonably necessary for competent representation. For lawyers in the few states still governed by the Code of Professional Responsibility—Disciplinary Rule 6-101(A)(2)—generally requires that lawyers not handle legal matters without adequate preparation. The only way for a lawyer to be fully prepared to discuss a specific matter of the law and, if necessary, argue about it on behalf of a client, is to have engaged in competent legal research. When a paralegal is engaged in legal research for a lawyer, under the supervision of the lawyer, the paralegal is engaged in one of the most important legal activities in which a paralegal is permitted to engage.

Eye on Ethics

A paralegal or legal assistant is not permitted to offer legal advice because they are not licensed to practice law. While paralegals and legal assistants work under the supervision of attorneys, giving legal advice is outside the scope of their knowledge and is unethical. A paralegal or legal assistant who gives legal advice is engaging in the unauthorized practice of law, which is illegal and can result in criminal punishment in some jurisdictions. The job of advising the client must be left to the person licensed to practice law: the attorney.

Lawyers rarely research the law for academic purposes. Their research centers on the facts of a client's case. As such, it is not enough just to find the law—the law must be analyzed as it pertains to the facts of the client's case. The lawyer must research and analyze the law so the legal argument portrays the client's position in the most favorable light. The argument can take the form of written documents such as pleadings filed with the court, or oral arguments as in the closing argument given in a court trial. Whether written or oral, it is very important for the law that has been uncovered to be analyzed as it relates to the client's case.

The legal research process is comprised of the following steps:

legal issue
The point in dispute between two or more parties in a lawsuit.

- Identify the pertinent facts in the case at hand.
- Identify the **legal issue** to be researched.
- Find the law applicable to the legal issue.
- Analyze the law as it relates to the legal issue and facts of the case at hand.
- Communicate the findings of the research and analysis.

GETTING STARTED

How does the legal professional begin legal research? A good researcher must ask some basic questions when given an assignment. The first question should be "What is the deadline for this assignment?" All legal research assignments will have deadlines. The attorney may have a deadline to file a pleading with the court, they may appear in court, or they may simply be trying to decide if they want to take on this particular client's case. The amount of time available will shape the overall approach to the legal research assignment. A researcher faced with a tight deadline must effectively manage time to finish the project by the said deadline.

Another important consideration is the form of the final research product. In the case fact pattern described earlier, the attorney has asked the research take the form of a legal memorandum. Other forms, that could be required, include briefings of pertinent case law or legal pleadings and briefs. Whatever the form, it is important to be clear on what the final work product should look like.

What is the scope that the research should take? Does the attorney want it limited to case law, statutes, or administrative procedures? Should online research tools be utilized? Some clients may not want to pay the fees and costs associated with having the attorney use online research tools such as Lexis or Westlaw. Understand the parameters under which the legal research should be conducted and stay within them.

jurisdiction
The power or authority of the court to hear a particular classification of case.

An important consideration is which **jurisdiction** controls the incident. The jurisdiction can limit or expand the research depending on the facts. For example, in the client's case presented in the case fact pattern, many cities have local smoking ordinances that may control the issue. The scope of the research could be limited to city ordinances. Is it a state or federal issue? Jurisdictional determinations are extremely important when conducting legal research. The legal researcher must avoid spending time researching a legal issue using the wrong types of legal materials.

Remember, most attorneys and legal practitioners have done a fair amount of legal research during their careers. These practitioners are a good source of information about where to get started. An attorney with substantial experience in an area of law can significantly reduce the

RESEARCH THIS

Examine the factual issues in the case fact pattern concerning the former employees and their allegations regarding exposure to second-hand smoke.

amount of time spent researching an issue by pointing you to past research which may only need to be updated. Asking an attorney or legal practitioner where to begin can prove invaluable.

HAVING A BASIC PLAN

strategy
A method for making, doing, or accomplishing something.

It is very important to outline a basic plan or **strategy** to legal research. There are important steps necessary to design a well thought out approach. The temptation exists to delve into legal authorities looking for pertinent legal research, but a good researcher takes time to think about the facts and develop a plan. Specific legal strategies will be discussed in the next chapter.

CREATING A LIST OF VOCABULARY TERMS

Every case will lend itself to creating a list of pertinent vocabulary terms. Some of these terms can be factual terms such as "second-hand smoke," while others may be legal terms such as "wrongful termination." It is important to sort through the facts of the case and separate the vocabulary terms into these two sections. Once you have determined the legal vocabulary, it will be easier to determine the legal issues based on them. The factual vocabulary will help you analyze the law as it relates to the facts of the case. Do not be concerned if you are not sure if a vocabulary term is factual or legal. Write it down where you think it fits best. As you conduct your legal research, the authorities will assist you in determining if you are correct.

FORMULATING THE LEGAL RESEARCH ISSUE

CYBER TRIP

You may obtain pertinent information regarding your vocabulary terms by searching them online. Various Web sites, both legal and nonlegal, can offer great assistance in learning more about your term. Some useful sites are

- www.google.com
- www.findlaw.com
- www.answers.com

If possible, attempt to identify the legal issue that needs to be researched. A good legal issue will contain the legal problem along with key facts. Think about your case and try to determine what the legal issue may be, as well as the key facts that support that issue. Again, do not be so concerned about being right or wrong. Your research will assist you in determining the proper course. The purpose of initially articulating a legal issue is just to get you started with your research. Your legal issue does not have to be a formal statement. It is simply a way to organize your thoughts and get you started. It is a preliminary assessment of the problem established by the facts of your case.

 A Day in the Life

The case fact pattern presented at the beginning of this chapter involves current topics. Many cities are enacting ordinances banning smoking from areas of the building, entire buildings, restaurants, and even beaches. For instance, Los Angeles has had smoke-free environments for years and the famous beach of Santa Monica is smoke-free. For facts regarding this area, the first place to begin legal research would be the local city ordinances. The issue of someone being harmed by inhaling second-hand smoke has been surging into the news lately. Even though this issue is timely, no law may have been created on this topic as of yet. Research of factual issues can help guide the attorney on how best to frame his client's argument. Maybe your client's case will be the first one in this area and thus establish a guideline for all those that follow.

FIGURE 1.1
Search Record

Source	Other Source	Other Source Searched	Case Cites

WRITING OUT YOUR PLAN

In order to proceed in an organized and efficient manner, it is important to write out your research plan. Your written plan should consist of the following:

- A vocabulary list of both factual and legal terms
- An initial legal problem or issue
- An outline of the sources to be checked to gather the law

Once you have created your vocabulary list, look up the terms in a legal dictionary and a legal thesaurus. These two sources will help expand your knowledge and your list of identifiable terms to search. Your vocabulary lists will also assist you in efficiently checking the indexes of the various sources of legal research to find the law pertinent to your facts more quickly.

Being organized and having a plan is essential to beginning your legal research. Keeping a record of the sources in which you are conducting your search, along with the results, can be extremely beneficial so that you do not duplicate your efforts. For example, you might create a table to track the sources you searched and the cases that were cited for each source. Figure 1.1 is a sample Search Record Table. As you conduct your searches for either your factual or legal terms, write down the sources as you review them along with pertinent cases that are cited in each source. Using such a table will enable you to streamline your research efforts.

Summary

Attorneys spend a great deal of time learning about the law. However, no matter how much time someone spends studying the law it is impossible for anyone to know all the law about every topic and from every jurisdiction. Therefore, even the most experienced attorneys must be able to do legal research. To add to this, the law changes constantly. Every year, thousands and thousands of laws change all over the United States. These changes could be anything from a city ordinance to a U.S. Supreme Court ruling. In order for a lawyer to make proper representations to courts on the status of the law as it relates to their clients' cases, it is imperative for them to be able to stay abreast of the constant changes in the law, especially in the jurisdiction where they practice. The process of finding the law is called legal research.

The legal research process is comprised of the following steps: (1) identify the pertinent facts in the case at hand; (2) identify the legal issue to be researched; (3) find the law applicable to the legal issue; (4) analyze the law as it relates to the legal issue and facts of the case at hand; and (5) communicate the findings of the research and analysis.

Remember, most attorneys and legal practitioners have done a fair amount of legal research during their careers. These practitioners are a good source of information about where to get started. An attorney with substantial experience in an area of law can significantly reduce the amount of time spent researching an issue by pointing you to past research which may only need to be updated. Asking an attorney or legal practitioner where to begin can prove invaluable.

It is very important to outline a basic plan or strategy to legal research. There are important steps necessary to design a well thought out approach. The temptation exists to delve into legal authorities looking for pertinent legal research, but a good researcher takes time to think about the facts and develop a plan.

Key Terms	jurisdiction 3	strategy 4
	legal issue 3	

Review Questions

1. Why is it important to conduct legal research?
2. What can happen to an attorney who argues bad law?
3. Can paralegals give legal advice to clients under the supervision of an attorney?
4. What is a legal issue?
5. What is the first question that should be asked when given a research assignment?
6. Why is jurisdiction important to legal research?
7. Why should you create vocabulary lists?
8. Define strategy.
9. A research plan should have which three elements?

Exercises

1. Create a research plan and vocabulary lists for the assignment given in the case fact pattern presented at the beginning of this chapter.
2. Look up in both a legal dictionary and a legal thesaurus all vocabulary terms you created for the case fact pattern and expand on the terms created. Create a legal issue.
3. Write down a list of places you might search when researching the issues in the case fact pattern presented at the beginning of this chapter.

Vocabulary Builders

Find and circle the following terms in the subsequent word search puzzle. The terms may appear up, down, sideways, or diagonal, and forward or backward, ignoring any spaces in phrases.

F	Z	A	B	D	Q	R	A	I	D	J	U	R	I	S	D	I	C	T	I	O	N	Q	U	S	B
A	E	I	B	P	R	N	I	C	Z	B	V	Y	H	U	S	Y	D	I	C	T	P	B	A	A	E
L	E	G	A	L	I	S	S	U	E	Q	R	D	S	A	N	M	V	I	D	S	Q	I	L	M	P
E	I	O	J	U	C	I	E	T	X	E	K	I	M	W	E	A	D	I	C	T	I	L	S	Z	A
N	H	U	K	T	Y	Q	P	F	S	C	I	C	Q	E	R	K	L	I	U	R	E	N	B	C	V
C	S	T	D	H	C	F	O	D	V	Y	F	T	N	T	Q	A	X	F	D	A	K	H	J	N	M
Y	M	D	S	B	B	N	L	C	E	C	D	I	N	V	D	G	U	E	T	T	D	I	C	T	I
C	E	I	L	W	A	S	C	U	I	L	L	A	E	C	C	Y	C	I	K	E	O	P	E	D	E
L	D	N	Q	C	L	K	Y	O	T	T	L	N	J	M	I	U	N	O	U	G	L	K	J	D	A
B	N	B	R	Y	L	U	C	E	U	P	C	A	O	R	P	E	J	U	R	Y	S	T	G	V	B
S	U	A	B	O	E	T	N	O	A	E	B	R	H	D	S	K	L	O	P	Y	M	S	C	E	I
K	C	L	P	D	T	R	E	C	T	O	R	Y	A	O	U	E	D	J	E	H	N	R	A	G	J
P	E	L	P	N	N	T	F	B	D	A	S	J	J	T	B	E	K	L	O	S	F	K	R	D	K
R	S	R	O	E	E	M	A	N	I	D	D	E	C	O	N	C	Y	C	L	O	P	E	A	D	I
O	O	Z	A	R	X	N	S	Y	R	J	D	I	R	E	C	Y	M	H	E	I	I	G	O	I	A
C	O	R	P	U	S	J	U	R	I	S	S	T	S	I	L	Y	R	A	L	U	B	A	C	O	V

ATTORNEY, JURISDICTION, LEGAL ISSUE, PLAN, STRATEGY, and VOCABULARY LIST.

Chapter 2

Introduction to Legal Research

CHAPTER OBJECTIVES

After reading this chapter, you should be able to:

• Identify the origins of the U.S. legal system in English history.

• Define "common law."

• Describe the basic structure of the U.S. legal system.

• Understand the significance of "federalism" and "separation of powers" for legal research.

• Appreciate why master legal researchers know "who publishes what."

• Distinguish primary authority from secondary authority.

• Explain why law librarians avoid giving patrons *the* answer to legal questions.

• Recognize the importance of getting the facts, and develop appropriate entry terms.

• Describe basic legal research strategy.

In this chapter, you will learn about the origins and nature of the U.S. legal system, law publishing, and what ties them together: the need to do legal research. You will learn about law books and law libraries, both physical and electronic. You will also learn about the legal research strategies.

THE U.S. LEGAL SYSTEM

jurisprudence
The science of law; namely, that science whose function is to ascertain the principles on which legal rules are based, so as not only to classify those rules in their proper order and show the relation in which they stand to one another, but also to settle the manner in which new or doubtful cases should be brought under the appropriate rules.

It is evident that to do legal research you must have an adequate understanding of the legal system. It is also evident that to have an adequate understanding of the legal system, you must be able to recognize the law in all its forms. In short, you must know the "sources of the law."

The U.S. legal system is complex. We inherited the sophisticated legal system of medieval England, and to avoid the tyranny of a king, modified it with the Constitution of the United States. As a result, to research U.S. law effectively, a legal researcher must know and appreciate a few fundamental facts, myths, and legends from world, English, and American history.

Law Is the Command of a Sovereign

What is the law? There are many answers to this question, and together the answers form our **jurisprudence,** a term used to describe both the philosophy of law and the law collectively.

Case Fact Pattern

Your child was born at City Hospital last week, and your father has given you $100 to open a bank account in your child's name. The clerk at the bank says you need a Social Security number to open the account. The clerk at the Social Security Administration says you need a birth certificate to get a number. The clerk at the Health Department says you can't get the birth certificate because City Hospital hasn't filed it yet. The clerk at City Hospital says it takes eight weeks to process the birth certificate, because it is necessary to get the doctor's signature. What are you going to do? Who are you going to believe? What is the law regarding birth certificates? How do you find out?

law
A set of rules and principles that govern any society.

sovereign
A person, body, or state in which independent and supreme authority is vested.

precedent
The holding of past court decisions that are followed in future judicial cases where similar facts and legal issues are present.

stare decisis
Decisions from a court with substantially the same set of facts should be followed by that court and all lower courts under it.

common law
Judge-made law; the ruling in a judicial opinion.

case of first impression
A case in which no previous court decision with similar facts or legal issue has arisen before.

U.S. Constitution
The fundamental law of the United States of America, which became the law of the land in March of 1789.

constitutional law
Based on federal constitution and arising from interpretations of the intent and scope of constitutional provisions.

federalism
Balanced system of national and state government in the U.S. Constitution; the federal government has jurisdiction over all matters related equally to all citizens of all states, and the state governments have specific authority in matters affecting only the citizens of the respective state entity.

Indeed, the leading encyclopedia covering "all the law of America" is entitled *American Jurisprudence.* For the purpose of legal research, one definition serves as a beacon for lawyers, law students, paralegals, and legal researchers of all kinds. Simply stated, **law** is the command of a sovereign.

It is easy to understand what a command is—someone telling you what you can or cannot do—but what is a sovereign? By definition, a **sovereign** is a person or entity with the power to command. The classic sovereign is the king. Who makes the laws, the commands, which people must follow? The classic answer, still true in many parts of the world today, is that the most powerful person, the one who can enforce obedience, is sovereign.

Common-Law Origins

Following the rule established for the preceding similar case, the **precedent,** is known as the doctrine of *stare decisis* (Latin for "stand by that decided"). By following precedent (the rules of law made by judges in deciding actual cases), the judges, over time, made rules of law common to all of England, known as the **common law.** Restated, the common law is the law made by judges in deciding actual cases—that is, a legal system emphasizing case law.

By following the doctrine of *stare decisis,* the judges put some predictability into their decisions: they would follow the reasoning of the most similar past case, unless they decided that its reasoning would not apply. The only kind of case not directly decided according to precedent was a **case of first impression**—a case without precedent.

The Origins of the Constitution of the United States

Ratified on June 21, 1788, and put into effect on April 30, 1789, the **U.S. Constitution** is the fundamental law of the land. Two aspects of the Constitution, two aspects of **constitutional law,** are of great significance to the legal researcher: federalism and the separation of powers. Both were designed, in part, to prevent any one person from attaining the power, and the inevitable tyranny, of a king.

Federalism

The preamble of the Constitution of the United States proclaims: "We the People of the United States . . . do ordain and establish this Constitution." Ultimate sovereignty was placed in the people, but immediately expressed in the Constitution. The Constitution created a new sovereign—the federal government of the United States of America. Under **federalism,** the federal government is a limited sovereign, having only the powers explicitly or implicitly granted it in the Constitution, primarily the powers granted the Congress in Article I, Section 8.

As the 10th Amendment reflects, the states retained sovereignty over all powers not granted to the federal government. Thus, the person researching U.S. law must be aware that there are 51 sovereigns in the United States: the federal government (including the District of Columbia) and 50 state governments. (See Figure 2.1.) The first step in legal research is to determine if the subject to be researched is a matter of federal law or state law, and if state law, of what state.

separation of powers
A form of checks and balances to ensure that one branch does not become dominant.

legislative
The branch of government that makes law.

ex post facto
"After the fact," by an act or fact occurring beyond some previous act of fact, and relating thereto.

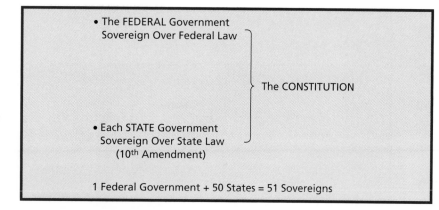

FIGURE 2.1   **The Federalism Compromise**

CYBER TRIP

The main research Web site for Congress is http://thomas.loc.gov, which was named to honor Thomas Jefferson.

CYBER TRIP

The official Web site for the President of the United States is www.whitehouse.gov.

CYBER TRIP

The official Web site for the U.S. Supreme Court is www.supremecourtus.gov.

Separation of Powers

As Articles I, II, and III reflect, the powers of the federal government, under the Constitution, are divided into three branches: legislative, executive, and judicial. This division, maintained by checks and balances, is the **separation of powers.**

Under Article I, the **legislative** branch, headed by Congress, makes new laws. When it enacts a law, it makes a reality in the future. Indeed, the ***ex post facto*** ("after the fact") clauses of the Constitution prohibit criminal laws from having a retroactive effect. **Statutes** are the laws the legislative branch makes, and law from the legislative branch is generally known as **statutory law.**

Under Article II, the **executive** branch, headed by the President, enforces the law. The executive branch sees that the laws are "faithfully executed." When the executive branch enforces a law, it is a reality in the present. To announce the exercise of a discretionary power, the executive may issue an **executive order.** The President, with the advice and consent of the Senate, also negotiates nation-binding agreements with foreign countries, known as **treaties.**

Under Article III, the **judicial** branch, headed by the Supreme Court, interprets the law. The judicial branch reviews the law, and makes law only in deciding actual legal controversies, known as **cases.** When the judicial branch interprets a law, its reality applies to events in the past, and a precedent is laid down for the future. Law from the judicial branch is generally known as **case law.**

Unstated in the Constitution, but understood by the lawyers at both the time the Constitution was written as well as today, is the fact that the Constitution did not displace the common law of England and colonial America. Unless a federal or state constitution or statute changed the common law, U.S. judges continued, and continue today, to apply the common law, as developed in the United States since the American Revolution.

In addition, especially under the legislative and executive branches, **administrative agencies** have been created. Since the typical legislator or executive does not have sufficient expertise to regulate a specialized area of the law such as aviation or radio transmission, administrative agencies, such as the Federal Aviation Administration (FAA) and the Federal Communications Commission (FCC), have been created and staffed by experts in the field. Within their specialized area of the law, administrative agencies may perform analogous legislative, executive, and judicial functions by making, enforcing, and interpreting their own **regulations.** (See Figure 2.2.)

Although the Constitution does not require the states to establish separation of powers in their constitutions, all the states have governments resembling the federal government. Thus, for the person researching U.S. law, there is another complexity. Not only are there 51 sovereigns, but also each sovereign has its own constitution, three branches, and administrative agencies. In a real sense, then, there are 204 significant sources of law in the United States—51 sovereigns, times four governmental units each: legislative, executive, and judicial branches, and administrative agencies.

statutes
A formal written enactment of a legislative body, whether federal, state, city, or county.

statutory law
Derived from the Constitution in statutes enacted by the legislative branch of state or federal government.

executive
The branch of government that enforces the law.

executive order
Order issued by the U.S. president having the force of law but without going through the typical process for enacting legislation.

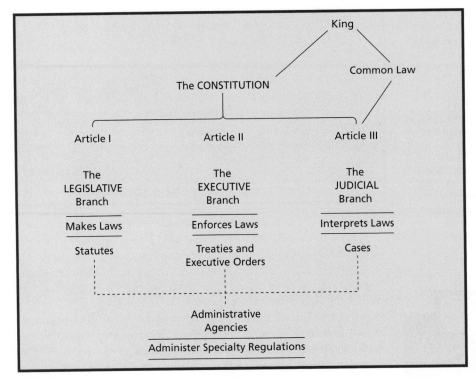

FIGURE 2.2   **The Separation of Powers Compromise**

LAW PUBLISHING

treaties
Compacts made between two or more independent nations with a view toward the public welfare.

judicial
Belonging to the office of a judge as a judicial authority.

cases
A general term for actions, causes, suits, or controversies, at law or in equity, that are contested before a court of law.

case law
Published court opinions of federal and state appellate courts; judge-created law in deciding cases, set forth in court opinions.

administrative agencies
Governmental bodies charged with administering and implementing particular legislation.

regulations
Rules or orders prescribed for management or government.

Who keeps track of the law coming from 51 sovereigns and the countless entities and subdivisions within them? The federal government and state governments publish some materials, but for a number of reasons, most legal publications are prepared by a private legal publishing industry. First, the law in its various forms—statutes, cases, regulations, and the like—is public property, free to be published by anyone. Second, private publishers are sometimes closer and more responsive to the legal marketplace, and so can create better products at less cost. Third, private publishers sometimes hire better writers and editors, invest more time and money, and advertise more effectively. Finally, and most importantly, private publishers have the incentive of making a profit.

In 1856, Hubert Howe Bancroft saw the need for law books in the growing West and founded the Bancroft-Whitney Company (BW) located in San Francisco, California. In 1873, Frank Shepard had the idea of creating books that systematically listed when judges had cited other cases and founded the Frank Shepard Company (Shepard's), eventually located in Colorado Springs, Colorado. In 1876, John B. West recognized the need for the systematic publication of state court decisions and founded the West Publishing Company (West) located in St. Paul, Minnesota. In 1882, James E. Briggs found a better way to publish the decisions of the U.S. Supreme Court and established The Lawyers Co-operative Publishing Company (LCP) located in Rochester, New York. In 1887, Matthew Bender had the vision to publish practice-oriented materials written by acknowledged experts, and he founded Matthew Bender & Company (Matthew Bender) in Albany, New York. Many other law publishers were similarly founded.

The late 1800s and early 1900s saw fierce competition for market share between the major competitors. In particular, West established a monopoly in the publishing of court decisions, and LCP established a monopoly in the publishing of selected decisions with analysis. Besides hundreds of thousands of pages of statutes and regulations, there are now about four million cases in U.S. case law.

By the late-1980s, the largest company, and the established leader, was West. West's main challenger was LCP. However, on the rise, due to its leadership in computer-assisted legal research with its LexisNexis service, was Mead Data Central, Inc. (MDC) of Miamisburg, Ohio, a subsidiary of the Mead Corporation of Dayton, Ohio. West then published a competing computer-assisted legal research service, Westlaw.

Today, there are only three major companies involved in the multibillion-dollar U.S. legal publishing industry. The largest company is Thomson, lead by its West division, often referred to as Thomson-West. The second largest company is Reed Elsevier, headed up by its LexisNexis division, and so usually referred to as LexisNexis. The third largest company is another international publishing conglomerate: Wolters Kluwer NV (Wolters Kluwer) of Amsterdam, Netherlands. All other legal publishers combined are smaller than any one of the big three: Thomson-West, LexisNexis, and Wolters Kluwer.

Why Master Legal Researchers Know "Who Publishes What"

This book carefully identifies "who publishes what." Why should you care who publishes what? You should care because similar law books and electronic files are not the same.

Law publishing is highly competitive. As a result, law publishers usually do not acknowledge their competitor's works in their publications, no matter how useful such references might be to the legal researcher. Yet, to paraphrase William Mark McKinney, law publishers are human. They miss cases, exclude them, or include them but index them poorly. Moreover, the style of a law book series or electronic files can change over time, as the result of changes in the law publisher's editorial policies. There is no such thing as a perfect law book or a perfect electronic file. If you can't find what you are looking for in one law publisher's book or electronic file, you need to know the alternatives. You need to know the competitor's book or electronic file that covers the same law source so you can try it instead.

Because international conglomerates have taken over the law publishing industry, as a general rule there are no guarantees about the quality of a given law book or electronic file. Today, most law books and electronic files are sold "as is." In 2005, for example, Reed Elsevier published on its public Web site a code of ethics that asserted high standards of ethical behavior, but also contained a waiver clause indicating that exceptions could be made for any employee. As a result, a legal researcher had a reason to doubt anything said or done by Reed Elsevier.

Perhaps the best reason why you should know who publishes what is simply this: Every master in the art of legal research knows who publishes what.

The Way to Win

What is the goal of legal research? It relates to the goal of any advocate in any case: to get the judge to say, "You win."

Stop and think. Why should a judge rule in your favor? *What is the strongest argument you can make to a judge?*

Human beings have a sense of simple justice, which is that *persons in like circumstances should be treated alike.* The challenge is to make the judge's basic sense of justice work in your favor.

The strongest argument you can make to a judge begins with someone else. Someone else was once in circumstances—whether factually, legally, or both—just like yours. If that person went to court and the judge said that he won, you can argue simple justice: persons in like circumstances should be treated alike. That person was in circumstances like yours, and he won. Since he won, the judge should say you win, because persons in like circumstances should be treated alike.

Do not lose sight of the essential purpose of legal research: *to find a case like yours, where the person like you won.* That is the strongest argument you can make to a judge. It's the way to get the judge to say "You win." (See Figure 2.3.)

As stated by Aaron Burr, the Vice President of the United States under Thomas Jefferson, "The law is what's boldly asserted and plausibly maintained." In every case, competent advocates boldly assert the law in their favor. The winner is the advocate who most plausibly maintains what he or she boldly asserts. The most plausible and maintainable assertion you can make is one backed by sound legal research. Tell the judge about the cases like yours, where people like you won. If your research is superior, the judge should conclude either that the cases you found are more like the case at hand than the cases your opponent found, where people like your opponent won, or that the cases cited are equally relevant, but more cases have gone your way. Either way, the judge should say, "You win."

FIGURE 2.3
Why Do Legal
Research?

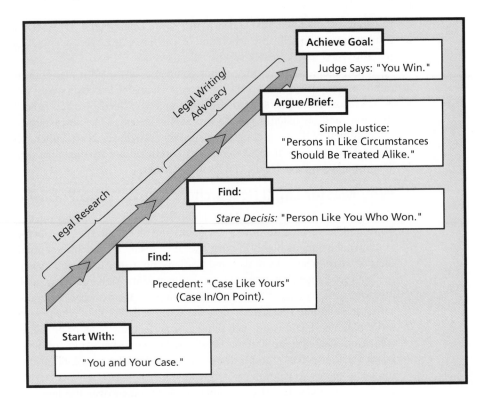

Authority: Primary and Secondary

Law is not only commands that are argued about, it is also something decided and commanded anew by the sovereign. You should understand the difference between the law itself—firmly rooted in, and established by, the sovereign—and a mere "bold assertion" of the law, however plausibly maintained by a nonsovereign.

At its best, law is a bold assertion plausibly maintained because a sovereign said it. Law is the command of a sovereign. In the United States, the Constitution of the United States is the supreme law of the land. As a result of federalism, law can come only from the federal government or from a state government. As a result of the separation of powers, law can come only from the appropriate branch or agency of the sovereign. The law is solely what the appropriate branch or agency commands.

The Constitution is the fundamental law. The legislature enacts statutes. The executive issues executive orders. The courts decide cases. Administrative agencies regulate special areas of the law. These acts—the Constitution, statutes, executive orders, court decisions, and administrative regulations—are authoritative acts of the sovereign and are known as **primary authority.** Primary authority is the law itself.

Everything else is **secondary authority.** Everything else includes encyclopedias, law review articles, newspaper polls, personal opinions, company policies, and teacher's assertions.

Any assertion of the law, no matter how bold, made by someone who is not the appropriate representative of the sovereign acting in that capacity, is not the law. It may be a fine expression of the law, it may explain the law and give it meaning, but it is not the law. (See Figure 2.4.)

Suppose you decide to put an item on layaway at a department store. The clerk says you must deposit 25 percent of the purchase price. You ask the clerk to accept 20 percent of the purchase price, which is all you have with you. The clerk snaps, "You must put 25 percent down. That's the law." Is it? Unless there is a statute, case, or regulation of the sovereign that says so, or a judge who will say so if you take the matter to court, it's not the law. The 25-percent requirement, however boldly asserted, is just a store *policy,* a guide to decision making, but it's not the law. The store, perhaps through the manager, could simply decide to change its policy and accept your 20-percent deposit, and no law would be broken.

Suppose your instructor tells you that you can't successfully be sued for negligence if you did not cause the harm to an individual, but the hurt person sues you anyway. The judge will not be impressed if you say: "My instructor said I can't lose." Your instructor is not a sovereign, nor is he or she the appropriate representative of a sovereign acting in that capacity, for deciding

primary authority
A primary source of law in the state or federal system that can be found in statutes, constitutions, rules of procedure, codes, and case law; the most fundamental place in which law is established.

secondary authority
Authority that analyzes the law, such as a treatise, encyclopedia, or law review article.

FIGURE 2.4
Legal Authority:
Primary and
Secondary

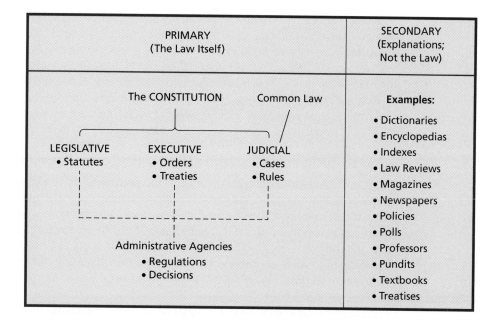

negligence law. The judge will be impressed if you say something like: "Your honor, may I tell you about several cases like mine, where the persons like me won?"

Does secondary authority have any value? Yes. Courts consider primary authority first and foremost, but if the primary authority is unclear, or if there is no primary authority on the issue at hand, the courts will consider secondary authority. The law in a given circumstance may have been better expressed by a legal author than by a representative of a sovereign. In a law review article, for example, a law professor may describe the best laws for the future and suggest a course for the development of those laws that a court would be wise to follow.

As a legal researcher, you must know how to research both primary authority and secondary authority. When you report the results of your research, however, cite to primary authority whenever and wherever possible. Primary authority is the law itself.

LAW BOOKS AND LAW LIBRARIES, BOTH PHYSICAL AND ELECTRONIC

When people with no legal training enter a physical law library for the first time, they are usually awed and overwhelmed. They find themselves surrounded by rows of impressive-looking books with strange titles. Those titles are equally strange when they appear in an electronic library. This book explains those impressive-looking books and their electronic counterparts. In particular, this book introduces you to the jargon of legal research. Legal research terms are explained and used, because once you understand the jargon of legal research, you can, very often, judge a law book, or its electronic counterpart, by its cover.

How to Judge a Law Book by Its Cover, and Other Parts

The title of a law book usually reflects its contents. Once you know the jargon, you know what's in the book. For example, books and electronic files that collect the opinions written by judges are called **reports.** Thus, if you see a book entitled *United States Reports,* you can reasonably infer that it contains opinions written by the appellate judges (the **justices**) on the U.S. Supreme Court.

Carefully examine every law book the first time you use it. If a book's title is not specific, examine the cover page. The cover page of the *South Western Reporter,* for example, indicates that it collects opinions from courts in Arkansas, Kentucky, Missouri, Tennessee, and Texas.

One part of any law book frequently neglected but well worth reading is its "foreword" or "preface." In prefaces, law book authors and editors often explain with great accuracy what is and what is not in their books. Many law books have guides explaining how to use the book.

Examine tables of contents. Like almanacs, dictionaries, encyclopedias, and other reference books, law books frequently contain more information than you might at first expect. Many law books have two tables of contents: one that summarizes the book in breadth and one that outlines the book in depth.

reports
Books and electronic files that collect the opinions written by judges.

justices
A title given to judges, particularly those of the U.S. Supreme Court and state supreme courts, and also to judges of appellate courts.

Be especially alert to law books containing tables of information, which are valuable tools for legal research. For example, some books covering federal law have "code" finding tables. If you know that your legal research problem involves a specific section of the *United States Code,* you can quickly find out if it is referred to in a given book by looking up that "code" section in the code-finding table for that book and consulting the references, if any, listed there.

Examine a law book's index. Most indexes are prepared directly from the text, so if a topic is in the index, it, or something about it, is in the book. If it's not in the index, it's probably not in the book. The quality of a book can often be determined by the depth and quality of its index.

How to Judge an Electronic File by Its Cover Page, and Other Parts

The title of an electronic file usually reflects its contents. Once you know the jargon, you know what's in the electronic file. You should carefully examine every electronic file the first time you use it. If you have the time and you will not be charged for doing so, systematically click everything you can, just to see what it is or what it does. Read all introductory materials, especially files labeled "About . . ." or "FAQ". **FAQ** is an acronym for "frequently asked questions." Examine tabs, tables of contents, and other guides. Electronic files frequently contain more information than you might first expect.

FAQ
An acronym for "frequently asked questions."

Visit Law Libraries, Both Physical and Electronic

Legal researchers work in law libraries, which may be physical, electronic, or both. Like all artists, you should develop a "professional curiosity" about your work. Just as musicians attend concerts and sculptors visit museums to gain more insight into their work, you should visit law libraries, both physical and electronic, whenever possible. In exploring a law library, and in considering the opportunities for doing research there, you will inevitably increase your knowledge and sharpen your skills.

This is not to say, however, that it will be easy to get in. Most physical law libraries are private, members-only operations. The leading electronic law libraries are expensive pay services.

Most physical county or court law libraries were created for the use of the judges in that county or court. The judges decide who can use their library, and they usually limit use to attorneys in the local bar association and their employees.

Some physical law libraries are run by associations of attorneys that limit use to attorneys who are dues-paying members and their employees. Most law firms limit the use of their libraries to their own partners, associates, and employees. The majority of law schools, on the other hand, limit use of their libraries to their own students and faculty.

Fortunately, the situation is not as bleak as it may first appear. Private libraries sometimes open up their memberships to law and paralegal students. The main branches of many college and public libraries have large law book collections, so you may find the law book you are looking for there. Furthermore, a lot of legal materials are now available for free in electronic files on the Internet.

The best bet for getting into a physical law library for free is to find the law libraries in your area that are members of the Federal Depository Library Program. Under this program, the library gets copies of federal government publications at no cost. In return, according to federal law, the library must be open to the public.

Even if a physical law library is a Federal Depository Library, you may run into obstacles. Since most books and electronic files in a law library require training for effective use, law librarians don't welcome the idea of having their doors open to everyone. Regular patrons of law libraries, trained in legal research, are generally quiet, responsible people who don't cause

CYBER TRIP

The Federal Depository Library Program is discussed at www.gpoaccess.gov/fdlp.html.

RESEARCH THIS

As stated in the text, you should carefully examine every law book and electronic file the first time you use it. Develop a "professional curiosity" about your work. Visit law libraries, both physical and electronic, whenever possible. In exploring a law library, and in considering the opportunities for doing research there, you will inevitably increase your knowledge and sharpen your skills.

Eye on Ethics

With all of the various books, manuscripts, journals and other legal documentation, it is very important to classify in advance what sources are considered primary authority and what sources are considered secondary authority. Even though some books may seem very authoritative and convincing in their approach or explanations, they may only be secondary authorities. Remember, only primary authorities can be cited to the court. Your attorney will be counting on you. Take the time to do it right!

trouble. The location of the law library may not be publicized, and you may be discouraged from entering. Accordingly, you may have to be a detective to find the library, and brave and tactful to get in. It is important that you act and dress appropriately, obey reasonable requests, and cultivate the impression that you belong there by your effective use of the library's resources.

Once law librarians become accustomed to your presence, they will be friendlier. If you need help finding what you are looking for, ask the reference librarian. If the librarian does not help you find exactly what you are looking for, the librarian's suggestions will usually lead you in the right direction, at least by getting you to think of a solution to your problem yourself.

There is one more thing you should be aware of when you visit a law library, either physical or electronic. Law librarians are concerned that their reference advice not be construed as legal advice. Don't ask a law librarian to find "the" answer to your legal problem. That's what lawyers do. Law librarians know that people do not ordinarily ask legal questions out of idle curiosity, and they are wary of accusations of unauthorized law practice, or legal malpractice, being made against them. A law librarian can suggest sources for you to use, but you have to do the research yourself.

THE BASIC STRATEGY FOR LEGAL RESEARCH

This book develops the subject of legal research from a bibliographic approach, emphasizing detailed descriptions of the various books and electronic files used. When bibliographic books describe a particular book or electronic file among others, they explain the purpose of the book or electronic file: why it exists. When you know the purpose of the book or electronic file, you ought to know *when* to use it: for its purpose. When bibliographic books describe a particular book or electronic file, they explain the structure of the book or electronic file: how it is organized. When you know the structure of the book or electronic file, you ought to know *how* to use it: by its structure.

Get the Facts

The basic strategy for legal research begins with getting the facts. The knowledge of legal research sources you acquire from this book will be useless if you don't know what you are looking for. As the old saying goes, "If you don't know where you are going, any road will take you there." If you are doing legal research and suddenly don't know what to do next, there is a good chance you forgot what you were looking for. Refresh your memory and go on, renewed in the understanding that a necessary part of legal research is to gather the facts about the case you are researching, both before you begin and as needed along the way.

Analyze the Facts

After you have gathered the facts (or have been given the facts as an assignment), you must analyze them. You must identify the legal issues that need to be researched and the relative importance of each issue. You must come up with the terms you will use as entry points in tables of contents, in indexes, or in computer word searches.

Your ability to analyze the facts will increase with experience. The more law you know and the more familiar you become with law books and other media, the easier it will be to identify the legal issues that need to be researched and their relative importance, along with appropriate terms to use as entry points.

One rule of thumb for analyzing fact patterns and for generating entry terms is the *TAPP Rule* used by indexers at LCP. The **TAPP Rule** is that legal researchers should be able to find the law

TAPP Rule
The rule of thumb that legal researchers should be able to find the law they are looking for by looking up terms representing the thing, act, person, or place involved in the case.

they are looking for by looking up terms representing the thing, act, person, or place involved in the case. For example, if an automobile is damaged when it hits a hole in a parking lot, a researcher should be able to find the relevant law by looking up things like "automobile" or "vehicle," acts like "maintenance" or "negligence," persons like "driver" or "property owner," and places like "parking lot" or even "hole."

The types of legal issues that arise, and their relative importance, generally mirror the litigation process. Does the court have jurisdiction? Has the statute of limitations run? Have all other procedural requirements been met? Does the plaintiff have a sound theory on which to sue? Does the defendant have a sound defense? Were the rules of evidence followed at trial? What relief is appropriate?

Many researchers find it useful to write out each issue they are researching in a complete sentence.

In collecting appropriate entry terms for a search in a variety of sources, consider synonyms and near synonyms (e.g., apartment, dwelling, home, homestead, house, residence, unit), understanding that your issue may be organized and indexed differently in different sources.

When the facts and issues are reasonably clear, and appropriate entry terms have come to mind, you are ready to find the law.

Five Steps

The basic legal research strategy for each issue has five overlapping phases or steps (see Figure 2.5.):

- Select the sovereign.
- Search mandatory "statutory" authority ("statutes in the sovereign").
- Search mandatory case authority ("cases in the sovereign").
- Search persuasive case authority ("cases in other sovereigns").
- Search persuasive secondary authority.

Select the Sovereign

The first step is to determine whether the issue is a matter of federal law or state law, and if of state law, of what state.

Because law is the command of a sovereign, you must first select the appropriate sovereign's law to search. And as a practical matter, most law books and electronic files cover either federal law or state law, or the law of a particular state. By selecting the appropriate sovereign's law to search, you avoid the mistake of searching another sovereign's law as mandatory authority.

FIGURE 2.5
Basic Search Strategy

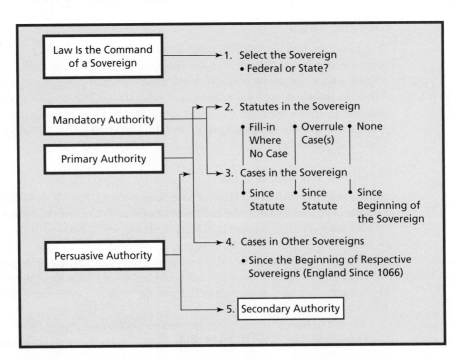

Determining whether the issue is a matter of federal law or of state law is not always easy. Indeed, some issues may involve both federal law and state law. With experience, you will develop the knack of recognizing which is which.

In general, federal law is law that relates to the Constitution of the United States, the federal government, or the powers granted to Congress in Article I, Section 8. State laws cover everything else. One twist is that the Constitution of the United States and the decisions of the U.S. Supreme Court interpreting the Constitution of the United States are, via the Supremacy Clause, mandatory authority for the states. When in doubt, search both federal law and state law.

Search Mandatory "Statutory" Authority

The second step is to search for relevant constitutional provisions, statutes, administrative regulations, and court rules in the appropriate sovereign, and any relevant federal treaties. Unless your issue is of constitutional import, involves a court rule, or is affected by a treaty, as a practical matter you need search only for statutes in the sovereign. An enabling statute, or a cross-reference in an annotated code, should indicate the existence of any relevant administrative regulations. If you expect to find constitutional provisions, court rules, treaties, or administrative regulations, search for them.

There are at least three reasons why searching for statutes in the sovereign is the second step: (1) you want to find primary authority—the law itself—as soon as possible; (2) you want to find mandatory authority—the law that must be followed within the sovereign—as soon as possible; and (3) the existence (or nonexistence) of statutes on your issue will direct the next step: the search for cases in the sovereign. Statutes are usually enacted either to fill in where there is no case precedent or to overrule existing case precedent. If the statute fills in where there was no case precedent, you only need to search for cases in the sovereign from the date of the statute. Likewise, if the statute overruled existing case precedent, you know that precedent is bad law, and, again, you only need to search for cases in the sovereign from the date of the statute. Moreover, if there is a statute in the sovereign, the case summaries in an annotated code will help you to find relevant cases in the sovereign from the date of the statute. If there is no statute in the sovereign, you know you must search for cases in the sovereign from as far back as the creation of the sovereign. Of course, the most authoritative precedents will be those from the most recent decisions from the higher-level courts with the most similarities to the case at bar.

In a similar fashion, administrative regulations will direct a search for administrative decisions.

Search Mandatory Case Authority

For the same reasons that searching for statutes in the sovereign is the second step, the third step is to search for relevant cases and administrative decisions in the sovereign. You want to find primary authority and mandatory authority as soon as possible, and the existence (or nonexistence) of statutes or administrative regulations in the sovereign will direct the search for cases or administrative decisions in the sovereign.

Remember that cases are more important than statutes because they can interpret statutes. Thus, the third step, the search for cases in the sovereign, must be completed after the second step, the search for statutes in the sovereign.

Find as many cases as you can. In the ideal search, you might find three types of cases to cite in support of your case: the landmark case, the leading case, and the local case. The **landmark case** is the first significant case, often the case of first impression for your issue, decided in your favor. The **leading case,** which may also be the landmark case, is the case opinion that reads like a textbook, laying out all the precedent on your issue, pro and con, and deciding in your favor. The **local case** is the most recent case from your local jurisdiction decided in your favor, pointing out that your local jurisdiction follows the precedent established by the landmark case and reaffirmed by the leading case.

The third step, the search for cases in the sovereign, completes the search for mandatory authority.

landmark case
A decision of the Supreme Court that significantly changes existing law.

leading case
A case opinion laying out all the precedent on an issue, and decided favorably.

local case
The most recent case from the local jurisdiction, decided favorably.

Search Persuasive Case Authority

If sufficient authority has not been found after the third step, the fourth step is to search for the remaining persuasive primary authority: the common law at large. The fourth step is to

A Day in the Life

The case fact pattern presented at the beginning of this chapter is based on a true story. When a legal researcher's child was born, the legal researcher wanted to promptly obtain the child's birth certificate. The legal researcher knew that a birth certificate was issued by the state and was ordinarily required in order to obtain a Social Security number. The legal researcher got into a runaround between the Health Department and the City Hospital. For two weeks, the legal researcher could not get the birth certificate from the Health Department, because the City Hospital had not yet filed it. The clerk at the City Hospital said that it took eight weeks to process birth certificates, and blamed the delay on the necessity of getting the doctor's signature.

The legal researcher analyzed the facts. The hospital had all the information needed for the birth certificate, and there seemed to be no reason why the law would give a doctor eight weeks to sign it. Because a birth certificate was required for everyone, the legal researcher figured that the state legislature probably enacted a law at some point governing the procedure for issuing birth certificates in the future. The state statute would be both primary authority and mandatory authority. The legal researcher searched the index of the state's statutes under the entry terms "Vital Statistics" and "Birth Certificates," and quickly found Ohio Revised Code § 3705.09(B) (1989), which provided that "When a birth occurs in or en route to an institution, the person in charge of the institution or his designated representative shall obtain the personal data, prepare the certificate, secure the signatures required, and file the certificate within 10 days with the local registrar of vital statistics." After the legal researcher confronted officials of the City Hospital with the law requiring a birth certificate to be filed within 10 days, an interesting thing happened. The birth certificate for the legal researcher's child was filed by the City Hospital with the Health Department the next day. The City Hospital did not explain why its clerk told the legal researcher that it took eight weeks.

search for relevant cases in other jurisdictions and sovereigns. The best precedents will be those from the most recent cases from the higher-level courts with the greatest similarities to the case at bar.

Statutes in other sovereigns are not considered persuasive authority because other sovereigns' legislatures can "dream up" whatever law they want. However, the existence of similar statutes in other sovereigns may support a policy argument based on the existence of a nationwide pattern or a trend.

The fourth step, the search for cases in the other sovereigns, completes the search for primary authority.

Search Persuasive Secondary Authority

If sufficient authority has not been found after the fourth step, the fifth step is to search for the remaining persuasive authority: secondary authority. Among secondary authorities, the most authoritative are well-reasoned law review articles and treatises, but, by definition, a court may be persuaded by other persuasive secondary authorities as well. When courts decide a case of first impression, they may cite almost anything that supports their decision.

Summary

Law is the command of a sovereign. The common law is the law made by judges in deciding actual cases. In the United States, however, the U.S. Constitution is the supreme law of the land, and the federal government and each state are sovereign; thus, there are 51 sovereigns. The powers of the federal government are divided into three branches: legislative, executive, and judicial. The legislative branch makes the law in the form of statutes. The executive branch enforces the law. The judicial branch interprets the law and makes the law—the common law—in deciding cases. Administrative agencies regulate specialized areas of the law.

Most legal publications are prepared by the private law publishing industry. Today, there are only three major companies, each an international publishing conglomerate, involved in the multibillion-dollar U.S. legal publishing industry. The largest company is Thomson, lead by its West division, and referred to as Thomson-West. The second largest company is Reed Elsevier, headed up by its LexisNexis division, known as LexisNexis. The third largest company is Wolters Kluwer NV, called Wolters Kluwer. All other legal publishers combined are smaller than any one of the big three. In view of the competitiveness of these publishers, and in view of the fact that most law books and electronic files are published with no guarantees, good legal researchers know the importance of "who publishes what."

Courts are run by judges, who are human beings. To get the judge to say, "You win," the strongest argument you can make is that persons in like circumstances should be treated alike. The purpose of legal research, then, is to find a case like yours where the person like you won, and tactfully point it out to the judge. Legal research is how the law, boldly asserted, is plausibly maintained. It is important to distinguish primary authority, the law itself, from secondary authority. You must know how to research both, but when you report the results of your research, cite to primary sources whenever and wherever possible. Mandatory authority is authority a court must follow. Persuasive authority, on the other hand, is authority a court *may* follow.

This book explains the law books and electronic files found in law libraries. Once you understand the jargon of legal research, you can, very often, judge a law book by its cover. You should check the title, the cover page, the table of contents, the preface, the tables, and the index. You can also judge an electronic file by its cover page. If you have the time and you will not be charged for doing so, systematically click everything you can, just to see what it is or does. Read all introductory materials, especially files labeled "About . . ." or "FAQ." You should visit law libraries, physical and electronic, whenever possible. Your best bet to get into a physical law library for free is to find the law libraries in your area that are members of the Federal Depository Library Program and, by federal law, must be open to the public. Act and dress appropriately, obey reasonable requests, and cultivate the impression that you belong by your effective use of the library's resources. Finally, be aware that law librarians are concerned that their reference advice not be construed as legal advice. A law librarian can suggest sources for you to use, but you have to do the research yourself.

The basic legal research strategy begins with getting the facts. After you have gathered the facts, you must analyze them. You must identify the legal issues that need to be researched and the relative importance of each issue. You must come up with the terms you will use as entry points in digests, indexes, and tables of contents, or in computer word searches. The basic legal research strategy for each issue has five overlapping phases or steps: (1) select the sovereign, (2) search mandatory "statutory" authority ("statutes in the sovereign"), (3) search mandatory case authority ("cases in the sovereign"), (4) search persuasive case authority ("cases in other sovereigns"), and (5) search persuasive secondary authority. The first step is to determine whether the issue is a matter of federal law or state law, and if of state law, of what state. The second step is to search for relevant constitutional provisions, statutes, administrative regulations, and court rules in the appropriate sovereign, and any relevant federal treaties. The second step will direct the third step: the search for cases and administrative decisions in the sovereign. If sufficient authority has not been found after the third step, the fourth step is to search for the remaining persuasive primary authority: relevant cases in other sovereigns that trace their origin to the Norman Conquest in 1066, as far back as the creation of that other sovereign, or, in the case of English law, as far back as the Norman Conquest in 1066. If sufficient authority has not been found after the fourth step, the fifth step is to search for the remaining persuasive authority: secondary authority.

Key Terms

administrative agencies   9
case law   9
case of first impression   8
cases   9
common law   8
constitutional law   8
executive   9

executive order   9
ex post facto   9
FAQ   14
federalism   8
judicial   9
jurisprudence   7
justices   13

landmark case   17
law   8
leading case   17
legislative   9
local case   17
precedent   8
primary authority   12
regulations   9
reports   13

secondary authority   12
separation of powers   9
sovereign   8
stare decisis   8
statutes   9
statutory law   9
TAPP Rule   15
treaties   9
U.S. Constitution   8

Review Questions

1. What is the "common law"?
2. What is the fundamental law in the United States?
3. How many sovereigns are there in the United States?
4. How are the powers of the federal government divided?
5. Why do master legal researchers know "who publishes what"?
6. Why should the legal researcher visit the law library?
7. Why is primary authority more important than secondary authority?
8. Why do law librarians avoid giving patrons "the" answer to legal questions?
9. What is the TAPP Rule and what is it good for?
10. What should you search first, cases or statutes? Why?

Exercises

Note: Because no particular law books or electronic files were discussed in this chapter, there are no exercises in this chapter involving the use of a particular law book or electronic file. Instead, the reader is encouraged to further explore the origins of the U.S. legal system, law publishing, and law libraries.

1. On what street in what city is the Rotunda/Exhibition Hall entrance to where the Constitution of the United States is currently located? (Tip: The answer can be found by searching www.archives.gov.) It is good for a legal researcher to be familiar with American history, especially the circumstances that lead to the writing of documents like the Declaration of Independence, the Constitution, and the Bill of Rights. The fundamentals of legal research come directly out of American history.

2. Use www.usace.army.mil to answer this question: In which U.S. Army Corps of Engineers' district do you live? As a general rule, the branches and agencies of the federal government of the United States have first-class Web sites. Notice that the USACE Web site seems to go on endlessly, demonstrating some of the awesome computing power possessed and used by the federal government, especially the Pentagon.

3. Who are the chief executive officers of the Thomson Corporation, Reed Elsevier PLC, and Wolters Kluwer NV? (Tip: The company Web sites are www.thomson.com, www.r-e.com, and www.wolters-kluwer.com.) Notice that these Web sites also seem to go on endlessly, demonstrating some of the awesome computing power possessed and used by these international conglomerates.

4. What is the first legal product listed under the list of products at www.thomson.com/legal ("PRODUCTS AND SOLUTIONS A–Z")? What is the first legal product listed under the list of products at www.lexisnexis.com/productsandservices?

5. What is the nearest law library to you that is a member of the Federal Depository Library Program? (Tip: The libraries are listed at www.gpoacess.gov/libraries.) If possible, visit the library in person. Does the library have a Web site on the Internet?

Vocabulary Builders

Find and circle the following terms in the following word search puzzle. The terms may appear up, down, sideways, diagonal, and forward or backward, ignoring any spaces in phrases

A	B	C	D	E	F	G	H	I	J	K	L	M	N	O	P	Q	R	S	T	U	V	W	X	Y	Z
A	B	A	S	I	C	L	E	G	A	L	R	E	S	E	A	R	C	H	B	C	D	E	F	G	H
W	A	L	E	S	A	C	O	N	S	T	I	T	U	T	I	O	N	A	L	L	A	W	I	J	K
L	M	N	O	P	Q	O	B	Y	E	D	W	A	R	D	N	O	L	F	I	R	A	S	T	U	V
W	X	Y	Z	A	B	M	C	D	E	F	G	H	J	U	D	I	C	I	A	L	I	J	K	L	M
N	O	P	Q	R	S	M	T	U	V	W	X	Y	Z	A	B	C	D	E	Y	F	G	H	I	J	K
L	M	N	O	P	Q	O	R	S	T	U	V	W	X	Y	Z	S	A	R	B	C	D	E	F	G	H
I	J	K	L	M	N	N	O	P	Q	R	E	S	T	U	V	W	O	X	Y	Z	A	B	C	D	E
F	G	H	I	J	K	L	M	N	O	P	Q	V	R	S	T	T	U	V	V	W	X	Y	Z	A	B
C	D	E	F	G	H	A	I	J	K	L	M	N	I	O	U	P	Q	R	E	S	T	U	V	W	X
Y	Z	A	B	C	D	W	E	F	G	H	I	J	K	T	L	M	N	O	P	R	Q	R	S	T	U
V	W	X	Y	Z	A	B	C	D	E	F	G	H	A	I	U	J	K	L	M	N	E	O	P	Q	R
S	T	U	V	P	R	E	C	E	D	E	N	T	W	X	Y	C	Z	A	B	C	D	I	E	F	G
S	I	S	I	C	E	D	E	R	A	T	S	H	I	J	K	L	E	M	N	O	P	Q	G	R	S
T	U	V	W	X	Y	Z	A	B	C	D	E	F	G	H	I	J	K	X	L	M	N	O	P	N	Q
R	S	T	U	V	W	X	Y	Z	L	E	G	I	S	L	A	T	I	V	E	A	B	C	D	E	F

CASE LAW, COMMON LAW, CONSTITUTIONAL LAW, EXECUTIVE, JUDICIAL, LEGISLATIVE, PRECEDENT, SOVEREIGN, STARE DECISIS, and **STATUTORY LAW.**

Chapter 3

Case Law

CHAPTER OBJECTIVES

After reading this chapter, you should be able to:

- Accurately describe a court's power to make law.

- Identify the parts of a judicial opinion.

- Understand the types of judicial opinions.

- Describe the courts in a three-level court system.

- Identify the federal reporters in the National Reporter System.

- Recognize the regional reporters in the National Reporter System.

- Identify major reporters outside the National Reporter System.

- Understand the significance of "unreported" opinions.

The purpose of this chapter is to introduce you to case law. You will learn where and how to locate case law, what is relevant case law, and how to identify the important parts of a case. In addition, you will be introduced to how case law is codified in the reporter system. You will also become familiar with the organization of the reporter system.

JUDICIAL POWER

As discussed previously, the U.S. legal system has roots in the common law. The common law is made and maintained by the courts. In a common-law system, the best argument you can make to a judge to win your case is there was a case like yours where the person like you won.

Court Sovereignty

Under the Constitution of the United States and under state constitutions, the power to interpret the law is given to the courts. In a common-law system, where the doctrine of *stare decisis* is followed, the interpretations themselves become precedents for future cases. Thus, in a sense, the courts not only interpret the law, they also make the law.

It is important not to lose sight of the constitutional separation of powers. The courts do not have sovereign power only when they interpret the law. A court must be confronted with a legal controversy—a case—in order to exercise sovereign power. Only in interpreting the law to decide a case can a court make a law. The court makes precedent**.**

Not only must a court be confronted with a legal controversy to interpret and make law, it must also be confronted with an *actual* legal controversy. Courts do not hear hypothetical or pretended controversies. Unless an actual case is filed and an actual legal controversy exists, the courts are without power to act. Otherwise, the courts would be "dreaming up" the law like the legislature, which would be fundamentally illegal. A fundamentally illegal act is **unconstitutional.**

unconstitutional
Not in accord with the principles set forth in the constitution of a nation or state.

Case Fact Pattern

You have recently been hired by a law firm as a paralegal to conduct legal research. One of the attorneys for the firm comes in and gives you your first assignment. It seems that a new client has come into the office to inquire as to his rights under the law and to seek the advice and representation of the firm. The client has been living with a person that he describes as his fiancée for the past five years. They have never been formally or legally married. The couple has recently broken up and now she is bringing suit against him alleging support and property rights. The attorney would like you to research the facts of the case and prepare a memorandum of law as to the issues and rights of the new client. The attorney suggests that you begin your legal research with the case of *Marvin v. Marvin* (1976) 18 Cal.3d 660 [134 Cal.Rptr. 815, 557 P.2d 106].

An infamous case, *In re Copeland* [66 Ohio App. 304, 33 N.E.2d 857 (Cuyahoga County Ct. App. 1940)], serves as a memorable example of the limits of judicial power. In *Copeland,* the appellate court was asked to review the disbarment of a judge:

> *Who was found guilty of having written, and caused to be published in a legal journal, an opinion in a fictitious cause purporting to have been heard and decided by him when he well knew that its published report would be relied upon by lawyers and judges as the decision of a court in a litigated controversy.*

The judge said:

> *[I]t was his purpose to edify the Bench and Bar by his thesis published under the guise of an authentic court finding . . . [and that] he employed this means for the purpose of stating his personal views on a hypothetical legal question for the benefit of the legal professional and the exaltation of his ego [66 Ohio App. At 305, 306].*

Maintaining the distinction between primary authority and secondary authority, the appellate court noted that the judge "by deception and concealment would foist his legal views upon his brethren as the judgment of a court of law," and said "[h]is effrontery in so doing is monstrously astounding." [66 Ohio App. at 305.]

In upholding the disbarment of the judge, the appellate court took care to point out that it was acting appropriately within the law: "We have pursued the authorities for like situations. We find none of and none are necessary." [66 Ohio App. at 307.] It was a deft declaration that the court, confronted by a real case, had dutifully searched the law, and finding none, exercised its sovereign power in its best judgment.

Citing primary authority in legal research is very important. Case law is primary authority. Constitutions, case law, and statutes are all considered primary authority. Case law is the legal opinions written by judges as they interpret the law to the particular facts of a case before them. As stated previously, the American legal system is based on precedent. A judge must look to the rulings made by other courts in the same jurisdiction in the same or similar legal and factual issues. By citing the precedents set in primary authorities, continuity and stability are maintained in the legal system.

Secondary authorities are those sources used to explain the law so that it is more easily understood. These sources are not to be relied on for their analysis. Secondary authorities consist of encyclopedias, journals, periodicals, and law reviews, to name a few. A secondary source usually is someone else's interpretation or analysis of the law. It should never be cited as primary authority. In fact, most secondary sources will provide references or citations to primary sources of law. The primary source should always be read and cited.

Legal Reasoning

In a common-law system, legal reasoning is often reasoning by **analogy.** When a court is called on to decide a case, it must compare the case to similar cases already decided and follow the most analogous case as precedent. Under the doctrine of *stare decisis,* if the court does not follow the precedent from the most analogous case, it must find a good reason for not doing so.

In deciding a case, a court is confronted with an actual legal controversy, known as the **case at bar.** Ordinarily, there is both a **plaintiff** (e.g., the person or legal entity that sought relief in the trial court) and a **defendant** (e.g., the person or legal entity responding to the

analogy
An inference that if two or more things agree in some respects, they will probably agree in others.

case at bar
The actual lawsuit that is being heard in the court or that is at issue.

plaintiff
The party initiating the legal action.

defendant
The party against whom a lawsuit is brought.

petitioner
Name designation of a party filing an appeal.

respondent
Name designation of the party responding to an appeal.

decision
The formal written resolution of a case; it explains the legal and factual issues that were presented, the resolution of the case, and the law that was used in reaching the ruling.

order
The rule of law or the specific authoritative directive from the court.

judgment
The court's final decision regarding the rights and claims of the parties.

decree
To determine or order judicially.

adjudication
The awarding by judicial decision.

mandatory authority
Authority that is binding upon the court considering the issue; a statute or regulation from the relevant jurisdiction that applies directly.

persuasive authority
A source of law or legal authority that is not binding on the court in deciding a case but may be used by the court for guidance.

binding authority
Another term for mandatory authority.

holding
That aspect of a court opinion which directly affects the outcome of the case.

case in point
An example that is used to justify similar occurrences at a later time.

on point
A statute or case is "on point" if it has direct application to the facts of a case currently before a tribunal for determination.

in point
Relevant or pertinent

plaintiff's claim). A plaintiff, especially a "plaintiff" expecting to be unopposed, may be termed a **petitioner,** and a defendant, especially a "defendant" opposing a petitioner, may be termed a **respondent.** The court must reason out the **decision,** the outcome of the case, declaring whether the plaintiff (or petitioner) wins or the defendant (or respondent) wins. A preliminary decision (e.g., a ruling on a motion) is known as an **order.** The final decision of a court entered into its records is its **judgment.** A determination of the rights and duties of the parties (e.g., in a divorce) is known as a **decree.** A judgment or decree is an **adjudication** of the case.

In deciding a legal controversy, a court usually weighs two types of authority: **mandatory authority** and **persuasive authority.** A court must follow mandatory authority (also referred to as **binding authority**), which consists of the laws properly enacted by its sovereign's legislature, and the law found in the opinions of its sovereign's next higher or highest court, if any. If a case follows precedent, the lower courts of the same jurisdiction are required to follow the ruling. If mandatory authority is lacking in any way, a court may consider persuasive authority, which consists of court opinions that are not mandatory within its sovereign, opinions by any other court tracing its origins to the Norman Conquest of 1066, and secondary authority. Nonbinding case law, such as case law from other jurisdictions that have decided the same or similar issues, is an example of persuasive authority. Persuasive authority is not binding on the court, but can do as the term implies, persuade the court to make a decision in a particular manner.

The court must reason its way through the legal controversy and arrive at a decision. The basic technique, honed over the centuries, is for the court to determine the point on which the case will turn, and if necessary, make a **holding**—a rule of law—upon which to decide the case.

Let us consider an example. Suppose a power failure causes the traffic light at an intersection to go out. Subsequently, two cars collide head on because both drivers, one driving on a two-lane highway and the other driving on a four-lane highway, each thought he had the legal right to proceed through the intersection. If the drivers sue each other, how does the court decide who wins?

The parties and the court do legal research. If there is a previous case like this one, known as a **case in point,** it is a simple matter to decide who wins. If a court in a previous case held that at an intersection a driver must yield to the car on the driver's right, then the driver of the car on the right wins.

If there isn't a previous case like the case at bar, then it is a case without precedent, known as a case of first impression. The matter now becomes much more complicated. Suppose there was no "right-of-way" rule in the sovereign, or the legislature had said right-of-way does not apply at an intersection with a traffic light. Then what? The case of *Marvin v. Marvin* (1976) 18 Cal.3d 660 [134 Cal.Rptr. 815, 557 P.2d 106] that appears in the case fact pattern was a case of first impression in California. The ruling in this case became a landmark decision and has been used as precedent in other cases since it was adjudicated in 1976.

If there is no previous case like the case at bar, the court must analogize from the case, however distant, that is most like the case at bar. To make a distinction, master legal researchers recognize that there is often a case **"on point"** that covers the issue implicitly, or by analogy, even if there is no case **"in point"** that covers the issue explicitly, or exactly.

Suppose in an earlier railroad crossing case, a court had reasoned the driver of a car must yield to a train because trains are bigger and heavier than cars, more difficult to stop, and, in a sense, a train's railroad is a "bigger" road than a car's highway. If the court in the case at bar decides the relative size of the roads is the key to deciding which driver must yield at a highway intersection, that becomes the rationale of the case. Making a new rule of law for highway intersections, the court holds that in the event of a traffic light failure, the driver on the smaller highway must yield to the driver on the bigger highway. Following the new rule, the court "logically" decides the driver on the four-lane highway wins.

Of course, this kind of reasoning by analogy is subject to argument. The court could have ruled the smaller car must yield to the larger car, or the legislature meant the right-of-way rule to apply only where there was no operating traffic light, and so on. The rationale of a case, the—distinction—is crucial. A different rationale will lead to a different holding and may result in a different decision in the case.

FIGURE 3.1
Legal Reasoning

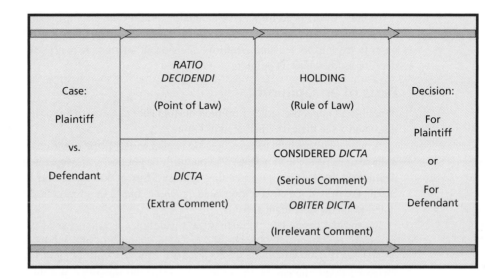

opinion
A formal statement by a court or other adjudicative body of the legal reasons and principles for the conclusions of the court.

dicta
Statements made by the court in a case that is beyond what is necessary to reach the final decision.

dictum
The singular use of *dicta*.

A court may also make extra comment in its **opinion,** not necessary to the decision, known as *dicta* (plural of **dictum**). Not being necessary to the decision, *dicta* are only secondary authorities. Irrelevant comment (e.g., the judge mentioning that as she decided the case it was snowing outside) is known as **obiter dicta.** Serious comment, however, a comment of importance to potential litigants, is known as **considered** *dicta* and has persuasive authority. For example, the court confronted with the highway intersection case might discuss how it would rule in a rail-crossing case. The comment is *dicta* because it is how the court would rule in a rail-crossing case. The comment is also *dicta* because it is not about the highway intersection case at bar, but because it is serious discussion that gives guidance to potential litigants in a future rail-crossing case. (See Figure 3.1.)

The nature of legal reasoning can also be understood with a nonlegal example. Suppose a parent must decide which of two children gets the last cookie in the cookie jar. How does the parent decide who eats the cookie?

The parent will decide after first making some distinction in the controversy. For example, the parent might decide the child who eats the cookie should have clean hands and rule that the first child to wash his hands gets the cookie. The parent might decide the child who gets the cookie should first eat all her vegetables and rule that the first child to eat all her vegetables gets the cookie. The parent might decide the children should be treated equally whenever possible and split the cookie in half. In any event, once a distinction is created, a rule can be formulated and a decision easily made. With a precedent established, it will be easier for the parent to decide later who gets the last piece of pie.

JUDICIAL OPINIONS

obiter dicta
An opinion voiced by a judge that has only incidental bearing on the case in question and is therefore not binding.

considered *dicta*
Opinions of a judge that do not embody the resolution or determination of the specific case before the court, but may tend to show how a court may decide a case in the future if the facts were a bit different than the facts being heard in the case at bar.

When confronted with a legal controversy, a court has the power to decide who wins. In the course of reasoning out a decision, a court ordinarily develops a rationale and a holding, but, from the winner's point of view, there is no necessity for the court to explain its reasoning. The winner has achieved the goal: the judge said to the winner, "You win."

However, a decision that "you lose" without explanation is not emotionally or intellectually satisfying for the loser. From the loser's point of view, simple justice requires that persons in like circumstances be treated alike, and the loser believes that in past cases most like his, the person like him won. The loser wants to know why the judge disagreed. To feel that justice has been done, the loser must be able to see how the judge based the decision against him on more analogous precedents.

Moreover, for other persons like the winner or loser, the decided case like theirs is a precedent. They want to understand why the winner won and to change their situation, if necessary, to assure themselves that they will win if their case goes to court in the future. In addition, other judges have an interest in understanding why the winner won, in the event they must decide a similar case.

Because of the need for a just explanation, and for the establishment of a rationale, holdings, and precedent, it is customary for a court, especially an appellate court reviewing a lower court case, to explain its reasoning and its decision in writing. A court's written explanation of its decision is known as its opinion.

Parts of an Opinion

A published appellate judicial opinion customarily consists of the following parts, in the order discussed. (See the case illustrated in Figure 3.2.)

A published appellate judicial opinion begins with the title of the case. Cases are usually titled in the names of the lead parties. The plaintiff, or plaintiffs, are separated from the defendant, or defendants, by *v.* or *versus*, meaning against. Thus, if John Doe and Richard Roe sue Sammy Smith, the title of the case, abbreviated, is *Doe v. Smith*. In a few states, the case title is reversed if and when the defendant appeals.

In criminal cases, the plaintiff is the sovereign. Criminal cases are titled "United States of America" or "State of," "People of," or "Commonwealth of" a state, versus the defendant or defendants (e.g., "United States of America v. Oliver North" is cited *United States v. North*.) In forfeiture cases, the case is titled in the name of the sovereign and the contraband seized (e.g., *One 1958 Plymouth Sedan v. Pennsylvania*).

Not all cases are contested. Some cases, such as bankruptcy, probate, and guardianship cases, are simply titled "*In the Matter of (whatever)*" or, in Latin, "*In re (whatever).*" Some cases can be brought on the application of one party and may be titled "*Ex parte (whatever).*"

If a person can sue as a named plaintiff with a collateral benefit to the general public, the case title may be "*State ex rel. (whatever v. whoever),*" indicating "State on the relation of the named plaintiff v. defendant." In maritime law, a case title may be simply the name of the affected ship (e.g., *The Titanic*).

appellant
The party filing the appeal.

appellee
The prevailing party who will respond to the appellant's argument.

plaintiff in error
Another name for the appellant in some states.

docket number
The number assigned to a case for its own administrative purposes.

synopsis
A short paragraph summary prepared by the publisher in unofficial reporters that identifies the issue, the procedural history, and the ruling of the court in the instant case.

headnotes
A key-numbered paragraph; an editorial feature in unofficial reporters that summarizes a single legal point in the court opinion.

syllabus
A short paragraph summary in the official reporter identifying issue, procedural history, and ruling of the court.

The case title usually indicates who appealed, known as the **appellant** or petitioner, and who answered the appeal, known as the **appellee** or respondent. In some states, a defendant-appellant may be known as the **plaintiff in error.**

Next, the court opinion contains the case's trial or appellate court docket number. The **docket number** is the court's serial number. There are two types of docket numbers. In most courts, the docket number indicates the year the case was filed and when it was filed in relation to the other cases filed that year. In abbreviations, the docket number may also indicate the month filed or the type of case (e.g., civil, criminal, or domestic relations). For example, "CV 92-3-120" might indicate "the 120th civil case filed in the third month of 1992." In some courts, the docket number indicates the sequence of filing from the day the court first opened for business. For example, "No. 12984" might mean "the 12,984th case filed in this court since it opened for business."

If necessary to avoid confusion, the opinion next states the name of the court deciding the case. The date of the decision is listed next, sometimes after the date the case was argued before the court.

Some publishers prepare a short paragraph summary of the entire case, known as the **synopsis,** which appears next. Following that, most publishers prepare brief summaries of the major legal points made in the opinion, called **headnotes,** because they are editor-made notations that appear before the court's opinion, often at the "head," or top, of the page. Also, the court, or a court employee known as the "Reporter of Decisions," may prepare an official summary or list of the major legal points in the opinion, referred to as the **syllabus.**

Next, the names (and sometimes the firms) of the attorneys who argued the case are listed. This information can be extremely valuable to a legal researcher because many attorneys, if asked, will share advice, wisdom, insight—even research references—gained from actually litigating a case like yours.

The justices who decided the case are usually listed next. Note that the abbreviations C.J., JJ., and J. indicate "Chief Justice," "Justices," and "Justice," and are not abbreviations for the first name of a justice.

Next in order is the opinion of the court, explaining the decision in the case. Most opinions begin with a brief overview of the case. The classic opinion then goes through the facts of the case in detail, the law that the court deemed applicable, the court's reasoning, and, finally, its decision.

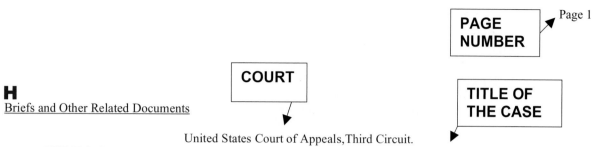

H

Briefs and Other Related Documents

United States Court of Appeals, Third Circuit.

THE U.S. SMALL BUSINESS ADMINISTRATION, as Receiver for Acorn Technology Fund, L.P.

v.

Peter E. CHIMICLES, Appellant

The U.S. Small Business Administration, as Receiver for Acorn Technology Fund, L.P.

v.

Leonard Barrack; Lynne Barrack, Appellants.

Nos. 04-4083, 05-1330.

Argued April 18, 2006.

May 10, 2006.

Background: Small Business Administration (SBA), as receiver of limited partnership licensed as a Small Business Investment Company (SBIC) pursuant to the Small Business Investment Act (SBIA), brought action against limited partners to enforce their capital contribution obligations under subscription agreements. The United States District Court for the Eastern District of Pennsylvania, James T. Giles, J., 2004 WL 2223304, denied limited partners' motions to stay proceedings pending mandatory arbitration, and they appealed.

4**Holding:**   The Court of Appeals, Michel, Circuit Judge, held that subscription agreements were not sufficiently related to partnership agreement between general partner and the limited partners for partnership agreement's arbitration clause to apply.

Affirmed.

West Headnotes

[1] Alternative Dispute Resolution 25T ☞213(5)

25T Alternative Dispute Resolution
    25TII Arbitration
        25TII(D) Performance, Breach, Enforcement, and Contest
            25Tk204 Remedies and Proceedings for Enforcement in General
                25Tk213 Review
                    25Tk213(5) k. Scope and Standards of Review. Most Cited Cases
Court of Appeals exercises plenary review over legal questions concerning the applicability and scope of an arbitration agreement.

[2] Alternative Dispute Resolution 25T ☞112

25T Alternative Dispute Resolution
    25TII Arbitration
        25TII(A) Nature and Form of Proceeding
            25Tk112 k. Contractual or Consensual Basis. Most Cited Cases
Despite the liberal policy in favor of enforcing arbitration agreements under the Federal Arbitration Act (FAA), a party cannot be forced to arbitrate unless that party has entered into a written agreement to arbitrate that covers the

FIGURE 3.2   Illustrative Case

RUNNING HEAD

dispute. 9 U.S.C.A. ß 1 et seq.

KEY NUMBER

[3] Partnership 289 ⟜366 ◄

289 Partnership
   289VIII Limited Partnership
      289k366 k. Relation Between Partners in General. Most Cited Cases
Even assuming that subscription agreements governing limited partners' capital contributions to limited partnership incorporated by reference the terms and conditions of the partnership agreement between general partner and the limited partners, the partnership agreement's arbitration provision did not apply to action to enforce the subscription agreements brought by partnership, or the Small Business Administration (SBA), as partnership's receiver; subscription agreements merely required the limited partners to agree "to be bound by all of the terms and conditions of the partnership agreement."

[4] Partnership 289 ⟜366

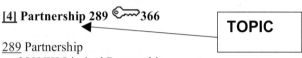

TOPIC

289 Partnership
   289VIII Limited Partnership
      289k366 k. Relation Between Partners in General. Most Cited Cases
Subscription agreements governing limited partners' capital contributions to limited partnership were not sufficiently related to partnership agreement between general partner and the limited partners for partnership agreement's arbitration clause to apply to action to enforce subscription agreements brought by Small Business Administration (SBA), as partnership's receiver; subscription agreements and the partnership agreements were separate, fully-integrated contracts, which stated that there were no other agreements between the parties.

*208 Michael D. Gottsch (Argued), M. Katherine Meermans, Chimicles & Tikellis LLP, Haverford, PA, for Appellant Peter E. Chimicles.
Eric Kraeutler, G. Jeffrey Boujoukos (Argued), Catharine E. Gillespie, Morgan, Lewis & Bockius LLP, Philadelphia, PA, for Appellants Leonard and Lynne Barrack.
Patrick L. Meehan, United States Attorney, Virginia A. Gibson, Assistant United States Attorney, Paul G. Shapiro (Argued), Assistant United States Attorney, Office of the United States Attorney, Philadelphia, PA, Patrick K. McCoyd, Tracey r. Seraydarian, Post & Schell, Philadelphia, PA, Thomas W. Rigby, Small Business Administration, Office of General Counsel/Litigation, Washington, DC, for Appellee United States Small Business Administration.

Before SLOVITER, AMBRO and MICHEL,[FN*] Circuit Judges.   ◄

JUDGES

    FN* Hon. Paul R. Michel, Chief Judge of the United States Court of Appeals for the Federal Circuit, sitting by designation.

AUTHOR OF OPINION

BEGIN OPINION

OPINION OF THE COURT
MICHEL, Circuit Judge. ◄
In these consolidated cases, Peter E. Chimicles appeals from an order of the United States District Court for the Eastern District of Pennsylvania, denying his motion to stay proceedings pending mandatory arbitration; Leonard and Lynn Barrack appeal a similar order.   Because we agree that these contractual disputes, each concerning an agreement without an arbitration provision, were not subject to an arbitration provision contained in a separate (but related) agreement, we affirm the district court's orders in both cases.

I. Background

This appeal concerns only two of the myriad of cases that revolve around Acorn Technology Fund, LP ("Acorn"), a

FIGURE 3.2   *(Continued)*

447 F.3d 207
447 F.3d 207
(Cite as: 447 F.3d 207)

New Jersey limited partnership founded in 1997.   Acorn's general partner was Acorn Technology Partners, LLC, a New Jersey limited liability corporation run by John B. Torkelsen.   Appellants Chimicles and the Barracks were private limited partners in this venture.   They both executed (1) a partnership agreement with Torkelsen acting on behalf of the general partner and (2) a subscription agreement with Acorn.   In the latter, each agreed to make capital contributions to the partnership in exchange for a limited partnership interest.

Acorn was licensed by the United States Small Business Administration ("SBA") as a Small Business Investment Company ("SBIC") pursuant to the Small Business Investment Act of 1958 ("SBIA"), 15 U.S.C. ß ß 661-697g. Once licensed, an SBIC can receive as much as $2 in federal matching funds for each private dollar it invests in qualified small businesses. 15 U.S.C. ß 683.   It must, however, conduct its activities according to the SBIA and its accompanying regulations. 13 C.F.R. ß 107.500.

On January 7, 2003, the United States filed an action against Acorn, alleging various violations of the SBIA and seeking appointment of a receiver.   On January 17, 2003, the SBA was appointed as receiver and, as such, was authorized to defend and pursue all "claims and causes of action available to Acorn, as warranted."   The district court also stayed all civil litigation "involving Acorn, the Receiver, or any of Acorn's past or present officers, directors, managers, agents or general or limited partners," unless specifically permitted by **209** the court. *Order for Operating Receivership, United States v. Acorn Technology Fund, L.P.,* No. 03-cv-0070 (E.D.Pa. Jan. 17, 2003). The instant cases, which were allowed to proceed despite the stay, involve the SBA's attempts to marshal Acorn's assets by making demands upon the limited partners for outstanding amounts owed on their investor subscription agreements.

A. Chimicles

Pursuant to an earlier agreement not relevant to this dispute, Chimicles subscribed to a $250,000 commitment as a private limited partner.   On September 15, 2000, he agreed to an additional $65,000, bringing his total commitment to $315,000.   It is undisputed that Chimicles fulfilled his $250,000 obligation but did not pay the additional $65,000, although he asserts that Torkelsen released him from this latter commitment.

By letter dated June 12, 2003, the SBA made a written demand upon Chimicles for the unpaid balance.   When he refused to honor his subscription commitment, the SBA filed a complaint against him, alleging breach of his subscription agreement with Acorn.   On January 16, 2004, Chimicles filed a motion to dismiss for lack of personal jurisdiction or, in the alternative, to stay the case pending mandatory arbitration.   On September 21, 2004, the motion was denied in its entirety.   A timely appeal followed.[FN1]

> FN1. Chimicles does not appeal the portion of the district court's order denying his motion to dismiss for lack of personal jurisdiction.

B. The Barracks

On April 7, 1998, the Barracks executed a subscription agreement for a $1 million limited partnership interest in Acorn.   They agreed to make an initial payment of $250,000 and three further payments of $250,000 over the next three years.   On September 15, 2000, the Barracks agreed to two additional payments of $250,000.   The Barracks have paid only $750,000 of their $1.5 million commitment, but they assert that Torkelsen encouraged them to invest by waiving in advance any penalties for failing to fulfill their subscription agreements.

By letter dated June 5, 2003, the SBA made a written demand upon the Barracks for the remaining $750,000. When they refused, the SBA sued the Barracks, alleging a breach of their subscription agreement. On September 22, 2004, the Barracks filed a motion to dismiss, or, in the alternative, to stay the case pending mandatory arbitration. Their motion was denied on January 5, 2005.   Like Chimicles, the Barracks appealed.

* * * * * *

FIGURE 3.2 *(Continued)*

447 F.3d 207   Page 4
447 F.3d 207
(Cite as: 447 F.3d 207)

These appeals were consolidated by order dated February 7, 2005.

HEADNOTE
REFERENCE

II. Jurisdiction and Standard of Review

[1][2] We have subject matter jurisdiction pursuant to 9 U.S.C. ß 16(a).   We exercise plenary review over legal questions concerning the applicability and scope of an arbitration agreement. *CTF Hotel Holdings, Inc. v. Marriott Int'l, Inc.*, 381 F.3d 131, 137 n. 10 (3d Cir.2004); *Harris v. Green Tree Fin. Corp.*, 183 F.3d 173, 176 (3d Cir.1999).   Despite the liberal policy in favor of enforcing arbitration agreements under the Federal Arbitration Act ("FAA"), 9 U.S.C. ß 1 et seq., a party cannot be forced to arbitrate unless "that party has entered into a written agreement to arbitrate that covers the dispute." ***210** *Bel-Ray Co., Inc. v. Chemrite Ltd.*, 181 F.3d 435, 440 (3d Cir.1999); 9 U.S.C. ß 2.

III. Discussion

The limited question before us is whether SBA's attempts to enforce the subscription agreements are subject to mandatory arbitration.   Appellants make similar arguments.   Essentially, both concede that the subscription agreements do not themselves provide for mandatory arbitration, but argue that the partnership agreements contain a valid (and broad) arbitration provision which applies to these disputes because the two agreements are sufficiently related.   Specifically, section 1.1 of the subscription agreement requires that investors agree to make capital contributions "in accordance with the terms and conditions described herein and in the Partnership Agreement, and to be bound by all of the terms and conditions of the Partnership Agreement."

If arbitration is required here, it must be imported from section 13.10 of the partnership agreement.   This provision states:
The General Partner and the Private Limited Partners, their successors, assigns, and/or their officers, directors, attorneys, shareholders, members or agents hereby agree that any and all controversies, claims or disputes arising out of or relating to this Agreement, the breach thereof, or the operation of the Partnership shall be settled by arbitration in Princeton, New Jersey, in accordance with the then prevailing commercial arbitration rules of the American Arbitration Association.   The Parties agree to abide by all decisions and awards rendered by the arbitrator, and such decisions and awards shall be final and conclusive and may be entered in any court having jurisdiction thereof as a basis of judgment.

The choice of venue clause in section 13.7 further provides that an "Action to enforce any provision of this Agreement or any action brought by the Partners against the General Partner or the Partnership shall be brought through arbitration in New Jersey, pursuant to Section 13.10 of this Agreement."

These arbitration provisions are noteworthy in two respects.   First, the agreement to arbitrate was made between the general partner and the private limited partners-i.e., the signatories to the partnership agreement.   Second, section 13.7 emphasizes that the arbitration clause was intended to apply to (1) actions to enforce provisions of the partnership agreement and (2) actions brought by the private limited partners.

[3] Acorn, however, was not a private limited partner, nor is the SBA as receiver acting as a private limited partner.   Even assuming arguendo that section 1.1 of the subscription agreement incorporates by reference the terms and conditions of the partnership agreement, the arbitration provision does not apply to an action brought by Acorn (or SBA as receiver).   Indeed, section 1.1 merely required the *investors* to agree "to be bound by all of the terms and conditions of the Partnership Agreement."

[4] Regardless, the district court correctly found that the subscription agreements and the partnership agreements are separate, fully-integrated contracts.   Section 3.5 of the subscription agreements provides that "[t]his instrument contains the entire agreement of the parties, and there are no representations, covenants or other agreements except as stated or referred to herein." Likewise, section 13.6 of the partnership agreements provides that "[t]his Agreement constitutes the complete and exclusive statement of the agreement between the Partners."

FIGURE 3.2   (*Continued*)

447 F.3d 207
447 F.3d 207
(Cite as: 447 F.3d 207)

*211 To support their argument for importing an arbitration clause from a related agreement, appellants rely heavily upon _Brayman Construction Corporation v. Home Insurance Company,_ 319 F.3d 622 (3d Cir.2003). This case is distinguishable. In _Brayman,_ a workers' compensation insurance policy was later supplemented by a retrospective premium agreement containing an arbitration clause that applied to any dispute that arose "between the Company and Insured." _Id._ at 623. Both contracts were signed by the same two parties. Neither attempted to enforce the arbitration provision against a third party.

Likewise, the decisions cited by appellants from other circuits enforced the arbitration clause against a party that had signed the agreement. _See Nat'l Am. Ins. Co. v. SCOR Reinsurance Co.,_ 362 F.3d 1288, 1289 (10th Cir.2004); _Pers. Sec. & Safety Sys. Inc. v. Motorola, Inc.,_ 297 F.3d 388, 392 (5th Cir.2002). In other words, the issue in those cases was the scope of arbitrable subject matter covered by the agreement, not whether both parties had agreed to arbitrate.

Finally, we note that even if we were to assume that disputes arising under the subscription agreement were otherwise subject to mandatory arbitration, appellants were unable to explain at oral argument why section 5.1.2 of the partnership agreement does not negate any obligation to arbitrate. Nor did Chimicles' post-argument memorandum provide a satisfactory response. Section 5.1.2 provides as follows:

Notwithstanding any provision in the Agreement to the contrary (except as expressly provided in this Section 5.1.2), in the event that the Partnership is subject to restricted operations (as such term is used in the SBIC Act) ᶠᴺ² and prior to the liquidation of the Partnership the SBA requires the General Partner and the Private Limited Partners to contribute any amount of their respective Commitments not previously contributed to the Partnership, the obligation to make such contributions shall not be subject to any conditions set forth in the Agreement other than limitations on the amount of capital which a Partner is obligated to contribute (a) within any specified time period or (b) prior to any specified date.

> FN2. The term "Restricted Operation Conditions" is defined at 13 C.F.R. ß 107.1820(e) and applies when, _inter alia,_ the "SBA determines that you have failed to comply with one or more of the substantive provisions of the Act." 13 C.F.R. ß 107.1820(e)(7). The occurrence of one of the enumerated "Restricted Operation Conditions" authorizes the SBA to avail itself of any of the remedies listed at 13 C.F.R. ß 107.1820(f).

Now that the SBA has been appointed as receiver and is attempting to marshal Acorn's assets, appellants' obligations to make contributions are no longer "subject to any conditions set forth in the Agreement," which we hold includes the arbitration provision set forth in section 13.10. Thus, even if imported into the subscription agreements, the arbitration provision of the partnership agreements would not apply to these disputes over unpaid investor commitments.

IV. Conclusion ◄  **DECISION**

For the aforementioned reasons, we affirm the district court's rulings that these disputes were not subject to mandatory arbitration.

C.A.3 (Pa.),2006.
U.S. Small Business Admin. v. Chimicles
447 F.3d 207

Briefs and Other Related Documents (Back to top)

• 05-1330 (Docket) (Feb. 7, 2005)
• 04-4083 (Docket) (Oct. 25, 2004)

FIGURE 3.2   _(Concluded)_

Source: Federal Reporter, Third Series, and _West's Federal Appendix_—Units of the National Reporter System, June 12, 2006. Reprinted with permission from Thomson/West.

affirm
Disposition in which the appellate court agrees with the trial court.

reverse
Disposition in which the appellate court disagrees with the trial court.

reversal
The act or instance of changing or setting aside a lower court's decision by a higher court.

vacate
Disposition in which the appellate court voids the decision of the lower court.

remand
Disposition in which the appellate court sends the case back to the lower court.

majority opinion
An opinion where more than half of the justices agree with the decision. This opinion is precedent.

concurring opinion
An opinion in which a judge who agrees with the ultimate results wishes to apply different reasoning from that in the majority decision.

An appellate court can make three kinds of decisions, in whole or in part, for or against the plaintiff, defendant, or both. The appellate court can **affirm,** which means it agrees with the decision of the lower court, and the party who won in the lower court wins. The appellate court can **reverse,** which means it disagrees with the decision of the lower court and either the party who lost in the lower court wins **(reversal)** or the case itself is dismissed **(vacated).** Or, the appellate court can **remand,** which means it found the proceedings in a lower court were not fair or complete, so it could not determine who should win and is therefore returning the case to the lower court for a new decision to be made after a fair and complete proceeding.

Types of Opinions

An appellate court opinion may consist of several opinions. Appellate courts consist of panels of three to nine justices. Each justice may have his own reasoning for voting to decide a case one way or the other, and each justice may write an opinion explaining his reasoning for voting the way he did.

For example, the custom in the U.S. Supreme Court is for the Justices to hear a case and then to meet in a private conference to vote on and decide the case. If the Chief Justice is in the majority, he or she assigns one of the Justices in the majority to write the opinion of the Court. If the Chief Justice is not in the majority, the Senior Associate Justice in the majority assigns one of the Justices in the majority to write the opinion of the Court.

If the other Justices who agree with the decision agree with the reasoning written by the assigned Justice, they simply "join" in the opinion of the Court. If a majority of the Justices join together in the opinion of the Court, the opinion is known as a **majority opinion,** and it, along with the decision, is considered precedent. If a Justice agrees with the decision but does not fully agree with the opinion of the Court, the Justice may write a separate opinion, known as a **concurring opinion,** in which other Justices may join.

On occasion, a majority of the Justices may agree on a decision, but a majority is unable to agree on the reasoning. The opinion of the Court is then known as a **plurality opinion,** in which other Justices who agree with the decision may join.

A Justice who disagrees with the decision of the Court may write an opinion explaining the disagreement, known as a **dissenting opinion,** in which other Justices who disagree with the decision may join.

Two other types of opinions exist. To signal unity (or to disguise differences), the majority agreeing with the decision may write a joint anonymous opinion, known as a ***per curiam*** ("by the court") **opinion.** If the court does not deem it necessary to write a full opinion, it may prepare a brief opinion, known as a **memorandum opinion.**

Memorandum opinions are ordinarily used for the granting or denial of an application for a writ of *certiorari* (e.g., "cert. granted" or "cert. denied"). A ***writ of certiorari*** is the written order of an appellate court with discretionary jurisdiction (usually the highest court in a three-level court system) stating that it chooses to review a lower-court decision and directing the lower court to produce its records for review.

JUDICIAL REPORTS

plurality opinion
A plurality *opinion* is the opinion from a group of *justices,* often in an *appellate court,* in which no single opinion received the support of a majority of the court. The final decision is determined by the *opinion* which received support from a mere *plurality* of the court. That is, the plurality opinion did not receive the support of half the justices, but received more support than any other opinion.

Court opinions (technically, copies of court opinions) are collected and published in books known as reports. (See Figure 3.3.) A set of reports is known as a **reporter.** Not all opinions are published in reports, for a number of reasons, including the level of the court involved, which is discussed next. Unreported decisions and the danger of decisions flooding the U.S. legal system are discussed in the final part of this section.

The federal court system and most state court systems are three-level court systems. (See Figure 3.4.) Some states, having less legal business, have a two-level court system.

The first level in both systems consists of trial courts. The purpose of the trial court is to determine the facts and make the original application of the law. Evidence is presented to a fact finder, judge, or jury, and after a verdict is reached, judgment is entered. In the vast majority of cases, the disagreement between the parties is more a disagreement about the facts than a disagreement about the law. When a trial court applies the law as understood by both parties, no new precedent is made. Because no new law is to be found by researching such a case, they are generally not reported. Trial court opinions are reported only if the trial judge

dissenting opinion
Opinion in which a judge disagrees with the results reached by the majority; an opinion outlining the reasons for the dissent, which often critiques the majority and any concurring opinions.

per curiam
A phrase used to distinguish an opinion of the whole court from an opinion written by any one judge.

memorandum opinion
A court's decision that gives the *ruling,* but no *opinion.*

writ of certiorari
Granting of petition, by the U.S. Supreme Court, to review a case; request for appeal where the Court has the discretion to grant or deny it.

reporter
Hardbound volumes containing judicial decisions.

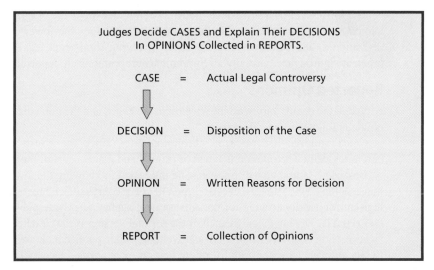

Judges Decide CASES and Explain Their DECISIONS
In OPINIONS Collected in REPORTS.

CASE = Actual Legal Controversy

DECISION = Disposition of the Case

OPINION = Written Reasons for Decision

REPORT = Collection of Opinions

FIGURE 3.3   **Case-Decision-Opinion Report**

takes the time to write an opinion to explain a novel application of the law in an unusual or unusually significant case.

The second and third levels of a three-level court system (combined in a two-level court system) consist of appellate courts. By reviewing the trial court record, weighing arguments presented in written briefs, and, if necessary, hearing oral arguments, appellate courts review the decisions of the trial courts, and in so doing, determine whether the trial courts properly applied the law. Appellate court opinions are generally reported because their opinions must be researched in order to find the law.

The second level of a three-level court system consists of intermediate appellate courts. Generally, the parties to a trial have a right to appeal (to have the acts of the trial judge reviewed), because of the broad discretionary powers given to the trial judge. However, experience shows that many appeals to intermediate appellate courts are without merit. Whether the result of bitterness, confusion, desperation, ignorance, or simply a dramatic attempt to establish a new precedent, parties often appeal even though the precedents are against them. There is an increasing tendency among the intermediate appellate courts to discourage publishers from reporting opinions in appeals having little or no merit, if only by not recommending certain opinions for publication. Sometimes, to conceal misdeeds by lawyers and judges, even meritorious appeals are not reported.

EXAMPLES		Federal Courts	Illinois Courts	New York Courts
Appellate Courts	"High," or "Supreme," Court	U.S. Supreme Court	Illinois Supreme Court	New York Court of Appeals
	Intermediate Appellate Court	U.S. Court of Appeals (by Circuit)	Illinois Appellate Court	Appellate Division N.Y. Supreme Court
Trial Courts		U.S. District Court (by District)	Illinois Circuit Court	New York Supreme Court

FIGURE 3.4   **Three-Level Court System**

The third level of a three-level court system consists of the "high," or final court, usually named the Supreme Court. The Supreme Court manages the lower courts and generally has discretion to accept for review only cases involving significant legal issues. Because of their inherent significance, virtually all Supreme Court opinions are reported.

Reported Opinions

Although the details vary with the sovereign, the court, and the publisher, the publication of court opinions follows a general pattern.

Court opinions are released chronologically, since the courts decide the cases filed chronologically. The opinion is typed or printed and made a part of the court's official record.

Because it is impractical for everyone interested in knowing the law to travel to every courthouse in the country to read every opinion to every court's official record, supreme courts (or the legislature) usually arrange for one government agency or private publisher to publish the **official reports.** The only significance of the official version is that it takes precedence if the unofficial version conflicts with the official version. Since publishers know that nobody would want to buy an inaccurate unofficial version, this rarely happens. "Unofficial" versions are carefully checked against the original and official versions, and they can, in fact, be more reliable than the "official" version. For example, when the editors of the Lawyers Cooperative Publishing Company (LCP) were preparing to reprint the company's unofficial *United States Supreme Court Reports, Lawyers' Edition* (L. Ed.) in 1905, they found many differences between the official records of the court and the court's "official" reports. On the advice of the court that the court records were "more official" than the "official" reports, the editors "reported from the records" to give lawyers the correct version.

If an individual court opinion is published separately, it is known as a **slip opinion.** A slip opinion can be important if the researcher is in need of the most recent decision the court made in a particular case. Slip opinions are issued in individual sheets and are collected chronologically until they are later arranged into digests. Court opinions are first collected for reporters in temporary pamphlets known as **advance sheets,** quickly assembled and distributed to customers to use until enough opinions have been released, and enough time has passed, for the publisher to be able to make a permanent bound volume. The advance sheets usually have the same pagination as the bound volume.

A reporter is a set of bound volumes that publish court opinions. When the features of a reporter change, or the marketing of the set changes, publishers sometimes start a new or higher numerical series of the reporter. For example, when West Publishing Company no longer reported U.S. District Court opinions in its *Federal Reporter* (F.), it started the *Federal Reporter, Second Series* (F.2d).

Court reports collect court opinions in a variety of combinations. Most reporters collect opinions by sovereign and court. LCP's *United States Supreme Court Reports, Lawyers' Edition, Second Series* (L. Ed. 2d), for example, collects the opinions of the U.S. Supreme Court. Some reporters collect opinions by geographic area or region. West's *South Eastern Reporter* (S.E.), for example, collects opinions from the southeastern states of Georgia, North Carolina, South Carolina, Virginia, and West Virginia. Some reporters collect opinions by subject. For example, *United States Tax Cases* (U.S.T.C.), published by Commerce Clearing House, Inc. (CCH), collects opinions in cases deciding federal tax law.

A bound reporter volume ordinarily contains several useful features. The full names and titles of the justices whose opinions appear in the volume may be listed. (See Figure 3.5.) If the bound volume is unofficial, there may be a cross-reference table showing where the official version of an opinion appears in the volume and vice versa. A table, in alphabetical order by case title, may

official reports
The publication of cumulated court decisions of state or federal courts in advance sheets and bound volumes as provided by statutory authority.

slip opinion
The first format in which a judicial opinion appears.

advance sheets
Softcover pamphlets containing the most recent cases.

 RESEARCH THIS

Look up the famous case of *Marbury v. Madison* first in the *United States Reporter* and then in the *United States Supreme Courts Reports.*

Notice how the case is depicted in each book. Note the differences in presentation and information presented.

indicate the opinions reported in the volume and the page on which they can be found. (See Figure 3.6.) Other tables may list and cross-reference statutes, court rules, and "words and phrases" interpreted by the opinions in the volume, and where those interpretations can be found.

Reporters are customarily identified by conventional abbreviations, so that a particular opinion can be simply cited by volume number, reporter abbreviation, and page number. For example, the famous U.S. Supreme Court opinion in *Marbury v. Madison*, decided in 1803, can be found in the first volume of the Government Printing Office's official reporter, the *United States Reporter*, wherein the opinion begins on page 137. It can also be found in the second volume of the *United States Supreme Courts Reports, Lawyers' Edition*, an unofficial reporter published by LCP, wherein the opinion begins on page 60. By custom, all of that can be said as follows:

FIGURE 3.5

Table of Judges

Source: From *West's Federal Supplement, Second Series,* a unit of the National Reporter System, Vol. 417 F.Supp.2d. Reprinted with permission from Thomson/West.

JUDGES OF THE
UNITED STATES COURTS
OF APPEALS

With Date of Appointment

DISTRICT OF COLUMBIA CIRCUIT

John G. Roberts, Jr.,
    Chief Justice .... 6–2–03 .... Washington, D.C.

CIRCUIT JUDGES

Douglas H. Ginsburg, C.J.	10–14–86	Washington
David Bryan Sentelle*	9–11–87	Washington
Karen LeCraft Henderson*	7–5–90	Washington
A. Raymond Randolph	7–16–90	Washington
Judith W. Rogers	3–11–94	Washington
David S. Tatel	10–7–94	Washington
Merrick B. Garland	3–20–97	Washington
Janice Rogers Brown	6–10–05	Washington
Thomas Beall Griffith	6–29–05	Washington

SENIOR CIRCUIT JUDGES

Harry T. Edwards	2–20–80	Washington
Laurence H. Silberman	10–28–85	Washington
Stephen F. Williams	6–16–86	Washington

FIRST CIRCUIT

David H. Souter
    Circuit Justice .... 10–9–90 .... Washington, D.C.

CIRCUIT JUDGES

Michael Boudin, C.J.*	5–26–92	Boston, Mass.
Juan R. Torruella*	10–4–84	San Juan P.R.
Bruce M. Selya*	10–14–86	Providence, R.I.
Sandra L. Lynch	3–17–95	Boston, Mass.
Kermit Lipez	7–24–98	Portland, Me.
Jeffrey R. Howard	5–3–02	Concord, N.H.

*Former U.S. District Judge.

FIGURE 3.6
Table of Cases

Source: From *West's Federal Supplement, Second Series,* a unit of the National Reporter System, Vol. 417 F.Supp.2d. Reprinted with permission from Thomson/West.

CASES REPORTED

ARRANGED UNDER THEIR RESPECTIVE CIRCUITS

DISTRICT OF COLUMBIA CIRCUIT

FIRST CIRCUIT

SECOND CIRCUIT

Marbury v. Madison, 5 U.S. (1 Cranch) 137, 2 L. Ed. 60 (1803). Being part of the jargon of legal research, reporter abbreviations are noted and used in this book wherever appropriate.

The National Reporter System

The backbone of legal research in the United States is the National Reporter System. Because of its national scope, the National Reporter System reporters are the most important for a legal researcher to become familiar with. A reference to a National Reporter System volume has meaning throughout the country. The National Reporter System essentially publishes for all states as well as federal reports. All states cases are available in the following:

- *Atlantic Reporter*
- *Northeastern Reporter*
- *Northwestern Reporter*
- *New York Supplement*
- *Pacific Reporter*
- *Southeastern Reporter*
- *Southern Reporter*
- *Southwestern Reporter*

The federal component of the National Reporter System is found in the following:

- *The Federal Supplement*
- *The Federal Reporter*
- *Federal Rules Decisions*
- *The Supreme Court Reporter*

The system also includes other titles such as the *Bankruptcy Reporter, Military Justice Reporter,* and *Federal Rules Decisions,* to name a few.

Federal Court Reports

One of the advantages for the legal researcher in utilizing the National Reporter System by West is that the editors will add material to aid the researcher in understanding, finding, and analyzing the cases that are published. Some of this material includes a summary paragraph at the beginning of the case briefly describing what the case is about. In addition, headnotes are presented that consist of point-by-point references of the law as it was considered by the court and applied to the case being presented. These headnotes are to be used with a feature that is unique to West—the key numbering system.

The editors at West have divided the law into approximately 400 general topics, and then further subdivided those topics into complex outlines. They assigned what is known as a key number to the smallest division within an outline. Each outline could contain several hundred to several thousand key numbers. These numbers are depicted in the headnotes by a picture of a little key with a number. Headnotes to cases are collected in jurisdictional digests and organized against these outlines and key numbers. If a legal researcher knows the particular topic and key number, it enables the researcher to examine all cases from a particular jurisdiction on the same point of law.

 RESEARCH THIS

Locate *The Supreme Court Reporter* and turn to the first case in any volume. Identify the summary, the headnotes, and the key numbers. Locate each of the areas of law as they are identified and applied in the case you chose. Note how the key numbering system provides a systematic approach to reviewing case law.

digest
A collection of all the headnotes from an associated series of volumes, arranged alphabetically by topic and by key number or summary of testimony with indexed references of a deposition.

A **digest** is a collection or compilation that embodies the chief matter of numerous books, articles, court decisions, and so on, disposed under proper heads or titles, and usually by an alphabetical arrangement for facility in reference. Most, but not all, jurisdictions have digests published by West. The key numbering system enables the researcher to look up specific areas of law from the published case and follow that area of law in various digests and encyclopedias more easily.

Digests also have other notable features. Many include volumes listed by topic. A Descriptive Word Index enables a researcher to look up related materials strictly from referencing the word much as you would look up a word in a dictionary. However, instead of finding just a definition of the word, you will find references to various parts of the volume in which the topics are discussed. Descriptive Word Indices are useful because they take common words, legal terms, and sometimes phrases, index them, and cross-reference them against topics and key numbers contained in other volumes. A Table of Cases or Plaintiff-Defendant and Defendant-Plaintiff Indices enable you to look up specific cases or parties to determine more information regarding the issues of those cases.

West publishes the intermediate federal courts of appeal and selected trial court opinions from district courts in the *Federal Reporter* (F.). However, in 1932, West dedicated this series in the *Federal Reporter, Second Series* (F.2d) and *Federal Reporter, Third Series* (F.3d) to just the U.S. Court of Appeals opinions. West then created the *Federal Supplement* (F.Supp.) and *Federal Supplement, Second Series* (F.Supp.2d) for the publishing of U.S. District Court opinions.

The federal courts of appeals are divided into 13 different regions, often known as *circuits*. Thus, these courts are often known as *circuit courts*. Eleven of the twelve circuit courts handle cases from different states—for example, the 11th Circuit Court of Appeals in Atlanta handles cases from Alabama, Florida, and Georgia. The 12th Circuit Court is the Court of Appeals for the District of Columbia, and is located in Washington. Additionally, there is also a United States Court of Appeals for the Federal Circuit, which hears certain specialized cases. (See Figure 3.7 and Figure 3.8.)

The federal district courts are the lowest federal courts of the three-level system. There are 94 judicial districts across the country, including judicial districts in the District of Columbia, Puerto Rico, the Virgin Islands, the Northern Mariana Islands, and Guam.

State Court Reports

The reports of state court opinions can be briefly summarized as follows. Every state at one time or another has arranged for the official publication of the opinions of the highest court, if not all appellate courts, by a local publisher. West's National Reporter System, which unofficially reports all the appellate court opinions of all states in a regional or specialized reporter, has become so prevalent, however, that several states have eliminated one or more of their little-used official state reporters, and most of them recognize the appropriate unit of the National Reporter System for their state as their official reporter. However, a few states, such as California and Illinois, do publish official reporters. West's National Reporter system covers the states with seven regional reporters that have been listed earlier.

FIGURE 3.7
West's Leading Federal Reporters

	1879 ⇓	1882 ⇓	1932 ⇓	1993 ⇓	1998 ⇓
U.S. Supreme Court			S. Ct.		
U.S. Courts of Appeals	F. Cas.	F.		F. 2d	F. 3d
U.S. District Courts/Special Courts	F. Cas.	F.		F. Supp.	F. Supp .2d
	Alphabetical	Chronological			
Note: Some Supreme Court cases are reported in F. Cas.					

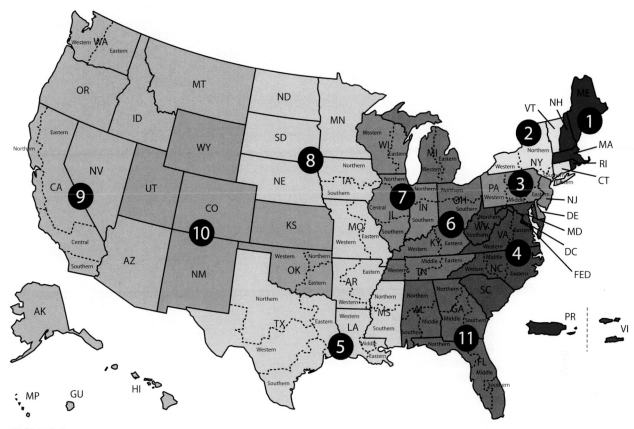

FIGURE 3.8   **U.S. Federal Judicial Circuits**

Source: Obtained from http://www.uscourts.gov/courtlinks.html.

The abbreviations of the current official reporter, if any, for the highest court in each state, or the current National Reporter System reporter covering the state, are presented in Table 3.1.

State court opinions are also available on the Lexis and Westlaw computer-based legal research systems, which will be discussed in Chapter 13.

Unreported Opinions

Appellate courts, both intermediate and supreme, are becoming increasingly concerned about the burdens placed on the legal system by an ever-growing flood of appellate court opinions. There are now millions of reported cases in U.S. case law, and the number grows by tens of thousands every year. Some argue that the information content of the average case has decreased to the point that the value to society of reporting every case is less than the cost of the forests cut down for the books and the valuable library and office space used to shelve them all.

Many appellate courts have sought to limit the number of their opinions reported. With increasing frequency, appellate courts are disposing of cases with memorandum of opinions or without opinions. Most appellate courts require attorneys who cite unreported opinions (which should be considered only as persuasive authority) to include a copy of the opinion in their briefs

 RESEARCH THIS

Remember the case at the beginning of the chapter, *Marvin v. Marvin* (1976) 18 Cal.3d 660 [134 Cal.Rptr. 815, 557 P.2d 106]? Locate the appropriate state reporter for this case and look it up. Identify who the plaintiff and defendant were, what the issue was, and what the court holding was. Once you have located it in the appropriate state reporter, locate the same case on the Internet. How does the reporting of this case on the Internet differ from what was published in the appropriate state reporter?

TABLE 3.1

National Reporter System

State	Reporter Abbreviation	State	Reporter Abbreviation
Alabama	So. 2d	Montana	Mont.
Alaska	P.3d	Nebraska	Neb.
Arizona	Ariz.	Nevada	Nev.
Arkansas	Ark.	New Hampshire	N.H.
California	Cal. 3d	New Jersey	N.J.
Colorado	P.3d	New Mexico	N.M.
Connecticut	Conn.	New York	N.Y.2d
Delaware	A.2d	North Carolina	N.C.
Florida	So. 2d	North Dakota	N.W.2d
Georgia	Ga.	Ohio	Ohio St. 3d
Hawaii	Haw.	Oklahoma	P.3d
Idaho	Idaho	Oregon	Or.
Illinois	Ill. 2d	Pennsylvania	Pa.
Indiana	N.E.2d	Rhode Island	A.2d
Iowa	N.W.2d	South Carolina	S.C.
Kansas	Kan.	South Dakota	N.W.2d
Kentucky	S.W.3d	Tennessee	S.W.3d
Louisiana	So. 2d	Texas	S.W.3d
Maine	A.2d	Utah	P.3d
Maryland	Md.	Vermont	Vt.
Massachusetts	Mass.	Virginia	Va.
Michigan	Mich.	Washington	Wash. 2d
Minnesota	N.W.2d	West Virginia	S.E. 2d
Mississippi	So. 2d	Wisconsin	Wis. 2d
Missouri	S.W.3d	Wyoming	P. 3d

CYBER TRIP

Besides Lexis and Westlaw, court opinions can be found on the Internet. The following sites are helpful when researching court opinions:

- www.legalonline. com/courts.htm

- www.findlaw.com/ casecode/supreme. html

- www.findlaw.com/ casecode/courts/index.html

- www.fedworld. gov/supcourt/index.htm

- www.usscplus.com

- www.law-cornell. edu

- www.law.indiana. edu

- www.washburn-law.edu

to the court. Some appellate courts have gone so far as to prohibit the citing of opinions in briefs where the opinions haven't been specifically marked by the appellate court as "for publication."

As a practical matter, legal researchers must try to find cases that support their case, even if those cases are unreported. Nothing informs the legal researcher better on what the law is on a particular topic than the reasoned opinion of a court, whether or not that opinion is reported. If a copy must be obtained of the unreported case in order to cite it, so be it. Even if a court prohibits the citation of an unreported case, one would be foolish not to tactfully make an argument—based on the unreported case—since it was known to have worked in the past.

How does the legal researcher find unreported cases on a given topic? The researcher must go beyond the methods used for finding reported cases. First, some publishing companies, recognizing the importance of unreported opinions, publish summaries and indexes to unreported decisions. For example, in Ohio, the Banks-Baldwin Law Publishing Company publishes the *Ohio Appellate Decisions Index,* which notes the key issues and facts in each case. As the publisher's catalog notes, there are "nearly 8,000 decisions issued each year by Ohio's 12 District Courts of Appeals, less than 10 percent of which are officially reported." Summaries of unreported decisions may also be found in local bar association newsletters.

Most "unreported" opinions, by definition not published in books, have nonetheless been entered into computer databases. Unreported cases can be searched and found on both Lexis and Westlaw computer-based legal research systems. Also, a search on the Internet can yield references to many unreported cases that are referenced in articles, Web sites, and the like.

As a last resort, an "unknown" unreported opinion can sometimes be obtained from the court through the docket number or through a court clerk familiar with the case.

 Eye on Ethics

Remember, when researching case law, it is important to cite the official report citation. Also, research your case to make sure that it has not been overruled in a subsequent case. It is important to cite primary authority whenever possible.

A Day in the Life

You have finished researching the case of *Marvin v. Marvin* (1976) 18 Cal.3d 660 [134 Cal.Rptr. 815, 557 P.2d 106]. You have learned from the case that California does not recognize common-law marriage, so the fact that your client and his partner were never married is definitely in his favor. You have learned that unmarried people who live together may enter into cohabitation agreements. These agreements are binding on all appellate courts and trial courts in California (which are lower courts in relation to the California Supreme Court). You report these facts back to the attorney who is handling the case. He indicates that he will further interview the client to determine if they entered into any cohabitation agreements while they were living together.

Summary

Under the Constitution of the United States and the state constitutions, the sovereign power to interpret the law, and in so doing *make* the law, is given to the courts. A court must be confronted with an *actual* legal controversy—a case—in order to exercise sovereign power. When a court is called on to decide a case, it must compare the case to similar cases already decided and follow the most analogous case as precedent. A court must follow mandatory authority, but it may consider persuasive authority. In making a decision, the court will determine the point on which the case will turn, and, if necessary, make a holding—a rule of law—upon which to decide the case.

Because of the need for a just explanation and for the establishment of the rationale behind the interpretation of the law, holdings, and precedent, it is customary for a court, especially an appellate court reviewing a lower-court case, to explain its reasoning and its decision in writing. A court's written explanation of its decision is known as its opinion. A published appellate judicial opinion customarily consists of the following parts: case title, docket number, name of the court, date of the decision, synopsis, headnotes, syllabus, attorneys' names, justices' names, overview of the case, the facts, the law, the court's reasoning, and the court's decision. The appellate court can affirm, which means it agrees with the decision of the lower court; it can reverse, which means it disagrees with the decision of the lower court; or it can remand, which means it found that the proceedings in the lower court were not fair or complete, and it is returning the case to the lower court. The types of opinions include the majority opinion, the concurring opinion, the plurality opinion, the dissenting opinion, the *per curiam* opinion, and the memorandum opinion.

Court opinions are collected and published in books known as reports. A set of reports is known as a reporter. Trial court opinions are reported only if the trial judge takes the time to write an opinion to explain a novel application of the law in an unusual or unusually significant case. Appellate court opinions are generally reported, because their opinions must be researched in order to find the law. Nevertheless, there is an increasing tendency among the intermediate appellate courts to discourage the publishers from reporting opinions in appeals having little or no merit. Court opinions are released chronologically. Supreme courts will usually arrange for one government agency or private publisher to publish the official reports for the court system. However, opinions are often published without special authority in unofficial reports. Court reports collect court opinions in a variety of combinations, but most collect opinions by sovereign and court. A bound reporter volume ordinarily contains several useful features, including the full names and titles of the justices, cross-reference tables, alphabetical tables of cases, and tables of statutes construed. Of all the reporters, the National Reporter System reporters are the most important for the legal researcher to be familiar with. One of the advantages for the legal researcher in utilizing the National Reporter System by West is that the editors will add material to aid the researcher in understanding, finding, and analyzing the cases that are published. Some of this material includes a summary paragraph at the beginning of the case briefly describing what the case is about. In addition, headnotes are presented that consist of point-by-point references of the law as it was considered by the court and applied to the case being presented. These headnotes are to be used with a feature that is unique to West—the key numbering system. The editors at West have divided the law into approximately 400 general topics, and then further subdivided those topics into complex outlines. They assigned what is known as a key number to the smallest division within an outline. Every state at one time or another has arranged for the official publication of the opinions of the highest court, if not all appellate courts, by a local publisher. West's National Reporter System, which unofficially reports all the appellate court opinions of all states in a regional or specialized reporter, has become so prevalent, however, that several states have eliminated one or more of their little-used official state reporters, and most of them recognize the appropriate unit of the National Reporter System for their state as their official reporter. However, a few states, such as California and Illinois, do publish official reporters.

Key Terms

adjudication 24	mandatory authority 24
advance sheet 34	memorandum opinion 32
affirm 32	*obiter dicta* 25
analogy 23	official reports 34
appellant 26	on point 24
appellee 26	opinion 25
binding authority 24	order 24
case at bar 23	*per curiam* opinion 32
case in point 24	persuasive authority 24
concurring opinion 32	petitioner 24
considered *dicta* 25	plaintiff 23
decision 24	plaintiff in error 26
decree 24	plurality opinion 32
defendant 23	remand 32
dicta 25	reporter 32
dictum 25	respondent 24
digest 38	reversal 32
dissenting opinion 32	reverse 32
docket number 26	slip opinion 34
headnotes 26	syllabus 26
holding 24	synopsis 26
in point 24	unconstitutional 22
judgment 24	vacated 32
majority opinion 32	*writ of certiorari* 32

Review Questions

1. What can a legislature do in making law that a court cannot do in making precedents?
2. What is the "holding" of a case?
3. What is a case law reporter?
4. Explain the difference between an official reporter and an unofficial reporter.
5. What is *stare decisis?*
6. Are headnotes written by the court?
7. How is a plurality opinion different from a majority opinion?
8. How are appellate courts different from trial courts?
9. What is a key number?
10. What is a digest?
11. What is the difference between a plaintiff and a petitioner?
12. What is an appellee?
13. When a court remands a case, what happens to it?
14. What is the difference between mandatory and persuasive authority?
15. List three examples of secondary authorities.

Exercises

1. Locate the *Federal Reporter, Second Series* (F.2d) and find the following case: *Warner Brothers Pictures, Inc. v. Columbia Broadcasting System, Inc.,* 216 F.2d 945. Answer the following questions:

   • Who are the parties to the action?

   • What is the name of the justice who wrote the opinion?

   • What is the official citation of the case?

   • What year was the case heard?

   • How many headnotes are there?

   • What was the holding?

2. List the 12 U.S. Federal Judicial Circuits and the states they cover.

3. Locate the case of *People v. Onofre,* 51 N.Y.2d 476, 415 N.E.2d 936 and answer the following questions:

   • In which reporter did you locate the case?

   • Is it the official reporter or the unofficial reporter?

   • What is the official state reporter for New York?

   • Which court heard the case?

   • When was the case heard?

   • What does "cert. denied" mean and why is it important to the case?

Vocabulary Builders

Find and circle the following "Top Ten" terms in the subsequent word search puzzle. The terms may appear up, down, sideways, or diagonal, and forward or backward, ignoring any spaces in phrases.

H	C	R	A	E	S	E	R	L	A	G	E	L	C	I	S	A	B	A	B	C	D	E	F	G	H
I	J	R	A	T	I	O	D	E	C	I	D	E	N	D	I	K	L	M	N	O	P	Q	R	S	T
U	V	W	T	P	X	Y	Z	A	B	C	D	E	F	G	H	I	J	K	L	M	N	O	P	Q	R
S	T	U	C	V	P	W	X	Y	Z	A	B	C	D	E	F	G	H	I	J	K	L	M	N	O	P
Q	R	S	I	T	U	E	V	W	X	Y	Z	A	B	C	D	A	E	F	G	H	I	J	K	L	M
N	O	P	D	Q	R	S	L	T	U	V	W	X	Y	Z	A	F	B	C	D	E	F	G	H	I	O
J	K	L	A	P	P	E	L	L	A	N	T	M	N	O	P	F	Q	R	S	T	U	V	W	P	X
Y	Z	A	B	C	D	E	F	G	E	H	I	J	K	L	M	I	N	O	P	Q	R	S	I	T	U
V	W	X	Y	Z	A	B	C	D	E	E	S	R	E	V	E	R	F	G	H	I	J	N	K	L	M
N	O	P	Q	R	S	T	U	V	W	X	Y	Z	A	B	C	M	D	E	F	G	I	H	I	J	K
L	M	N	O	P	Q	R	S	T	W	R	I	T	O	F	C	E	R	T	I	O	R	A	R	I	U
V	W	X	Y	Z	A	B	C	D	E	F	G	H	I	J	K	D	L	M	N	N	O	P	Q	R	S
T	U	V	W	X	Y	Z	A	B	C	D	E	F	G	H	I	J	K	L	M	N	O	P	Q	R	S
T	U	V	W	X	Y	Y	T	I	R	O	H	T	U	A	E	V	I	S	A	U	S	R	E	P	Z
A	M	A	N	D	A	T	O	R	Y	A	U	T	H	O	R	I	T	Y	B	C	D	E	F	G	H
I	J	K	L	M	N	O	P	Q	R	S	T	U	I	F	L	O	N	D	R	A	W	D	E	Y	B

AFFIRM, APPELLANT, APPELLEE, DICTA, MANDATORY AUTHORITY, OPINION, PERSUASIVE AUTHORITY, RATIO DECIDENDI, REVERSE, and **WRIT OF CERTIORARI.**

Chapter 4

Case Finders

CHAPTER OBJECTIVES

After reading this chapter, you should be able to:

- Identify the essential parts of a case citation.

- Describe how law students find cases when they begin law school.

- Explain the purpose of a memorandum of law and its use in finding cases.

- Recognize briefs as potential case finders.

- Compare and contrast a digest with an index.

- Explain "digest topics" and "key numbers."

- Describe the digest method in detail.

- Identify digest equivalents created by LexisNexis.

- Recognize the limitations of digests as case finders.

- List the major case finders discussed in other chapters of this book.

In this chapter, you will begin to learn how lawyers and legal researchers "find a case like yours where the person like you won." This chapter provides an overview of all the methods of finding cases, with an emphasis on searching specialized indexes known as digests. In particular, you will learn about Thomson/West's digest method, and the electronic equivalent created by LexisNexis.

This chapter provides an overview of all the methods of finding cases, but both by design and by necessity some resources used as case finders are discussed in more detail in later chapters. Other than common starting points—such as casebooks, lawyers, memorandums, and briefs—and other than the specialized indexes of the law known as digests, the remaining methods are only summarized at the end of this chapter, being discussed in detail in later chapters.

CASE FINDERS GENERALLY

chronologically
In or by real-time sequence.

topically
By subject or by topic.

As discussed in Chapter 2, courts have power only to decide actual cases. Actual cases occur **chronologically,** in real-time sequence. As noted in Chapter 3, most reporters report cases chronologically as the courts decide them. Yet, the goal of legal research is to find cases like yours, where the person like you won. In other words, the goal of legal research is to find cases on your topic, or **topically.** If the cases are reported chronologically, how do you find them topically? This is the most fundamental problem in legal research. The solution is using a case finder.

Case Fact Pattern

After receiving your report about the *Lynch v. Donnelly* case and discussing your findings with the mayor, the law director asks you to prepare a memorandum on the subject of public religious displays. The law director wants you to find as many cases as you can and focus the memorandum on the facts of each case. Heading out of the office on the way to court, the law director mentions that "we" have only the state digest in the office, so you'll have to go down to the County Law Library to use the federal digests. Because of the city's tight budget, the law director says you are to use the law books at the County Law Library before asking the law director for permission to use any expensive electronic legal research service. Before you realize it, the law director is gone. Which digests will you use?

Two types of case finders are available: indexes and collections. The value of an index is that the publisher has taken the time to systematically record the location of cases by topic to speed up your research. The value of a collection is that the publisher has taken the time to arrange the cases by topic to reduce the amount of your research. The law's unique indexing case finder, the digest, is discussed in this chapter. The law's unique collection case finder, the annotation, will be discussed in Chapter 5.

Citations

As noted in Chapter 3, case reporters are customarily identified by conventional abbreviations. No matter what type of case finder you use, the reference to the location at which a case opinion may be found in a reporter is customarily given by a **citation** (or **cite**). The citation is usually a reference to the first page of the report of an opinion in a reporter, but it may also be a reference to a specific succeeding page of the opinion, known as a **jump cite** or **pinpoint cite.** Since an opinion may be reported in more than one reporter (for example, in an official reporter and in an unofficial reporter), it may be found in more than one location. A reference to an alternate location for a case opinion is known as a **parallel citation** (or **parallel cite**).

A variety of styles exist for citing cases and other sources, but one convention is universal. Cases are always cited by volume number, reporter abbreviation, and page (or paragraph) number, in that order. For example, instead of referring to "the U.S. Supreme Court opinion in the case of Moore against the City of East Cleveland, decided in 1977, starting on page 494 of Volume 431 of the *United States Reports,* published by the U.S. Government Printing Office," the custom is to cite the case as follows: *Moore v. City of East Cleveland,* 431 U.S. 494 (1977). An example of a jump cite to the portion of the *Moore* opinion on page 497 of Volume 431 of the *United States Reports* would be as follows: *Moore v. City of East Cleveland,* 431 U.S. 494, 497 (1977). As an example of a citation including a parallel cite, instead of referring to "the New York Court of Appeals opinion in the case of Palsgraf against the Long Island Railroad Co., decided in 1928, starting on page 339 of Volume 248 of the *New York Reports,* and also starting on page 99 of Volume 162 of the *North Eastern Reporter,* the custom is to cite the case as follows: *Palsgraf v. Long Island Railroad Co.,* 248 N.Y. 339, 162 N.E. 99 (1928).

Giving conventional legal citations to legal authorities is important because of the distinction between primary authority and secondary authority. Unless you are an official representative of a part of a sovereign acting in that capacity (that is, a legislator, executive, judge, or administrator), what you say about the law is not the law itself. It's not primary authority. It is, at best, only secondary authority. When you make a bold assertion about the law, a lawyer or legal researcher will want you to give at least one conventional reference to a primary authority, or a respected secondary authority, that also said so, or implied so. Then, if the lawyer or legal researcher has any doubt as to whether you have stated or interpreted the law accurately, he or she can look up your reference and decide for him or herself. Get in the habit of citing legal authority, especially primary authority, for your legal assertions.

This book intentionally delays the detailed discussion of citation until after the different major sources of the law are covered. Many people find the specific rules of citation and different systems of citation easier to understand if they have first become familiar with the sources the citations describe.

citation or cite
Information about a legal source directing you to the volume and page in which the legal source appears.

jump cite or pinpoint cite
The page reference in a citation that directs the reader to the cited material in the case.

parallel citation or parallel cite
A citation of a case text found in two or more reporters.

Casebooks

The case finder that lawyers first learn about in law school, and the case finder lawyers in practice most frequently forget about, is the law school casebook. Although a law school casebook is designed to be used in law school, it contains a lot of case law information that can be useful at other times for other purposes, such as basic legal research. A casebook can be used as a starting point for finding cases like yours where a person like you won, particularly when no other resource is readily available.

Most U.S. law schools claim to teach the law by the so-called Socratic method first introduced at Harvard Law School by Christopher Columbus Langdell in 1871. Teaching a course in contract law, Langdell provided his students with a book, now known as a **casebook,** containing a series of carefully selected cases on each topic he covered. Langdell had his students read the cases he collected in his book, then, in class, he carefully questioned them in order to teach them to discover for themselves the rules of law that could be found in the cases.

casebook

A law school textbook containing a series of selected cases on each topic to be covered.

Langdell's teaching method caught on and became the standard in law schools across the nation. The method has been severely criticized at times, and rightly so, because if not properly done, if the questioning is not carefully built around the student's knowledge, the students are tortured rather than taught. Nevertheless, the method, in some form or another, has remained a part of the law school experience.

Because of the Socratic, or "casebook," method, professors and scholars at leading law schools have, over the years, written hundreds of casebooks for use in law school courses in almost every subject. What better way is there to find a case on your topic than to use the work of a scholar committed to studying the law? The only limit is that a given casebook may not cover your particular topic or the casebook may be more time-consuming to use than other case finders.

For example, three renowned professors of criminal law, Yale Kamisar, Wayne R. LaFave, and Jerold H. Israel, co-authored *Modern Criminal Procedure: Cases, Comments, and Questions*, published as part of the "American Casebook Series" by Thomson/West. It is an excellent source of significant and instructive cases on the topics that have arisen in modern criminal procedure.

The principal publishers of casebooks are Thomson/West (including Foundation Press), and Little, Brown and Company. Casebooks may be purchased from the publisher or from a law school bookstore. Most lawyers keep at least some of their casebooks from law school. Casebooks may also be found in physical law libraries.

Lawyers

Similar to a professor or scholar, whose business is it to keep up-to-date on the law? The answer, of course, is a lawyer. By definition, a **lawyer** is a legal expert. The "average" lawyer has gone to law school, studied for a bar exam, performed legal research, given advice, and handled—through negotiations, hearings, trials, and appeals—a variety of cases. Another obvious and frequently forgotten potential case finder is the "average" lawyer.

lawyer

A legal expert.

Suppose you work in a large law firm and have been given an extensive legal research project. One way to get started is to ask the lawyers in the firm what they know about your topic. There is a good chance that somewhere in their past or in their law practice, at least one of them had a reason to become familiar with your topic. In fact, some lawyers, just to stay current in the law, read advance sheets religiously. Lawyers may, at times, astonish you with what they know "off the tops of their heads." They remember case names, cites, relevant books, their notes from a continuing education seminar, and other similar sources they can and will refer you to. This information might have taken you hours to discover on your own or you might have missed some of it completely.

In short, lawyers are generally well-trained and experienced legal experts. Use their expertise to help you find your case.

Memorandums

In a well-run law office, the discoveries of the firm's lawyers and legal researchers may already be recorded and relevant to your topic. When a client comes into a law office for advice, it is a common and sensible practice for a lawyer to have the client's legal questions thoroughly researched before any "100%" advice is given.

The usual scenario is for a partner to pose the client's legal question to an associate or paralegal and to have the associate or paralegal research the question in detail. So as not to prejudice the research, the associate or paralegal is not told who in the fact pattern the partner represents.

The associate or paralegal is then directed to prepare a **memorandum of law,** a written discussion of a legal question, objectively reporting the law favoring each side in the fact pattern, as found after researching the topic. The "memo" may also include the researcher's opinion as to who, based on her research, she believes will win if the case goes to court. With a well-written memo in hand, a lawyer can confidently advise the client of the arguments pro and con, and the likelihood of the client winning in court.

To avoid duplicating research that has already been done by someone else in the firm, well-run law offices keep a copy of every memorandum ever prepared by lawyers in their offices, indexed by topic. If you work in such a firm, you should check if your topic has already been researched and written up in a memo. If so, all you may have to do is update it.

Although all law practices have their own styles and formats concerning legal memoranda prepared in their offices, there are some basic components that are typically found in most legal memorandum. For instance, the memo should begin with basic information concerning whom it was for, who wrote it, the subject matter, and the date that it was created. A typical heading might look something like the following:

memorandum of law

Analysis and application of existing law setting forth the basics for filing a motion.

MEMORANDUM OF LAW

To:

From:

Date:

Subject:

After the heading, such as the previous one, a basic legal memorandum should contain four subsections. These subsections are (1) statement of the facts, (2) issue, (3) discussion or analysis, and (4) conclusion. The statement of the facts section should consist of a concise statement of the facts relevant to the research and the case. The issue section should contain the issue or the question that needs to be researched. The discussion or analysis section is the section of the memorandum that is the most important. In this section, all relevant legal research is analyzed to the specific facts and legal question of your case. By an analysis of the law to your facts, a conclusion can be formed about how a particular issue may be handled under the law. The conclusion is the summary of how a particular issue may be handled under the law. A legal memorandum containing the preceding elements is well structured and useful.

Briefs

When a case is appealed, appellate courts ordinarily require the lawyers to present their arguments to the court in writing. A formal written argument to a court is known as a **brief.** A brief, as the name suggests, should be brief. Concise arguments are usually more powerful and persuasive than extended arguments. Lawyers often deal with complex legal issues and complicated fact patterns; therefore, a well-written brief may be quite lengthy.

Unlike a memorandum, which is objective in nature and intended to be used only within the firm, a brief is public advocacy. In a brief, lawyers argue their client's cause, putting forth the best arguments available for the client, such as cases like their client's where the person like their client won. Unlike a memorandum, a brief is filed with the court and available to the public.

brief

A formal written argument presented to the court.

Components of a Legal Brief

A legal brief, like the legal memorandum, has some essential legal components. The first component is the case caption. As can be seen in Figure 4.1, the case caption identifies the parties to the action, the docket number of the case, the jurisdiction where the case has been filed, the title of the brief, and typically the name of the attorney who is filing the brief. If the brief is particularly

FIGURE 4.1
Excerpt from a Brief

IN THE UNITED STATES COURT OF APPEALS FOR THE SIXTH CIRCUIT

No. 88-1271

JAMES A. TRAFICANT, JR.,
Petitioner-Appellee

v.

COMMISSIONER OF INTERNAL REVENUE,
Respondent-Appellant

ON APPEAL FROM THE DECISION OF THE UNITED STATES TAX COURT

BRIEF FOR THE APPELLEE

STATEMENT OF THE ISSUES

1. Whether the Tax Court correctly found that taxpayer failed to report $108,000 on his 1980 income tax return and that the underpayment of tax was due to fraud within the meaning of Section 6653(b) of the Internal Revenue Code.
2. Whether the Tax Court abused its discretion in the following procedural rulings:
   A. Refusing to permit taxpayer to act as a *pro se* co-counsel with his attorney before the Tax Court.
   B. Limiting the scope of taxpayer's cross-examination as a result of taxpayer's Fifth Amendment claim.
   C. Admitting into evidence the audio tapes of taxpayer's conversation at the Carabbias' home.
   D. Declining taxpayer's motions to have the Tax Court judge disqualified.

TABLE OF AUTHORITIES	**Page**
Cases:	
Action Realty Co. v. *Will,* 427 F. 2d 843 (7th Cir. 1970)	44
Akland v. *Commissioner,* 767 F. 2d 618 (9th Cir. 1985)	22
American Trucking Associations, 310 U.S. 534 (1940)	43
Anderson v. *Bessemer City,* 470 U.S. 564 (1985)	18, 20, 22
Anthracite Coal Antitrust Litigation, In re, 82 F.R.D. 364 (M.D. Pa. 1979)	37
Backos v. *United States,* 82 F.R.D. 743 (E.D. Mich. 1979)	37, 38
Bahoric v. *Commissioner,* 363 F. 2d 151 (9th Cir. 1966)	23
Barksdale v. *Emerick,* 853 F. 2d 1359 (6th Cir. 1988)	44–46
Baxter v. *Palmigiano,* 425 U.S. 308 (1976)	36
Beaver v. *Commissioner,* 55 T.C. 85 (1970)	23
Biggs v. *Commissioner,* 440 F. 2d 1 (6th Cir. 1971)	21, 22
Bradford v. *Commissioner,* 796 F. 2d 303 (9th Cir. 1971)	23
Browning v. *Foltz,* 837 F. 2d 276 (6th Cir. 1988), cert. denied, 57 U.S.L.W. 3453 (Sup. Ct., Jan. 10, 1989)	45
By-Prod Corp. v. *Armen-Berry Co.,* 668 F. 2d 956 (7th Cir. 1982)	41
Cirillo v. *Commissioner,* 314 F. 2d 478 (3d Cir. 1963)	23
Cupp v. *Commissioner,* 65 T.C. 68 (1975), *aff'd* without published opinion, 559 F. 2d 1207 (3d Cir. 1977)	30
Daiflon v. *Allied Chemical Corp.,* 534 F. 2d 221 (10th Cir. 1976), cert. denied, 429 U.S. 886 (1976)	43
Dellacroce v. *Commissioner,* 83 T.C. 269 (1984)	37
Factor v. *Commissioner,* 281 F. 2d at 100 (9th Cir. 1960)	23
Franklin v. *Franklin,* 283 S.W. 2d 483 (Mo. (1955)	37
Grudin v. *Commissioner,* 536 F. 2d 295 (9th Cir. 1976)	23
Habersham-Bey v. *Commissioner,* 78 T.C. 304 (1982)	23
Helvering v. *Mitchell,* 303 U.S. 391 (1938)	21, 26–28

D. *The Tax Court properly declined taxpayer's motions to have the Tax Court judge disqualified*

FIGURE 4.1
(*continued*)

**CYBER
TRIP**

The briefs filed
with a court can
sometimes be
found online.
Check the
particular court's
official Web
site and other
related Web
sites. For the
United States
Supreme Court,
for example,
briefs can be
found on the
court's official
Web site, www.
supremecourtus.
gov, and on
Findlaw at
http://supreme.
lp.findlaw.com/
supreme_court/
briefs/index.html.
The briefs of the
Office of the
Solicitor General
of United States
are available at
www.usdoj.gov/
osg/briefs/search.
html.

table of authorities
Section of the appellate
brief that identifies cases,
statutes, constitutional
provisions, and all other
primary and secondary au-
thorities contained within
the brief.

> Taxpayer claims (Br. 41–50) that Judge B. John Williams, the Tax Court judge who heard this case, was required to recuse himself from this case pursuant to 28 U.S.C. Section 455,[27] because his statements during a pretrial hearing and his prior employment by the Government reveal bias in favor of the United States. To prevail on appeal, taxpayer must show that Judge Williams abused his discretion in failing to disqualify himself. *Barksdale v. Emerick,* 853 F. 2d 1359, 1361 (6th Cir. 1988). Taxpayer fails to demonstrate any abuse of discretion because these allegations of partiality are unsupported by the facts in this case.
>
> It is well-established that a judge whose impartiality might reasonably be questioned must recuse himself from the trial. *Barksdale v. Emerick, supra; Roberts v. Bailar,* 625 F. 2d 125 (6th Cir. 1980). To be sufficient, a litigant's claims of judicial bias must contain specific facts and reasons; conclusory allegations and speculations are not sufficient. *Action Realty Co.* v. *Will,* 427 F. 2d 843 (7th Cir. 1970).
>
> [27]It is not clear whether 28 U.S.C. Section 455 applies to Tax Court judges since they are not defined as "judges of the United States." Compare 28 U.S.C. Section 451 with Section 7443 of the Internal Revenue Code (26 U.S.C.) (judges of the United States Tax Court serve for a fifteen-year term (although they may be reappointed) rather than serve during "good behavior"); *cf., Sharon v. Commissioner,* 66 T.C. 515, 533–534 (1978), *aff'd* 591 F. 2d 1273 (9th Cir. 1978), cert. denied, 442 U.S. 941 (1948). But in any event, regardless of the specific applicable statute, taxpayer's claims of prejudice are unsupported by the record.

lengthy, perhaps over ten pages, as is the case in some jurisdictions, a table of contents may be the next component. Some jurisdictions require a table of contents if the brief is over a certain page limit. Make sure you know the requirements of your jurisdiction in order to properly construct your brief. Some briefs also require a **table of authorities** listing the page numbers in the brief where a particular legal citation is referenced.

Like the legal memorandum, a brief should contain a statement of facts section. This section will set forth the factual dispute being presented to the court. The statement of facts should be written to portray the client's case in the strongest manner and should contain all facts of your client's case relevant to the legal problem. The brief should also contain a section stating the legal issue, typically referred to as the statement of the issue or the question presented. This section sets forth the legal question before the court for resolution. Often, more than one legal question will be set forth, stated in question form.

The argument section is critical to any brief and should follow the statement of issue section. In this section, the facts are analyzed to the law. The next section is critical to any brief. The argument is the main section of the brief and will usually be the lengthiest part of the brief. This is the section where the client's facts are analyzed to the law. The argument section presents the reasons the court should rule in favor of the client and the law it should use to make its decision. The argument section tells the court why it should rule in favor of the client, and the law it should use to make its decision. Every brief should end with a conclusion. The conclusion is a brief summary of the main points, indicating the desired ruling. Every brief ends with a signature block for the attorney who is filing the brief.

Libraries that serve appellate courts frequently collect the briefs and records filed in the cases before the court. Copies of the briefs and records may be available in other libraries as well. If you know a case is relevant to yours, you can often find cases not only by reading the court's opinion, but also by reading the briefs filed by each party's lawyer in the case. You can find cases by using the work of a lawyer doing what a lawyer does best: arguing a client's cause.

DIGESTS

Soon after the West Publishing Company began publishing cases chronologically in the various units of the National Reporter System, the editors realized lawyers and legal researchers needed a way of finding the cases reported by topic. Their solution was to create a specialized index of the reported cases and the rules of law found therein, known as a digest. The Thomson/West digest is still in use today, both physically in law books and electronically as a part of Westlaw. In the early-2000s, an electronic equivalent was created by LexisNexis.

Because digests are essentially indexes, they are not themselves cited as authority. Because digest paragraphs and headnotes are summaries, cases found with digests should always be read and understood before they are cited as authority. Headnotes are utilized by West reporters to identify topics and key numbers throughout their citators, annotations, and digests. A researcher can follow a topic and key number through the West system to identify primary and secondary sources that involve the same topic.

How a Digest Is Like an Index

To appreciate what a digest is, you should first understand how an ordinary index is created and used.

Indexes help where the topics within a text are presented in a varied or sequential order, like chronological order. Since it is impractical for researchers to read an entire book just to find one piece of information or to determine that the one piece of information is not in the book, an index allows researchers to go directly to the information desired without reading the whole book, or to quickly determine that the book, or a portion of it, does not contain the information they desire.

entries
In an index, words or phrases used to note key concepts, words, and phrases in the text indexed.

To create an ordinary index, the text to be indexed is read by an editor and divided up into key concepts, words, and phrases. As the editor notes all the key concepts, words, and phrases in a word or a few words known as **entries,** indenting subordinate concepts under major ones where appropriate, the editor records their location in the text by the page numbers at which they appear, known as **references.** The major entries, followed by the subordinate entries beneath them, are then arranged alphabetically (in the order of the alphabet from A to Z) carrying the page references with the entries. In final editing, references to other entries, known as **cross-references,** are noted, and the index is complete.

references
In an index, page numbers indicating the location in the text at which key concepts, words, or phrases appear.

To use an ordinary index, the researcher makes an educated guess as to the editor's choice of words for the major entry for the concept, word, or phrase sought in the text, and then, if appropriate, for the subordinate entry. If and when an appropriate entry is found, the researcher notes the page reference. The researcher then turns to the appropriate page and reads or scans the page until the desired concept, word, or phrase is found.

cross-references
In an index, references to other entries.

Case law research is analogous to researching a particular concept, word, or phrase in a large book. (See Figure 4.2.) The cases are reported chronologically, but a legal researcher like you wants to find cases only like yours. It is obviously impractical for you to read every case in every reporter every time you want to find a case like yours or to discover that there has been no case like yours. A digest is a specialized index that allows you to go directly to the case like yours without reading every case, or to quickly determine there has been no case like yours.

Thomson/West's editors prepare their digests in the process of preparing case opinions for publication in the National Reporter System. LexisNexis editors follow a similar process in preparing case opinions for publication. As discussed next, Thomson/West publishes digests for all of American law, digests that cover only federal law, and digests that cover only the law of particular states.

digests or digest paragraphs
A collection of all the head notes from an associated series of volumes, arranged alphabetically by volume or by key number or summary of testimony with indexed references of a deposition.

Each case opinion received for publication is read by an editor, who notes portions of the opinion, usually whole sentences and paragraphs, that seem to be legally significant, because they appear to describe the rules of law being laid down or followed as precedent. The editor summarizes these points of law into headnotes, notations to be placed ahead of the judges' opinion in the reporter (and generally falling at the top or "head" of a page). Thomson/West and other digest editors make similar, if not identical, summaries to the entries in the digest, referred to as **digests** or **digest paragraphs.** With each digest paragraph, the editor records the location of its source in the reporter by legal citation reference: the volume, reporter, and page.

FIGURE 4.2
Finding Tools

	Organization	Entry	Reference
Ordinary Index	A–Z	Word or Phrase	Page Number
Digest	Outline	Paragraph	Citation (Volume–Reporter–Page)

RESEARCH THIS

Thomson/West publishes a digest for every state, except Delaware, Nevada, and Utah. At a law library, locate the state digest for your state or for a neighboring state. Look at one of the main volumes of the digest. Carefully examine every feature of the volume. Look ahead to Figure 4.6 in this book, then follow a case law reference in the digest—a case citation—to the case's location in a reporter. See the connection between the digest volume and the reporter volume. Understand how a digest is simply a specialized index of the law.

Unlike an index, the headnotes and the digest paragraphs are not arranged alphabetically. Instead, they are keyed to an outline of the law. Thomson/West sets up theirs this way. Technically, the outline is an organization of classifications from general to specific known as a **taxonomy.** Headnotes, after being keyed to the outline, are numbered sequentially and remain ahead of the opinion in the reporter for each case. The paragraph origin in the text of the opinion for each headnote is indicated in the text by the headnote number in brackets (e.g., [5]). The digest paragraphs reflecting the headnotes are classified to the digest according to the outline.

Modified over the years, Thomson/West's outline has seven main divisions: Persons, Property, Contracts, Torts, Crimes, Remedies, and Government. Each main division is divided into subdivisions, and the subdivisions are divided into **topics,** which are the major divisions in the outline. The outline contains more than 400 topics. (See Figure 4.3.) Each topic is then separately outlined according to the nature of the topic, creating thousands of subtopics. The lines in the topic outline are numbered sequentially. (See Figure 4.4.)

taxonomy
An organization of classifications from general to specific.

topics
The major divisions in a subject outline.

FIGURE 4.3
Outline of the Law
Source: From *West's Federal Practice Digest—Volume 1.* Reprinted by permission of Thomson/West.

Digest Topics are arranged for your convenience by Seven Main Divisions of Law. Complete alphabetical list of Digest Topics with topic numbers follows this section.

1. PERSONS
2. PROPERTY
3. CONTRACTS
4. TORTS
5. CRIMES
6. REMEDIES
7. GOVERNMENT

1. PERSONS

RELATING TO NATURAL PERSONS IN GENERAL
Civil Rights
Dead Bodies
Death
Domicile
Food
Health
Holidays
Intoxicating Liquors
Names
Seals
Signatures
Sunday
Time
Weapons

PARTICULAR CLASSES OF NATURAL PERSONS
Absentees
Aliens
Chemical Dependents
Children Out-of Wedlock
Citizens
Convicts
Indians
Infants
Mental Health
Slaves
Spendthrifts

PERSONAL RELATIONS
Adoption
Attorney and Client
Child Custody

FIGURE 4.3
(*continued*)

Child Support
Executors and Administrators
Guardian and Ward
Husband and Wife
Labor and Employment
Marriage
Parent and Child
Principal and Agent
Workers' Compensation

ASSOCIATED AND ARTIFICIAL PERSONS
Associations
Beneficial Associations
Building and Loan Associations
Clubs
Colleges and Universities
Corporations
Exchanges
Joint-Stock Companies and Business Trusts
Limited Liability Companies
Partnership
Religious Societies

PARTICULAR OCCUPATIONS
Accountants
Agriculture
Auctions and Auctioneers
Aviation
Banks and Banking
Bridges
Brokers
Canals
Carriers
Commerce
Consumer Credit
Consumer Protection
Credit Reporting Agencies
Detectives
Electricity
Explosives
Factors
Ferries
Gas
Hawkers and Peddlers
Innkeepers
Insurance
Licenses
Manufactures
Monopolies
Pilots
Public Amusement and Entertainment
Railroads
Seamen
Shipping
Steam
Telecommunications
Towage

Trade Regulation
Turnpikes and Toll Roads
Urban Railroads
Warehousemen
Wharves

2. PROPERTY

NATURE, SUBJECTS, AND INCIDENTS OF OWNERSHIP IN GENERAL
Abandoned and Lost Property
Accession
Adjoining Landowners
Confusion of Goods
Improvements
Property

PARTICULAR SUBJECTS AND INCIDENTS OF OWNERSHIP
Animals
Annuities
Automobiles
Boundaries
Cemeteries
Common Lands
Copyrights and Intellectual Property
Crops
Fences
Fish
Fixtures
Franchises
Game
Good Will
Logs and Logging
Mines and Minerals
Navigable Waters
Party Walls
Patents
Public Lands
Trademarks
Waters and Water Courses
Woods and Forests

PARTICULAR CLASSES OF ESTATES OR INTERESTS IN PROPERTY
Charities
Condominium
Dower and Curtesy
Easements
Estates in Property
Joint Tenancy
Landlord and Tenant
Life Estates
Perpetuities
Powers
Remainders
Reversions
Tenancy in Common
Trusts

FIGURE 4.3
(*continued*)

**PARTICULAR MODES OF ACQUIRING
OR TRANSFERRING PROPERTY**
Abstracts of Title
Adverse Possession
Alteration of Instruments
Assignments
Chattel Mortgages
Conversion
Dedication
Deeds
Descent and Distribution
Escheat
Fraudulent Conveyances
Gifts
Lost Instruments
Mortgages
Pledges
Secured Transactions
Wills

3. CONTRACTS

**NATURE, REQUISITES, AND INCIDENTS
OF AGREEMENTS IN GENERAL**
Contracts
Customs and Usages
Frauds, Statute of
Interest
Usury

**PARTICULAR CLASSES
OF AGREEMENTS**
Bailment
Bills and Notes
Bonds
Breach of Marriage Promise
Champerty and Maintenance
Compromise and Settlement
Covenants
Deposits and Escrows
Exchange of Property
Gaming
Guaranty
Implied and Constructive Contracts
Indemnity
Joint Adventures
Lotteries
Principal and Surety
Public Contracts
Rewards
Sales
Subscriptions
Vendor and Purchaser

**PARTICULAR CLASSES OF IMPLIED
OR CONSTRUCTIVE CONTRACTS
OR QUASI CONTRACTS**
Account Stated
Contribution
Implied and Constructive Contracts

**PARTICULAR MODES OF
DISCHARGING CONTRACTS**
Novation
Payment
Release
Subrogation
Tender

4. TORTS

Assault and Battery
Collision
Conspiracy
False Imprisonment
Forcible Entry and Detainer
Fraud
Libel and Slander
Malicious Prosecution
Negligence
Nuisance
Products Liability
Seduction
Torts
Trespass
Trover and Conversion
Waste

5. CRIMES

Abortion and Birth Control
Adulteration
Adultery
Arson
Bigamy
Breach of the Peace
Bribery
Burglary
Compounding Offenses
Controlled Substances
Counterfeiting
Criminal Law
Disorderly Conduct
Disorderly House
Disturbance of Public Assemblage
Embezzlement
Escape
Extortion and Threats
False Personation
False Pretenses
Fires
Forgery
Homicide
Incest
Insurrection and Sedition
Kidnapping
Larceny
Lewdness
Malicious Mischief
Mayhem
Neutrality Laws
Obscenity

FIGURE 4.3
(*continued*)

Obstructing Justice
Perjury
Prostitution
Racketeer Influenced and Corrupt
    Organizations
Rape
Receiving Stolen Goods
Rescue
Riot
Robbery
Sodomy
Suicide
Treason
Unlawful Assembly
Vagrancy

6. REMEDIES

REMEDIES BY ACT OR AGREEMENT OF PARTIES
Accord and Satisfaction
Arbitration
Submission of Controversy

REMEDIES BY POSSESSION OR NOTICE
Liens
Lis Pendens
Maritime Liens
Mechanics' Liens
Notice
Salvage

MEANS AND METHODS OF PROOF
Acknowledgment
Affidavits
Estoppel
Evidence
Oath
Records
Witnesses

CIVIL ACTIONS IN GENERAL
Action
Declaratory Judgment
Election of Remedies
Limitation of Actions
Parties
Set-Off and Counterclaim
Venue

PARTICULAR PROCEEDINGS IN CIVIL ACTIONS
Abatement and Revival
Appearance
Costs
Damages
Execution
Exemptions
Homestead
Judgment

Jury
Motions
Pleading
Pretrial Procedure
Process
Reference
Stipulations
Trial

PARTICULAR REMEDIES INCIDENT TO CIVIL ACTIONS
Arrest
Assistance, Writ of
Attachment
Bail
Deposits in Court
Garnishment
Injunction
Judicial Sales
Ne Exeat
Receivers
Recognizances
Sequestration
Undertakings

PARTICULAR MODES OF REVIEW IN CIVIL ACTIONS
Appeal and Error
Audita Querela
Certiorari
Exceptions, Bill of
New Trial
Review

ACTIONS TO ESTABLISH OWNERSHIP OR RECOVER POSSESSION OF SPECIFIC PROPERTY
Detinue
Ejectment
Entry, Writ of
Interpleader
Possessory Warrant
Quieting Title
Real Actions
Replevin
Trespass to Try Title

FORMS OF ACTIONS FOR DEBTS OR DAMAGES
Account, Action on
Action on the Case
Assumpsit, Action of
Covenant, Action of
Debt, Action of

ACTIONS FOR PARTICULAR FORMS OR SPECIAL RELIEF
Account
Cancellation of Instruments
Debtor and Creditor

FIGURE 4.3
(*continued*)

Divorce
Partition
Reformation of Instruments
Specific Performance

CIVIL PROCEEDINGS OTHER THAN ACTIONS
Habeas Corpus
Mandamus
Prohibition
Quo Warranto
Scire Facias
Supersedeas

SPECIAL CIVIL JURISDICTIONS AND PROCEDURE THEREIN
Admiralty
Bankruptcy
Equity
Federal Civil Procedure

PROCEEDINGS PECULIAR TO CRIMINAL CASES
Double Jeopardy
Extradition and Detainers
Fines
Forfeitures
Grand Jury
Indictment and Information
Pardon and Parole
Penalties
Searches and Seizures
Sentencing and Punishment

7. GOVERNMENT

POLITICAL BODIES AND DIVISIONS
Counties
District of Columbia
Municipal Corporations
States
Territories
Towns
United States

SYSTEMS AND SOURCES OF LAW
Administrative Law and Procedure
Common Law
Constitutional Law
International Law
Parliamentary Law
Statutes
Treaties

LEGISLATIVE AND EXECUTIVE POWERS AND FUNCTIONS
Bounties
Census

Commodity Futures Trading Regulation
Consumer Protection
Customs Duties
Drains
Eminent Domain
Environmental Law
Highways
Inspection
Internal Revenue
Levees and Flood Control
Pensions
Postal Service
Private Roads
Public Contracts
Public Utilities
Schools
Securities Regulation
Social Security and Public Welfare
Taxation
Unemployment Compensation
Weights and Measures
Zoning and Planning

JUDICIAL POWERS AND FUNCTIONS, AND COURTS AND THEIR OFFICERS
Amicus Curiae
Clerks of Courts
Contempt
Court Commissioners
Courts
Federal Courts
Judges
Justices of the Peace
Removal of Cases
Reports
United States Magistrates

CIVIL SERVICE, OFFICERS, AND INSTITUTIONS
Ambassadors and Consuls
Asylums
Attorney General
Coroners
District and Prosecuting Attorneys
Elections
Newspapers
Notaries
Officers and Public Employees
Prisons
Registers of Deeds
Sheriffs and Constables
United States Marshals

MILITARY AND NAVAL SERVICE AND WAR
Armed Services
Military Justice
Militia
War and National Emergency

FIGURE 4.4
Outline of the Topic

Source: West's Federal
Practice Digest—Volume 12A
Bridges—Citizens. Reprinted
by permission of Thomson/
West.

CEMETERIES

SUBJECTS INCLUDED

Lands used for burial of the dead, whether in churchyards or other places, and regulations relating thereto
Organization, franchises and powers of companies formed to provide and maintain such places
Rights, duties and liabilities of such companies and of purchasers of lots or other rights or privileges in respect of property

SUBJECTS EXCLUDED AND COVERED BY OTHER TOPICS

Burial, personal rights, duties and liabilities, see DEAD BODIES
Decedents' estates, liabilities of, see EXECUTORS AND ADMINISTRATORS
Sanitary regulations, see HEALTH AND ENVIRONMENT
Zoning restrictions, see ZONING AND PLANNING

For detailed references to other topics, see Descriptive-Word Index

_____

Analysis

☞1. Power to establish and regulate.
  2. Lands constituting cemeteries.
  3. Statutory and municipal regulations.
  4. Establishment by municipalities.
  5. Companies and associations.
  6. Location.
  7. _____ In general.
  8. _____ Consent of adjacent landowners.
  9. _____ Consent of public authorities.
10. Acquisition of and title to lands.
10.1. _____ In general.
11. _____ Mode of acquiring lands.
12. _____ Title and rights acquired.
13. _____ Power to sell or mortgage or lease.
14. _____ Abandonment.
15. Title and rights of owners of lots in general.
16. Right of burial.
17. Care of grounds, lots, and graves.
18. Tombstones and monuments.
19. Trespasses.
20. _____ In general.
21. _____ Disinterments.
22. _____ Offenses.

key number system
A detailed system of classification that currently divides the law into more than 400 separate categories or topics.

The numerical designation of a line in a topic outline is known as a **key number system.** Since there are key numbers under each topic, a key number has no significance in itself. A topic with a key number has significance. If you can determine the topic and key number combination or combinations for cases like yours, the "key number" will "unlock" the entry to the digest paragraphs summarizing the cases like yours in the digest. (See Figure 4.5.)

Using a digest is analogous to using an ordinary index, but more is involved. Instead of (1) alphabetically searching entries to (2) find a short entry giving you (3) a page reference to (4) turn to and search the text to check if the information you want is there (as you would with an ordinary index), the digest method is (1) conceptually searching an outline of the law to determine the appropriate topic and key number combinations to (2) find a long entry (that is, a digest paragraph under the appropriate topic and key number combinations in a digest) giving you (3) a citation reference (volume, reporter, and page) to (4) select the correct reporter, turn to the correct page, and search the text to check the similarity of the case to yours.

FIGURE 4.5
**Digest Summary
of Case**

Source: West's *Federal
Practice Digest—Volume 12A
Bridges—Citizens.* Reprinted
by permission of Thomson/
West.

CEMETERIES
For references to other topics, see Descriptive-Word Index

Research Notes
Bogert, Trusts and Trustees.

☞ *1-2.* *For other cases see earlier editions of this digest, the Decennial Digests, and Westlaw.*

Library references
C.J.S. Cemeteries.

☞ **3. Statutory and municipal regulations.**

Library references
C.J.S. Cemeteries §§ 3, 4, 11.

N.D.Ill. 1988. Illinois Cemetery Care Act and Illinois public policy prevent party from owning exclusive right to information contained in cemetery's books and records without also owning or operating cemetery. Ill. S.H.A. ch. 21, 64.1 et seq.

In re Memorial Estates, Inc., 90 B.R. 886.

E.D.N.Y. 1991. Fact that New York statute requiring cemetery plot to be offered to cemetery at original purchase price plus 4% interest before being sold on open market could have had disproportionate impact on Jewish fraternal organizations did not make statute inconsistent with First Amendment where lack of proportion did not result from discriminatory motive; any disproportionality occurred as result of Jewish immigrants forming benevolent societies and purchasing cemetery plots. U.S.C.A. Const. Amend. 1; N.Y.McKinney's N–PCL § 1513(c); N.Y.McKinney's Insurance Law § 4522.

Warschauer Sick Support Soc. v. State of N.Y., 754 F.Supp. 305.

☞ *4-12.* *For other cases see earlier editions of this digest, the Decennial Digests, and Westlaw.*

Library references
C.J.S. Cemeteries.

☞ **10. Acquisition of and title to lands.**

☞ **13. ____ Power to sell or mortgage or lease.**

N.D.Ill. 1988. Class of owners of mausoleum rights and burial rights and class of cemetery's union employees were not entitled to intervene in foreclosure action against mortgagor cemetery, where bankruptcy court, which was hearing case due to bankruptcy of mortgagor cemetery, made it clear the foreclosure action and counterclaims of third party to which mortgagor cemetery had attempted to sell assets including unused burial spaces would not in any way affect rights of class of union employees or class of purchasers.

In re Memorial Estates, Inc., 90 B.R. 886.

Bankruptcy judge's failure to consider and include issue of third party's allegedly exclusive right to information contained in cemetery's books and records provided no basis for striking proposed findings and conclusions of bankruptcy judge with respect to foreclosure action brought by mortgagee against mortgagor cemetery; whether third party, to which cemetery had attempted to sell assets including unused burial spaces, needed books and records, and whether third party had right to exclusive use of information in the books and records was irrelevant to the foreclosure proceedings.

In re Memorial Estates, Inc., 90 B.R. 886.

Mortgage securing cemetery premises did include "unused burial spaces," under Illinois law.

In re Memorial Estates, Inc., 90 B.R. 886.

Under Illinois law, "unused burial spaces" were subject to mortgage after mortgagor cemetery attempted to sell unused burial spaces to third party; cases established that common-law rule providing purchasers for value of burial space were not subject to cemetery's mortgage applied only to individual purchasers of burial spaces for direct interment purposes, and third party was corporate retailer of cemetery lots, so common-law rule subordinating mortgage to individual's right to be buried in burial space that he purchased for value did not apply.

In re Memorial Estates, Inc., 90 B.R. 886.

Under Illinois law, third party that attempted to purchase unused burial spaces from mortgagor cemetery was not bona fide purchaser that took free of mortgage securing cemetery premises that

FIGURE 4.5
(*continued*)

covered unused burial spaces; regardless of whether the third party paid valuable consideration for the burial spaces, the third party did have actual notice of the mortgage before it acquired rights to burial spaces, so third party could not qualify as bona fide purchaser.

In re Memorial Estates, Inc., 90 B.R. 886.

Mortgagee had failed to prove that third party which attempted to purchase mortgagor cemetery's assets including unused burial spaces assumed mortgagor cemetery's mortgage obligations, and third party was accordingly not liable for attorney fees and costs incurred as a result of mortgagee's foreclosure as provided for by mortgage, under Illinois law,

although mortgagee argued third-party implicitly assumed mortgage obligations.

In re Memorial Estates, Inc., 90 B.R. 886.

Security agreement between mortgagor cemetery and mortgagee, providing that in event of default, mortgagee could take and maintain possession of real estate and all documents, books, records, papers, and accounts of cemetery precluded third party from purchasing exclusive right to information contained in cemetery's books and records, where cemetery defaulted on note before attempted transfer of books and records to third party.

In re Memorial Estates, Inc., 90 B.R. 886.

For cited U.S.C.A. sections and legislative history, see United States Code Annotated

A Digest Walk-Through

Let's walk through a Thomson/West example, examining the digest method in more detail. (See Figure 4.6.) Suppose you want to find a case that ruled whether or not a cemetery plot was an "interest in land" such that a contract for the transfer of one would have to be in writing.

Determination of a Topic and Key Number Combination from a Topic Outline

The first step in the Thomson/West digest method is to determine the appropriate topic and key number combinations to be searched. One obvious approach to doing this is to become thoroughly familiar with Thomson/West's outline of the law. Set out in Figure 4.3, the outline can be found in the front of any of Thomson/West's digest volumes. Ideally, you would recognize that a cemetery plot is a type of property, and thus the appropriate major division of the outline to search is

FIGURE 4.6
The Digest Method

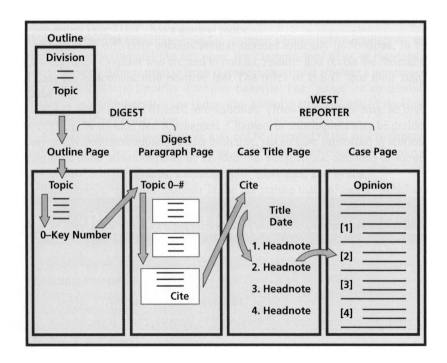

"Property." Under the major division "Property," you would go to the subdivision "Particular Subjects and Incidents of Ownership." Under that subdivision, "Cemeteries" is the relevant topic.

To view the outline of the topic, you would find the first few pages of the topic in the appropriate digest volume in the appropriate digest set, each set being organized alphabetically by topic. You would scan the outline of the topic—Cemeteries—for a line such as "Cemetery plots as interests in land," and pick up the line's key number.

Determination of a Topic and Key Number Combination from a Descriptive-Word Index

Another approach to finding topics and key numbers is to use Thomson/West's "Descriptive-Word Index" volumes for the appropriate digest set. (See Figure 4.7.) The index contains a variety of catch words as entries, with references to topic and key number combinations, intended to allow researchers to find the best combination or combinations that will enable them to uncover cases like theirs.

Determination of a Topic and Key Number Combination from a Case Report or Other Thomson/West Publication

If you have already found one case like yours, another approach is to use West's tables of cases for the appropriate digest set. These tables list the topic and key number combinations in which digest paragraphs have been made for each case. These topic and key number combinations can also be picked up directly from the headnotes in the report of the case like yours in the National Reporter System. This leads to yet another approach, which is, generally, to get suggested topic and key number combination cross-references from other Thomson/West publications.

Thomson/West publishes an array of books, and most are tied together by topic and key number references.

Thomson/West publishes the National Reporter System. Specialized reporters cover the federal and specialized courts, and regional reporters cover the state courts. Headnotes with topic and key number take you back and forth between court opinions and Thomson/West's digests.

As discussed in this chapter, Thomson/West's American Digest System, and other Thomson/West digests, index the reporters. Searches of reporters and digests, including topics and key numbers, can be made electronically on Westlaw.

Thomson/West's annotated federal code, *United States Code Annotated* (U.S.C.A.) contains topic and key number research references. Thomson/West also publishes *Black's Law Dictionary* and a wide variety of form books and textbooks. Thomson/West's one-volume treatises for students, known as hornbooks, include digest references.

Search the Appropriate Digest Using a Topic and Key Number Combination

After determining the appropriate topic and key number combinations to search, the next step in the digest method is to search the appropriate digest sets under the appropriate topic and key number combinations. Under each topic and key number, you will find all the digest paragraphs classified to that topic and key number combination from all the cases. Under some topic and key number combinations, there are only a few of these fine-print summaries, which you can quickly read and review. Under other topic and key number combinations, however, there may be hundreds of these fine-print summaries, which may take you hours to read and review.

Using Its Citation Found in a Digest, Find the Case in a Reporter

If you find a summary in a digest that appears to indicate a case like yours, the next step in the digest method is to use the citation (volume-reporter-page) to find the case in the National Reporter System.

Select the appropriate reporter, turn to the proper page, and search the text to check if the case is one like yours. Sometimes this can be quickly done by finding the headnotes with your topic and key number combinations and using the bracketed headnote numbers in the text to locate the part of the opinion discussing your topic. Because digest paragraphs are summaries, however, you may find upon reading the case you have been referred to that it is not really a case like yours.

FIGURE 4.7
Descriptive-Word Index

Source: West's *Federal Practice Digest, 4th*—Volume 97 Descriptive Word Index A–Ci. Reprinted by permission of Thomson/West.

CEMETERIES

References are to Digest Topics and Key Numbers

CHARITABLE gift, devise or trust,
Care and improvement, **Char** ⟜ **15**

COMPANIES, **Cem** ⟜ **5**

DEDICATION,
Property, **Dedi** ⟜ **10**

EMINENT domain,
Acts and regulations constituting taking, **Em Dom** ⟜ **2(1.1)**
Cemeteries as public use, **Em Dom** ⟜ **42**
Taking property of another cemetery, **Em Dom** ⟜ **47(4)**

ESTABLISHMENT, **Cem** ⟜ **1, 4**
Municipal corporations, **Mun Corp** ⟜ **734**

EXEMPTIONS,
Income tax-federal, **Int Rev** ⟜ **4056**
Property taxes, **Tax** ⟜ **245**
Public improvement assessments, **Mun Corp** ⟜ **434(4)**

GIFTS,
Care and improvement, **Cem** ⟜ **15**

INCOME tax-federal,
Exemptions, **Int Rev** ⟜ **4056**

LANDS constituting, **Cem** ⟜ **2**

LEASE of land, **Cem** ⟜ **13**

LOCATION,
Consent,
Adjacent landowners, **Cem** ⟜ **8**
Public authorities, **Cem** ⟜ **9**

LOTS,
Care, **Cem** ⟜ **17**
Charitable gift, **Char** ⟜ **15**
Exemption from legal process, **Exemp** ⟜ **51**
Title to property, **Cem** ⟜ **15**

MORTGAGES, **Cem** ⟜ **13**

MUNICIPAL corporations,
Establishment by, **Cem** ⟜ **4**
Regulations, **Cem** ⟜ **3**

NUISANCE,
Private nuisance, **Nuis** ⟜ **3(7)**

OFFENSES, **Cem** ⟜ **22**

POWERS and duties,
Establishment and regulation, **Cem** ⟜ **1**

PROPERTY taxes,
Exemptions, **Tax** ⟜ **245**

SALE of land, **Cem** ⟜ **13**

STATUTES, **Cem** ⟜ **3**

TOMBS and tombstones, **Cem** ⟜ **18**

TRESPASS, **Cem** ⟜ **20**
Disinterments, **Cem** ⟜ **21**

VETERANS, **Armed S** ⟜ **123**

CENSORS AND CENSORSHIP

OBSCENITY. See heading **OBSCENITY**, generally.

PRISONERS,
Rights and restrictions, **Prisons** ⟜ **4(6)**

RADIO, **Tel** ⟜ **429-437**

SCHOOLS and school districts. **Schools** ⟜ **164-168**

SPEECH, freedom of. See heading **SPEECH, FREEDOM OF**, generally.

TELEVISION, **Tel** ⟜ **429-437**

CENSUS

APPORTIONMENT and reapportionment. See heading **ELECTION DISTRICTS OR PRECINCTS, APPORTIONMENT** and reapportionment.

CHILDREN and minors,
Schools and school districts, **Schools** ⟜ **43**

MUNICIPAL corporations, **Census** ⟜ **9**

REDISTRICTING. See heading **ELECTION DISTRICTS OR PRECINCTS, APPORTIONMENT** and reapportionment.

SCHOOLS and school districts. **Schools** ⟜ **43**

STATE, **Census** ⟜ **8**

STATISTICAL adjustment, **Census** ⟜ **7**

UNITED States,
Generally, **Census** ⟜ **1**
Compilation of returns, **Census** ⟜ **7**
Constitutional law, **Census** ⟜ **2**
Enumeration, **Census** ⟜ **4**
Methodology, **Census** ⟜ **4**
Officials, **Census** ⟜ **3**
Publication of returns, **Census** ⟜ **7**
Questionnaires, **Census** ⟜ **4**
Refusal to furnish information, **Census** ⟜ **5**
Reports, **Census** ⟜ **6**
Returns,
Compilation, **Census** ⟜ **7**
Making, **Census** ⟜ **6**
Publication, **Census** ⟜ **7**
Statistical sampling, **Census** ⟜ **4, 7**
Statutes, **Census** ⟜ **2**
Undercounting, **Census** ⟜ **4**

VOTER tabulation districts, **Census** ⟜ **7**

The Supplementation of Physical Digest Volumes by Pocket Parts

In going through these steps of a digest search, a legal researcher must be aware that most physical digests are supplemented by cumulative annual pocket parts. For the latest citations, check the pocket part.

Thomson/West's American Digest System

West Publishing Company began preparing digests in 1890. The digest sets indexing the case opinions in all the various units of the National Reporter System are known as the American Digest System.

In the same way that West reported federal cases before the National Reporter System started, in a special reporter, *Federal Cases,* West digested the cases before it made its topic and key number outline of the law in a special digest. This special digest, the *Century Digest,* covers the years 1658–1896.

Since 1897, West has published a series of digests according to its topic and key number outline of the law. Each major digest covers a 10-year period and is known as a decennial digest. Because of the tremendous growth in case law in the past few decades, West started, with the Ninth Decennial, to issue the "decennials" in five-year parts. The Eleventh Decennial, Part 2, is a four-year part. Until the next decennial part is published, the most recent coverage is collected in a series known as the General Digest. Thus, the American Digest System, which contains over 400 volumes, includes the following sets:

> *1658–1896 Century Digest, 1897–1906 First Decennial, 1907–1916 Second Decennial, 1916–1926 Third Decennial, 1926–1936 Fourth Decennial, 1936–1946 Fifth Decennial, 1946–1956 Sixth Decennial, 1956–1966 Seventh Decennial, 1966–1976 Eighth Decennial, 1976–1981 Ninth Decennial, Part 1, 1981–1986 Ninth Decennial, Part 2, 1987–1991 Tenth Decennial, Part 1, 1991–1996 Tenth Decennial, Part 2, 1996–2001 Eleventh Decennial, Part 1, 2001–2004 Eleventh Decennial, Part 2, 2004– General Digest (11ᵗʰ Series).*

The dates of coverage of the different digests have been mentioned so that you will know if one or more of these digests are relevant to your search. To thoroughly search a topic from the present back to 1658, it is necessary to search in each of 16 sets under the appropriate topic and

 Eye on Ethics

The library I use doesn't have that book or electronic file mentioned in *Basic Legal Research*. Are "they" doing something unethical? No, absolutely not! It is not unethical for a particular library to not have a particular book or electronic file.

Law books and electronic files are expensive, and libraries have limited budgets. Educators and librarians must make tough choices when deciding which law books and electronic files a particular library needs in order to meet the most common needs of their students or users. The availability of materials in a nearby library or elsewhere is an important consideration and choices must be made on a case-by-case basis. It is unrealistic to expect every library to have every book or electronic file mentioned in *Basic Legal Research*.

The American Bar Association (ABA), for example, does not require a school to have the national units of the Thomson/West American Digest System in the school's library in order for the school to have an ABA-approved paralegal program. Paralegal students do not commonly

use the national units. The money it would cost to provide the units can be better spent elsewhere in the paralegal program. The national units of the Thompson-West American Digest System are mentioned in *Basic Legal Research* because some paralegal students have access to a library that contains them, and every paralegal should at least know of them.

In gathering information for *Basic Legal Research,* six different physical law libraries were consulted: a personal law library, a county law library, a law school law library, a regional law library, a state supreme court law library, and the Library of Congress. Each library had at least one resource that was not available (or not readily available) at another library. In the coverage of modern law books and electronic files, *Basic Legal Research* generally favors inclusion rather than exclusion. With the possible exception of the Library of Congress, no library contains all of the law books and electronic files mentioned in *Basic Legal Research*.

key number combination, and, because it used a different numbering system, in the Century Digest under the appropriate number located in the cross-reference *Table of Key Numbers Section for Century Digest* found in West's First and Second Decennials.

Other Digests

Because of the massive size of the American Digest System, many legal researchers ignore the entire system and use Thomson/West's special digests, digests published by LexisNexis, and other publications.

Thomson/West publishes the information contained in the American Digest System in special digests. Except for Delaware, Nevada, and Utah, Thomson/West publishes a digest for every state. The state digests are much more focused and are easier to use than the decennials. To search for case law in a given state, including decisions in federal cases from that state, search the state's digest under the appropriate topic and key number combinations.

West publishes regional digests covering some of the regional reporters in the National Reporter System. The digest paragraphs are arranged alphabetically by the states in the region. The regional digests currently published include the *Atlantic Digest, Second Series,* the *North Western Digest, Second Series,* the *Pacific Digest, Five Series,* and the *South Eastern Digest, Second Series.*

Thomson/West currently publishes *West's Federal Practice Digest, 4th,* for federal cases covering cases since December 1975. Under each topic and key number combination, the digest paragraphs are arranged chronologically by court level for the Supreme Court and the Courts of Appeals, then alphabetically through the District Courts. In addition, under the topic "Patents," Key Number 328, there is a numerical list of all patents adjudicated since December 1975, and under the Topic "Trade Regulations," Key Number 736, there is an alphabetical list of the trademarks and trade names adjudicated since December 1975.

West's Federal Practice Digest, 4th, completely replaces *West's Federal Practice Digest, 3d,* which covered cases from December 1975 into 1983. Federal cases before December 1975 are digested in the following sets:

- 1961–Nov. 1975   West's Federal Practice Digest, 2d
- 1939–1960   Modern Federal Practice
- 1789–1938   Federal Digest

The dates of coverage have been mentioned so that you will know if one or more of these digests are relevant to your search. If you are only searching for federal cases after November 1975, you need only search in *West's Federal Practice Digest, 4th.*

As might be expected, Thomson/West publishes a digest covering only the opinions of the U.S. Supreme Court, the *U.S. Supreme Court Digest.*

LexisNexis also publishes a U.S. Supreme Court digest, the *Digest of United States Supreme Court Reports,* more commonly known by the title on the spine: *U.S. Supreme Court Digest, Lawyers' Edition,* originally published by LCP. Of course, LCP and LexisNexis could not use West's topic and key number system. LexisNexis editors create unique headnotes for the opinions in L. Ed. and L. Ed. 2d and classify them to the L. Ed. Digest according to nearly 400 unique digest titles originally created by LCP, similar to the titles created by LCP for what was its national encyclopedia, *American Jurisprudence, Second Series.* Each digest title is outlined according to the nature of the title, and each line is given a section number.

The L. Ed. Digest includes an extensive table of cases in several volumes, an index to L. Ed., L. Ed. 2d, and other annotations. Thomson/West publishes digests to cases and annotations in its various annotation series originally published by LCP.

It also publishes digests for some of its specialized reporters, including *West's Bankruptcy Digest* and *West's Education Law Digest,* along with the *Military Justice Digest* and the *U.S. Claims Court Digest.*

LexisNexis and the Search Advisor

In 1999, LexisNexis began a multimillion-dollar project to make its own case law summaries and headnotes for the approximately four million cases in U.S. case law, and in the process make an index of the law to compete with Thomson/West's Key Number System. In 2004, LexisNexis publicly announced that a group of nearly 600 case law editors had completed three million summaries.

FIGURE 4.8
U.S. Supreme Court Digest, Lawyers' Edition

Source: From *Digest of the United States Supreme Court Reports, Lawyers' Edition, Volume 4.* Reprinted by permission of LexisNexis.

CEMETERIES

Scope of Topic: This topic covers the general subject of cemeteries and burial grounds or plots.

Treated elsewhere are matters as to gifts for cemetery purposes (see CHARITIES) and the exemption of cemeteries from taxation (see TAXES). Matters as to procedure and proof are treated in such topics as DAMAGES; EVIDENCE; PLEADING; and TRIAL.

§   1   Generally.
§   2   Public regulation.

D§ 1 Generally.

Research References

14 Am Jur 2d, Cemeteries §§ 1, 2, 4–8, 11, 12, 19–27, 30–45, 47, 48

Liability of cemetery in connection with conducting or supervising burial services. 42 ALR4th 1059.

Civil liability of undertaker in connection with transportation, burial, or safeguarding of body. 53 ALR4th 360.

Dead bodies: liability for improper manner of reinterment. 53 ALR4th 394.

Liability for desecration of graves and tombstones. 77 ALR4th 108.

Enforcement of preference expressed by decedent as to disposition of his body after death. 54 ALR3d 1037.

SHEPARD'S® Citations Service. For further research of authorities referenced here, use SHEPARD'S to be sure your case or statute is still good law and to find additional authorities that support your position. SHEPARD'S is available exclusively from LexisNexis™.

Cross References

Gifts to or for cemetery, see CHARITIES § 4.

Race or color, discrimination because of, see CIVIL RIGHTS.

Interference with the burial ground of a religious society is a public nuisance and may be enjoined as such. Beatty v Kurtz, 2 Pet 566,

7 L Ed 521

Under the charter of the Glenwood cemetery, the lot holders had a right to demand that the ground immediately available for burial should remain set apart for that object; that the cemetery should be forever under the protection of a perpetual corporation, charged with the duty of laying out and ornamenting the grounds, capable of receiving gifts and bequests, and empowered to make bylaws for the regulation of the corporation; and while all the property need not be laid out into lots, it should all be available for the general objects of the institution. Close v Glenwood Cemetery, 107 US 466, 2 S Ct 267,

27 L Ed 408

§ 2 Public regulation.

Research References

14 Am Jur 2d, Cemeteries §§ 3, 9, 10, 13–18, 28, 29, 52

Zoning regulations in relation to cemeteries. 96 ALR3d 921.

The availability for burial purposes of large tracts of land within the limits of the city of San Francisco cannot be alleged by a cemetery association owning a burial ground within those limits, to invalidate, under the Federal Constitution, an ordinance forbidding the burial of the dead within the limits of the city and county of San Francisco. Laurel Hill Cemetery v San Francisco, 216 US 358, 30 S Ct 301,

54 L Ed 515

LexisNexis headnotes are classified to its Search Advisor taxonomy. Available electronically on Lexis.com, the Search Advisor helps a legal researcher search for cases topically.

In 2003, LexisNexis added a "More Like This Headnote" feature to Lexis.com. As a result, LexisNexis created the electronic equivalent of a digest search. Analogous to a legal researcher finding the Thomson/West topic and key number for cases like their case, and searching digests under that topic and key number, a Lexis.com user can find a LexisNexis headnote, classified to the Search Advisor, for cases like their case, and retrieve more cases like the headnote by using the "More Like This Headnote" feature.

The Limitations of Digests

Digests have a number of limitations as case finders. In theory, you find the single Thomson/West topic and key number combination, or a similar combination in a similar digest (such as a Search Advisor topic on Lexis.com), go to the appropriate digest volume or electronic file, and there find all the cases like yours neatly summarized. In practice, though, difficulties can pop up at every step.

It is not always a simple matter to find the appropriate topic and key number combination, or a similar topic in a similar system. In the Thomson/West digest search example used earlier, concerning cases that ruled whether or not a cemetery plot is an "interest in land" such that a contract for the transfer of one would have to be in writing, a researcher might just as logically try to search under the major division "Contracts" instead of "Property," then under "Nature, Requisites, and Incidents of Agreements in General," and under the topic "Frauds, Statute of," with a completely different key number. You may find that the cases like yours can be found under several different topic and key number combinations, or under several topics in a similar system.

In fact, as West Publishing Company founder John B. West discovered, his own editors sometimes disagreed about the "correct" classification of a case. Writing in the *Law Library Journal,* West noted:

> *The digester bound to a fixed classification soon finds himself sorely pressed to make certain cases "fit the classification." I remember three excellent digesters who spent an entire day in disagreeing as to whether seal fishery cases should be classified under the topic "Fish" or that of "Game" in the Digest Scheme. It is the old story of the camel's head in the tent. What seems at first a plausible pretext for forcing some novel case or new principle into a topic or subdivision to which it does not naturally belong, leads to hopeless confusion [West, Multiplicity of Reports, 2 LAW LIBR. J. 4 (1909)].*

To keep up with changes in technology and the law, Thomson/West has occasionally changed topics and key numbers, including going to subdivided key numbers (e.g., a key number such as "37.15[2]"). This change can cause confusion, since a researcher going back in time must also trace the changes in the topics and key numbers.

Again, once a legal researcher gets to a digest under a particular topic and key number, or to a topic under a similar system, there may be hundreds of digest paragraphs or cases to search. Regarding Thomson/West's digests, Westlaw allows a digest search to be done electronically, but even electronic digest searches can be imperfect.

Finally, digest paragraphs, like headnotes, have been frequently called into question. An editor, in the rush to prepare headnotes for a reporter and digest paragraphs for a digest, may unavoidably miss significant points of law in the opinion, or misstate points, where the cases are read chronologically rather than topically. Moreover, headnotes and digest paragraphs, like the entries in an ordinary index, can be very superficial and give very little information or guidance.

Attorney Jesse Franklin Brumbaugh, as far back as his 1917 book *Legal Reasoning and Briefing* (Indianapolis: Bobbs-Merrill, 1917), noted these and other deficiencies in digests. He wrote:

> *First the topical divisions may be so poorly chosen that the subject-matter is either not all covered, or there may result the most confusing overlapping. In such instances, unless the decisions are repeated, there may be all the way from one to a dozen places where good fishing may be had for the point desired. Furthermore, another blight of a peculiarly insidious type may follow from a careless classification of materials under the topics chosen. Presuming that excellent divisions into topics have been made, the entire field covered and the topics being mutually exclusive, still it does not follow that the material of the law will have been properly pigeonholed under the best topic. This will direct the searcher to cases that, while they may contain the point desired, were not decided upon this point and discuss it as merely incidental thereto, if not merely as dicta. The effect is to lead to false practice, the quoting of precedents not four-square to the proposition. It leads the hurried practitioner to use dictum for "The Law," and is all the more dangerous because so insidious an evil [p. 237].*

Brumbaugh concluded that the worst feature of a digest is that it "involves such a tremendous waste of time on the part of the searcher in overcoming these logical discrepancies [p. 237]." He advised, "That set of books which supplies the lawyer with the case or cases which he desires in the simplest, quickest and most reliable manner is, other things being equal, the most valuable to him."

OTHER CASE FINDERS

It is important to understand that many other case finders are not discussed in detail in this chapter. The more you perform legal research, the more you will come to realize that case citations are included in virtually every law book and electronic file, and thus, *virtually every law book and electronic file is a potential case finder.* Once you have a case cite, you have overcome the fundamental problem that cases are reported chronologically.

Remember that this book is divided into chapters. This chapter provides an overview of all the methods of finding cases, but both by design and by necessity, some resources used as case finders are discussed in more detail in later chapters. Other than common starting points such as casebooks, lawyers, memorandums, and briefs, and other than the specialized indexes of the law known as digests, the remaining methods are only summarized here and discussed in detail in later chapters.

The following sections briefly discuss the other principal case finders. They will be discussed in more detail in later chapters in this book.

A.L.R. Annotations

Partially in response to West's digest system, LCP developed a specialized series of collection case finders known as annotations. Eventually published by Thomson/West, these annotations are called the *American Law Reports* (A.L.R.).

Legal Research by Computer

Case reporters, case finders, and many other legal sources are available in electronic files. Through word searching texts by computer, legal researchers can, in effect, make their own indexes of the source being searched. Lexis.com, Westlaw, and other sources on the Internet, are discussed in Chapter 13.

Shepard's Citations

Shepard's Citations, a hybrid of case indexing and case collecting through tables of case cites, were developed to allow attorneys to check the status of cases as precedent, but they can also be used as imperfect case finders. *Shepard's Citations* published by LexisNexis, and the competing service, *Key-Cite,* are published by Thomson/West.

 ## A Day in the Life

In your job as a paralegal for the City Law Department, the law director has asked you to prepare a memorandum on the subject of public religious displays. The law director wants you to find as many cases as you can and focus the memorandum on the facts of each case. Because of the city's tight budget, however, you are to use the law books at the County Law Library before asking the law director for permission to use any expensive electronic legal research service.

As a practical matter, the law director has asked you to find cases in the traditional manner: using the physical digests created by West Publishing Company and now published by Thomson/West, and the physical digest created by LCP and now published by LexisNexis. The fact that you already have one of the cases like yours, *Lynch v. Donnelly,* 465 U.S. 668, 79 L. Ed. 604, 104 S. Ct. 1355 (1984), is a great help. If you go to the report of the case at 104 S. Ct. 1355, you can pick up the topics and key numbers of the relevant headnotes, then search those topics and key numbers in the relevant Thomson/West digests like the *U.S. Supreme Court Digest* and *West's Federal Practice Digest, 4th.* Likewise, if you go to the report of the case at 79 L. Ed. 604, you can pick up the LCP classification of the relevant headnotes and use them for a digest search in the *U.S. Supreme Court Digest, Lawyers' Edition.*

Knowing that a digest search is not always perfect, and knowing that virtually every law book and electronic file is a potential case finder, in your effort to find as many cases as you can, you extend your search to other sources. Before long, you have found many cases involving the subject of public religious displays. You understand how lawyers and paralegals can spend many hours engaged in legal research. Indeed, an entire day in the life of a legal researcher can be easily spent in a law library, engaged in research based on a single case.

Secondary Authority

Secondary authority includes everything that is not primary authority. Again, since case citations are included in virtually every law book and legal electronic file, virtually every law book and legal electronic file is a potential case finder.

Summary

The fundamental problem in legal research is that cases are reported chronologically, but a legal researcher wants to find cases topically. The solution is to use a case finder—either an index or a collection. A case is customarily cited by its location in a reporter: volume-reporter-page. There are some obvious case finders that should not be ignored. Because of the Socratic, or "casebook," method, professors and scholars at leading law schools have, over the years, written hundreds of casebooks in almost every subject. Lawyers may astonish you with what they know "off the tops of their heads." In a well-run law firm, a memorandum of law (an in-house written discussion of a legal question) may already have been prepared. In the courthouse, you may find briefs—the formal written arguments filed with the court—for cases like yours.

West Publishing Company's solution to the fundamental legal research problem was to create a specialized index of the reported cases known as a digest. Thomson/West puts together its digests in the process of preparing case opinions for publication in the National Reporter System. If you can determine the topic and key number combination or combinations for cases like yours, the "key number" will "unlock" the entry to the digest paragraphs summarizing cases like yours in the digest. Thomson/West's digest sets indexing the case opinions in the various units of the National Reporter System are known as the American Digest System. Thomson/West publishes a digest for almost every state, some regional digests, and federal digests, including the U.S. Supreme Court Digest. LexisNexis publishes the U.S. Supreme Court Digest, Lawyers' Edition. In 1999, LexisNexis began a multimillion-dollar project to make its own case law summaries and headnotes, classified to its Search Advisor taxonomy. In 2003, with the addition of the "More Like This Headnote" feature to Lexis.com, LexisNexis created the electronic equivalent of a digest search. Digests have a number of limitations as case finders, stemming from the difficulties inherent in classifying the law.

The more you perform legal research, the more you will come to realize that case citations are included in virtually every law book and electronic file. Consequently, virtually every law book and legal electronic file is a potential case finder. Besides casebooks, lawyers, memorandums, briefs, and digests, other case finders include annotations, legal research by computer, *Shepard's Citations*, and other secondary sources.

Key Terms

brief   47
casebook   46
chronologically   44
citation   45
cite   45
cross-references   50
digest paragraphs   50
digests   50
entries   50
jump cite   45
key number system   56

lawyer   46
memorandum of law   47
parallel citation   45
parallel cite   45
pinpoint cite   45
references   50
table of authorities   49
taxonomy   51
topically   44
topics   51

Review Questions

1. What are the essential parts of a case citation?
2. What is a casebook?
3. Why is a memorandum of law prepared?
4. Why is a brief prepared?

5. How is a digest similar to an ordinary index?
6. What is a key number? Does the number mean anything by itself?
7. What are the steps in the digest method? (Hint: Review Figure 4.6.)
8. What is the digest equivalent created by LexisNexis?
9. What are the limitations of digests as case finders?
10. The structure of this chapter, primarily covering digests but also briefly summarizing other legal resources, is based on what fact about virtually every law book and legal electronic file?

Exercises

1. Use *West's* Federal Practice Digest, 4th, to answer this question: Under the topic outline "Crops," what is the key number for cases discussing "Ownership in general"?

2. Use West's Federal Practice Digest, 4th, to answer this question: What is the cite of the case decided by the Seventh Circuit Court of Appeals in 1988 and digested under the Topic "Equity," Key Number 67?

3. Use West's Federal Practice Digest, 4th, to answer this question: Does the law favor escheat? Under what topic and key number is there a digest paragraph supporting your answer? What is the cite of the case under that digest paragraph? (Tip: Remember that digests are secondary authority and that you should read any case and be satisfied that it supports your case before you cite it in a brief.)

4. Use the U.S. Supreme Court Digest (Thomson/West) to answer these questions: Can the states add conditions to those imposed by Congress for the naturalization of aliens? Under what topic and key number is there a digest paragraph supporting your answer? What is the U.S. cite of the case under that digest paragraph?

5. Use the U.S. Supreme Court Digest, Lawyers' Edition (LCP, now published by LexisNexis) to answer these questions: In an action for malicious prosecution, is having acted upon the advice of counsel a good defense? Under what topic and section number is there a digest paragraph supporting your answer? What is the U.S. cite of the case under that digest paragraph?

Vocabulary Builders

Find and circle the following terms in the subsequent word search puzzle. The terms may appear up, down, sideways, or diagonal, and forward or backward, ignoring any spaces in phrases.

C	B	Y	E	D	W	A	R	D	N	O	L	F	I	A	B	C	D	E	F	G	H	I	J	K	L
M	H	N	O	P	Q	R	S	T	U	V	W	X	Y	Z	A	B	C	D	E	F	G	H	I	J	K
L	M	R	N	O	P	R	E	F	E	R	E	N	C	E	S	C	I	P	O	T	Q	R	S	T	U
V	W	X	O	Y	Z	A	B	C	D	E	F	G	H	I	J	K	L	M	N	O	O	P	Q	R	S
T	U	V	W	N	X	Y	Z	A	B	C	D	E	F	G	H	I	J	K	L	M	N	P	O	P	Q
R	S	T	U	V	O	W	C	I	T	A	T	I	O	N	X	Y	K	Z	A	B	C	D	I	E	F
G	H	I	J	K	L	L	M	N	S	O	P	Q	R	S	T	O	U	V	W	X	Y	Z	A	C	B
Y	L	L	A	C	I	P	O	T	E	K	L	M	N	O	O	P	Q	R	S	T	U	V	W	X	S
Y	Z	A	B	C	D	E	F	G	G	F	E	I	R	B	G	H	I	J	K	L	M	N	O	E	P
Q	R	S	T	U	V	W	X	Y	I	Z	A	B	E	C	D	E	F	G	H	I	J	K	I	L	M
N	O	P	Q	R	S	T	U	V	D	C	W	S	X	Y	Z	A	B	C	D	E	F	R	G	H	I
J	K	L	M	N	O	P	Q	R	S	T	A	U	V	W	X	Y	Z	A	B	C	T	D	E	F	G
H	I	J	K	L	M	N	O	P	Q	C	R	L	S	T	U	V	W	X	Y	N	Z	A	B	C	D
E	F	G	H	I	J	K	L	P	A	R	A	L	L	E	L	C	I	T	E	M	N	O	P	Q	R
S	T	U	V	W	X	Y	Z	A	B	C	D	E	F	Y	G	H	I	J	K	L	M	N	O	P	Q
R	S	T	U	V	W	X	Y	B	A	S	I	C	L	E	G	A	L	R	E	S	E	A	R	C	H

BRIEF, CASEBOOK, CHRONOLOGICALLY, CITATION, DIGEST, ENTRIES, PARALLEL CITE, REFERENCES, TOPICALLY, and **TOPICS.**

Chapter 5

Annotations

CHAPTER OBJECTIVES

After reading this chapter, you should be able to:

- Recognize the purpose and use of annotations.

- Compare and contrast annotations and digests.

- Identify and use the various annotation series.

- Judge the quality of the various annotation series.

- Identify and use the various parts of an A.L.R. annotation.

- Find A.L.R. annotations using the digest method.

- Find A.L.R. annotations using the index method.

- Find A.L.R. annotations using miscellaneous methods.

- Identify and use A.L.R. supplementation.

- Understand the limitations of A.L.R. in legal research.

In this chapter, you will learn about a system for finding cases based on searching collections of the same—a process known as annotations. Emphasis is placed on the *American Law Reports* (A.L.R.) system originally published by The Lawyers Co-operative Publishing Company (LCP) and now published by Thomson/West.

ANNOTATIONS, GENERALLY

annotation
An in-depth analysis of a specific and important legal issue raised in the accompanying decision, together with an extensive survey of the way the issue is treated in various jurisdictions.

annotate
To note or to mark up.

Unlike a digest, which is a method of finding cases in a specialized index of the law, an **annotation** is a method of finding cases in a specialized collection of the law.

The word **annotate** means to note. A common scholarship technique is to annotate—to note, or to mark up—a book or text. When a passage makes an important point, needs explanation, or deserves comment, a scholar often records related points, explanations, and comments right in the margin. Having all the related points, explanations, and comments collected in one spot, it is easy to study the subject in detail. A scholar can easily find what he or she wants to know about a particular point using these notes.

Annotation, in its ordinary sense, is especially useful in the law. Legal researchers are usually seeking to find all the cases, explanations, and comments available on a particular point of law. If someone has already read, analyzed, and synthesized the relevant law, and put it into note form for you, your research is virtually complete. All you have to do is read the notes.

Annotations are best used early in the legal research process. They are designed to be a fast method for finding case law. If an annotation exists on the point you are researching and you can

Case Fact Pattern

While you are at the county law library researching public religious displays, you notice that the library has several hundred volumes of a law book series known as A.L.R. Although you came to the county law library to use the Thomson/West digests, you wonder if you can find cases on public religious displays in A.L.R. as well, so the next day you take time to peruse the A.L.R. collection on the subject.

find it, you may be taken right to the heart of your issue. An annotation is similar to a memorandum of law.

The *American Law Reports* (A.L.R.) is an important secondary source of legal information. It is a shortcut in two significant ways. First, when you use an A.L.R. annotation, the A.L.R. editor has already done a West digest search for you. Even in a simple annotation, the A.L.R. editor searches all the relevant West Topics and Key Numbers. For example, in an annotation such as "Mausoleum as Nuisance," 1 A.L.R. 546, the A.L.R. editor searches the West digests under both the subject (Cemeteries), and the cause of action (Nuisance). It is not uncommon for an A.L.R. editor to search through 20 or more West Key Numbers in preparing an A.L.R. annotation.

Second, the A.L.R. editor has read all of the cases relevant to the point annotated and is in a position to analyze them for you. The A.L.R. editor sifts through, chooses, compares, and weighs all the cases on the point annotated, summarizes them, organizes them by fact pattern or legal holding, and lists them pro and con. With a good annotation, you know the status of the common law on your point. In the words of a state Supreme Court Justice (Chief Justice Ron George), A.L.R. provides the service of "separating the wheat from the chaff."

A.L.R. ANNOTATIONS

Over 800 volumes of A.L.R. have been published since 1919 in eight different series. A.L.R.-style annotations also appear in the *United States Supreme Court Reports, Lawyers' Edition* (L. Ed. and L. Ed. 2d).

Early A.L.R. annotations contained few parts and sections, while modern A.L.R. annotations contain a number of them. A.L.R.'s style and content have also changed over the years.

Series

The A.L.R. system of annotations consists of eight series (see Figure 5.1). The original A.L.R. (First Series) was published from 1919 to 1948 in 175 volumes. Starting in 1936, annotations were often written to support articles in LCP's encyclopedia, *American Jurisprudence.*

A.L.R. Second Series (A.L.R. 2d) was published from 1948 to 1965 in 100 volumes. The principal reason for the new series was to give LCP salesmen a "new" book to sell. Minor editorial changes included a section-numbered scheme (outline) and an index preceding each long annotation. A small group of editors wrote most of the annotations, and few limitations were placed on their writing. Within the company, LCP editors were viewed as "creative law writers."

In the late 1950s, A.L.R.-style annotations were included in L. Ed., and, in L. Ed. 2d, they became a permanent feature.

FIGURE 5.1
The A.L.R. Series

A.L.R. (1st)	1919–1948	175 Volumes
A.L.R. 2d	1948–1965	100 Volumes
A.L.R. 3d	1965–1980	100 Volumes
A.L.R. Fed.	1969–2005	Over 100 Volumes
A.L.R.4th	1980–1992	90 Volumes
A.L.R.5th	1992–2	Several Volumes
A.L.R.6th	2005–Present	Several Volumes
A.L.R. Fed.2d	2005–Present	Several Volumes

Eye on Ethics

Although the business of law publishing has not always been conducted in an ethical manner, there are some little-known people who have worked in the business of law publishing who have become ethical heroes.

Perhaps the greatest hero in law publishing was Ernest Schopler, a Jewish German lawyer who came to the United States in 1938 after Nazi Germany prohibited Jews from practicing law. He became an American lawyer and found work as an A.L.R. editor for The Lawyers Co-operative Publishing Company (LCP). After Nazi Germany was defeated in World War II, he returned to Germany as an American lawyer with the United States Office of Military Government.

Using his expertise in both German and American law, Ernest Schopler was the lawyer who, with blue-pencil in hand, actually denazified German law.

He later returned to the United States and LCP, and became their greatest A.L.R. editor. Because of the quality of his work, he was promoted to Managing Editor of the *United States Supreme Court Reports, Lawyer's Edition* (L.Ed), and was responsible for the addition of A.L.R.– style annotations to L.Ed.

Thomas Jefferson, the Third President of the United States, once said: "The study of law . . . qualifies a man to be useful to himself, to his neighbors, and to the public." That describes Ernest Schopler.

A.L.R. Third Series (A.L.R.3d) was published from 1965 to 1980 in 100 volumes. There was a subtle but definite shift in writing style from "great book" to "product." Arbitrary limitations were imposed on the editors, including a strict budget. A.L.R.3d added new features, such as a larger typeface for "improved readability" (which also reduced the number of annotations per volume) and a box of "Total Client Service Library" references (that "billboarded" other LCP products).

In 1969, to capture the tremendous growth of federal law during the 1960s, and to sell another book, LCP put federal law annotations in a separate series: A.L.R. Federal (A.L.R. Fed.). A.L.R. Fed. has been published from 1969 to 2005 in approximately 200 volumes.

By 1974, all A.L.R. editors were required to follow a strict style and content rulebook. A narrow interpretation of relevancy was imposed. Commentary was limited to "practice pointers." Each A.L.R. annotation became a narrow, carefully budgeted, slice of law.

A.L.R. Fourth Series (A.L.R.4th) was published from 1980 to 1992 in 100 volumes. The strict rulebook style is evident. By 1987, LCP removed the phrase "creative law writing" from its editor recruiting materials.

As the result of a joint venture with LCP, in 1986, Mead Data Central made electronic versions of A.L.R.2d, A.L.R.3d, A.L.R.4th, and A.L.R. Fed. available on its Lexis computer research service.

RESEARCH THIS

To understand anything well, you need to spend some time with it. A.L.R. is no exception. If nothing else, examine the first volumes in each series. Thomson/West has continued the LCP tradition of providing an introduction to the new series in the first volume in each series.

Volume 1 of A.L.R. Federal is an example. On page vii there is a foreword. The foreword notes the extraordinary growth in federal litigation in the 1960s that caught the attention of the editors of A.L.R. The foreword states that the growth of federal law created a

need-to-know that A.L.R. Federal was designed to meet.

Note the features and lack of features of 1 A.L.R. Fed. It has a "SUBJECTS ANNOTATED In This Volume" feature similar to a digest, and a "TABLE OF CASES Reported in This Volume" similar to a simple index, but it does not have a simple table of contents. Note, among other things, that the body of an annotation is printed in two columns. Notice how the volume is supplemented by a pocket part. Compare and contrast 1 A.L.R. Fed with the latest volume of A.L.R. Fed. 2d.

A.L.R. Fifth Series (A.L.R.5th) was published from 1992 to 2005 in 125 volumes. Under Thomson management, several cosmetic changes were made with A.L.R.5th, including expanded research references, West digest references, and extensive jurisdiction tables. Reported cases were collected at the end of each volume.

After Thomson's purchase of West in 1996, electronic versions of A.L.R., A.L.R.2d, A.L.R.3d, A.L.R.4th, A.L.R.5th, and A.L.R. Fed. were put on Thomson/West's Westlaw computer research service. LexisNexis apparently obtained a license to continue to publish electronic versions of A.L.R.2d, A.L.R.3d, A.L.R.4th, A.L.R.5th, and A.L.R. Fed., because they appear on the Lexis. com computer research service.

A.L.R. Sixth Series (A.L.R.6th) and A.L.R. Federal Second Series (A.L.R. Fed. 2d) were begun in 2005, and were created to be Thomson/West exclusives. They are not published by LexisNexis. They feature further expanded research references, and integration with Thomson/West's A.L.R. digest, *West's ALR Digest,* first published in 2004 and featuring Key Number topics.

Parts and Sections

Modern A.L.R. annotations contain the parts and sections shown in Figure 5.2.

Prior to A.L.R.5th, an annotation was preceded by a reported case. Now the reported cases appear at the end of each volume. The reported case is an example of the point annotated. A.L.R. editors attempt to collect leading cases wherein the point annotated is a "major feature" of the case. The case is summarized, and headnotes are made and classified to an A.L.R. digest. When available, the briefs of counsel on appeal are summarized just before the opinion of the court.

When LCP published A.L.R., the reported case in A.L.R.4th was a state case, the reported case in A.L.R. Fed. was a Court of Appeals, District Court, or other lower federal court case, and the reported case in L. Ed. 2d was a U.S. Supreme Court case. Under Thomson/West, the reported case in A.L.R. Fed. 2d may be any federal court case. Under LexisNexis, the reported case in L. Ed. 2d continues to be a U.S. Supreme Court case.

FIGURE 5.2
A.L.R. Parts and Sections

Source: American Law Reports, ALR4th Cases and Annotations— Volume 77. Courtesy of The Lawyers Co-operative Publishing Company and Bancroft-Whitney Co. Reprinted by permission of Thomson/West.

ANNOTATION

LIABILITY FOR DESECRATION OF GRAVES AND TOMBSTONES

by

Danny R. Veilleux, J.D.

TOTAL CLIENT-SERVICE LIBRARY® REFERENCES

14 Am Jur 2d. Cemeteries §§ 39–42; 22 Am Jur 2d, Damages §§ 251 et seq.; 22 Am Jur 2d, Dead Bodies §§ 102–106, 142, 145–147, 151, 154, 155; 38 Am Jur 2d, Fright, Shock, and Mental Disturbance §§ 1 et seq.

Annotations: See the related matters listed in the annotation.

5A Am Jur Pl & Pr Forms (Rev), Cemeteries, Forms 43, 71–77; 8 Am Jur Pl & Pr Forms (Rev), Dead Bodies, Form 6

4 Am Jur Legal Forms 2d. Cemeteries §§ 54:121.5, 54:124 ; 7 Am Jur Legal Forms 2d, Dead Bodies §§ 84:31–84:38

43 Am Jur Proof of Facts 2d 1, Intentional Infliction of Emotional Distress

3 Am Jur Trials 637, Selecting the Remedy

US L Ed Digest, Cemeteries § 1: Damages §§ 153, 154

ALR Digests, Cemeteries §§ 11, 12, 12.5, 13: Corpse §§ 16-18: Damages § 339

Index to Annotations, Cemeteries; Dead Bodies: Emotional Injury: Exhumation and Disinterment

VERALEX®: Cases and annotations referred to herein can be further researched through the VERALEX electronic retrieval system's two services, **Auto-Cite®** and **SHOWME®**. Use Auto-Cite to check citations for form, parallel references, prior and later history, and annotation references. Use SHOWME to display the full text of cases and annotations.

FIGURE 5.2
(continued)

Liability for desecration of graves and tombstones

I. Preliminary Matters

§ 1. Introduction
[a] Scope
[b] Related matters
§ 2. Summary and background
[a] Generally
[b] Practice pointers

II. General Considerations Affecting Right to Maintain Action

A. Theories of Recovery

§ 3. Interference with actual or constructive interest in burial lot
§ 4. Interference with "right of burial"
[a] Theory followed
[b] Theory rejected
§ 5. Injury to tombstone or monument
[a] Generally
[b] —Recovery without regard to title or possession of burial lot
[c] —Recovery requiring ownership of tombstone
§ 6. Breach of contract
§ 7. Mental suffering—generally
[a] General view permitting recovery
[b] View permitting recovery if there is physical injury or pecuniary loss
[c] View permitting recovery without physical injury or pecuniary loss—generally
[d] —If defendant's actions are willful, wanton, malicious, or the like
[e] View permitting recovery without evidence of gross negligence, bad faith, or the like
[f] View permitting recovery if defendant's actions are willful, wanton, malicious, or the like
§ 8. —Recovery for negligent infliction of emotional distress
§ 9. —Recovery for intentional infliction of emotional distress
§ 10. —Recovery in action for breach of contract
[a] Recovery granted
[b] Recovery denied

B. Degree of Kinship to Deceased

§ 11. Action by "heirs at law" or "next of kin"—generally

TABLE OF JURISDICTIONS REPRESENTED

Consult POCKET PART in this volume for later cases

US: § 25
Ala: §§2[b], 3, 7[a, f], 9, 11[b], 12[b], 15[a, b], 16[a, c], 17[b], 19[a-c, f], 22[a], 29, 30, 34, 37[b], 44, 46[a]
Ark: §§ 2[b], 9, 14[b], 38
Colo: §§ 2[b], 7[f], 22[d]
Fla: §§ 9, 22[e]
Ga: §§ 2[b], 3, 5[b], 7[d, f], 13[a], 15[a], 16[b], 17[e], 18, 19[a, b, f], 20[a, b], 21, 24, 34, 37[c, d], 39, 41, 5[a, b], 50, 51
Ind: § 23
Iowa: §§ 2[b], 3, 5[a], 13[a], 14[a], 15[b], 18, 26[c]

FIGURE 5.2
(*continued*)

Kan: §§ 4[a], 7[a], 16[c]
Ky: §§ 2[b], 3, 7[a, b, f], 11[b, c], 12[a, c], 14[c], 15[a, c], 18, 19[a, g, h], 37[b], 42[a], 43, 45[a], 46[a-c]
La: §§ 2[b], 3, 4[b], 6, 7[a, d, f], 10[b], 14[a, d], 19[b], 20[a], 23, 25, 28, 31, 37[a], 40, 47, 48
Me: §§ 2[b], 3, 7[f], 17[d], 26[b]
Md: §§ 3, 17[b], 34
Mass: §§ 2[b], 3, 7[f], 13[d], 17[b, c], 27, 34
Mich: §§ 3, 5[a], 13[a], 19[f]], 25, 29
Minn: §§ 3, 32
Mo: §§ 2[b], 3, 7[a], 17[b], 35
NH: §§ 5[a], 13[a, c]
NY: §§ 3, 4[a], 5[a, b], 7[a], 11[a, d], 12[b], 13[a, c], 15[a], 17[b], 22[c], 32, 33
NC: §§ 2[b], 3, 5[b], 7[a, c], 11[a, c], 13[a, b], 19[a], 24, 49, 51

Ohio: §§ 4[a, b], 7[d], 8, 14[b], 24, 34
Okla: §§ 3, 19[a], 36
Or: §§ 2[b], 7[c, e], 12[a], 22[a], 27
Pa: § 2[b]
Puerto Rico: §§ 6, 24, 28
RI: §§ 3, 15[b]
SC: §§ 2[b], 3, 7[a], 14[a], 18, 19[d, e], 34, 48
Tenn: §§ 2[b], 3, 7[c, e], 14[a], 17[b], 22[b], 26[c]
Tex: §§ 2[b], 3, 4[a], 5[c], 6, 7[a-d], 10[a], 12[a], 19[h], 21, 22[a, b, e], 26[a], 31, 34, 42[b], 45[a]
Utah: §§ 3, 7[a], 17[b], 22[c]
W Va: §§ 2[b], 3, 7[a, e], 12[a], 14[a], 17[a], 19[b], 24, 46[a]
Wis: § 2[b]

I. Preliminary Matters

§ 1. Introduction

[a] Scope

This annotation[1] collects and analyzes the reported cases in which the courts have determined whether and to what extent a party may be held civilly[2] liable for the

[Text omitted]

Speiser, Krause, and Gans, 4 The American Law of Torts § 16:34 (1987).

§ 2. Summary and background

[a] Generally

Although the right to maintain an action for the desecration of a grave or tombstone is well established, no uniform theory of recovery has emerged. Courts do, however, generally recognize that relatives of the deceased may demand legal protection to prevent the burial place from unnecessary disturbance,[7] despite adherence to the general view that there can be no property right in a dead body.[8]

Frequently, courts have permitted recovery for the desecration of a grave or tombstone based on the view that the offending party has committed a trespass to the burial lot. According to this view, an action may be maintained by individuals having an actual or constructive possessory interest in the soil to which the decedent's remains have been committed (§ 3). Although some courts have reasoned that an interred body becomes a part of the soil,[9] and others have quoted the familiar adage that dust has returned to dust and ashes to ashes, they have generally recognized that the peculiar nature of an interest in a burial lot requires the application of principles different from those applied to ordinary property rights. Since parties with an interest in a burial lot, including those who purchase the lot, do not generally acquire the fee to the soil,[10] some courts view the desecration of the grave as a violation of a "quasi-property" interest obtained by those receiving express or implied permission to bury their dead.

Another theory that has been used to support a cause of action for the desecration of a grave or tombstone is that the offensive conduct violates the "right of burial" which entitles certain individuals to control the burial or other legal disposition of the deceased (§ 4[a]). Some courts, however, have expressly rejected this theory, to the extent that it limits the cause of action for the desecration of a grave to parties having such . . .

---

1. The present annotation supersedes the annotation at 172 ALR 554.
2. On the subject of criminal liability, see 81 ALR3d 1071; and 52 ALR3d 701, which discuss the mis-
7. 14 Am Jur 2d, Cemeteries § 39.
8. 22A Am Jur 2d, Dead Bodies § 2.
9. 22A Am Jur 2d, Dead Bodies § 70.
10. 14 Am Jur 2d, Cemeteries § 25.

The annotation begins with a short title and the name of the purported author. Keep in mind that an annotation is a cooperative effort. The purported author is usually the editor who read all the cases and prepared the first rough draft, but if that editor has left the publisher, the purported author may be a revising editor. In any event, a revising editor may make substantial changes in the first editor's content and emphasis. The reported case materials may be prepared by a third editor, the indexing materials may be prepared by clerical assistants, and the supplementary materials may be prepared by still other editors and clerical assistants.

An annotation in A.L.R.6th or A.L.R. Fed. 2d next contains a summary of the topic or point annotated.

When LCP published A.L.R., the next part of the annotation was the **TCSL Box.** Cross-references to other units of the LCP's Total Client Service Library were listed.

The next part of an annotation is a detailed logical section-numbered outline originally known as a **scheme,** but referred to by Thomson/West as a **Schematic Article Outline.** After standardized §§ 1 and 2, or under Thomson/West, standardized §§ 1–3, the subject is outlined beginning with the next section. The analysis may be legal, factual, or both, depending on the subject annotated.

Under Thomson/West, the next part is an extensive listing of Research References, including references to related annotations. The part following that is a legal word and fact index of the annotation.

When LCP published A.L.R., the next part was the "Table of Jurisdictions Represented." Under Thomson/West, there is an expanded Jurisdictional Table of Cases, Laws, and Rules. The **jur table** is useful in determining if the annotation cites any cases from a given state or federal circuit.

The most important part of an A.L.R. annotation is the **Scope,** which was § 1[a] under LCP and is § 1 under Thomson/West. The Scope states, with some specificity, the purported contents of the annotation. The scope statement may indicate the annotation contains less than the title of the annotation might imply. To keep annotations artificially short, A.L.R. editors are usually prohibited from making reference to cases in the annotation not literally within the scope of the annotation as perceived by the revising editor, even though the revising editor may not have read all the cases. Moreover, doubts about problem cases are usually resolved in favor of exclusion, rather than inclusion.

When LCP published A.L.R., § 1[b], "**Related matters,**" was a list of similar, related annotations, along with a token sample of law articles and treatises on the point annotated. Under Thomson/West, these kinds of references are included in the Research References. When LCP published A.L.R., if a statute or court rule was particularly relevant to the point annotated, a copy was included in a § 1[c]. Under Thomson/West, these are included in the Table of Cases, Laws, and Rules.

Section 2, "Summary and comment," is a summary of the law found in the preparation of the annotation, but not a free commentary by the editor who read all the cases. Each statement is required to be supported by a citation to another part of the annotation or another outside source. **Practice pointers,** which was § 2[b] under LCP and is § 3 under Thomson/West, are "useful hints" on how to handle a case involving the topic or point annotated.

Beginning with § 3 under LCP and § 4 under Thomson/West, the cases are collected according to the scheme. Each section, or part of a section, begins with an introductory paragraph defining the type of cases to follow. Each case is then set out—sketched—in a paragraph known as a **setout.** If there are numerous repetitive cases, the case cites are merely listed with sample setouts. Since a setout is but a sketch of a case, it may not reflect the true nature of the case. Thus, cases found in A.L.R. should be read in full and analyzed before being cited in a brief.

When published by LCP, if an annotation contained only a few cases, it did not have a scheme, index, jurisdiction table, or numbered sections.

How an A.L.R. Annotation Is Prepared

Just as it is important to understand how a digest is prepared to begin to understand its limitations, it is important to understand how an annotation is prepared to begin to understand its limitations.

An A.L.R. annotation begins with topic selection. Selectors read current cases looking for emerging legal issues of interest to the average lawyer. The goal is to find an interesting case to lead a "hot" topic. If the expense of making an annotation on a given topic can be justified to management, a selection memo is prepared for an editor.

TCSL Box
When LCP published A.L.R., the part of an A.L.R. annotation that listed cross-references to other units of LCP's Total Client Service Library.

scheme or Schematic Article Outline
The detailed logical section-numbered outline of an A.L.R. annotation.

jur table
The "Jurisdictional Table of Cases, Laws, and Rules" or "Table of Jurisdictions Represented" in an A.L.R. annotation.

Scope
The part of an A.L.R. annotation that states the purported contents of the annotation.

Related matters
When LCP published A.L.R., the part of an A.L.R. annotation that listed similar, related annotations, along with a token sample of law review articles and treatises on the point annotated.

Practice pointers
The part of an A.L.R. annotation that contains "useful hints" on how to handle a case involving the topic or point annotated.

setout
The paragraph sketch of a case in an A.L.R. annotation.

The editor begins by making an exhaustive search of the subject, including secondary sources of all kinds. The editor separately researches each annotation, then collects and reads all the relevant cases in, on, and around the point being annotated. While actual techniques vary, editors are instructed to read each case once, decide if it is explicitly on point, prepare setouts, and then organize the setouts within a scheme. The rough draft is then edited by a revising editor to keep each annotation within the strict "rulebook" style. True commentary and creativity are thus kept to a minimum.

Again, an important part of the process is the A.L.R. editor's search of the West Digest System. West topics and key numbers that are searched for each annotation are kept on file, along with other key sources searched, and these topics and key numbers are used as the basis for supplementing each annotation in the future.

How to Use the A.L.R.

When using the A.L.R. a step-by-step approach can be helpful. The following is a list of research steps to assist the researcher when using the A.L.R.

1. Decide if the legal issue is one that involves state or federal law.

2. Identify descriptive words that can be utilized to research the legal issue.

3. If the legal question involves a state law issue, check the general A.L.R. Index or Digest for a cite to an article.

4. If the legal question involves federal law, consult the A.L.R. Fed. Index or Digest for a cite to an article.

5. Locate the appropriate article in the appropriate volume of the A.L.R.

6. Identify the sources of primary law in the jurisdiction involving your legal issue.

7. Check the pocket part or other supplement to ensure that you have the most recent information.

8. Check the history of the annotations to determine if there are articles that supersede the one you are using.

A.L.R. ANNOTATION FINDERS

While annotations are essentially finding tools, there are so many of them that there are "finding tools" to find annotations. Thus, several ways exist to find an A.L.R. annotation.

A.L.R. Indexes

Over the years, LCP published a complex series of "Word" and "Quick" indexes for A.L.R. annotations. Finally, in 1986, LCP simplified the matter somewhat with the publication of a five-volume set, the *Index to Annotations,* covering all LCP annotations except those in A.L.R. (First Series), which were still indexed with the *A.L.R. First Series Quick Index.* In 1992, Thomson replaced it with a six-volume set simply named the *ALR Index.* In 1999, Thomson/West replaced it with a new six-volume set also named the *ALR Index.* It is kept up-to-date with a pocket supplement.

LCP indexers described the A.L.R. indexes as "word-fact" indexes. To search for law relating to an automobile accident, for example, one can search traditional legal words like *negligence* and *due care,* along with fact words like *automobile* and *highway.* Under each entry are the appropriate annotation titles and their citations. (See Figure 5.3.)

A.L.R. Digests

LCP published a digest for A.L.R. (First Series), a digest for A.L.R.2d, and a digest for A.L.R.3d, A.L.R.4th, and A.L.R. Fed. combined. The law was classified under a few hundred topics similar to the topics in LCP's encyclopedias. Under each topic were annotation titles and their citations, along with digest paragraphs prepared for the reported cases and their citations.

In 2004, Thomson/West replaced all the previous A.L.R. digests with *West's ALR Digest.* The digest is a total reclassification according to Thomson/West's Key Number taxonomy. (See Figure 5.4.)

FIGURE 5.3
A.L.R. Index

Source: ALR Index - Index C-D. Reprinted with permission from Thomson/West.

ALR INDEX

Adverse possession
  governmental unit, acquisition of title to land by adverse possession by state or other governmental unit or agency, **18 ALR3d 678, § 4, 10[,a e]**
  use of property by public as affecting acquisition of title by adverse possession, **56 ALR3d 1182, § 5[b]**
Airport, zoning regulations limiting use of property near as taking of property, **18 ALR4th 542, § 4[a]**
Autopsy, liability for wrongful autopsy, **18 ALR4th 858, § 11[c]**
Burial services, liability of cemetery in connection with conducting or supervising burial services, **42 ALR4th 1059**
Charities and charitable contributions, validity, as for charitable purpose, of trust for maintenance or care of private cemetery, burial lot, tomb, or monument, or erection of tomb or monument, **47 ALR2d 596**
Cotenants, rights and remedies as between cotenants of cemetery lots respecting burials therein, **10 ALR2d 219**
Cremation
  negligence, liability in action based upon negligence, for injury to, or death of, person going upon cemetery premises, **63 ALR3d 1252, § 7[a]**
  zoning regulations in relation to cemeteries, **96 ALR3d 921, § 3 [a]**
Death of person going upon cemetery premises, liability in action based upon negligence for, **63 ALR3d 1252**
Desecration of graves and tombstones, liability for, **77 ALR4th 108**
Disinterment in criminal cases, **63 ALR3d 1294**
Easements
  eminent domain, unsightliness of powerline or other wire, or related structure, as element of damages in easement condemnation proceeding, **97 ALR3d 587, § 3[b], 6**
  locating easement of way created by necessity, **36 ALR4th 769, § 7[a], 8[a]**

  private easement, loss by nonuse, **62 ALR5th 219, § 46[b], 63[b]**
Eminent domain
  location, validity of public prohibition or regulation of location of cemetery, **50 ALR2d 905**
  measure of damages for condemnation of cemetery lands, **42 ALR3d 1314**
  municipal power to condemn land for cemetery, **54 ALR2d 1322**
Emotional injury, recoverability of compensatory damages for mental anguish or emotional distress for breach of service contract, **54 ALR4th 901, § 4, 5[d], 6, 7, 11[b]**
Estate taxes, deductibility from testator's gross estate, under 26 U.S.C.A. § 2055, of bequests for public, charitable, and religious uses, **46 ALR Fed 246, § 5, 13, 17**
Frauds, statute of, exceptions to rule that oral gifts of land are unenforceable under statute of frauds, **83 ALR3d 1294, § 5[a]**
Funerals and funeral directors
  liability in action based upon negligence, for injury to, or death of, person going upon cemetery premises, **63 ALR3d 1252**
  supervision, cemetery's liability in connection with conducting or supervising burial services, **42 ALR4th 1059**
Gift for maintenance or care of private cemetery or burial lot, or of tomb or of monument, including the erection thereof, as valid trust, **47 ALR2d 596**
Graverobbing, construction and application of graverobbing statutes, **52 ALR3d 701**
Leases, availability of tax exemption to property held on lease from exempt owner, **54 ALR3d 402, § 3, 13[a]**
Life tenants, implication of right of life tenant to entrench upon or dispose of corpus from language relating to the extent of his dominion over the corpus, or the beneficial purpose of the provision for the life tenant, **31 ALR3d 169, § 7[13, 24]**

FIGURE 5.4
A.L.R. Digests

A.L.R (1st), A.L.R. 2d, A.L.R.3d, A.L.R.4th, A.L.R.Fed. A.L.R.5th, A.L.R.6th. A.L.R.Fed 2d.

A.L.R. (First) Digest   A.L.R. Second Digest   A.L.R. 3d, 4th, and Federal Digests

**CYBER
TRIP**

A.L.R. customers
are kept apprised of
new and upcom-
ing annotations by
a free newsletter
shipped with each
volume. The newslet-
ter for A.L.R.6th is
known as *ALR 6th
Alert.* The newsletter
for A.L.R. Fed. 2d is
known as *ALR Fed-
eral 2d Alert.* They
can be viewed at the
ALR Alert Center at
http://west.thomson.
com/alr/resources/
alerts.

**Total Client Service
Library (TCSL)**
LCP's marketing slogan for
its national law book sets,
which were thoroughly
cross-referenced with
each other.

Total Client Service Library

Although L. Ed. was the first set of books published by LCP, the company's defining set, its backbone, was A.L.R. Just as each A.L.R. annotation was researched and written individually, without reference to a master outline, so each LCP publication was researched and written individually, without reference to a master outline. Just as LCP struggled to develop organizational tools—digests and indexes—for A.L.R., the company also struggled to develop a system of organization for its array of books.

A partial solution came in the mid-1930s. After preparing A.L.R. annotations for several years, some A.L.R. editors were sitting around at lunch one day discussing their work. One remarked that so many A.L.R. annotations had been written that an encyclopedia could be made out of them. The editor-in-chief overheard him and said, "Let's do it." As a result, in 1936, *American Jurisprudence* (Am. Jur.)—and later, *American Jurisprudence 2d* (Am. Jur. 2d)—was born.

Whereas A.L.R. provided a point-by-point treatment of the law, Am. Jur. provided an overview of the law, built on, and citing, among other things, A.L.R. annotations and the cases within A.L.R. annotations. As it turned out, some annotations had to be written to fill in gaps in coverage for the new encyclopedia, but the close relationship indicates why Am. Jur. 2d is an excellent tool for finding A.L.R. annotations.

From 1953 to 1964, LCP created a series of national form books. Each picked up the "Am Jur" moniker: *Am Jur Legal Forms* (1953) [and *Am Jur Legal Forms 2d* (1971)], *Am Jur Pleading and Practice Forms* (1956) [now *Am Jur Pleading and Practice Forms, Revised* (1967)], *Am Jur Proof of Facts* (1959) [and *Am Jur Proof of Facts 2d* (1974)], and *Am Jur Trials* (1964).

Finding that lawyers liked buying "coordinated" books, in 1961 LCP's marketing department devised a slogan for LCP's national sets: the **Total Client Service Library (TCSL)**. Every new national set LCP created was then made part of the TCSL, including among others, *A.L.R. Federal* (1969), *United States Code Service* (U.S.C.S.) (1972), *Federal Procedural Forms, Lawyers' Edition* (1975) (to be discussed in Chapter 9), *Bankruptcy Service, Lawyers' Edition* (1979), and *Federal Procedure, Lawyers' Edition* (1981). Auto-Cite was added in 1982.

LCP's editorial department supported the TCSL "coordination" claim by thoroughly cross-referencing each set in the TCSL with every other set in the TCSL, and in particular, with A.L.R. It is important to remember, however, that each was independently researched and written, and thus, as with A.L.R. itself, some law may have fallen through the cracks.

Thomson/West Publications

Since Thomson purchased West in 1996, references to A.L.R. annotations have increasingly appeared in Thomson/West publications. A.L.R. annotations can be word-searched using the Westlaw computer research system.

LexisNexis Publications

To the extent that LexisNexis publishes former LCP publications, references to A.L.R. annotations continue to appear in those publications.

A.L.R. ANNOTATION SUPPLEMENTATION

Cases are frequently decided after an A.L.R. annotation on the point has already been published. A.L.R. annotations are kept up-to-date by supplementary material that collects these "later cases." The method of supplementation has changed frequently over the years. (See Figure 5.5.)

Blue Books

To supplement A.L.R. (First Series) annotations, LCP published the *A.L.R. Blue Book of Supplemental Decisions.* The volumes in this set simply list cites to later cases on each annotation topic.

Later Case Service

To supplement A.L.R.2d annotations, LCP published the *A.L.R. 2d Later Case Service.* Instead of simply listing cites to later cases on each annotation topic, each case is keyed to the appropriate section of the annotation supplemented.

FIGURE 5.5
A.L.R.
Supplementation

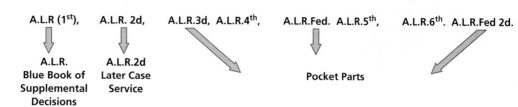

FIGURE 5.6

Annotation History Table

Source: *ALR Index - Index C–D.* Reprinted by permission of Thomson/West.

ANNOTATION HISTORY TABLE

This table lists annotations in ALR (First Series), ALR2d, ALR3d, ALR4th, ALR5th through Volume 69, ALR Fed through Volume 155, which have been superseded or supplemented by later annotations. Consult the pocket part in this volume for later history.

ALR (First Series)

1 ALR 148	Superseded 99 ALR2d 7	2 ALR 1522
Superseded 74 ALR2d 828	2 ALR 6	Superseded 157 ALR 1359
1 ALR 222	Supplemented 49 ALR2d	2 ALR 1576
Subdiv VIII Superseded 71	982	Superseded 77 ALR2d
ALR2d 1140	2 ALR 61	1182
1 ALR 329	Superseded 14 ALR3d 783	3 ALR 242
Superseded 36 ALR2d 861	2 ALR 225	Superseded 72 ALR2d 342
1 ALR 343	Supplemented 41 ALR2d	3 ALR 312
Superseded 51 ALR2d	1263	Superseded 24 ALR2d 194
1404	2 ALR 287	3 ALR 610
1 ALR 383	Superseded 11 ALR4th	Superseded 12 ALR2d 611
Superseded 13 ALR4th	345	3 ALR 664
1153	2 ALR 345	Superseded 48 ALR2d 894
1 ALR 449	Superseded 44 ALR2d	74 ALR4th 90
Superseded 28 ALR2d 662	1242	3 ALR 824
1 ALR 528	2 ALR 545	Superseded 13 ALR3d 848
Superseded 87 ALR4th 11	Superseded 54 ALR3d 9	3 ALR 833
1 ALR 546	2 ALR 579	Superseded 22 ALR3d
Superseded 50 ALR2d	Superseded 50 ALR2d	1346
1324	1161	3 ALR 902
1 ALR 834	2 ALR 592	Superseded 57 ALR3d
Superseded 91 ALR2d	Superseded 12 ALR3d 933	1083
1344	2 ALR 867	3 ALR 1003
1 ALR 861	Superseded 25 ALR3d 941	Superseded 98 ALR3d 605
Superseded 41 ALR2d	2 ALR 1008	3 ALR 1096
1213	Superseded 90 ALR2d	Superseded 89 ALR3d 551
1 ALR 884	1210	3 ALR 1104
Superseded, as to private	2 ALR 1068	Superseded 8 ALR4th 886
easements 25 ALR2d 1265	Superseded 6 ALR3d 1457	3 ALR 1109
1 ALR 1163	2 ALR 1368	Superseded 92 ALR2d
Superseded 28 ALR4th	Superseded 56 ALR3d	1009
482	1182	3 ALR 1130
1 ALR 1267	2 ALR 1376	Supplemented 41 ALR2d
Superseded 87 ALR2d 271	Superseded 45 ALR2d	739
1 ALR 1368	1296	3 ALR 1279
Superseded 46 ALR2d	2 ALR 1389	Subdiv II Superseded 100
1140	Superseded 28 ALR3d	ALR2d 227
1 ALR 1528	1344	3 ALR 1304
Superseded 13 ALR3d 42	2 ALR 1428	Superseded 82 ALR2d 611
1 ALR 1632	Superseded 61 ALR5th	
Superseded 53 ALR2d 572	739	
1 ALR 1688		

Pocket Supplementation

To supplement A.L.R.3d and later annotations, Thomson/West continues the LCP tradition of publishing annual cumulative pocket parts for each volume. Again, each case is keyed to the appropriate section of the annotation supplemented.

Annotation History Table

superseding annotation
An annotation that replaces another annotation.

Another method used to keep annotations up-to-date is to issue superseding or supplementing annotations. If the subject matter of an annotation, or a part of it, has changed significantly, a **superseding annotation** may be prepared. The subject will be rewritten as if there were no annotation on the point. If there have been a lot of cases on an annotated point, but no fundamental changes, a **supplementing annotation** may be prepared. The new cases are discussed with reference to the original annotation.

supplementing annotation
An annotation that provides additional cases on a topic or point already annotated.

To check if a particular annotation, or a part of it, has been superseded or supplemented, refer to the supplemental service for that series of annotations or to the Annotation History Table in the last volume of the *ALR Index.* (See Figure 5.6.) To check if a particular annotation supersedes or supplements another annotation, refer to the scope section of the annotation.

THE LIMITATIONS OF A.L.R. ANNOTATIONS

If your point is annotated, you may find more cases, and quicker, with an A.L.R. annotation than with West's digests. But, relatively speaking, less and less of U.S. case law is being annotated. A.L.R. annotations collect (and West's digests index) reported cases, but more and more of U.S. case law is going unreported. When there is no A.L.R. annotation on your point, you must turn to other sources. Moreover, even if there is an annotation on your point, it merely collects "in point" cases, without real commentary.

 ## A Day in the Life

You are at the county law library, researching public religious displays, when you take a look at A.L.R.

You begin your research in the *ALR Index.* Because the *ALR Index* is a multivolume set, you need an entry term to decide which volume to look in. The terms "religious" and "religion" come to mind, so you look in the volume containing the R index. Fortunately, there is a main entry for RELIGION AND RELIGIOUS SOCIETIES. The next logical term is "displays." You're in luck. You quickly find an entry for "Display of religious structures, erection, maintenance, or display of religious structures or symbols on public property as violation of religious freedom, 36 ALR3d 1256."

You find where A.L.R.3d is shelved and pull out volume 36. You go to page 1256. You find the annotation, but you are concerned about the age of the annotation. The annotation at 36 A.L.R.3d 1256 was published in 1971. You know from your West Digest search that many cases on the topic of public religious displays were decided after 1971. Is the annotation at 36 A.L.R.3d 1256 the best there is on the topic? Will you have to read and analyze all the cases since 1971 on your own?

You start to check the pocket supplement for 36 A.L.R.3d 1256 when you realize that you skipped a step. Each volume in the *ALR Index* has a pocket supplement. You go back to the "R" volume in the *ALR Index* and check the supplement. Bingo! Under RELIGIONS AND RELIGIOUS SOCIETIES you find what you almost overlooked—an entry for a superseding annotation—"Display of religious symbols, First Amendment challenges to the display of religious symbols on public property, 107 ALR5th 1." The superseding annotation was published in 2003, and is exactly what you need. Most importantly, you've learned a fundamental lesson in legal research the easy way: Don't forget to check the supplement!

Summary

The annotation method of finding cases is based on finding cases in a specialized collection of law. If someone has already read, analyzed, and synthesized the relevant law for you, and put it into note form, your research is virtually complete. *American Law Reports* (A.L.R.) is the super-annotated set. It was LCP's special case finder prepared by reading cases topically.

There are eight series of A.L.R. annotations: A.L.R. (First Series), A.L.R.2d, A.L.R.3d, A.L.R.4th, A.L.R.5th, A.L.R.6th, A.L.R. Fed., and A.L.R. Fed. 2d. A.L.R.-style annotations also appear in L. Ed. and L. Ed. 2d. The reported cases serve as examples of the topics or points annotated. Large annotations have a detailed logical section-numbered outline known as a scheme. When using a modern annotation, be aware of its scope statement and the fact that commentary and creativity have been artificially limited.

Annotations can be found with the *ALR Index to Annotations* and *West's ALR Digest*. References to annotations are also found in LCP's Total Client Service Library volumes (such as *American Jurisprudence*) and other sources.

Modern annotations are complemented by pocket supplementation. To check if an annotation has been supplemented or superseded, consult the Annotation History Table in the last volume of the *ALR Index*.

A.L.R. is an unusual case finder. If your point is annotated, you may find more cases quicker with an A.L.R. annotation than with West's digests.

Key Terms

annotate 69	Scope 75
annotation 69	setout 75
jur table 75	superseding annotation 80
practice pointers 75	supplementing annotation 80
related matters 75	TCSL Box 75
Schematic Article Outline 75	Total Client Service Library (TCSL) 78
scheme 75	

Review Questions

1. What is the purpose and use of an annotation?

2. What are the differences between an annotation and a digest?

3. What are the current annotation series?

4. What series of A.L.R. was written by a small group of creative law writers, without rulebooks or artificial limitations of any kind?

5. What are the parts and sections of a modern A.L.R. annotation and what is their purpose?

6. What is the index for modern A.L.R. annotations?

7. What is the digest for modern A.L.R. annotations?

8. In what other ways can you find an A.L.R. annotation?

9. How are modern A.L.R. annotations supplemented?

10. Why might an A.L.R. annotation not contain "All the case law on your point"—as it was advertised in the mid-1980s?

Exercises

1. Use the annotation at 21 A.L.R.4th 383 to answer the following questions: What is the annotation's title? Does the Scope exclude certain cases? What section discusses silverware? In what section is there a case from New Hampshire? What is the title of the first case setout in § 6?

2. Use the annotation at 82 A.L.R. Fed. 248 to answer the following questions: What is the annotation's title? Does the Scope exclude certain cases? What section discusses cases involving newspapers reporters? In what section is there a case from the Eighth Circuit?

What is the title of the first case setout in § 10?

3. Use the pocket supplement to the annotation at 64 A.L.R.4th 323 to answer the following question: What is the cite of the first case listed that supplements § 22 of the annotation?

4. Use the *ALR Index* to answer the following question: What is the cite of the

A.L.R. annotation that discusses liability for death on a golf course?

5. Use the Annotation History Table to answer this question: What is the cite of the A.L.R. annotation, if any, that superseded 49 A.L.R.2d 679?

Vocabulary Builders

Find and circle the following "Top-Ten" terms in the word search puzzle. The terms may appear up, down, sideways, or diagonal, and forward or backward, ignoring any spaces in phrases.

Y	R	A	R	B	I	L	E	C	I	V	R	E	S	T	N	E	I	L	C	L	A	T	O	T	A
B	C	D	N	B	A	S	I	C	L	E	G	A	L	R	E	S	E	A	R	C	H	E	F	U	G
H	I	A	N	N	O	T	A	T	I	O	N	J	K	L	E	M	N	O	P	Q	R	S	T	O	U
V	W	X	Y	Z	O	A	B	C	D	E	F	G	H	I	J	M	K	L	M	N	O	P	Q	T	R
S	T	U	V	W	X	T	Y	Z	A	B	C	D	E	F	G	H	E	I	J	K	L	M	N	E	O
P	Q	R	S	T	U	V	A	W	X	Y	Z	A	B	C	D	L	E	H	F	G	H	I	J	S	K
L	M	N	O	P	Q	R	S	T	T	U	V	W	X	Y	B	Z	A	B	C	C	D	E	C	F	G
H	I	J	K	L	M	N	O	P	E	Q	R	S	T	A	U	V	W	X	Y	S	Z	H	A	B	C
D	E	F	G	H	I	J	K	L	M	N	O	P	T	Q	R	S	T	U	V	W	E	X	Y	Z	A
B	C	D	E	F	G	H	I	J	K	L	M	R	N	O	P	Q	R	S	T	M	U	V	W	X	Y
Z	A	G	N	I	D	E	S	R	E	P	U	S	U	P	P	L	E	M	E	N	T	I	N	G	B
C	D	E	F	G	H	I	C	J	K	J	L	M	N	O	P	Q	R	S	T	U	V	W	X	Y	Z
A	B	C	D	E	F	G	O	H	I	J	K	L	M	N	O	P	Q	R	S	T	U	V	W	X	Y
Z	A	B	C	D	E	F	P	G	H	I	J	K	L	M	N	O	P	Q	R	S	T	U	V	W	X
Y	Z	A	B	C	D	E	E	F	G	H	I	J	B	Y	E	D	W	A	R	D	N	O	L	F	I
P	R	A	C	T	I	C	E	P	O	I	N	T	E	R	S	K	L	M	N	O	P	Q	R	S	T

ANNOTATE, ANNOTATION, JUR TABLE, PRACTICE POINTERS, SCHEME, SCOPE, SETOUT, SUPERSEDING, SUPPLEMENTING, and TOTAL CLIENT SERVICE LIBRARY.

Chapter 6

Statutory Law

CHAPTER OBJECTIVES

After reading this chapter, you should be able to:

• Define basic legislative terminology.

• Understand the nature of legislative history.

• Identify the official chronological source of federal legislation.

• Explain how federal legislation is found topically.

• Identify the official code of federal legislation.

• Describe the benefits of an "annotated" code.

• Recognize the indexes available for annotated codes.

• Compare and contrast Thomson/West's annotated code with LexisNexis's annotated code.

• Recognize the limitations of annotated codes.

• Describe the usual features of state and local codes.

In this chapter, you will learn about the books and electronic files that track the law made by the legislative branch. Emphasis is placed on federal legislation and its publication.

LEGISLATION

enactment
The legislative process that results in the making of a statute.

Congress
A two-year period in which the legislature of the United States meets; the same as the two-year term of a representative.

session
The sitting of a court, legislature, council, commission, and so on for the transaction of its proper business.

bill
A proposed permanent law.

The legislative branch of government makes the law. Unlike judges, who must be confronted with an actual legal controversy and interpret the law to make precedent, legislators simply "dream up" the law. The legislative branch makes statutes. Thus, law from the legislative branch is known as statutory law. (See Figure 6.1.) The legislative process resulting in the creation of a statute is known as **enactment.** Because the federal legislative process is illustrative of the legislative processes in the states, the federal legislative process is discussed in detail in this chapter.

Federal law is made in the sense of being "dreamed up" by Congress. Congress meets in two-year periods, each one known as a **Congress,** with 1789–1790 called the 1st Congress and 2005–2006 known as the 109th Congress. The 20th Amendment, § 2, of the Constitution of the United States, requires Congress to "assemble at least once in every year, and such meeting shall begin at noon on the 3d day of January, unless they shall by law appoint a different day." Accordingly, each Congress consists of a first and a second **session,** each approximately one year in length.

A proposed permanent law introduced in the House of Representatives or in the Senate is known as a **bill** (introduced with the words "Be it enacted"). Bills introduced in the House of

Case Fact Pattern

On your way back to the office after researching public religious displays, you learn that a train carrying hazardous materials has derailed near the center of the city. Tank cars are on fire, spewing poisonous smoke and gas, and several thousand residents have been forced to evacuate. When you get back to the office, you find the law director and everyone else watching the mayor's press conference on TV. The mayor is asked why trains carrying such hazardous cargo were allowed to pass through the city. The mayor says he doesn't know, but he's going to ask the law director to find out what the city can do about it. The law director tells you to put the public religious display project on hold. Instead, your assignment is to find out which federal laws apply to the transportation of hazardous materials and if those laws preempt (prohibit) any state or local law.

act
A bill considered and passed by one house of the Congress of the United States of America.

engrossed bill
The final, officially signed copy of an act.

enrolled bill
A final, officially signed copy of a parchment of a bill that has passed both houses of the Congress of the United States of America.

veto
To return to the Congress a bill without the President's signature that had been presented to the President by Congress, with the result that the bill does not become law, unless the President's return is overridden by a two-thirds vote of each house.

pocket veto
The untimely non-return of a bill presented to the President, with the result that a return thereafter cannot be overridden because the houses of Congress have adjourned.

joint resolution
A proposed temporary (time-oriented) law.

Representatives during a Congress are numbered sequentially beginning with H.R. 1. Bills introduced in the Senate during a Congress are numbered sequentially beginning with S. 1.

In each house, committees study bills. Public hearings may be held, after which the committees report their recommendations to the full house. Placed on the calendar, bills come up for debate, possible amendment, and a vote. Bills considered and passed by one house (each an **act;** and each corrected, final, officially signed copy known as an **engrossed bill**) are sent to the other house for consideration and passage. Substantial differences between versions may be ironed out by a joint conference committee, followed by a vote in each house.

As specified by Article 1, Section 7, of the Constitution of the United States, bills that pass both houses (each corrected, final, officially signed copy on parchment known as an **enrolled bill**) are presented to the President for signature (approval), return without a signature **(veto)**, timely non-return (abstention), or untimely non-return **(pocket veto)**. A bill becomes law if the President signs it, if the President returns it within 10 days (Sunday excepted) and the veto is overridden by a two-thirds vote in each house, or if the President does not return it within 10 days (Sunday excepted) and the houses of Congress have not adjourned.

Bills not passed during a Congress must be reintroduced to be considered again for passage. Bills should be compared and contrasted with joint resolutions, concurrent resolutions, and simple resolutions.

A **joint resolution** (designated H.J. RES. or S.J. RES.) is a proposed temporary (time-oriented) law (introduced with the words "Be it resolved"), such as an extension of a law about to expire or a one-time expenditure. Joint resolutions are passed like bills, except that a proposed

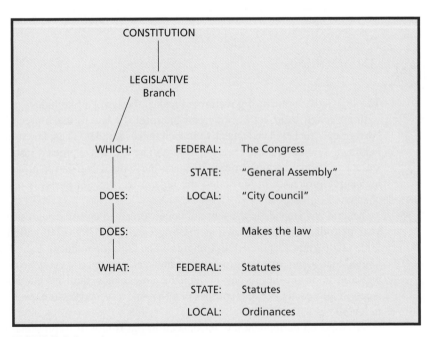

FIGURE 6.1   **The Legislative Branch**

CYBER TRIP

The C-SPAN cable television network covers the day-to-day activities of Congress, the federal government, and related political activities. C-SPAN is available on the Internet at www.c-span.org. Bills from the 101st Congress (1989) to the present can be searched for at the Library of Congress Web site at http://thomas.loc.gov/.

Eye on Ethics

It is unethical for a legislator to seek passage of a new law solely for the benefit of the legislator, rather than for the good of the people. However, the nature of legislation—the "dreaming up" of new laws—certainly creates an environment in which unethical conduct can occur. Paralegals in positions related to the legislative process should beware.

Lobbyists are people in the business of trying to persuade legislators to pass laws favorable to the lobbyist or his or her clients. It is ethical to try to persuade a legislator to pass a certain law. It is also ethical for a legislator to listen to lobbyists, but a legislator may not make any agreement with a lobbyist that constitutes taking a bribe or accepting a kickback. A legislator is prohibited from participating in graft, which is taking advantage of a position of trust to dishonestly obtain money or property.

The 1939 movie *Mr. Smith Goes to Washington* is an excellent work of fiction exploring the problem of unethical legislation. Starring Jimmy Stewart as Senator Jefferson Smith, the movie contains many depictions of reality that still ring true today. Paralegals will identify with Jean Arthur as Clarissa Saunders, the aide to Senator Smith who performs all the functions of a paralegal.

constitutional amendment must be passed by a two-thirds vote of each house and need not be presented to the President (see Figure 6.2).

A **concurrent resolution** (designated H. CON. RES. or S. CON. RES.) is a proposed *administrative* (not legislative) statement of Congress, such as an expression of congressional opinion or the creation of a joint committee, which must be passed by each house to become effective, but is not a law commanding all. Similarly, a **simple resolution** (designated H. RES. or S. RES.) is a proposed *administrative* (not legislative) statement of one house, such as an expression of the house's opinion or the creation of a committee, which must be passed to become effective, but is not a law commanding all.

concurrent resolution
A proposed administrative (not legislative) statement of Congress.

simple resolution
A proposed administrative (not legislative) statement of one house of Congress.

legislative history
The transcripts of the legislative debates leading up to the passage of the bill that became the law or statute.

Legislative History

The laws enacted by the legislature are subject to interpretation by the courts. While it is true that in interpreting a statute a court may consider **legislative history,** the committee reports, floor debates, and other information considered by the legislature in enacting a bill or joint resolution, this is ordinarily done only when the statute has never been interpreted by a court before. Most legal research texts bury this fact in a blizzard of information about the sources of legislative history.

If a statute has never been interpreted by a court before, a court may seek to determine the intent of the legislature in passing the law and apply the law in a manner consistent with that intent. But a court is not bound by legislative intent. A court is bound only by the wording of the statute if the statute is constitutional. More important, once a statute has been interpreted by a court, that interpretation becomes a precedent that has persuasive, if not mandatory, authority. A court can be bound by another court's interpretation of a statute.

As a practical matter, then, the only time a legal researcher need research legislative history is if a court is deciding a case of first impression as to interpreting a statute. If the statute has already been interpreted, legislative history is usually discussed and determined, if at all, in the first few case opinions under the statute.

A detailed discussion of legislative history is beyond the scope of this book. In summary, legislative intent can be inferred from amendments, committee reports, debates, and hearings.

Legislative intent may be inferred by comparing the original version of a bill or joint resolution with any amendments, and whether or not those amendments were enacted. The original version of a bill and its amendments can be found by working with the official record of Congress, the *Congressional Record* (Cong. Rec.), and by checking the bill number in the *History of Bills and Resolutions* part of the *Congressional Record Index* for the appropriate session of Congress.

FIGURE 6.2
Joint Resolution

109TH CONGRESS
1ST SESSION

H. J. RES. 59

JOINT RESOLUTION

Expressing the sense of Congress with respect to the women suffragists who fought for and won the right of women to vote in the United States.

Whereas one of the first public appeals for women's suffrage came in 1848 when Lucretia Mott and Elizabeth Cady Stanton called a women's rights convention in Seneca Falls, New York, on July 19, 1848;

Whereas Sojourner Truth gave her famous speech titled "Ain't I a Woman?" at the 1851 Women's Rights Convention in Akron, Ohio;

Whereas in 1869, suffragists formed two national organizations to work for the right to vote: the National Woman Suffrage Association and the American Woman Suffrage Association;

Whereas these two organizations united in 1890 to form the National American Woman Suffrage Association;

Whereas in 1872, Susan B. Anthony and a group of women voted in the presidential election in Rochester, New York;

Whereas she was arrested and fined for voting illegally;

Whereas at her trial, which attracted nationwide attention, she made a speech that ended with the slogan "Resistance to Tyranny Is Obedience to God";

Whereas on January 25, 1887, the United States Senate voted on women's suffrage for the first time;

Whereas during the early 1900s, a new generation of leaders joined the women's suffrage movement, including Carrie Chapman Catt, Maud Wood Park, Lucy Burns, Alice Paul, and Harriot E. Blatch;

Whereas women's suffrage leaders devoted most of their efforts to marches, picketing, and other active forms of protest;

Whereas Alice Paul and others chained themselves to the White House fence;

Whereas the suffragists were often arrested and sent to jail, where many of them went on hunger strikes;

Whereas almost 5,000 people paraded for women's suffrage up Pennsylvania Avenue in Washington, DC; and

Whereas on August 26, 1920, the 19th Amendment to the United States Constitution granted women in the United States the right to vote: Now, therefore, be it

Resolved by the Senate and House of Representatives of the United States of America in Congress assembled, That it is the sense of Congress that women suffragists should be revered and celebrated for working to ensure the right of women to vote in the United States.

Passed the House of Representatives July 25, 2005. Attest:

Clerk.

CYBER TRIP

The *Congressional Record* from 1994 to the present is available on the Internet at www.gpoaccess.gov/crecord/index.html.

If a committee recommends passage of a bill or joint resolution, the committee usually writes a report explaining its recommendation. Legislative intent may be inferred from a committee report. Thomson/West's *United States Code Congressional and Administrative News* (U.S. Code Cong. & Admin. News) publishes selected committee reports for significant enacted legislation.

A significant bill or joint resolution may be debated on the floor in each house of Congress. Legislative intent may be inferred from the debate, especially from statements by a sponsoring legislator about the scope of the legislation. Such statements can be found in the *Congressional Record.*

FIGURE 6.3
Enactment of a Bill

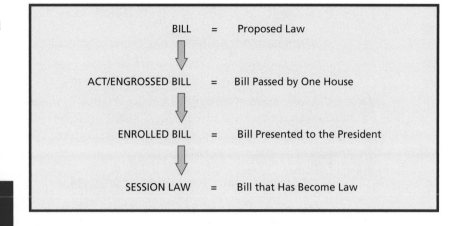

session law
A bill or a joint resolution that has become law during a particular session of the legislature; the second format in which new statutes appear as a compilation of the slip laws.

public law
A law that applies to everyone.

private law
A law that applies only to an individual or to a few individuals.

slip law
A copy of a particular law passed during a session of the legislature; the first format in which a newly signed statute appears.

A shortcut is to find a legislative history that has already been compiled. Sources that may help include *Sources of Compiled Legislative Histories,* Wolter Kulwer's *Public Laws—Legislative Histories Microfiche,* and LexisNexis's *Legislative History Service.* The most widely used indexes of legislative history are the *Congressional Information Service/Index* ("CIS Index") and the *CCH Congressional Index.*

Many legislative history materials are available at Lexis.com, the Westlaw Web site, and other sources on the Internet.

Because of the nature of legislative history research, it is appropriate to obtain the assistance of a librarian familiar with the resources available in a given library. Similarly, "legislative history" on a current bill or joint resolution may be found by contacting the local office of your congressman or congresswoman, or one of your senators, and asking for assistance.

The only major difference between federal legislation and state legislation is the availability of legislative history. While state legislative history theoretically exists, sources of state legislative history are usually nonexistent. State committee reports and floor debates are rarely published. At best, a state legislative bureau may be able to provide summaries of proposed legislation. Legislative history may be limited to a drafting committee's commentary collected in the state's annotated code (discussed next).

After a Bill Becomes Law

A bill or joint resolution that has become law during a particular session of the legislature is known as a **session law.** (See Figure 6.3.) Most laws apply to everyone, and each is known as a **public law.** During each Congress, public session laws are numbered sequentially beginning with Public Law No. 1 (Pub. L. No. 1). Some laws apply only to an individual or a few individuals, and each is known as a **private law.** During each Congress, private session laws are numbered sequentially beginning with Private Law No. 1 (Priv. L. No. 1).

A copy of a particular law passed during a session of the legislature is known as a **slip law.** Slip laws are collected and officially published in numerical order by the U.S. Government Printing Office in the *United States Statutes at Large* (Stat.). Slip laws are also published by Thomson/West in U.S. Code Cong. & Admin. News (see Figure 6.4) and by LexisNexis in its advance sheets to the *United States Code Service* (U.S.C.S.).

The Stat. includes enacted bills, joint resolutions, and concurrent resolutions. Simple resolutions are included in the *Congressional Record.*

FEDERAL CODES

The *United States Statutes at Large* (Stat.), published by the U.S. Government Printing Office, is the official chronological source of federal legislation. Legal researchers, however, want to find the law on a given topic. If statutes come out chronologically, how do you find them topically? The solution is to use a specialized collection. Since the number of pages of statutes

FIGURE 6.4

Example of Slip Law

Source: Native American Technical Corrections Act of 2006, published in *United States Code Congressional and Administrative News,* 109th Congress – Second Session. Reprinted by permission of Thomson/West.

PUBLIC LAW 109–221 [H.R. 3351]; May 12, 2006

NATIVE AMERICAN TECHNICAL CORRECTIONS ACT OF 2006

For Legislative History of Act, see Report for P.L. 109–221 in U.S.C.C. & A.N. Legislative History Section

An Act To make technical corrections to laws relating to Native Americans, and for other purposes.

Be it enacted by the Senate and House of Representatives of the United States of America in Congress assembled,

SECTION 1.   SHORT TITLE; TABLE OF CONTENTS.

25 USCA
§ 1451
NOTE

(a)   SHORT TITLE.—This Act may be cited as the "Native American Technical Corrections Act of 2006".

(b)   TABLE OF CONTENTS.—The table of contents of this Act is as follows:

Sec. 1.   Short title; table of contents.

TITLE I—TECHNICAL AMENDMENTS AND OTHER PROVISIONS RELATING TO NATIVE AMERICANS

Sec. 101.   Alaska Native Claims Settlement Act technical amendment.
Sec. 102.   ANCSA amendment.
Sec. 103.   Mississippi Band of Choctaw transportation reimbursement.
Sec. 104.   Fallon Paiute Shoshone tribes settlement.

TITLE II—INDIAN LAND LEASING

Sec. 201.   Prairie Island land conveyance.
Sec. 202.   Authorization of 99–year leases.
Sec. 203.   Certification of rental proceeds.

TITLE III—NATIONAL INDIAN GAMING COMMISSION FUNDING AMENDMENT

Sec 301.   National Indian Gaming Commission funding amendment.

TITLE IV—INDIAN FINANCING

Sec. 401.   Indian Financing Act Amendments.

TITLE V—NATIVE AMERICAN PROBATE REFORM TECHNICAL AMENDMENT

Sec. 501.   Clarification of provisions and amendments relating to inheritance of Indian lands.

TITLE I—TECHNICAL AMENDMENTS AND OTHER PROVISIONS RELATING TO NATIVE AMERICANS

SEC. 101.   ALASKA NATIVE CLAIMS SETTLEMENT ACT TECHNICAL AMENDMENT.

43 USCA
§ 1629b

(a)(1)   Section 337(a) of the Department of the Interior and Related Agencies Appropriations Act, 2003 (Division F of Public Law 108-7; 117 Stat. 278; February 20, 2003) is amended—

(A)   in the matter preceding paragraph (1), by striking "Section 1629b of title 43, United States Code," and inserting

"Section 36 of the Alaska Native Claims Settlement Act (43 U.S.C. 1629b)";

43 USCA
§ 1629b
43 USCA

(B)   in paragraph (2), by striking "by creating the following new subsection:" and inserting "in subsection (d), by adding at the end the following:"; and

§ 1629b
43 USCA
§ 1629b

(C)   in paragraph (3), by striking "by creating the following new subsection:" and inserting "by adding at the end the following:".

43 USCA
§ 1629e

(2)   Section 36 of the Alaska Native Claims Settlement Act (43 U.S.C. 1629b) is amended in subsection (f), by striking "section 1629e of this title" and inserting "section 39".

FIGURE 6.4
(*continued*)

43 USCA
§ 1629e

(b) (1) Section 337(b) of the Department of the Interior and Related Agencies Appropriations Act, 2003 (Division F of Public Law 108-7; 117 Stat. 278; February 20, 2003) is amended by striking "Section 1629e(a)(3) of title 43, United States Code," and inserting "Section 39(a)(3) of the Alaska Native Claims Settlement Act (43 U.S.C. 1629e(a)(3))".

(2) Section 39(a)(3)(B)(ii) of the Alaska Native Claims Settlement Act (43 U.S.C. 1629e(a)(3)(B)(ii)) is amended by striking "(a)(4) of section 1629b of this title" and inserting "section 36(a)(4)".

(c) The amendments made by this section take effect on February 20, 2003.

43 USCA
§ 1629b
NOTE
43 USCA
§ 1613a

SEC. 102. ANCSA AMENDMENT.

All land and interests in land in the State of Alaska conveyed by the Federal Government under the Alaska Native Claims Settlement Act (43 U.S.C. 1601 et seq.) to a Native Corporation and reconveyed by that Native Corporation, or a successor in interest, in exchange for any other land or interest in land in the State of Alaska and located within the same region (as defined in section 9(a) of the Alaska Native Claims Settlement Act (43 U.S.C. 1608(a)), to a Native Corporation under an exchange or other conveyance, shall be deemed, notwithstanding the conveyance or exchange, to have been conveyed pursuant to that Act.

SEC. 103. MISSISSIPPI BAND OF CHOCTAW TRANSPORTATION REIMBURSEMENT.

The Secretary of the Interior is authorized and directed, within the 3-year period beginning on the date of enactment of this Act, to accept funds from the State of Mississippi pursuant to the contract signed by the Mississippi Department of Transportation on June 7, 2005, and by the Mississippi Band of Choctaw Indians on June 2, 2005. The amount shall not exceed $776,965.30 and such funds shall be deposited in the trust account numbered PL7489708 at the Office of Trust Funds Management for the benefit of the Mississippi Band of Choctaw Indians. Thereafter, the tribe may draw down these moneys from this trust account by resolution of the Tribal Council, pursuant to Federal law and regulations applicable to such accounts.

SEC. 104. FALLON PAIUTE SHOSHONE TRIBES SETTLEMENT.

(a) SETTLEMENT FUND.—Section 102 of the Fallon Paiute Shoshone Indian Tribes Water Rights Settlement Act of 1990 (Public Law 101–618; 104 Stat. 3289) is amended—

(1) in subsection (C)—

(A) in paragraph (1)—

(i) by striking the matter preceding subparagraph (a) and inserting the following: "Notwithstanding any

code
Set of volumes that groups statutes by subject matter and is well indexed in order to make the statutes more accessible for research purposes.

codification
The process of collecting the permanent public statutes topically, adding amendments, and deleting expired, repealed, or superseded statutes.

positive law
A codified law passed as a statute; the law actually enacted.

prima facie
Accepted on its face, but not indisputable.

issued each year is much less than the number of pages of case opinions, and legislation often expires, is repealed, or is later superseded, legislatures have undertaken to have all their permanent public statutes in force organized topically. Such a topical collection of statues is known as a **code.** The process of collecting permanent public statutes topically, adding amendments, and deleting expired, repealed, or superseded statutes, is known as **codification.**

The statutes of the U.S. government were first codified by commissioners in the *Revised Statutes of 1875.* The *Revised Statutes of 1875* was introduced as a bill, which also repealed the public laws then in *Statutes at Large.* With the bill's passage, the codification became **positive law**—meaning the law was "actually enacted."

This first codification, known as the first edition, was later discovered to contain errors and improper additions, and a second edition was authorized by Congress in 1878, but never enacted into positive law. The second codification was only ***prima facie*** (accepted on its face, but not indisputable) evidence of the law as actually enacted. The one official source again became *Statutes at Large.* Congress did not codify its statutes again until 1926.

TABLE 6.1
Titles and Status of U.S.C.

1. General Provisions [positive law]	27. Intoxicating Liquors
2. The Congress	28. Judiciary and Judicial Procedure [positive law]
3. The President [positive law]	
4. Flag and Seal, Seat of Government and the States [positive law]	29. Labor
5. Government Organization and Employees [positive law]	30. Mineral Lands and Mining
	31. Money and Finance [positive law]
6. [Surety bonds] [superseded by Title 31]	32. National Guard [positive law]
7. Agriculture	33. Navigation and Navigable Waters
8. Aliens and Nationality	34. [Navy] [superseded by Title 10]
9. Arbitration [positive law]	35. Patents [positive law]
10. Armed Forces [positive law]	36. Patriotic Societies and Observations [positive law]
11. Bankruptcy [positive law]	
12. Banks and Banking	37. Pay and Allowances of the Uniformed Services [positive law]
13. Census [positive law]	
14. Coast Guard [positive law]	38. Veterans' Benefits [positive law]
15. Commerce and Trade	39. Postal Service [positive law]
16. Conservation	40. Public Buildings
17. Copyrights [positive law]	41. Public Contracts
18. Crimes and Criminal Procedure [positive law]	42. The Public Health and Welfare
	43. Public Lands
19. Customs Duties	44. Public Printing and Documents [positive law]
20. Education	
21. Food and Drugs	45. Railroads
22. Foreign Relations and Intercourse	46. Shipping [positive law]
23. Highways [positive law]	47. Telegraphs, Telephones, and Radiotelegraphs
24. Hospitals and Asylums	
25. Indians	48. Territories and Insular Possessions
26. Internal Revenue Code	49. Transportation [positive law]
	50. War and National Defense; and Appendix

CYBER TRIP

The *United States Code* is available on the Internet at www.gpoaccess.gov/uscode/index.html. Note that this version of the United States Code may not be as up-to-date as the unofficial versions published by Thomson/West or LexisNexis.

CYBER TRIP

The Office of Law Revision Counsel Web site is available on the Internet at http://uscode.house.gov.

titles
The major topical divisions of a code, such as the 50 topical divisions of the United States Code.

sections
The subdivisions of statutes under each title of a code.

United States Code (U.S.C.)

In 1926, committees of the House and Senate collected the current laws in the *Revised Statutes of 1875* and the current laws in *Statutes at Large* since 1873, and created the *United States Code* (U.S.C.), published by the Government Printing Office. Since 1926, a new edition of U.S.C. has been issued every six years. Since 1932, cumulative supplements have been issued each intervening year. U.S.C. has a general index.

The U.S.C. officially collects federal statutes topically in 50 **titles.** In 1982, the Office of Law Revision Counsel was created to collect, restate, and revise the federal statutes one title at a time for enactment into positive law. The titles of U.S.C. and their status are provided in Table 6.1.

U.S.C. titles may be divided into subtitles. Titles or subtitles may be divided into chapters, which may be divided into subchapters. Chapters or subchapters may be divided into parts, which may be divided into subparts. Under each title, statutes are organized in **sections.** Sections (which may have letter additions) may be divided into subsections. Sections or subsections may be further divided into paragraphs, subparagraphs, sentences, and words.

For example, the word *business* in the tax statute that defines a "Subchapter S" corporation (that is, a corporation that may be taxed like a partnership) is the 19th word in the only sentence in the first paragraph of the first subsection of § 1361, which falls in part I of Subchapter S of Chapter 1 of Subtitle A of Title 26 of the U.S.C. Going back:

1. Title 26: Internal Revenue Code of 1986 as amended.

2. Subtitle A: Income Taxes.

3. Chapter 1. Normal Taxes and Surtaxes.

4. Subchapter S. Tax Treatment of S Corporations and Their Shareholders.

5. Part 1. In General.

RESEARCH THIS!

As a result of the wide availability of the Internet, statutory law has become the most accessible. As we've seen, the *United States Code* is available on the Internet at www.gpoaccess. gov/uscode/index.html. To see, for example, the federal district courts established in your state, search Title 28 – Judiciary and Judicial Procedure, Part I – Organization of the Courts, Chapter 5 – District Courts, 28 U.S.C. §§ 81-131.

See if the statutory code for your state is available for free on the Internet. Search your state's name and "statute" or "code" on a search engine such as www.google.com. Browse through the results.

For example, the Laws of New York can be found at http://public.leginfo.state.ny.us/ menugetf.cgi.

6. Section 1361. S Corporation defined.

7. Subsection (a). S Corporation defined.

8. Paragraph 1. In general.

9. Only sentence.

10. Nineteenth word.

Statutes are cited by title number, code abbreviation, and section number. For example, the statute that makes it a federal crime to assassinate the President of the United States, Section 1751 of Title 18 of the U.S.C., is cited 18 U.S.C. § 1751. The "Subchapter S" definition discussed previously would be cited 26 U.S.C. § 1361 (a)(1).

The concept of positive law is discussed in the U.S.C. at 1 U.S.C. § 204(a). It is important to note, however, that the courts have uniformly held that if there is a conflict in wording between the chronological Stat. and the topical U.S.C., the chronological version, the Stat., controls.

Annotated Codes

The official U.S.C., published by the U.S. Government Printing Office, lacks a few basic features of importance to legal researchers.

First, as a government publication, the U.S.C. is not always published in a timely manner. A statute may be enacted and not appear in the U.S.C. or in a U.S.C. supplement for several months.

Second, the U.S. Government Printing Office does not publish an array of law books on par with Thomson/West or LexisNexis. As a result, the U.S.C. does not provide useful cross-references to other law books.

Third, as discussed earlier, the laws enacted by the legislature are subject to interpretation by the courts. The U.S.C. does not include summaries of court opinions that have interpreted particular statutes.

Filling the void, Thomson/West and LexisNexis publish their own versions of the U.S.C., using the same title and section numbering system.

Thomson/West publishes the *United States Code Annotated* (U.S.C.A.) and LexisNexis publishes the *United States Code Service* (U.S.C.S.). (See Figure 6.5.) Each is an **annotated code,**

annotated code
A code that provides, in addition to the text of the codified statutes, such information as cases that have construed the statute, law review articles that have discussed it, the procedural history of the statute, cross-references to superceded codifications, cross-references to related statutes, and other information.

FIGURE 6.5
Federal Codes
NOTE: These federal codes all have the same title and section numbering system.

Publisher	Title	Features
U.S. Government Printing Office	U.S.C.	Official; unannotated
West	U.S.C.A.	Unofficial; annotated
LCP	U.S.C.S.	Unofficial; annotated

containing case summaries of the courts' interpretation of each statute. Each federal annotated code is a multivolume set, with each title of the U.S.C. contained in one or more volumes of the set. Each statute is set out, followed by history notes, research references, and case summaries. The history notes usually include references to Public Law numbers and the Stat. Each federal annotated code is kept current by cumulative annual pocket parts and replacement volumes (including paperback bound supplements), as well as by a current service.

Finding a Relevant Code Section

Unless a legal researcher already has a reference to a particular code section, the most common method of entry into a federal annotated code is through an index. Each federal annotated code has a general index for the set and a "volume index"—also known as a "title index" or "topic index" (that is, an index of just one title, found in the last volume of the set containing statutes from that title). Since the volume indexes are usually much more detailed than the general index, you should generally use the volume index if you know the title in which the statute you are looking for will be found.

It is interesting to note that the general index for the U.S.C. was prepared under contract by West Publishing Company (West) and that the indexers at The Lawyers Co-operative Publishing Company (LCP) used that public domain index in preparing their general index of the federal code.

The next most common method of entry into a federal annotated code is to work with the tables of contents in the front of each volume and at the front of each chapter of a title.

The U.S.C. and both federal annotated codes also contain tables showing where statutes in the Stat. may be found in the U.S.C., where a section can be found in a revised title, and other similar tables. Both federal annotated codes also contain tables of acts by popular names.

United States Code Annotated (U.S.C.A.)

Since 1927, West and its successor Thomson/West have published the *United States Code Annotated* (U.S.C.A.). The U.S.C.A. follows the format and language of the U.S.C., which, as discussed previously, is only *prima facie* evidence of the law, unless the relevant title has been enacted into positive law.

The U.S.C.A., as a major Thomson/West publication, lists topic and key number research references for a statute, references to other West publications, and references to specific sections of the *Code of Federal Regulations* (C.F.R.). Following West Publishing Company's philosophy of comprehensive publishing, the set includes extensive case summaries, apparently drawn from headnotes in the National Reporter System and/or digest paragraphs from West's digests. The case summary section is entitled "Notes of Decisions." (See Figure 6.6.)

The U.S.C.A. also includes volumes covering the Constitution of the United States and federal court rules.

The U.S.C.A. is available electronically on Thomson/West's Westlaw computer legal research service. The physical version of the U.S.C.A. is kept up-to-date by pocket parts, while the electronic version of the U.S.C.S. is kept up-to-date electronically. Another way to check on the status of a statute is to use the *Shepard's Citations*.

United States Code Service (U.S.C.S.)

Since 1972, LCP and its federal code successor LexisNexis have published the *United States Code Service* (U.S.C.S.). The U.S.C.S. follows the format of the U.S.C., but its text follows the language in the Stat., which, as discussed earlier, controls when there is a conflict with the U.S.C. The titles of the U.S.C. are conveniently listed on the inside front cover of each volume. The U.S.C.S. also includes advance sheets with cumulative tables and slip laws.

The U.S.C.S., once part of LCP's Total Client Service Library, lists research references to other publications (especially A.L.R. annotations), references to law review articles, and references to the *Code of Federal Regulations* (C.F.R.). Following a philosophy of selective publishing, LCP's editors prepared case summaries for U.S.C.S., known as **casenotes,** only when a case

casenotes
Case summaries in the United States Code Service (U.S.C.S.).

FIGURE 6.6
Excerpt from the U.S.C.A.

Source: United States Code Annotated - Title 42 The Public Health and Welfare – 6321 to 7000. Reprinted by permission from Thomson/West.

Notification requirements respecting released substances, see 42 USCA § 9603.

Permits to include requirements for use and disposal of sludge that implement regulations unless requirements have been included in permit issued under provisions of this subchapter, see 33 USCA § 1345.

"Qualified hazardous waste facility" means any facility for disposal of hazardous waste by incineration or entombment if facility is subject to final permit requirements under this subchapter, see 26 USCA § 142.

Remedial actions provided by the President upon condition that State assure availability of hazardous waste disposal facility in compliance with requirements of this subchapter, see 42 USCA § 9604.

Reports and studies concerning additional hazardous wastes and construction and operation of hazardous waste facilities, see 42 USCA § 9651.

Requirements for facilities, including those under this subchapter, to establish and maintain evidence of financial responsibility, promulgated no earlier than five years after Dec. 11, 1980, see 42 USCA § 9608.

Rules for protection from hazards at inactive or depository uranium mill tailings sites consistent with standards required by this subchapter, see 42 USCA § 2022.

§ 6921. Identification and listing of hazardous waste

(a)   Criteria for identification or listing

Not later than eighteen months after October 21, 1976, the Administrator shall, after notice and opportunity for public hearing, and after consultation with appropriate Federal and State agencies, develop and promulgate criteria for identifying the characteristics of hazardous waste, and for listing hazardous waste, which should be subject to the provisions of this subchapter, taking into account toxicity, persistence, and degradability in nature, potential for accumulation in tissue, and other related factors such as flammability, corrosiveness, and other hazardous characteristics. Such criteria shall be revised from time to time as may be appropriate.

(b)   Identification and listing

(1) Not later than eighteen months after October 21, 1976, and after notice and opportunity for public hearing, the Administrator shall promulgate regulations identifying the characteristics of hazardous waste, and listing particular hazardous wastes (within the meaning of section 6903(5) of this title), which shall be subject to the provisions of this subchapter. Such regulations shall be based on the criteria promulgated under subsection (a) of this section and shall be revised from time to time thereafter as may be appropriate. The Administrator, in cooperation with the Agency for Toxic Substances and Disease Registry and the National Toxicology Program, shall also identify or list those hazardous wastes which shall be subject to the provisions of this subchapter solely because of the presence in such wastes of certain constituents (such as identified carcinogens, mutagens, or teratagens [1]) at levels in excess of levels which endanger human health.

(B) does not accept hazardous wastes identified or listed under this section, and

(2) the owner or operator of such facility has established contractual requirements or other appropriate notification or inspection procedures to assure that hazardous wastes are not received at or burned in such facility.

(Pub.L. 89–272, Title II, § 3001, as added Pub.L. 94–580, § 2, Oct. 21, 1976, 90 Stat. 2806, and amended Pub.L. 96–482, § 7, Oct. 21, 1980, 94 Stat. 2336; Pub.L. 98–616, Title II, §§ 221(a), 222, 223(a), Nov. 8, 1984, 98 Stat. 3248, 3251, 3252; Pub.L. 104–119, § 4(1), Mar. 26, 1996, 110 Stat. 833.)

[1] So in original. Probably should be "teratogens".

HISTORICAL AND STATUTORY NOTES

Revision Notes and Legislative Reports
1976 Acts. House Report No. 94–1491(Parts I and II), see 1976 U.S. Code Cong. and Adm. News, p. 6238.

FIGURE 6.6
(*continued*)

1980 Acts. Senate Report No. 96–172 and House Conference Report No. 96–1444, see 1980 U.S. Code Cong. and Adm. News, p. 5019.

1984 Acts. House Report No. 98–198 and House Conference Report No. 98–1133, see 1984 U.S. Code Cong. and Adm. News, p. 5576.

1996 Acts. House Report No. 104–454, see 1996 U.S. Code Cong, and Adm. News, p. 593.

References in Text

Chapter 51 of Title 49, referred to in subsec.(d)(7)(A), is 49 U.S.C.A. § 5101 et seq.

Amendments

1996 Amendments. Subsec. (d)(5). Pub. L. 104–119, § 4(1), substituted "under this section" for "under section 6921", which, due to prior editorial translation, required no change in text.

1984 Amendments. Subsec. (b)(1). Pub. L. 98–616. § 222(b), added "The Administrator, in cooperation with the Agency for Toxic Substances and Disease Registry and the National Toxicology Program, shall also identify or list those hazardous wastes which shall be subject to the Provisions of this subchapter solely because of the presence in such wastes of certain constituents (such as identified carcinogens, mutagens, or teratagens) at levels in excess of levels which endanger human health."

Subsec. (d). Pub.L. 98–616, § 221(a), added subsec. (d).

Subsecs. (e) to (h). Pub.L. 98–616, § 222(a), added subsecs. (e), (f), (g) and (h).

Subsec. (i). Pub.L. 98–616, § 223(a), added subsec. (i).

1980 Amendments. Subsec. (b). Pub.L. 96–482 designated existing provisions as par. (1) and added pars. (2) and (3).

Transfer of Functions

For transfer of certain enforcement functions of Administrator or other official of the Environmental Protection Agency under this chapter to Federal Inspector, Office of Federal Inspector for the Alaska Natural Gas Transportation System, see note set out under section 6903 of this title.

Administrative Burdens; Small Quantity Generators; Retention of Current System; Report to Congress

Section 221(e) of Pub.L. 98–616 provided that: "The Administrator of the Environmental Protection Agency, in conjunction with the Secretary of Transportation, shall prepare and submit to the Congress a report on the feasibility of easing the administrative burden on small quantity generators, increasing compliance with statutory and regulatory requirements, and simplifying enforcement efforts through a program of licensing hazardous waste transporters to assume the responsibilities of small quantity generators relating to the preparation of manifests and associated recordkeeping and reporting requirements. The report shall examine the appropriate licensing requirements under such a program including the need for financial assurances by licensed transporters and shall make recommendations on provisions and requirements for such a program including the appropriate division of responsibilities between the Department of Transportation and the Environmental Protection Administration. Such report shall be submitted to the Congress not later than April 1, 1987."

Ash Management and Disposal

Pub.L. 101–549, Title III, § 306, Nov. 15, 1990, 104 Stat. 2584, provided that: "For a period of 2 years after the date of enactment of the Clean Air Act Amendments of 1990 [Nov. 15, 1990], ash from solid waste incineration units burning municipal waste shall not be regulated by the Administrator of the Environmental Protection Agency pursuant to section 3001 of the Solid Waste Disposal Act [this section]. Such reference and limitation shall not be construed to prejudice, endorse or otherwise affect any activity by the Administrator following the 2-year period from the date of enactment of the Clean Air Act Amendments of 1990 [Nov. 15, 1990]."

Educational Institutions; Accumulation, Storage and Disposal of Hazardous Wastes; Study

Section 221(f) of Pub.L. 98–616, as amended Pub.L. 107–110, Title X, § 1076(aa), Jan. 8, 2002, 115 Stat. 2093, provided that:

"(1) The Administrator of the Environmental Protection Agency shall,

FIGURE 6.6
(*continued*)

in consultation with the Secretary of Education, the States, and appropriate educational associations, conduct a comprehensive study of problems associated with the accumulation, storage and disposal of hazardous wastes from educational institutions. The study shall include an investigation of the feasibility and availability of environmentally sound methods for the treatment, storage or disposal of hazardous waste from such institutions, taking into account the types and quantities of such waste which are generated by these institutions, and the nonprofit nature of these institutions.

"(2) The Administrator shall submit a report to the Congress containing the findings of the study carried out under paragraph (1) not later than April 1, 1987.

"(3) For purposes of this subsection—

"(A) the term 'hazardous waste' means hazardous waste which is listed or identified under Section 3001 of the Solid Waste Disposal Act [this section];

"(B) the term 'educational institution' includes, but shall not be limited to,

"(i) secondary schools as defined in section 9101 of the Elementary and Secondary Education Act of 1965 [20 U.S.C.A. § 7801]; and

"(ii) institutions of higher education as defined in section 1201(a) of the Higher Education Act of 1965 [section 1141(a) of Title 20]."

[Except as otherwise provided, amendments by Pub.L. 107–110 effective Jan. 8, 2002, see Pub.L. 107–110, § 5, set out as a note under 20 U.S.C.A. § 6301.]

Regulation Under the Solid Waste Disposal Act

Pub.L. 99–499, Title 1, § 124(b), Oct. 17, 1986, 100 Stat. 1689, provided that "Unless the Administrator of the Environmental Protection Agency promulgates regulations under subtitle C of the Solid Waste Disposal Act [this subchapter] addressing the extraction of wastes from landfills as part of the process of recovering methane from such landfills, the owner and operator of equipment used to recover methane from a landfill shall not be deemed to be managing, generating transporting, treating, storing, or disposing of hazardous or liquid wastes within the meaning of that subtitle. If the aqueous or hydrocarbon phase of the condensate or any other waste material removed from the gas recovered from the landfill meets any of the characteristics identified under section 3001 of subtitle C of the Solid Waste Disposal Act [this section] the preceding sentence shall not apply and such condensate phase or other waste material shall be deemed a hazardous waste under that subtitle, and shall be regulated accordingly."

Small Quantity Generator Waste; Administrator of Environmental Protection Agency; Information and Education; Waste Generators

Section 221(b) of Pub.L. 98–616 provided that: "The Administrator of the Environmental Protection Agency shall undertake activities to inform and educate the waste generators of their responsibilities under the amendments made by this section [enacting subsec. (d) of this section] during the period within thirty months after the enactment of the Hazardous and Solid Waste Amendments of 1984 [Nov. 8, 1984] to help assure compliance."

Study of Existing Manifest System for Hazardous Wastes as Applicable to Small Quantity Generators; Submittal to Congress

Section 221(d) of Pub.L. 98–616 provided that: "The Administrator of the Environmental Protection Agency shall cause to be studied the existing manifest system for hazardous wastes as it applies to small quantity generators and recommend whether the current system shall be retained or whether a new system should be introduced. The study shall include an analysis of the cost versus the benefits of the system studied as well as an analysis of the ease of retrieving and collating information and identifying a given substance. Finally, any new proposal shall include a list of those standards that are necessary to protect human health and the environment. Such study shall be submitted to the Congress not later than April 1, 1987."

CROSS REFERENCES

Application of special study wastes described in this section to special study wastes provisions relating to national contingency plan, see 42 USCA § 9605.

FIGURE 6.6
(*continued*)

"Hazardous substance" as meaning any hazardous waste having characteristics identified under this section, see 33 USCA § 1319.

"Municipal or commercial waste" as meaning solid waste excluding solid waste identified and listed under this section, see 33 USCA § 2601.

Revision of hazard ranking system, see 42 USCA § 9625.

AMERICAN LAW REPORTS

Right to intervene in federal hazardous waste enforcement action. 100 ALR Fed 35.

LIBRARY REFERENCES

Administrative Law
Hazardous waste management, generally, see 40 CFR § 260.1 et seq.

American Digest System
Environmental Law ⬅ 415.
United States ⬅—41.
Key Number System Topic Nos. 149E, 393.

Corpus Juris Secundum
C.J.S. United States § 54.

Encyclopedias
61C Am. Jur. 2d Pollution Control §§ 1151, 1152, 1158, 1163, 1177, 1207, 1234, 1238, 1247, 1258, 1274, 1282.

Forms
Jurisdiction and venue in district courts, matters pertaining to, see West's Federal Forms § 1001 et seq.
Preliminary injunctions and temporary restraining orders, matters pertaining to, see West's Federal Forms § 5271 et seq.
Sentence and judgment, see West's Federal Forms § 7801 et seq.

Law Review and Journal Commentaries
City of Chicago v. Environmental Defense Fund: Searching for plain meaning in unambiguous ambiguity. Richard J. Lazarus and Claudia M. Newman, 4 N.Y.U.Envtl. L.J. 1 (1995).
Defense contractor recovery of cleanup costs at contractor owned and operated facilities. Cheryl Lynch Nilsson, 38 A.F.L.Rev. 1 (1994).
Emerging federal law of mine waste: Administrative, judicial and legislative developments. John R. Jacus and Thomas E. Root, 26 Land & Water L.Rev. 461 (1991).

appeared to add something new to the law. The casenote section is entitled "Interpretive Notes and Decisions." (See Figure 6.7.)

The U.S.C.S. also includes volumes covering the Constitution of the United States and federal court rules.

The U.S.C.S. is available electronically using LexisNexis's Lexis.com computer legal research service. The physical version of the U.S.C.S. is kept up-to-date by pocket parts, while the electronic version of the U.S.C.S. is kept up-to-date electronically. Again, another way to check on the status of a statute is to use the *Shepard's Citations*.

The Limitations of Codes

A legal researcher should bear in mind that similar to headnotes, digest paragraphs, and A.L.R. setouts, U.S.C.A. case summaries and U.S.C.S. casenotes are finding aids that do not always accurately reflect the detail of a case opinion. They are written in a competitive environment and usually give only the holding of a court without its reasoning.

FIGURE 6.7
Excerpt from the U.S.C.S.

Source: United States Code Service - Lawyers Edition. Reprinted by permission of Matthew Bender and Company Inc. A member of the LexisNexis Group.

§ 60102. Purpose and general authority

(a) Purpose and minimum safety standards. (1) Purpose. The purpose of this chapter [49 USCS §§ 60101 et seq.] is to provide adequate protection against risks to life and property posed by pipeline transportation and pipeline facilities by improving the regulatory and enforcement authority of the Secretary of Transportation.

(2) Minimum safety standards. The Secretary shall prescribe minimum safety standards for pipeline transportation and for pipeline facilities. The standards—

(A) apply to owners and operators of pipeline facilities;

(B) may apply to the design, installation, inspection, emergency plans and procedures, testing, construction, extension, operation, replacement, and maintenance of pipeline facilities; and

(C) shall include a requirement that all individuals who operate and maintain pipeline facilities shall be qualified to operate and maintain the pipeline facilities.

(3) Qualifications of pipeline operators. The qualifications applicable to an individual who operates and maintains a pipeline facility shall address the ability to recognize and react appropriately to abnormal operating conditions that may indicate a dangerous situation or a condition exceeding design limits. The operator of a pipeline facility shall ensure that employees who operate and maintain the facility are qualified to operate and maintain the pipeline facilities.

(b) Practicability and safety needs standards. (1) In general. A standard prescribed under subsection (a) shall be—

(A) practicable; and

(B) designed to meet the need for—

(i) gas pipeline safety, or safely transporting hazardous liquids, as appropriate; and

(ii) protecting the environment.

(2) Factors for consideration. When prescribing any standard under this section or section 60101(b), 60103, 60108, 60109, 60110, or 60113, the Secretary shall consider—

(A) relevant available—

(i) gas pipeline safety information;

(ii) hazardous liquid pipeline safety information; and

(iii) environmental information;

(B) the appropriateness of the standard for the particular type of pipeline transportation or facility;

(C) the reasonableness of the standard;

(D) based on a risk assessment, the reasonably identifiable or estimated benefits expected to result from implementation or compliance with the standard;

(E) based on a risk assessment, the reasonably identifiable or estimated costs expected to result from implementation or compliance with the standard;

(F) comments and information received from the public; and

(G) the comments and recommendations of the Technical Pipeline Safety Standards Committee, the Technical Hazardous Liquid Pipeline Safety Standards Committee, or both, as appropriate.

(3) Risk assessment. In conducting a risk assessment referred to in subparagraphs (D) and (E) of paragraph (2), the Secretary shall—

(A) identify the regulatory and nonregulatory options that the Secretary considered in prescribing a proposed standard;

(B) identify the costs and benefits associated with the proposed standard;

(C) include—

(i) an explanation of the reasons for the selection of the proposed standard in lieu of the other options identified; and

(ii) with respect to each of those other options, a brief explanation of the reasons that the Secretary did not select the option; and

FIGURE 6.7
(*continued*)

(D) identify technical data or Other information upon which the risk assessment information and proposed standard is based.

(4) Review. (A) In general. The Secretary shall—

(i) submit any risk assessment information prepared under paragraph (3) of this subsection to the Technical Pipeline Safety Standards Committee, the Technical Hazardous Liquid Pipeline Safety Standards Committee, or both, as appropriate; and

(ii) make that risk assessment information available to the general public.

(B) Peer review panels. The committees referred to in subparagraph (A) shall serve as peer review panels to review risk assessment information prepared under this section. Not later than 90 days after receiving risk assessment information for review pursuant to subparagraph (A), each committee that receives that risk assessment information shall prepare and submit to the Secretary a report that includes—

(i) an evaluation of the merit of the data and methods used; and

(ii) any recommended options relating to that risk assessment information and the associated standard that the committee determines to be appropriate.

(C) Review by Secretary. Not later than 90 days after receiving a report submitted by a committee under subparagraph (B), the Secretary—

(i) shall review the report;

(ii) shall provide a written response to the committee that is the author of the report concerning all significant peer review comments and recommended alternatives contained in the report; and

(iii) may revise the risk assessment and the proposed standard before promulgating the final standard.

(5) Secretarial decision making. Except where otherwise required by statute, the Secretary shall propose or issue a standard under this Chapter [chapter] only upon a reasoned determination that the benefits of the intended standard justify its costs.

(6) Exceptions from application. The requirements of subparagraphs (D) and (E) of paragraph (2) do not apply when—

(A) the standard is the product of a negotiated rulemaking, or other rulemaking including the adoption of industry standards that receives no significant adverse comment within 60 days of notice in the Federal Register;

(B) based on a recommendation (in which three-fourths of the members voting concur) by the Technical Pipeline Safety Standards Committee, the Technical Hazardous Liquid Pipeline Safety Standards Committee, or both, as applicable, the Secretary waives the requirements; or

(C) the Secretary finds, pursuant to section 553(b)(3)(B) of title 5, United States Code, that notice and public procedure are not required.

(7) Report. Not later than March 31, 2000, the Secretary shall transmit to the Congress a report that—

(A) describes the implementation of the risk assessment requirements of this section, including the extent to which those requirements have affected regulatory decision making and pipeline safety; and

(B) includes any recommendations that the Secretary determines would make the risk assessment process conducted pursuant to the requirements under this chapter a more effective means of assessing the benefits and costs associated with alternative regulatory and nonregulatory options in prescribing standards under the Federal pipeline safety regulatory program under this chapter [49 USCS §§ 60101 et seq.].

(c) **Public safety program requirements.** (1) The Secretary shall include in the standards prescribed under subsection (a) of this section a requirement that an operator of a gas pipeline facility participate in a public safety program that—

(A) notifies an operator of proposed demolition, excavation, tunneling, or construction near or affecting the facility;

FIGURE 6.7
(*continued*)

(B) requires an operator to identify a pipeline facility that may be affected by the proposed demolition, excavation, tunneling, or construction, to prevent damaging the facility; and

(C) the Secretary decides will protect a facility adequately against a hazard caused by demolition, excavation, tunneling, or construction.

(2) To the extent a public safety program referred to in paragraph (1) of this subsection is not available, the Secretary shall prescribe standards requiring an operator to take action the Secretary prescribes to provide services comparable to services that would be available under a public safety program.

(3) The Secretary may include in the standards prescribed under subsection (a) of this section a requirement that an operator of a hazardous liquid pipeline facility participate in a public safety program meeting the requirements of paragraph (1) of this subsection or maintain and carry out a damage prevention program that provides services comparable to services that would be available under a public safety program.

(4) Promoting public awareness. (A) Not later than one year after the date of enactment of the Accountable Pipeline Safety and Accountability Act of 1996 [enacted Oct. 12, 19961], and annually thereafter, the owner or operator of each interstate gas pipeline facility shall provide to the governing body of each municipality in which the interstate gas pipeline facility is located, a map identifying the location of such facility.

(B)(i) Not later than June 1, 1998, the Secretary shall survey and assess the public education programs under section 60116 and the public safety programs under section 60102(c) and determine their effectiveness and applicability as components of a model program. In particular, the survey shall include the methods by which operators notify residents of the location of the facility and its right of way, public information regarding existing One-Call programs, and appropriate procedures to be followed by residents of affected municipalities in the event of accidents involving interstate gas pipeline facilities.

(ii) Not later than one year after the survey and assessment are completed, the Secretary shall institute a rulemaking to determine the most effective public safety and education program components and promulgate if appropriate, standards implementing those components on a nationwide basis. In the event that the Secretary finds that promulgation of such standards are not appropriate, the Secretary shall report to Congress the reasons for that finding.

(d) Facility operation information standards. The Secretary shall prescribe minimum standards requiring an operator of a pipeline facility subject to this chapter [49 USCS §§ 60101 et seq.] to maintain, to the extent practicable, information related to operating the facility as required by the standards prescribed under this chapter [49 USCS §§ 60101 et seq.] and, when requested, to make the information available to the Secretary and an appropriate State official as determined by the Secretary. The information shall include—

(1) the business name, address, and telephone number, including an operations emergency telephone number, of the operator;

(2) accurate maps and a supplementary geographic description, including an identification of areas described in regulations prescribed under section 60109 of this title, that show the location in the State of—

(A) major gas pipeline facilities of the operator, including transmission lines. . .

STATE CODES

Just as the legislative process of the federal government is illustrative of the legislative processes in the states, the books covering the legislative branch of the federal government are illustrative of the books covering the legislative branches of the states.

In general, state legislatures meet in sessions. The session laws are published separately as slip laws and in official chronological collections similar to the Stat. (for example, *Laws of*

A Day in the Life

The case fact pattern presented at beginning of this chapter is based on a true story. On February 26, 1989, a train carrying hazardous materials derailed in Akron, Ohio. Tank cars were on fire, spewing poisonous smoke and gas, and several thousand residents were forced to evacuate for several days. At a press conference, the mayor wondered aloud whether the city could do something to prevent hazardous materials from being transported through the city.

By examining the table of contents to U.S.C.A. or U.S.C.S. you can see that Title 49 of the United States Code contains federal laws on the subject of transportation. By using the volume table of contents, the index for the entire code, or, ideally, the index for the volume, you find 49 U.S.C. §§ 5101-5126, concerning the transportation of hazardous materials. The issue of preemption is specifically addressed at 49 U.S.C. § 5125. Historical references are made in the annotated code to the original Hazardous Materials Transportation Act, which had the purpose of establishing uniform national standards for the transportation of hazardous materials to avoid a patchwork of state and local standards. Because you are using an annotated code, you find references to several cases interpreting the legislation. By reading and studying those cases, you learn about the basic law of hazardous materials transportation.

To make a long story short, you find that state and local laws regulating hazardous materials transportation are preempted by the federal law, unless the state and local laws are compatible with the federal law. Every city and town is inclined to prohibit the transportation of hazardous materials through their city or town, but if every city and town did so, there would be no way to transport hazardous materials that need to be transported by rail or by truck. Raw materials that are hazardous to transport are usually transported because they are ultimately used to benefit people and society. For example, the tank cars that caught fire in Akron contained butane. Among other things, butane is used in the making of surgical gloves. Cities and towns must share the risk of transporting butane by rail or by truck, if their citizens want surgeons to have and use inexpensive surgical gloves.

Washington). Again, since legal researchers need to find legislation topically, an official topical code is authorized in each state (for example, *Revised Code of Washington*), which may or may not be positive law. The code is usually available in an annotated form (for example, *Revised Code of Washington Annotated*).

Again, unless a legal researcher already has a reference to a particular code section, the most common method of entry into a state annotated code is through an index. For example, in Ohio, each state annotated code has a general index for the set and more-detailed volume indexes for each title.

The codes set out each statute, followed by history notes, research references, and case summaries. Tables usually correlate earlier and later versions of the code. State codes also generally include some type of legislative service such as a source of recent legislation.

State codes generally include volumes covering the state constitution and court rules.

While the *Martindale-Hubble Law Dictionary* includes a "law digests" volume comparing various state laws, and some loose-leaf services contain comparative charts, no one book collects the text of the law from each state. All statutes electronic files can be searched on Lexis.com and Westlaw, but no one book collects the statutes of all 50 states.

Under Article I, Section 10, Clause 3 of the Constitution of the United States, states may enter into interstate compacts (for example, to resolve boundary disputes or to create a port authority) with the consent of Congress. The text of an interstate compact can be located in the session laws of the respective sovereigns. The congressional consent may be found in the *United States Statutes at Large*. The text may be located in the annotated codes of the respective states. Cases interpreting interstate compacts are digested in Thomson/West digests and in LexisNexis's L. Ed. Digest.

LOCAL CODES

enabling act
A statute creating and/or empowering a local government or agency.

Local governments exist only after the appropriate sovereign's legislature passes an **enabling act** allowing or creating the local government. The enabling act, along with the sovereign's constitution, gives the local government its power. When a local governmental body, such as a city

ordinance
A legislative act of a local government.

council, legislates, it makes an **ordinance.** Ordinances may be collected topically in a code.

Small private publishers usually publish the codified ordinances of a local government. It can be difficult, if not impossible, to locate a copy of a local government's code outside the territory of the local government. If a copy is not available at the local law or public library, a legal researcher may have no choice but to review the code in the local government's offices.

Local codes are rarely annotated. However, local codes, especially local traffic laws, often mimic the state's statutes. When this is so, the state's annotated code may be consulted for case authority interpreting the statute/ordinance.

If the desired ordinance cannot be located in the local code by working the table of contents, you may find that the local code has a general index you can search.

Summary

The legislative branch of government makes statutes. Federal law is made in the sense of being "dreamed up" by Congress. A proposed permanent law introduced in the House of Representatives or in the Senate is known as a bill. A bill that passes both houses is presented to the President and becomes law if the President signs it, if the President returns it within 10 days (Sunday excepted) and the veto is overridden by a two-thirds vote in each house, or if the President does not return it within 10 days (Sunday excepted) and the houses of Congress have not adjourned. Bills should be compared and contrasted with joint resolutions, concurrent resolutions, and simple resolutions. The laws enacted by the legislature are subject to interpretation by the courts. As a practical matter, the only time a legal researcher need research legislative history is if a court is deciding a case of first impression as to interpreting a statute. Legislative intent can be inferred from amendments, committee reports, debates, and hearings. While state legislative history theoretically exists, sources of state legislative history are usually nonexistent. Slip laws are collected and officially published in chronological order by the U.S. Government Printing Office in the *United States Statutes at Large* (Stat.).

Statutes come out chronologically, but they may be found topically with a specialized collection known as a code. The process of collecting permanent public statutes topically, adding amendments, and deleting expired, repealed, or superseded statutes is known as codification. The *United States Code* (U.S.C.) officially collects federal statutes topically in 50 titles. Titles may be divided into subtitles, chapters, subchapters, parts, and subparts. Under each title, statutes are organized into sections. Sections may be divided into subsections, paragraphs, subparagraphs, sentences, and words. Statutes are cited by title number, code abbreviation, and section number. The U.S.C. does not provide useful cross-references to other law books and it does not include summaries of court opinions that have interpreted particular statutes. Thomson/West and LexisNexis each publish a federal annotated code. Each is a multivolume set, with each title of the U.S.C. contained in one or more volumes of the set. Each statute is set out, followed by history notes, research references, and case summaries. Each federal annotated code is kept current by cumulative annual pocket parts and replacement volumes, as well as a current service. Each has a general index and volume indexes for each title. Thomson/West publishes the *United States Code Annotated* (U.S.C.A.), which lists topic and key number research references for a statute, along with references to other publications. LexisNexis publishes the *United States Code Service* (U.S.C.S.), which similarly lists research references to other publications. A legal researcher should bear in mind that similar to headnotes, digest paragraphs, and A.L.R. setouts, casenotes are finding aids that do not always accurately reflect the detail of a case opinion or even refer you to every case.

Like the federal legislature, state legislatures meet in sessions. The session laws are published separately as slip laws, in official chronological collections, and in official topical codes, usually in annotated form. The most common method of entry into a state annotated code is through an index. The codes set out each statute, followed by history notes, research references, and case summaries. There is no one book that collects the statutes of all the states.

Local governments exist only after the legislature of the appropriate sovereign passes an enabling act allowing or creating the local government. When a local governmental body, such as a city council, legislates, it makes an ordinance. Ordinances may be collected topically in a code. The codified ordinances of a local government are usually published by small private publishers. A legal researcher often has no choice but to review the code in the local government's offices.

Key Terms

act   84
annotated code   91
bill   83
casenotes   92
code   89
codification   89
concurrent resolution   85
Congress   83
enabling act   100
enactment   83
engrossed bill   84
enrolled bill   84
joint resolution   84
legislative history   85

ordinance   101
pocket veto   84
positive law   89
prima facie   89
private law   87
public law   87
sections   90
session   83
session law   87
simple resolution   85
slip law   87
titles   90
veto   84

Review Questions

1. What is the difference between a bill, a joint resolution, a concurrent resolution, and a simple resolution?
2. When do you need to research legislative history?
3. What is the official chronological source of federal legislation?
4. What is codification?
5. What is the official code of federal legislation?
6. What are the benefits of an annotated code?
7. How are the federal annotated codes indexed?
8. What research reference does the U.S.C.A. have that the U.S.C.S. doesn't have? What research reference does the U.S.C.S. have that the U.S.C.A. doesn't have?
9. Why shouldn't you cite a casenote in a brief?
10. Is there an annotated code for your state?

Exercises

1. Use the *United States Code Congressional and Administrative News* to answer these questions: What is the title of Public Law 100-235, 101 Stat. 1724? Pursuant to the law, what federal agencies must provide computer system security training to their employees who use computers? As the bottom of 101 Stat. 1730 indicates, what was the bill designation, the date the bill passed the House of Representatives, and the date the bill passed the Senate?
2. Use 33 U.S.C.A. § 494 to answer these questions: What topic and key number is listed under "Library References"? Under "Notes on Decisions," what is the full cite of the Alabama District Court opinion discussing the duty to provide bridge tenders?
3. Use the volume index to Title 4 of U.S.C.S. to answer this question: What statute provides that a star will be added to the flag of the United States on the admission of each new state? Turn to that statute to answer this question: On what day are new stars added to the flag?
4. Use U.S.C.S. to answer these questions: How many stars does 4 U.S.C.S. § 1 require for the flag of the United States? What is the effective date of 4 U.S.C.S. § 1?
5. Use the Interpretive Notes and Decisions of 17 U.S.C.S. § 102 to answer these questions: What is the outline number of casenotes discussing the copyrightability of the plot of a play? Is the plot of a play copyrightable?

Vocabulary Builders

Find and circle the following "Top-Ten" terms in the word search puzzle. The terms may appear up, down, sideways, or diagonal, and forward or backward, ignoring any spaces in phrases.

A	A	S	I	C	A	B	C	D	E	F	G	H	I	Z	K	E	L	M	N	O	P	Q	R	S	T
C	E	G	A	L	U	V	W	X	Y	Z	A	B	C	D	D	E	F	G	H	I	J	K	L	M	N
Y	E	S	E	A	R	C	H	O	W	A	L	Y	R	O	T	U	T	A	T	S	P	V	Q	R	S
P	Y	T	U	V	W	X	Y	Z	A	B	C	D	C	E	F	G	H	I	J	K	E	L	M	N	O
X	D	W	A	R	D	P	Q	R	S	T	U	D	V	W	X	Y	Z	A	B	T	C	L	D	E	F
L	O	L	F	I	G	H	I	J	K	L	E	M	N	S	E	C	T	I	O	N	S	O	T	P	Q
E	S	T	U	V	W	X	Y	Z	A	T	B	C	S	D	E	F	G	H	I	J	K	L	M	I	N
L	P	Q	R	S	T	U	V	W	A	X	Y	E	Z	A	B	C	D	E	F	G	H	I	J	K	T
B	M	N	O	P	Q	R	S	T	T	U	R	V	W	X	Y	Z	A	B	C	D	E	F	G	H	N
M	J	K	L	M	N	O	O	P	Q	G	R	S	T	U	V	W	X	Y	Z	A	B	C	D	E	E
A	G	H	I	J	K	N	L	M	N	N	O	P	Q	R	S	T	U	V	W	X	Y	Z	A	B	M
E	D	E	F	G	N	H	I	O	J	K	L	M	N	O	P	Q	R	S	T	U	V	W	X	Y	T
R	Z	A	B	A	C	D	C	O	D	I	F	I	C	A	T	I	O	N	E	F	G	H	I	J	C
P	K	I	M	N	O	P	Q	R	S	T	U	V	W	X	Y	Z	A	B	C	D	E	F	G	H	A
Z	L	J	K	L	M	N	O	P	Q	R	S	T	U	V	W	X	Y	Z	A	B	C	D	E	F	N
L	E	G	I	S	L	A	T	I	V	E	H	I	S	T	O	R	Y	G	H	I	J	K	L	M	E

ANNOTATED CODE, BILL, CODIFICATION, CONGRESS, ENACTMENT, LEGISLATIVE HISTORY, SECTIONS, STATUTORY LAW, TITLES, and **VETO.**

Chapter 7

Constitutional Law, Court Rules, and Other Promulgations

CHAPTER OBJECTIVES

After reading this chapter, you should be able to:

- Recognize the nature of constitutional law.

- Identify the source of the text of the Constitution.

- Identify the official version of the Constitution.

- Identify the annotated sources of the Constitution.

- Find the text of state constitutions.

- Describe the benefits of an "annotated" code.

- Understand the nature of court rules.

- List the different kinds of court rules.

- Identify the annotated sources of the federal court rules.

- Find state court rules.

- Find treaties and executive orders.

In this chapter, you will learn about the sources of law under the Constitution and under the legislative, executive, and judicial branches of government, other than case law, statutory law, and administrative law.

charter
The documents that form a government; the fundamental law of a local government.

CONSTITUTIONAL LAW

The documents that form a government are known as that government's **charter.** In a loose sense, documents such as the Declaration of Independence and the Federalist Papers are part of the charter of the United States of America. In a strict sense, the charter of the United States of

Case Fact Pattern

In your research of the federal laws that apply to the transportation of hazardous materials and the issue of preemption, you see references to the Supremacy Clause of the Constitution of the United States. Your mind is full of questions.

Where is the Supremacy Clause in the Constitution? What exactly does it state? How have the courts interpreted it in other kinds of cases?

constitution
The written fundamental law of a sovereign, such as the Constitution of the United States.

preamble
The introductory statement of legal intent, such as the "We the People" portion of the Constitution of the United States.

Bill of Rights
Set forth the fundamental individual rights government and law function to preserve and protect; the first ten amendments to the Constitution of the United States.

America is its written fundamental law, its **constitution,** the Constitution of the United States. Law directly derived from this fundamental document is known as constitutional law. (See Figure 7.1.)

Federal Constitution

Law is the command of a sovereign, and in the United States of America the people are sovereign. As the **preamble** (the introductory statement of legal intent) states, the people have exercised their power through the Constitution of the United States "to form a more perfect Union, establish Justice, insure domestic Tranquility, provide for the common defence, promote the general Welfare, and secure the Blessings of Liberty." As Article VI, Clause 2, of the Constitution provides, the Constitution, federal laws made pursuant to it, and treaties made under it, are the supreme law of the land. The Constitution returns some powers to the people, including the power to amend the Constitution and the power to vote.

The Constitution was drafted at the Constitutional Convention held in Philadelphia in the summer of 1787. Signed by 39 delegates on September 17, 1787, the Constitution became effective, by its terms, when it was ratified by the ninth state, which was New Hampshire, on June 21, 1788. The federal government began operating under the Constitution on April 30, 1789.

The Constitution is organized into articles, sections, and clauses. Articles I, II, and III cover the branches of the federal government. Article I covers the legislative branch; Article II covers the executive branch; and Article III covers the judicial branch. Article IV covers the states. Article V covers the amendment process. Articles VI and VII cover miscellaneous matters.

There have been 27 amendments (technically, additional articles) to the Constitution. The first ten amendments, ratified by three-fourths of the states on December 15, 1791, are known as the **Bill of Rights.** The 27th amendment was certified on May 18, 1992. (See Figure 7.2.)

The Constitution is the most widely available law in the United States. The text is routinely reproduced in almanacs, encyclopedias, and dictionaries, especially law dictionaries. The text is also found in law, history, and political science texts, and in patriotic pamphlets and prints. Ironically, few people have ever read the Constitution from beginning to end. This fundamental

FIGURE 7.1
Outline of the U.S. Constitution

Preamble	**We the People** of the United States, in Order to form a more perfect Union, establish Justice, insure domestic Tranquility, provide for the common defence, promote the general Welfare, and secure the Blessings of Liberty to ourselves and our Posterity, do ordain and establish this Constitution for the United States of America.	
Articles	Article 1	Legislative Branch
	Article 2	The Presidency
	Article 3	The Judiciary
	Article 4	The States
	Article 5	The Amendment Process
	Article 6	The Constitution's Legal Status
	Article 7	Ratification
Signers		39 Delegates
Amendments		1—27

CYBER TRIP

A hypertext interpretation of *The Constitution of the United States* by the Congressional Research Service can be found on Cornell University Law School's Legal Information Institute Web site at www.law.cornell.edu/anncon/index.html.

Amendment	Issue
First	Freedom of speech, freedom of the press
Second	Right to keep and bear arms
Third	No quartering of soldiers in private homes
Fourth	Search and seizure
Fifth	Right to due process – Self-Incrimination protection
Sixth	Rights of accused persons
Seventh	Right of trial by jury
Eight	Cruel and unusual punishment prohibited
Ninth	The peoples' rights
Tenth	Powers reserved by the states

FIGURE 7.2   Bill of Rights – Quick Reference

document, important to legal researchers because it explains the structure of the government and the sources of law, is reproduced in Appendix A.

Where is the official version of the Constitution of the United States? The Constitution is on parchment, under glass, bathed in helium, and is displayed in the intentionally dim light of the Exhibition Hall Rotunda of the National Archives in Washington, D.C.

Annotated Constitutions

judicial review
The doctrine that the clauses of the Constitution, like statutes, are subject to interpretation by the courts, and, in particular, by the U.S. Supreme Court.

Under the doctrine of **judicial review,** the clauses of the Constitution, like statutes, are subject to interpretation by the courts, particularly by the U.S. Supreme Court. In fact, since the Constitution was designed to be a flexible general guide for the government, it is subject to more interpretation than a statute, which, by design, is usually quite specific. Legal researchers usually need to refer to an **annotated constitution,** a version of the Constitution containing case summaries of how the courts have interpreted the Constitution.

annotated constitution
A version of a Constitution containing case summaries of how the courts have interpreted it.

Three annotated constitutions are preferred by most legal researchers for researching constitutional law. The most readily available annotated constitutions are the *United States Code Annotated* (U.S.C.A.) and the *United States Code Service* (U.S.C.S.). Both sets have volumes in which each clause of the Constitution is set out, followed by the usual code treatment: history notes, research references, and case summaries. The U.S.C.A., published by Thomson/West gives digest topic and key number references. The U.S.C.S., published by LexisNexis, gives other references.

Both U.S.C.A. and U.S.C.S. may be entered by a volume index, and are kept current by cumulative annual pocket parts and a specialized service.

The third source, much less widely available physically, is a one-volume annotated constitution entitled *The Constitution of the United States of America.* Published pursuant to a congressional resolution (see 2 U.S.C. § 168), it is prepared by the Congressional Research Service of the Library of Congress. Significant cases are woven into the analysis following each clause.

Other sources of case authority and interpretation concerning the Constitution can be found in a variety of publications. Both Thomson/West and LexisNexis publish digests covering the Supreme Court. LexisNexis publishes annotations in the *United States Supreme Court Reports, Second Lawyers' Edition* (L. Ed. 2d) that cover points ruled on by the Supreme Court. Numerous treatises and periodicals are also available covering legal issues of all kinds, including constitutional law.

RESEARCH THIS

Not surprisingly, the text of the Constitution of the United States can be found on the Internet. For example, the text can be found on the U.S. Government Printing Office Web site at http:// www.gpoaccess.gov/constitution/index.html. Use the Internet to answer this question: What does Article II, Section 1, Clause 5 of the Constitution of the United States provide?

State and Local Constitutions

promulgated
Made official and public.

Just as the people as a whole have acted as sovereign for the federal government, the people of each state have **promulgated** (made official and public) a constitution to be the fundamental law for their state. Just as the federal constitution can be found with a federal annotated code, state constitutions are usually found with their state annotated code, either as a separate volume or in an appendix. Again, an annotated version includes case summaries of how the courts have interpreted the constitution. Often cross-references are provided to similar constitutional provisions in other states and in the federal constitution, so a legal researcher can research case interpretations in other states as persuasive authority. Like codes, entry into an annotated state constitution may be made through a general or a volume index.

Another source of state constitutions is a three-volume set, *Constitutions of the United States: National and State,* prepared by the Columbia University Legislative Drafting Research Fund.

The fundamental law of a local government agency is usually known as its charter. Like local ordinances, a legal researcher may have no choice but to review the local charter in the local government's offices.

COURT RULES

The courts have the power to decide real cases. Insofar as the sovereign's constitution and statutes empower and direct the judicial process, the courts are bound to follow them. However, if no constitutional clauses or statutes direct the judicial process, the judicial branch has the inherent power to promulgate its own rules governing its own activities in deciding cases. It is common for high-level courts to govern the lower courts and to establish uniform procedures through a system of court rules.

For example, suppose your local county courthouse opens at 8:30 a.m. Why is it 8:30 a.m. instead of, say, 9:00 a.m.? The Constitution of the United States does not provide when state courts must open for the day. The state constitution probably does not provide when the state's courts must open for the day. The state statutes probably do not provide when the state's courts must open for the day. Since the court must open sometime to decide cases, and the relevant constitutions and statutes do not provide a time, the state courts then have the inherent authority to set the opening time by rule. If the high or supreme court does not set the time, then an intermediate court might set the time. If not, the matter will be left to the discretion of the local trial judges. If they enter a rule on the public journal of the court, that's the time. If they do not, the matter will be left to the discretion of the individual judge. It is extremely important to check the local rules of the court in which a document is being filed or a case is being heard. To violate a court rule can sometimes lead to the judge dismissing the case because of a technicality. If a client's case is mishandled because the local court rules were not followed, an attorney can be sued for malpractice, face sanctions, or perhaps even disbarment.

Who makes the rules governing the filing of a civil lawsuit in a U.S. District Court? The U.S. Supreme Court does, but not because of inherent power. The Constitution provides twice, in Article I, § 8, and in Article III, § 1, that Congress has the power to create the lower federal courts. This is the legislative branch's check on the power of the judicial branch provided by the framers of the Constitution. Under Title 28 of the *United States Code* (U.S.C.), Congress has created the lower federal courts, but, under 28 U.S.C. § 2072, Congress has delegated to the Supreme Court the authority to make rules of procedure for the District Courts. Who makes the rules of procedure for cases before the Supreme Court? The Supreme Court. Since the Constitution is silent on the matter, the Supreme Court has the inherent power and authority to make its own rules.

There are rules covering virtually every procedural act possible in the judicial branch. There are rules of civil procedure, criminal procedure, evidence (trial procedure), and appellate procedure and practice. There are rules of juvenile procedure, traffic court, claims court, and bankruptcy. There are rules governing attorneys, judges, admission to the bar, grievances, and discipline. There are "codes" of rules regarding ethics and judicial conduct. Most court rules are rules of superintendence (general applicability). Almost every court also has local rules applicable only to that court. In assisting in the handling of a case in court, read and follow the local rules of the court.

Major publishers often publish court rules in pamphlet form. Thomson/West, for example, publishes the rules of most states, including the federal courts in the state, in pamphlets titled by the state, "Rules of Court," year, and volume.

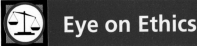

Eye on Ethics

Remember that the ethics applicable to lawyers, and indirectly applicable to paralegals, are usually published as court rules. In addition to any ethical codes directly applicable to a paralegal, an ethical paralegal is familiar with the ethical codes that apply to lawyers in the paralegal's state.

Publishers also publish pamphlets covering specific areas of law, which include the relevant statutes and court rules. Thomson/West, for example, publishes the *Federal Criminal Code and Rules,* covering the relevant portions Titles 18, 21, 28, and 46 of the U.S.C., and the Federal Rules of Criminal Procedure, Rules Governing Section 2254 Cases, Rules of Procedure for the Trial of Misdemeanors Before United States Magistrates, Federal Rules of Evidence, Federal Rules of Appellate Procedure, and Rules of the Supreme Court.

FIGURE 7.3
Excerpt from U.S. Code Annotated

Source: U.S. Code Annotated, Title 28 – Federal Rules of Civil Procedure. Reprinted by permission of Thomson/West.

II. COMMENCEMENT OF ACTION; SERVICE OF PROCESS, PLEADINGS, MOTIONS, AND ORDERS

Rule 3.   Commencement of Action

A civil action is commenced by filing a complaint with the court.

PRACTICE COMMENTARY

by David D. Siegel

Paradoxically, most of what has to be said about Rule 3 is said in the course of the extensive Commentaries on Rule 4, set out following Rule 4 further on in this volume. But a warning to plaintiffs about to rely on Rule 3 in a case in which subject matter jurisdiction is based on diversity of citizenship is urgent enough to repeat here, under Rule 3 itself.

Rule 3 provides the rule of federal practice that the filing of the complaint marks the commencement of the action. The moment of filing is the key time to look to determine whether the statute of limitations has been satisfied. As long as the complaint has been filed on or before the last day—the assumption would run—the action is timely and the summons and complaint can be served at any time during the 120 days that follow. (The 120-period comes from Rule 4[j].)

The foregoing is true enough as a general principle when jurisdiction is based on a federal question, or any other ground of jurisdiction except diversity of citizenship. When diversity is the jurisdictional basis for the federal action, however, Rule 3 emphatically does not govern for purposes of the statute of limitations. The rule applicable in a diversity case to determine whether the statute of limitations has been satisfied is taken from the law of the state in which the federal court happens to be sitting.

If that state's law is the same as Rule 3, deeming the action commenced when the complaint is filed even if the summons has not yet been served, perhaps the plaintiff can take Rule 3 at face value. But even there—if the case is a diversity case—state law may have little connected tidbits that differ from federal practice. Perhaps, for limitations purposes, state law will require service in a shorter time (following the filing of the complaint) than the 120 days allowed by Federal Rule 4(j), for example. In a diversity case, all matters connected with the statute of limitations should be consulted in forum state law. Indeed, since it may be difficult to determine whether a given item is to come from state or from federal law in a particular state, or in a particular fact pattern, the best bet is to take such proceedings—whenever the statute of limitations is in any way involved—as will satisfy both federal and forum state requirements. The governing ideology here is that discretion is the better part of valor, and even the valiant do best to bow and scrape when the statute of limitations threatens.

If forum state law is not the same as Rule 3; if the forum state deems the statute of limitations satisfied not merely upon the filing of the complaint, but at some later. . .

Annotated Court Rules

Like constitutional clauses, court rules are subject to interpretation by the courts, and in particular, by the court that promulgated them. A legal researcher may need to refer to an annotated version of the court rules—a version of the court rules containing case summaries of how the courts have interpreted the court rules.

Just as an annotated constitution can be found with a federal annotated code, annotated federal court rules are found with a federal code, either in a separate volume or at the end of the volume of the relevant title. The principal federal annotated codes—the U.S.C.A. and the U.S.C.S.— have been previously discussed with regard to statutes. The U.S.C.S. covers federal rules in special "Court Rules" volumes, while the U.S.C.A. follows the relevant title method, locating, for example, the Federal Rules of Criminal Procedure at the end of Title 18, and the Federal Rules of Civil Procedure at the end of Title 28. In both sets, each rule is followed by the usual code treatment: history notes, research references, and case summaries. The U.S.C.A., published by Thomson/West, gives digest topic and key number references. The U.S.C.S., published by LexisNexis, gives other references. Again, both sets may be entered by a volume index, and both sets are kept current by cumulative annual pocket parts and a current service. (See Figures 7.3 and 7.4.)

Just as annotated federal court rules can be found with a federal annotated code, annotated state court rules are usually found with their state annotated code, either in a separate volume or at the end of the volume of the relevant title.

Other sources of case authority and interpretation concerning court rules can be found in a variety of publications. Thomson/West publishes *Federal Rules Decisions* (F.R.D.) as part of its National Reporter System. LexisNexis's *United States Supreme Court Digest, Lawyers' Edition* contains court rules volumes. A.L.R. annotation sometimes covers points ruled on by the courts, including court rules. There are numerous treatises and formbooks covering legal matters of all kinds, including those arising under court rules.

FIGURE 7.4
Excerpt from U.S.C.S. Court Rules

Source: U.S.C.S. Court Rules – Federal Rules of Civil Procedure. Reprinted by permission of LexisNexis.

Rule 2, n 13

actions whether in cases at law, in equity or in admiralty and therefore, facts of each case and not nature of action decide question of whether summary judgment should be granted. Suro v Llenza (1982, DC Puerto Rico) 531 F Supp 1094.

14. Damages

Rule of law that in absence of express statutory provision court of equity is without power to assess exemplary or punitive damages is not changed by Rule 2, for it does not abolish distinction between law and equity. Coca-Cola Co. v Dixi-Cola Laboratories, Inc. (1946, CA4 Md) 155 F2d 59, 68 USPQ 242, 69 USPQ 360, cert den (1946) 329 US 773, 91 L Ed 665, 67 S Ct 192, 71 USPQ 328 and cert den (1946) 329 US 773, 91 L Ed 665, 67 S Ct 192, 71 USPQ 328.

Rule that court of equity may not award punitive damages without express statutory authority is inapplicable where complaint alleges both legal and equitable causes of action and contains prayer for both injunction and damages. Sperry Rand Corp. v A-T-0, Inc. (1971, CA4 Va) 447 F2d 1387, 171 USPQ 775, cert den (1972) 405 US 1017, 31 L Ed 2d 479, 92 S Ct 1292, 173 USPQ 193 and reh

den (1972, CA4 Va) 459 F2d 19 and cert den (1972) 409 US 892, 34 L Ed 2d 150, 93 S Ct 117, 93 S Ct 119, 175 USPQ 385.

Procedural dilemma which formerly barred derivative suit for three fold damages under Antitrust Laws (15 USCS §§ I et seq.) has been eliminated by adoption of Federal Rules. Kogan v Schenley Industries, Inc. (1956, DC Del) 20 FRD 4.

Damages for infringement of design patent may be recovered either by action at law or upon bill in equity for injunction to restrain such infringement, under Rule 2. Ross v Plastic Playthings, Inc. (1956, DC NY) 138 F Supp 887, 109 USPQ 12.

15. Appeal

Policy of Rules, in abolishing procedural distinctions between law and equity rid in establishing single unified practice, must not be subverted by allowing appeal from order denying demand for jury trial, on theory that it is in effect same as interlocutory injunction. Morgantown v Royal Ins. Co. (1949) 337 US 254, 93 L Ed 1347, 69 5 Ct 1067.

Rules do not obliterate distinction between law and equity in application of 28 USCS § 1292 concerning appeals from interlocutory-injunctions. Gatliff Coal Co. v Cox (1944, CA6 Ky) 142 F2d 876, 14 BNA LRRM 782, 8 CCH LC-62199.

FIGURE 7.4
(*continued*)

II. COMMENCEMENT OF ACTION; SERVICE OF PROCESS, PLEADINGS, MOTIONS, AND ORDERS

Rule 3. Commencement of Action
A civil action is commenced by filing a complaint with the court.

HISTORY ANCILLARY LAWS AND DIRECTIVES

Other provisions:
Notes of Advisory Committee 1. Rule 5(e) defines what constitutes filing with the court.
2. This rule governs the commencement of all actions, including those brought by or against the United States or an officer or agency thereof regardless of whether service is to be made personally pursuant to Rule 4(d), or otherwise pursuant to Rule 4(e).
3. With this rule compare former Equity Rule 12 (Issue of Subpoena—Time for Answer) and the following statutes (and other similar statutes) which provide a similar method for commencing an action:
U.S.C., Title 28, former: § 45 (District courts; practice and procedure in certain cases under interstate commerce laws). § 762 (Petition in suit against United States). § 766 (Partition suits where United States is tenant in common or joint tenant).
4. This rule provides that the first step in an action is the filing of the complaint. Under Rule 4(a) this is to be followed forthwith by issuance of a summons and its delivery to an officer for service. Other rules providing for dismissal for failure to prosecute suggest a method available to attack unreasonable delay in prosecuting an action after it has been commenced.

TREATIES

treaty
A nation-binding agreement with a foreign country.

international law
The rules governing sovereign countries by their consent: the law of nations.

executive agreement
A President's agreement with a foreign country that is not nation-binding.

CYBER TRIP

Recent "Senate Treaty Documents" can be searched at the U.S. Government Printing Office Web site, GPO Access, at www.gpoaccess.gov/serialset/cdocuments/index.html.

A nation-binding agreement with a foreign country is known as a **treaty.** Treaties are part of the rules governing sovereign countries by their consent—the law of nations—known as **international law.** Article II, Section 2, Clause 2, of the Constitution of the United States provides that the President "shall have Power, by and with the Advice and Consent of the Senate, to make Treaties; provided two-thirds of the Senators present concur." If the President makes an agreement with a foreign country, but does not seek the advice and consent of the Senate, it is known as an **executive agreement.** The President may abide by an executive agreement, but his successor may ignore it, since it is, by definition, not nation-binding.

Article VI, Clause 2, of the Constitution of the United States provides that along with the Constitution and the laws made pursuant to it, "all Treaties made, or which shall be made, under the Authority of the United States, shall be the supreme Law of the Land; and the Judges in every State shall be bound thereby, any Thing in the Constitution or laws of any State to the Contrary notwithstanding." As the supreme law of the land, treaties affect everyone. Since the 97th Congress, a hyphenated number identifies treaties. The first number refers to the Congress in which the treaty was submitted, while the second number is a sequence number. For example, Treaty 106-2 refers to the second treaty sent to the 106th Congress.

Treaties have been published in a variety of publications. Currently, all treaties and executive agreements in which the United States is a party are published as pamphlets in the *Treaties and Other International Acts Series* (T.I.A.S.), bound in volumes as *United States Treaties and Other International Agreements* (U.S.T.), each published pursuant to 1 U.S.C. § 112a by the U.S. Department of State. They are indexed by the *United States Treaties and Other International Agreements Cumulative Index.* Treaties and executive agreements are also published in *United States Statutes at Large* (Stat.) by the U.S. Government Printing Office.

Treaties in Force is an annual publication of the U.S. Department of State. It can be used, along with the monthly *Department of State Bulletin* and its monthly and annual indexes, to determine the current status of a treaty or executive agreement. *Treaties in Force* lists all currently effective treaties and executive agreements by both country and subject.

Some treaty publications concern particular subjects. Wolters Kulwer publishes *Commerce Clearing House, Tax Treaties,* which covers treaties involving tax law. C. Kappler's *Indian Affairs, Laws and Treaties* deals with treaties involving Indian tribes.

A Day in the Life

Where is the Supremacy Clause in the Constitution? What exactly does it state? How have the courts interpreted it in other kinds of cases? These questions were not assigned to you. They occurred to you on your own. One of the beautiful things about being skilled in legal research is that you can find the answers to your own questions about the law.

You could have used U.S.C.A. or other sources, but in learning about the statutory volumes of U.S.C.S., you remember seeing the Constitution volumes of U.S.C.S. Using the index to search for the Supremacy Clause, you find that it is Clause 2 of Article VI. "This Constitution, and the Laws of the United States which shall be made in Pursuance thereof; and all Treaties made, or which shall be made, under the Authority of the United States, shall be the supreme Law of the Land; and the Judges of every State shall be bound thereby, any Thing in the Constitution or Laws of any State to the Contrary notwithstanding."

Under the Interpretative Notes and Decisions for Article VI, Clause 2, there are numerous case-note headings under Part II entitled CONFLICTS BETWEEN STATE OR LOCAL ACTION AND FEDERAL PRE-EMPTION AFFECTING PARTICULAR MATTERS. The casenote headings under Subpart A run from "A" (Abortion) to "W" (Wiretaps), and include a casenote heading for "Pollution; hazardous materials." The casenotes under that heading generally indicate how, in matters related to pollution and hazardous materials, federal law usually preempts state law.

CYBER TRIP

Treaties in Force is available on the U.S. Department of State Web site. See www.state.gov/s/l/treaties.

Like constitutional clauses and court rules, treaties are subject to interpretation by the courts. Thus, a legal researcher may need to refer to an annotated version of a treaty. LexisNexis's annotated code, U.S.C.S., includes volumes of treaties by year of ratification, with casenotes.

Summary

The charter of the United States of America is its written fundamental law, the Constitution of the United States. In the United States, the people are sovereign and exercise their power through the Constitution. The Constitution, organized into articles, sections, and clauses, now includes 26 amendments. The clauses of the Constitution are subject to interpretation by the courts. The most readily available annotated constitutions are the constitutional volumes of the United States Code Annotated (U.S.C.A.) and the United States Code Service (U.S.C.S.). Both set out each clause of the Constitution, followed by history notes, research references, and case summaries. Both sets may be entered by a volume index. Just as the federal Constitution can be found with a federal annotated code, state constitutions are usually found with their state annotated code.

If no constitutional clauses or statutes direct the judicial process, the judicial branch has inherent power to promulgate its own rules governing its own activities in deciding cases. It is common for high-level courts to govern the lower courts and to establish uniform procedures through a system of court rules. There are rules covering virtually every procedural act possible in the judicial branch. Major publishers often publish court rules in pamphlet form. Court rules are subject to interpretation by the courts, and so a legal researcher may need to refer to an annotated version. Annotated federal court rules are found with the annotated federal codes, either in a separate volume or at the end of the volume of the relevant title. Annotated state court rules are usually found with their annotated state code.

A nation-binding agreement with a foreign country is known as a treaty. If the President makes an agreement with a foreign country, but does not seek the advice and consent of the Senate, it is known as an executive agreement. Treaties have been published in a variety of publications. Currently, all treaties and executive agreements in which the United States is a party are published in Treaties and Other International Acts Series (T.I.A.S.) and in United States Statutes at Large (Stat.). Treaties in Force can be used, along with the Department of State Bulletin, to determine the current status of a treaty or an executive agreement. Treaties are subject to interpretation by the courts. The United States Code Service (U.S.C.S.) includes volumes of treaties with casenotes.

Key Terms

annotated constitution   106
Bill of Rights   105
charter   104
constitution   105
executive agreement   110

international law   110
judicial review   106
preamble   105
promulgated   107
treaty   110

Review Questions

1. What is the fundamental law?

2. Where can you find the text of the Constitution of the United States on the Internet?

3. Where is the original Constitution of the United States?

4. Why would you use an annotated federal code to study a clause of the Constitution?

5. Where would you expect to find the text of your state constitution?

6. Where do the courts get the power to make court rules?

7. Name some of the different kinds of court rules.

8. Why would you use an annotated federal code to study a federal court rule?

9. Where would you expect to find your state's rules of civil procedure?

10. Which resource contains the information needed to verify the validity of a treaty?

Exercises

1. Use the Constitution volume index to U.S.C.A. to answer this question: What is the article-section-clause cite for the part of the Constitution requiring the testimony of two witnesses to convict someone of treason?

2. Use the Constitution volumes of U.S.C.A. to answer these questions: What topic and key number is listed as a Library Reference for Article V? According to the case summaries, can a constitutional amendment be ratified by a referendum of the voters of a state? What is the U.S. cite of the first case summary regarding ratification by referendum?

3. Use the Constitution volume index to U.S.C.S. to answer this question: What is the article-section-clause cite for the part of the Constitution discussing the oath of Senators trying an impeachment?

4. Use the Constitution volumes of U.S.C.S. to answer these questions: What is the volume-series-page cite of the first L. Ed. 2d annotation listed under the Research Guide for Article VI, Clause? According to the casenotes, was West Virginia's workmen's compensation act held to have violated a treaty between the United States and Italy in 1928?

5. Use the Federal Rules of Evidence volumes of U.S.C.A. in Title 28 to answer these questions: What is the last topic and key number listed as a Library Reference for Federal Rule of Evidence 604? According to the case summaries, must an oath include the word "solemnly"? Give the full citation of the case summary supporting your answer.

Vocabulary Builders

Find and circle the following "Top-Ten" terms in the subsequent word search puzzle. The terms may appear up, down, sideways, or diagonal, and forward or backward, ignoring any spaces in phrases.

A	B	C	D	E	F	G	H	I	J	I	K	L	M	N	O	P	Q	B	A	S	I	C	R	S	T
C	O	N	S	T	I	T	U	T	I	O	N	A	L	L	A	W	U	L	E	G	A	L	V	W	X
Y	Z	A	B	C	D	E	F	G	H	I	J	T	K	L	M	N	O	R	E	S	E	A	R	C	H
P	E	X	E	C	U	T	I	V	E	A	G	R	E	E	M	E	N	T	Q	R	S	T	U	V	W
X	Y	Z	A	B	D	E	T	A	G	L	U	M	O	R	P	C	D	E	F	G	H	I	J	C	K
L	M	N	O	P	Q	R	S	T	U	V	W	X	Y	Z	N	A	C	B	C	D	E	F	G	H	H
E	I	J	K	L	M	N	O	P	Q	R	S	T	U	V	W	A	X	O	Y	Z	A	B	C	A	D
L	E	F	G	H	I	J	K	L	M	N	O	P	Q	R	S	T	T	U	N	V	W	X	Y	R	Z
B	A	B	C	D	E	F	G	S	T	H	G	I	R	F	O	L	L	I	B	G	H	I	J	T	K
M	L	M	N	O	P	Q	R	S	T	U	V	W	X	Y	Z	A	B	C	O	D	R	E	R	E	F
A	N	N	O	T	A	T	E	D	C	O	N	S	T	I	T	U	T	I	O	N	G	E	H	R	I
E	J	K	L	M	N	O	P	Q	R	S	T	U	V	W	X	Y	Z	A	B	C	A	D	S	E	F
R	G	H	I	J	K	L	M	N	O	P	Q	R	S	T	U	V	W	X	Y	T	Z	L	A	S	B
P	C	D	E	F	G	H	I	J	K	L	M	N	O	P	Q	R	S	T	Y	U	V	W	L	X	Y
Z	A	B	C	D	E	F	G	H	I	J	K	L	M	N	O	P	Q	R	S	T	U	V	W	A	X
B	Y	E	D	W	A	R	D	N	O	L	F	I	Y	Z	A	B	C	D	E	F	G	H	I	J	W

ANNOTATED CONSTITUTION, BILL OF RIGHTS, CHARTER, CONGRESS, CONSTITUTIONAL LAW, EXECUTIVE AGREEMENT, INTERNATIONAL LAW, PREAMBLE, PROMULGATED, and **TREATY.**

Chapter 8

Administrative Law

CHAPTER OBJECTIVES

After reading this chapter, you should be able to:

- Understand why administrative agencies were created.

- Compare and contrast the duties and powers of administrative agencies and executive departments.

- Find regulations chronologically.

- Find regulations topically.

- Compare and contrast administrative and executive orders.

- Recognize administrative decisions.

- Recognize the nature and use of loose-leaf services.

- Identify the basic features of loose-leaf services.

- Identify the major federal tax services.

Administrative agencies are an important feature of the United States governmental system. As the government grows and becomes more complex, the need for administrative agencies to assist the government in conducting its business grows. The United States Constitution grants to Congress and the executive branches of government the power to create necessary agencies. In fact, there are well over 100 federal administrative agencies. Administrative agencies administer some of the government's business which enables other parts of the government to conduct business.

ADMINISTRATIVE AGENCIES AND EXECUTIVE DEPARTMENTS

As technology advances and society grows more complex, a sovereign's legislative, executive, and judicial branches become increasingly unable to manage all the details of government. The gaps are filled and the details are managed by the branches of government creating specialized governmental entities, known in the broad sense as **administrative agencies.**

administrative agency
A governmental body charged with administering and implementing particular legislation.

For example, when the transmission and reception of electromagnetic radiation (such as radio waves) were developed in the early 1900s, few, if any, of the federal government's legislators, executives, or judges had sufficient expertise in electronics or physics to be able to govern its development. When the nation's first commercial radio station, KDKA in Pittsburgh, Pennsylvania, went "on the air" in 1920, the average legislator, executive, or judge did not foresee that someday there would be hundreds of radio stations across the country and countless radio-wave transmitting devices (e.g., automatic garage door openers) with potentially conflicting signals, causing "interference" with each other. When the need to govern the details of radio became apparent, such as the need to assign

Case Fact Pattern

At the bankruptcy firm where you work, one of the firm's new clients has come into the office very upset. Debt collectors have been calling her at all hours of the day and night, sometimes waking her at 5:00 in the morning, demanding payment. The collectors are from a collection agency, threatening legal action. The assigned attorney asks you to research the client's rights as they relate to collection of debts. Which administrative agency deals with this issue and how do you locate this type of information to conduct thorough research?

stations to particular frequencies of amplitude modulation (AM) or frequency modulation (FM), the legislature acted by creating a body of experts to manage the problem.

Under its constitutional authority to regulate interstate commerce, Congress, with the Federal Communications Act of 1934, created an independent agency, the Federal Communications Commission (FCC), to manage radio communications. The FCC grants radio station licenses, assigns frequencies, and is responsible for tracking down and stopping unauthorized radio broadcasts. One requirement of the FCC is familiar to almost everyone. Licensed broadcast stations must identify themselves on the air at least once every hour ("station identification").

In the narrow sense, an administrative agency is an "independent agency," a governmental entity distinct from the three branches of government, created to independently govern a limited specialized area of the law. (See Figure 8.1.) Since an administrative agency is distinct from the three branches of government, it has to answer only to the three branches of government in a formal way. For example, if the National Labor Relations Board (NLRB) wants to order a particular company committing an unfair labor practice against a union to reinstate a particular employee with back pay, it need not ask for specific permission from any of the three branches of government. The legislature has granted general authority in the National Labor Relations Act, the executive has appointed members to the NLRB with the power to act, and the judiciary will enforce the orders of the NLRB to act as the judiciary interprets to be within the mandate of the act.

Under the executive branch of government, groups of specialists may be organized to assist the executive in carrying out the functions of the executive branch. (See Figure 8.2.) Among administrative agencies, these organizations are known as **executive departments.** The heads of executive departments do not run entities distinct from the executive branch. They must answer to the executive both formally and informally. For example, if the Secretary of the Department of Defense wants to eliminate a major weapon system, it must be with the approval of the executive, the President, who is the commander in chief. Similar "executive departments" may also be

executive department
That branch of government charged with carrying out the laws enacted by the legislature.

FIGURE 8.1

Administrative Agencies

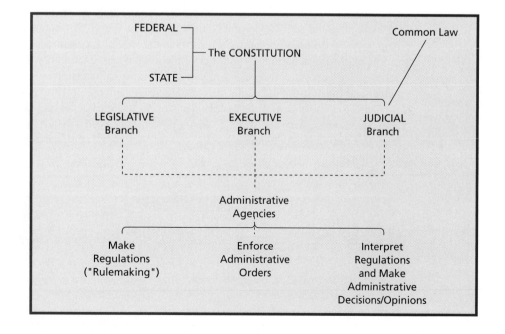

FIGURE 8.2

The Executive Branch

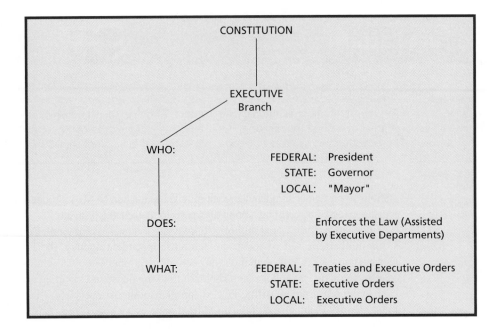

CONSTITUTION

EXECUTIVE
Branch

WHO:

FEDERAL: President
STATE: Governor
LOCAL: "Mayor"

DOES:

Enforces the Law (Assisted by Executive Departments)

WHAT:

FEDERAL: Treaties and Executive Orders
STATE: Executive Orders
LOCAL: Executive Orders

legislative department

That department of government whose appropriate function is the making or enactment of laws, as distinguished from the judicial department, which interprets and applies the laws, and the executive department, which carries them into execution and effect.

created under the legislative branch (e.g., the General Accounting Office and the Library of Congress) and are known as **legislative departments.**

The technical distinction between administrative agencies and executive departments has been blurred in two ways. First, administrative agencies and executive departments are generally required by the sovereign to follow similar operating procedures. In the federal government, for example, each must follow the Administrative Procedure Act, which requires them to notify the public of proposed rule changes, hold public hearings, and the like. Second, the names given to the various administrative agencies and executive departments are often confusingly similar, yet widely varied.

An administrative agency, or a part of it, may be called, among other things, an administration, agency, authority, board, bureau, commission, corporation, department, division, foundation, office, or service. For example, local weather reports, watches, and warnings originate from offices of the National Weather Service (NWS), which is part of the National Oceanographic and Atmospheric Administration (NOAA), which is part of the U.S. Department of Commerce, which is, of course, an executive department of the President.

Usually the best way to sort out "who's who" is to consult an almanac, encyclopedia, directory, or manual. For the federal government, an extremely useful text is the *U.S. Government Manual,* prepared annually by the National Archives. The *U.S. Government Manual* is a "road map" to the federal government. Each entity in the federal government is covered, with emphasis on the executive departments and independent agencies. Each entity and its function are described in a concise narrative, usually with citations to its statutory source of authority. The names and functions of the major officials are also listed. (See Figure 8.3.)

The *U.S. Government Manual* includes several useful indexes and tables. Appendix A lists agencies that have been abolished, or whose powers have been transferred and to where they have been transferred (e.g., the powers of the former Materials Transportation Bureau [MTB] of the Department of Transportation [DOT] are now exercised by the Office of Hazardous Materials

 RESEARCH THIS

Locate the *U.S. Government Manual.* Find the appropriate appendix and answer the following question. What is the commonly used abbreviation and acronym for the Department of Homeland Security? How about for the Federal Trade Commission?

FIGURE 8.3

Excerpt from the U.S. Government Manual

Source: U.S. Government Printing Office.

Office of the Vice President of the United States

Eisenhower Executive Office Building Washington, DC 20501
Phone, 202–456–7549

Assistant to the President, Chief of Staff to the Vice President, and Assistant to the Vice President for National Security Affairs	I. Lewis Libby
Counsel to the Vice President	David Addington
Principal Deputy Assistant to the Vice President for National Security Affairs	Victoria Nuland
Deputy Chief of Staff to the Vice President	C. Dean McGrath, Jr.
Assistant to the Vice President for Legislative Affairs	Brenda Becker
Assistant to the Vice President for Domestic Policy	Kevin O'Donovan
Executive Assistant to the Vice President	Debra Heiden
Assistant to the Vice President for Operations	Claire O'Donnell
Chief of Staff to Mrs. Cheney	Stephanie Lundberg
Deputy Assistant to the Vice President and Director of Scheduling	Elizabeth Kleppe
Director of Correspondence for the Vice President	Cecelia Boyer
Press Secretary to the Vice President	Kevin Kellems
Assistant to the Vice President for Homeland Security Affairs	Carol Kuntz
Deputy Assistant to the Vice President for Advance	Dan Wilmot

The Office of the Vice President serves the Vice President in the performance of the many detailed activities incident to his immediate office.

Council of Economic Advisers

1800 G Street NW, Washington, DC 20502
Phone, 202–395–5084. Internet www.whitehouse.gov/cea.

Chairman	Harvey S. Rosen
Members	Kristin J. Forbes, (VACANCY)
Chief of Staff	Gary D. Blank

The Council of Economic Advisers primarily performs an analysis and appraisal of the national economy for the purpose of providing policy recommendations to the President.

The Council of Economic Advisers (CEA) was established In the Executive Office of the President by the Employment Act of 1946 (15 U.S.C. 1023). It now functions under that statute and Reorganization Plan No. 9 of 1953 (5 U.S.C. app.), effective August 1, 1953.

The Council consists of three members appointed by the President with the advice and consent of the Senate. One of the members is designated by the President as Chairman.

The Council analyzes the national economy and its various segments;

Transportation [OHMT]). Appendix B is the famous "alphabet soup" table listing the acronyms for all the governmental agencies (e.g., CIA, FAA, FBI, NRC) and what they stand for (e.g., Central Intelligence Agency, Federal Aviation Administration, Federal Bureau of Investigation, Nuclear Regulatory Commission, respectively). (See Figure 8.4.) Appendix C contains governmental organizational charts.

FIGURE 8.4

Excerpt from the U.S. Government Manual, *Appendix A*

Source: U.S. Government Printing Office.

Appendices

APPENDIX A: Commonly Used Abbreviations and Acronyms

ADA	Americans with Disabilities Act of 1990	BRS	Biotechnology Regulatory Service (Agriculture)
ADB	Asian Development Bank	BTS	Bureau of Transportation Statistics
AFDB	African Development Bank		Directorate of Border and Transportation Security (Homeland Security)
AFDF	African Development Fund		
AFIS	American Forces Information Service (Defense)		
AGRICOLA	Agricultural Online Access	BVA	Board of Veterans' Appeals
AmeriCorps* NCCC	National Civilian Community Corps	CBO	Congressional Budget Office
AmeriCorps* VISTA	Volunteers in Service to America	CBP	Customs and Border Protection
AMS	Agricultural Marketing Service	CCC	Commodity Credit Corporation
Amtrak	National Railroad Passenger Corporation	CDBG	Community Development Block Grant
APH	American Printing House for the Blind (Education)	CEA	Council of Economic Advisers
APHIS	Animal and Plant Health Inspection Service	CEQ	Council on Environmental Quality
ARS	Agricultural Research Service	CFR	*Code of Federal Regulations*
ATF	Bureau of Alcohol, Tobacco, Firearms, and Explosives	CFTC	Commodity Futures Trading Commission
BBG	Broadcasting Board of Governors	COPS	Office of Community Oriented Policing Services (Justice)
BEA	Bureau of Economic Analysis	CRS	Congressional Research Service
BIA	Bureau of Indian Affairs	CSREES	Cooperative State Research, Education, and Extension Service
BIC	Business Information Center (SBA)		
BIF	Bank Insurance Fund	CSS	*See* NSA/CSS
BIS	Bureau of Industry and Security (Commerce)	DAU	Defense Acquisition University
BLM	Bureau of Land Management	DDESS	Department of Defense Domestic Dependent Elementary and Secondary Schools
BLS	Bureau of Labor Statistics		

Monitor Publishing Co. publishes several "Yellow Book" directories for the federal government. The *Federal Yellow Book,* for example, is described by the company as the "who's who in federal departments and agencies."

There are now hundreds of administrative agencies in the federal and state governments. The number of administrative agencies is an accurate reflection of the complexity of society and its technological advances.

Administrative Regulations

Like the sovereign's legislature, administrative agencies may "dream up" laws, so long as they are within the scope of the authority, the specialized area of law, given to the administrative agency by the legislature. To reflect the difference between the broad powers of the legislative branch and the limited powers of an administrative agency, however, the terminology is different. Whereas a legislature enacts statutes, an administrative agency issues regulations. Whereas a legislature legislates, an administrative agency **regulates.** Whereas statutes are made as the result of a legislature's enactment, regulations are made as the result of an administrative agency's **rulemaking.**

Prior to 1936, there was no official source for federal regulations. Ignorance of federal regulations and the resulting confusion were rampant. The situation came to a head in the infamous Supreme Court case *Panama Refining Co. v. Ryan* [293 U.S. 388 (1935)]. The Panama Refining Company was prosecuted for violating an administrative regulation, and the case reached the Supreme Court on appeal before it was discovered that the regulation in question had been revoked before the prosecution had begun.

To clear up some of the confusion, in 1936, Congress passed the Federal Register Act [49 Stat. 500, 44 U.S.C. § 1504 et seq.]. The National Archives was given the duty of preparing and publishing (through the Government Printing Office) the *Federal Register* (Fed. Reg.). Published daily, except on Saturdays, Sundays, or legal holidays and the day following, the *Federal Register* is the official chronological source of federal regulations. For any federal administrative regulation or ruling to have legal effect, it must be published in the *Federal Register*. The types of actions that are published in the *Federal Register* are

- Enacted or amended rules or regulations
- Proposed rules
- Notices of administrative hearings
- Presidential proclamations

Each daily *Federal Register* is about the size of a magazine, and bound volumes of the set are truly massive. The pages of the set are numbered consecutively throughout the year and run into five figures. (See Figure 8.5.) Weekly, quarterly, and annual indexes are issued, but they are not cumulative. The Congressional Information Service publishes the *CIS Federal Register Index,* however, which is cumulative.

Administrative Codes

Just as statutes made by legislatures are collected topically in books called codes, regulations made by administrative agencies are also collected topically in books also called codes, or more specifically, **administrative codes.** As with the codification of statutes, the codification of regulations adds amending regulations to regulations currently in force and removes expired, repealed, or superseded regulations.

The official administrative code of the federal government, consisting of the topical collection of federal regulations, is the *Code of Federal Regulations* (C.F.R.), prepared and published (through the Government Printing Office) by the National Archives under the Federal Register Act. The C.F.R. is published in pamphlets in 50 titles, generally parallel to the 50 titles of the *United States Code* (U.S.C.) or the *United States Code Annotated* (U.S.C.A.). For example, 21 C.F.R. refers to the regulations regarding food and drugs, while 21 U.S.C.A. also refers to the regulations concerning food and drugs. The title numbers are the same. The paralleling of the title numbers allows for easier cross-referencing and researching by the legal researcher.

The covers of the pamphlets are white and another color. To keep the code up-to-date, approximately one-quarter of the pamphlets are replaced each calendar quarter. The covers of the new year's pamphlets are white and a color contrasting from the previous year's color (e.g., 1990 was blue; 1991 was maroon). The updating of the C.F.R. is different from the *United States Code.* The *United States Code* is updated by the publication of pocket part supplements.

Margin glossary

regulate
To direct by rule or restriction; to subject to governing principles or laws.

rulemaking
The power to prescribe rules of procedure to be followed under the topics and issues directed by a certain administrative agency.

administrative agency regulations and rules (administrative codes)
Processes and guidelines established under the particular administrative section that describe acceptable conduct for persons and situations under the control of the respective agency.

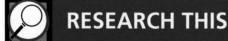

RESEARCH THIS

Locate the *Code of Federal Regulations.* Find the appropriate section and answer the following question. What is the definition of a frozen dessert?

FIGURE 8.5

Excerpt from the Federal Register

Rules and Regulations

Federal Register
Vol. 71, No. 131
Monday, July 10, 2006

This section of the FEDERAL REGISTER contains regulatory documents having general applicability and legal effect, most of which are keyed to and codified in the Code of Federal Regulations, which is published under 50 titles pursuant to 44 U.S.C. 1510.

The Code of Federal Regulations is sold by the Superintendent of Documents. Prices of new books are listed in the first FEDERAL REGISTER issue of each week.

OFFICE OF PERSONNEL MANAGEMENT

5 CFR Part 534

RIN 3206-AL01

Senior Executive Service Pay

AGENCY: Office of Personnel Management.

ACTION: Final rule.

SUMMARY: The Office of Personnel Management is issuing final regulations to provide agencies with the authority to increase the rates of basic pay of certain members of the Senior Executive Service whose pay was set before the agency's senior executive performance appraisal system was certified for the calendar year involved. The final regulations allow an agency to review the rate of basic pay of these employees and provide an additional pay increase, if warranted, up to the rate for level II of the Executive Schedule upon certification of the agency's senior executive performance appraisal system for the current calendar year.

DATES: *Effective Date:* The final regulations will become effective on July 10, 2006.

FOR FURTHER INFORMATION CONTACT:
Jo Ann Perrini by telephone at (202) 606–2858; by FAX at (202) 606-0824; or by e-mail at *pay-performance-policy@opm.gov*.

SUPPLEMENTARY INFORMATION: On March 3, 2006, the Office of Personnel Management (OPM) issued proposed regulations to provide agencies with the authority to increase the rates of basic pay of certain members of the Senior Executive Service (SES) whose pay was set before the agency's senior executive performance appraisal system was certified under 5 CFR part 430, subpart D, for the calendar year involved (71 FR 10913). We proposed that agencies be authorized to review the rates of basic pay set for these SES members and provide an additional pay increase, if warranted, up to the rate for level II of the Executive Schedule upon certification of the agency's senior executive performance appraisal system for the current calendar year. The additional pay increase would not be considered a pay adjustment for the purpose of applying 5 CFR 534.404(c) ("the 12-month rule").

The 30-day public comment period ended on April 3, 2006. During the public comment period, OPM received comments from eight Federal agencies and one association of Federal executives. All of the commenters fully support OPM's proposed regulations. Therefore, we are adopting the proposed regulations as final.

"Certification Gap"

Under the new SES performance-based pay system, an agency must set and adjust the rate of basic pay for an SES member on the basis of the employee's performance and/or contribution to the agency's performance, as determined by the agency through the administration of its performance management system(s) for senior executives. Under 5 U.S.C. 5382(b), the maximum rate of the SES rate range may not exceed the rate for level III of the Executive Schedule unless the agency's senior executive performance appraisal system is certified under 5 U.S.C. 5307(d). By law, such certification must be made on a calendar year basis. (See 5 U.S.C. 5307(d) and 5 CFR part 430, subpart D.) Therefore, an agency may not set or adjust pay for an SES member at a rate above the rate for level III until its senior executive performance appraisal system is certified for the calendar year involved. Since many agencies' senior executive performance appraisal systems are not certified at the beginning of a calendar year,

FIGURE 8.5
(*continued*)

there is a gap from the time an agency may set or adjust pay above level III (in the previous calendar year) to the time an agency may set or adjust pay above level III upon certification of its senior executive performance appraisal system (in the next calendar year).

The regulations at 5 CFR 534.404(e)(2) allow agencies that eventually receive certification of their senior executive performance appraisal system(s) to provide an additional pay increase to certain SES members, such as a new appointee with superior leadership skills, an SES member accepting a position with substantially greater responsibility, or an SES member who is critical to the mission of the agency and who is likely to leave the agency. This is accomplished by providing for an additional exception to the "12-month rule."

The requirement in 5 U.S.C. 5307(d) that senior executive performance appraisal systems be certified on a calendar year basis may be changed only through legislation. Although the commenters fully support OPM's efforts to close the "certification gap," several recognized the need for a long-term solution and recommended a legislative change to allow senior executive performance appraisal systems to be certified on an annual basis (i.e., once every 12 months), rather than on a calendar year basis, as required by current law.

Effective Date

Under 5 CFR 534.404(e)(2), the decision to provide an additional pay increase to an SES member may not be made effective before the date the agency's senior executive performance, appraisal system is certified under 5 CFR part 430, subpart D, or after December 31st of the calendar year for which the agency's system is certified. An agency asked whether the effective date for providing an additional pay increase would be the effective date of the final regulations or the date the agency's senior executive performance appraisal system is certified. If an agency's senior executive performance appraisal system is certified for calendar year 2006 before the final regulations become effective, the earliest date an agency may provide an additional pay increase would be the effective date of the final regulations. The agency has no authority to provide an additional pay increase until the final regulations become effective. However, if an agency's senior executive performance appraisal system is certified for calendar year 2006 after the final regulations become effective, the earliest date an agency may provide an additional pay increase would be the date the agency's senior executive performance appraisal system is certified.

To bring a pamphlet of C.F.R. up to date, one must consult the *Federal Register.* A monthly pamphlet, *LSA: List of CFR Sections Affected,* lists regulatory changes made since a particular title pamphlet was last published. The *Federal Register* also has a list "CFR Parts Affected" cumulated on the last day of each month, and cumulated daily back to the last day of the previous month. The *LSA* only lists the section of the code that has been changed. It refers you to the *Federal Register* to see what the actual change is.

The C.F.R. includes an annual index volume. Its entries are coordinated with the Office of the Federal Register's *Thesaurus of Indexing Terms* developed in 1980 (see 45 Fed. Reg. 2998, Jan. 15, 1980). The index also includes tables in a "Finding Aids" section.

When researching administrative regulations, the following steps may be helpful:

- First, locate the topic of interest in an index that leads you to the appropriate title and section. The *Thesaurus of Indexing Terms* or the tables of the "Finding Aids" section can help you locate your topic and guide you to the appropriate volume.

- Once you have located your title and section for your topic, it is essential to make sure the regulation has not had a recent change. Check the *LSA* to find out if a change has been made. If a change was made to the regulation, check the appropriate part of the *Federal Register* to determine the part of the regulation that has been changed.

- Remember, the volume numbers of the C.F.R. correspond to the volume numbers of the *United States Code* and the *United States Code Annotated.* This may help you in your research. These two sources are updated with pocket part supplements. Remember to check the pocket parts to see if any changes have been made.

Eye on Ethics

Remember, as officers of the court, lawyers are required to refer to the most recent versions of codes and statutes. As the paralegal doing research for an attorney, it is important to ensure that the most recent version of any code or statute is being cited to the court.

The text of the C.F.R. is also available on the Lexis (GENFED; CFR file) and Westlaw (CFR database) computer-assisted legal research systems. If there is a conflict in language between the *Federal Register* and C.F.R., the *Federal Register* version controls.

State administrative regulations are often published topically in state administrative codes. (See Appendix III.) Often, a free copy of current codified regulations can be obtained simply by calling or writing the relevant agency.

Administrative Orders and Executive Orders

administrative order
Administrative acts having force of law, designed to clarify or implement a law or policy.

proclamation
The act of publicly proclaiming or publishing; a formal declaration; an avowal; a public announcement giving notice of a governmental act that has been done or is to be done.

administrative law judge
One who presides at an administrative hearing; with power to administer oaths, take testimony, rule on questions of evidence, regulate the course of proceedings, and make agency determinations of fact.

administrative decision
The issuing of an order or determination by the administrative law judge adjudicating the issues at the hearing and explaining his or her reasoning behind the determination.

When the administrator of an administrative agency formally exercises discretionary "executive" power, the administrator makes an **administrative order.** When the executive of the executive branch formally exercises discretionary executive power, the executive makes an executive order. For example, Congress has given the President the discretion to suspend trade with a foreign country for 30 days without congressional consent. If the President wants to exercise the discretion to suspend trade with a foreign country for 30 days, the President does so by issuing an executive order. By custom, executive orders having no continuing legal effect, such as declaring a certain day to be "National Whatever Day," are known as **proclamations.** Presidential documents can be found in a variety of sources. The Office of Federal Register sources include the *Federal Register,* Title 3 of the C.F.R., the *Codification of Presidential Proclamations and Executive Orders,* and the *Weekly Compilation of Presidential Documents,* the latter includes lists of laws approved, nominations, and other material released by the White House. Proclamations and executive orders are also found in *United States Code Congressional and Administrative News* (U.S. Code Cong. & Admin. News) and in advance pamphlets to the *United States Code Service* (U.S.C.S.). Proclamations also appear in *United States Statutes at Large* (Stat.). State administrative and executive orders are rarely published, but they are in some states (e.g., Michigan).

Administrative Decisions

Since there may be a continuing need to interpret administrative regulations, many administrative agencies exercise judicial-like functions. For example, the Office of Hearings and Appeals of the Social Security Administration hears disputes concerning whether a person is disabled enough to be entitled to Social Security disability benefits. The "judge" in an administrative hearing is known as an **administrative law judge.** The administrative law judge's decision may be explained in an **administrative decision.**

Administrative decisions may or may not be appealed to the courts, depending on the subject matter involved. For example, decisions of the federal government's Employees' Compensation

RESEARCH THIS

Use the index to the C.F.R. to locate the volume of the C.F.R. that deals with unfair or deceptive acts and practices. Which administrative agency handles these types of issues? Can you locate the code that can help you answer the questions related to the harassment of the firm's client by the debt collector? What is the volume number of the C.F.R. that refers to this issue?

Appeals Board cannot be appealed to the courts because the board interprets a voluntary compensation act, the Federal Employee's Compensation Act, and not a liability act, such as the Federal Employers' Liability Act.

Like judicial opinions, administrative decisions are published in reports. The Government Printing Office publishes federal administrative decisions of various agencies in a variety of specialized reporters. These Government Printing Office publications are usually available at major federal depository libraries. Decisions of major federal administrative agencies are also published, usually in loose-leaf form, by private publishers. State administrative decisions, except in the areas of tax law and workers' compensation, are rarely published.

Attorney General Opinions

attorney general
Is the chief law officer of the sovereign and represents the sovereign in legal matters generally and gives advice and opinions to the heads of the government as requested.

An **attorney general** is the chief lawyer for a sovereign. The attorney general gives legal advice to officials in the executive branch, especially about the proper operation of governmental entities and agencies. When an executive official asks the attorney general for advice, it is a common practice, especially in the various states, for the attorney general to answer with a formal written opinion: an official memorandum of law.

Although the opinion of an attorney general is official, it is essentially advice and not considered primary authority. However, the opinions of attorneys general are ordinarily followed by governmental officials and are considered very persuasive authority.

The opinions of the attorneys general are usually published by the appropriate sovereign. Many are also available on the Lexis (e.g., GENFED; USAG file) and Westlaw (e.g., USAG database) computer-assisted legal research systems. They are usually annotated in the sovereign's annotated codes. Citations to opinions of attorneys general are also cited in *Shepard's Citations.*

LOOSE-LEAF SERVICES

loose-leaf service
A service that publishes recently decided court decisions in loose-leaf binders, such as *U.S. Law Week,* provides for information to be easily updated. The loose pages are used to replace the existing pages in the notebook to ensure that the most current information is available.

A **loose-leaf service** is a law publication, usually a set of books, issued in notebook form.

Until recently, the law was published in notebook form only where the law was so complex and changed so rapidly that it was impractical to publish it in the permanent bound volumes or in permanent bound volumes with pocket supplements. The advantage of a loose-leaf service, where the publisher could keep the service up-to-date simply by periodically issuing new or replacement pages to be inserted into the set, was compatible with the need to keep up with the complex nature of, and rapid changes in, the law.

Recently, however, some publishers have shifted to publishing in notebook form simply because it is cheaper for them to do so. In 1986, for example, the Lawyers Co-operative Publishing Company (LCP) started several publications as loose-leaf services, rather than as a set of bound volumes, in part because it had acquired the ability to make notebooks at its own manufacturing plant. Moreover, some publishers simply prefer to offer their supplementation in loose-leaf form. Sometimes, instead of issuing individual replacement pages, publishers issue whole replacement sections, thereby making the updating of the loose-leaf service quicker, simpler, and more convenient.

Understand that in the age of computer databases, the value of the permanent bound volume has declined. Information in a computer database, properly backed up, is almost as permanent as the information in a bound volume. It can be searched electronically and doesn't take up nearly as much shelf space as information in a book. Today, the importance of printed material is more in its readability than in its permanency. In terms of readability, a loose-leaf service is just as readable as a bound volume.

Loose-leaf services are published for complex and rapidly changing areas of the law. The section of law that is most complex—involving specialized areas of the law—and which changes most rapidly, is administrative law. Most loose-leaf services cover areas of the law dealing with money, where the practitioners of the law tend to be those who can afford to pay for an up-to-date notebook service. As a result, most loose-leaf services cover tax and business law.

CYBER TRIP

Loose-leaf services can be searched on the Bureau of National Affairs, Inc. Web site at www.bna.com.

Most of the major national loose-leaf services are published by one of four major private publishers: Bureau of National Affairs, Inc. (BNA); Commerce Clearing House, Inc. (CCH); Prentice-Hall Information Services (P-H), a division of Simon & Schuster, Inc.; and Research Institute of America (RIA). Loose-leaf services are available in almost every conceivable tax and business-related area of the law, including income tax, estate tax, pensions, securities, labor law, employment discrimination law, and the like. Loose-leaf services can usually be located in law libraries according to the Library of Congress Classification system discussed in Appendix IV. Many of these services, such as the BNA, are available online on the Internet and can sometimes be searched more easily than publications.

Almost every major loose-leaf service begins with a section explaining how to use the set, including summaries of the contents, indexes, tables, and other available finding aids. Most loose-leaf services are organized according to sections or paragraph numbers, which are relatively permanent, rather than by page number. There are page numbers, but they are there only to keep track of the pages in the set. Pages may be added to the set, but they are kept under a particular section or paragraph number by adding letters after page numbers (e.g., a page 12A to be added after page 12 but before page 13).

One excellent feature of a loose-leaf service is the ease in which the publisher can bring together in one place all the sources of law, primary and secondary, on a particular subject, even while the law is changing. Instead of a researcher having to look in one book for a statute, another for a regulation, another for a textbook discussion, and another for a case opinion, a loose-leaf service can be designed to bring all of this information together on a particular topic in consecutive pages of the notebook. Replacement pages containing minor or major changes can be sent to the customer.

Loose-leaf services ordinarily contain the text of the statutes, legislative history, and regulations concerning a particular topic, along with a text discussion, tables, and indexes. Recent material the publisher has not had time to edit into the main text may be included in a "current developments" section.

Tax Services

The complexity of tax law is well known, as is its political nature, making it subject to frequent changes and revisions. Tax law is ideally suited to treatment in loose-leaf services. Accordingly, the three major federal tax loose-leaf services deserve special mention.

CCH publishes the *Standard Federal Tax Reporter.* It is organized in the format of the Internal Revenue Code (26 U.S.C.). After each code section, relevant regulations are presented, followed by a text discussion of the topic of the code section, followed by case summaries. CCH supports its commitment to tax law by publishing a general tax case reporter, *United States Tax Cases* (U.S.T.C.), and a reporter of U.S. Tax Court memorandum opinions, *Tax Court Memorandum Decisions* (T.C.M.). CCH also publishes a tax handbook, *U.S. Master Tax Guide,* keyed to the *Standard Federal Tax Reporter.*

RIA publishes the 35-volume *Federal Tax Coordinator 2d.* Rather than following the Internal Revenue Code section by section, RIA has broken down the law by topic. Major topic headings are lettered from A to V, with each federal code section and regulation reprinted by topic in the appropriate volume. The text is broken down into paragraphs cited by letter heading and paragraph number (e.g., V-2118). There are multiple finding aids for the set, including a topical index, and finding tables from the Internal Revenue Code, regulations, rulings, and cases. A companion set, *Tax Action Coordinator,* includes a tax analysis of legal forms and a complete set of tax forms. RIA also publishes a two-volume streamlined set, *Tax Guide,* and a tax handbook, the *Master Federal Tax Manual,* keyed to the *Federal Tax Coordinator 2d.* The entire RIA editorial staff consists of tax attorneys and accountants, who seek to write RIA services in "clear business English."

P-H publishes *Federal Taxes 2d.* Whereas P-H's first tax service was organized around the Internal Revenue Code (26 U.S.C.), like CCH's *Standard Federal Tax Reporter, Federal Taxes 2d* is broken down by topic, similar to RIA's *Federal Tax Coordinator 2d.* P-H supports its commitment to tax law by publishing a general tax case reporter, the *American Federal Tax Reports 2d* (A.F.T.R.2d) and a reporter of U.S. Tax Court memorandum opinions, *Memorandum Decisions of the Tax Court* (T.C.M.).

A Day in the Life

Returning to the research assignment given to you regarding harassing telephone calls made to the client concerning the collection of debts, the paralegal's first step in determining the client's rights is to find out which government administrative agency deals with these types of issues. The second step is to locate the regulations pertaining to the issue.

Using one of the available indexes to the *U.S. Governmental Manual*, the paralegal determines the Federal Trade Commission regulates issues of consumer protection. Next, the paralegal would go to the appropriate pages that describe the Federal Trade Commission's responsibilities and references.

The Fair Debt Collection Practices Act is regulated by the FTC. It is located at 15 U.S.C. 1601. This Act states that no debt collector can harass a debtor by calling them before 8:00 a.m. or after 9:00 p.m. It also states that a debt collector cannot make false or misleading statements such as they are going to institute legal action against the debtor unless they intend to do so.

Summary

The details of government are increasingly being managed by specialized governmental entities known as administrative agencies. Technically, an administrative agency is an "independent agency," a governmental entity distinct from the three branches of government, created to independently govern a limited specialized area of the law, which only has to answer to the three branches of government in a formal way. Executive departments are groups of specialists organized to assist the executive in carrying out the functions of the executive branch. The heads of executive departments must answer to the executive both formally and informally. An administrative agency, or a part of it, may be called, among other things, an administration, agency, authority, board, bureau, commission, corporation, department, division, foundation, office, or service. Usually the best way to sort out "who's who" is to consult an almanac, encyclopedia, or government directory or manual. For the federal government, a useful text is the *U.S. Government Manual,* which includes several useful indexes and tables. Appendix B is the famous "alphabet soup" table listing the acronyms for all the governmental agencies and what they stand for. An administrative agency issues regulations. The *Federal Register* (Fed. Reg.) is the official chronological source of federal regulations. Regulations made by administrative agencies are collected topically in books known as codes. The official topical collection of federal regulations is the *Code of Federal Regulations* (C.F.R.). When the executive of the executive branch formally exercises discretionary executive power, the executive makes an executive order. Executive orders having no continuing legal effect are known as proclamations. Presidential documents can be found in a variety of sources. Many administrative agencies exercise judicial-like functions. An administrative law judge's decision may be explained in an administrative decision. Administrative decisions may or may not be appealed to the courts, depending on the subject matter involved. Administrative decisions are published in reports.

A loose-leaf service is a law publication, usually a set of books, issued in notebook form. Until recently, the law was published in notebook form only where the law was so complex and changed so rapidly that it was impractical to publish it in the permanent bound volumes or in permanent bound volumes with pocket supplements. Recently, however, some publishers have shifted to publishing in notebook form simply because it is cheaper for them to do so. Most loose-leaf services are published for complex and rapidly changing areas of the law, and the law that is most complex (involving specialized areas of the law), and changes most rapidly, is administrative law. Most loose-leaf services cover tax and business law. There are loose-leaf services available in almost every conceivable tax and business-related area of the law. Most loose-leaf services are organized according to sections or paragraph numbers, which are relatively permanent, rather than by page number. There are page numbers, but they are there only to keep track of the pages in the set. One feature of a loose-leaf service is that it brings together in one place all the sources of law, primary and secondary, on a particular subject, even while the law is changing. Loose-leaf services can be searched online. Loose-leaf services ordinarily contain the text of the statutes, legislative history, and regulations concerning a particular topic, along with a text discussion, tables, and indexes. Tax law is ideally suited to treatment in loose-leaf services. The three major federal tax loose-leaf services are CCH's *Standard Federal Tax Reporter,* RIA's *Federal Tax Coordinator 2d,* and Prentice-Hall's *Federal Taxes 2d.*

Key Terms

administrative agency 114	executive departments 115
administrative codes 119	legislative departments 116
administrative decision 122	loose-leaf service 123
administrative law judge 122	proclamations 122
administrative order 122	regulates 119
attorney general 123	rulemaking 119

Review Questions

1. Why are administrative agencies created?

2. How is an independent administrative agency different from an executive department?

3. What do you call the process of making regulations?

4. What is the official chronological source of federal regulations?

5. What is the official topical source of federal regulations?

6. What is significant about the volume numbers for the *United States Code* and the C.F.R.?

7. How is a proclamation different from other executive orders?

8. What do you call an administrative law judge's written reasons for his decision?

9. What is an attorney general?

10. What is a loose-leaf service?

11. Why is a loose-leaf better than a statutory code, an administrative code, a textbook, and a case reporter?

12. What are the major federal tax services?

Exercises

1. What steps must one take to become a citizen of the United States? Using the *U.S. Governmental Manual,* identify the two administrative agencies that have regulations and procedures for this process. Remember, since the attacks on the United States on September 11th, 2001, a new administrative agency was created that plays a role in the procedures necessary for citizenship.

2. Locate the Americans with Disabilities Act in the United States Code index, 42§12101. Using the table of contents for this section, provide the citation for the section that requires implementation of regulations for equal opportunities of employment for individuals with disabilities. Use the annotations in the section to locate the appropriate part of the C.F.R. that references the same act. Provide the C.F.R. citation for the section.

3. Go to the United States Department of Labor Web site at www.dol.gov and locate the Family and Medical Leave Act. Provide the appropriate citation for the site as listed on the Web site. What is the maximum leave a person can take from work for the birth of a child?

Vocabulary Builders

Find and circle the following terms in the subsequent word search puzzle. The terms may appear up, down, sideways, or diagonal, and forward or backward, ignoring any spaces in phrases.

A	D	M	I	N	I	S	T	R	A	T	I	V	E	A	G	E	N	C	Y	B	W	Q	U	S	H
L	E	G	I	S	L	A	T	I	V	E	D	E	P	A	R	T	M	E	N	T	S	B	A	A	E
A	E	E	Y	C	Y	D	D	O	B	Q	R	D	S	A	N	W	V	I	D	S	Q	I	T	M	X
C	I	O	J	U	C	I	E	T	X	E	K	I	M	W	E	A	D	I	C	T	I	T	S	Z	E
T	H	U	K	T	Y	A	D	M	I	N	I	S	T	R	A	T	I	V	E	C	O	D	E	S	C
I	S	T	D	N	C	F	O	D	V	Y	F	T	V	T	Q	A	X	F	D	R	K	H	J	N	U
C	M	D	S	E	B	N	L	C	E	C	D	E	G	V	D	G	U	E	N	X	D	I	C	T	T
E	U	I	L	M	A	S	C	U	I	L	R	O	E	C	C	Y	C	E	K	L	O	P	E	A	I
B	D	R	Q	E	L	K	Y	O	T	W	S	N	J	M	I	U	Y	O	U	T	L	K	C	D	V
O	N	B	Z	T	L	U	C	E	A	P	C	A	O	R	P	G	J	U	R	O	S	I	G	V	E
O	U	A	B	A	E	T	N	L	A	E	B	R	H	D	E	K	L	O	P	Y	D	S	C	E	O
K	C	L	P	T	I	R	E	C	T	O	R	Y	A	N	U	E	D	J	E	O	N	R	A	G	R
S	E	L	P	S	N	Y	F	B	D	A	S	J	E	T	B	E	K	L	I	S	F	K	R	D	D
R	S	R	O	E	E	M	F	N	I	D	D	R	C	O	N	C	Y	R	L	O	P	E	A	D	E
O	O	Z	A	R	X	N	S	Y	R	J	A	I	R	E	C	Y	E	H	E	I	I	G	O	I	R
L	E	G	A	L	F	O	R	M	S	L	S	E	C	U	N	P	U	M	A	K	L	P	G	F	H

ADMINISTRATIVE AGENCY, ADMINISTRATIVE CODES, ATTORNEY GENERAL, EXECUTIVE ORDER, and **LEGISLATIVE DEPARTMENTS.**

Chapter 9

Secondary Sources: General

CHAPTER OBJECTIVES

After reading this chapter, you should be able to:

- Begin legal research in an unfamiliar area of the law.

- Use *Corpus Juris Secundum* (C.J.S.).

- Use *American Jurisprudence 2d* (Am. Jur. 2d).

- Understand when commercial law outlines may be useful.

- Recognize the benefits of the various legal dictionaries such as *Black's Law Dictionary, Ballentine's Law Dictionary,* and Gifis's *Law Dictionary.*

General secondary sources of the law are reference books that are often used as a starting point for research in an unfamiliar area of the law, as a tool for legal self-study, or as a source of information about a particular lawyer or law firm. General secondary sources of law can provide explanations of legal issues. These sources are not citable or quotable materials but are used to locate primary sources of law.

ENCYCLOPEDIAS

An encyclopedia is a comprehensive work that covers all of the subjects within a particular branch of knowledge (or all branches of knowledge). While an encyclopedia covers all of a branch of knowledge and includes some detail, it is essentially a summary that does not include everything. An encyclopedia does not replace all other books on a given subject, it just ties them together. A **legal encyclopedia** brings together all branches of knowledge for particular legal subjects.

legal encyclopedia
A multivolume compilation that provides in-depth coverage of every area of the law.

A famous saying about the law, variously attributed, is that "the law is a seamless web." This is true in two senses. First, the law of property overlaps the law of contracts, which overlaps the law of torts, which overlaps criminal law, and so on. Second, the various forms of sovereign commands (from case opinions, to statutes, and back to court rules) mesh with each other to form "the" law. It has always been the dream of legal researchers to be able to read one text statement of the law bringing it all together. West Publishing Company (West) and Lawyers Cooperative Publishing (LCP) publish three national encyclopedias covering all of U.S. law: *Guide to American Law, Corpus Juris Secundum* (C.J.S.), and *American Jurisprudence 2d* (Am. Jur. 2d).

Using Legal Encyclopedias

Using a legal encyclopedia is fairly simple. If the legal topic that needs to be researched is known, it can simply be looked up alphabetically in the same manner in which one would use any

Case Fact Pattern

The lead story on the local news program you are watching concerns the beating of a suspect by police officers during an arrest. The beating appears particularly brutal. You wonder what the law is regarding the use of excessive force by police officers.

---

encyclopedia. If the exact topic is not known but a legal question is, the following procedure may be helpful. For example, the legal question might be "When is a police officer guilty of using excessive force while making an arrest?" In this instance, the following procedure is helpful.

- Go to the index that is found usually as the last volume in the set of encyclopedias.
- Following the preceding case fact pattern, the legal question is "What constitutes 'excessive force' by a police officer during an arrest?"
- Review the facts and determine some word(s) that can be checked in the index. For instance, the word "police" can be looked up in the index. If the legal encyclopedia *American Jurisprudence* is being utilized, the index will refer you alphabetically to the volume that contains "Sheriffs and Police" as the topic.
- Within that section, the term "excessive force" or "force" can be looked up within the "Sheriffs and Police" section. At that point, the researcher will be directed to a numerical section within the topic that will further explain the issue.
- Once the specific topic is identified, the legal encyclopedia will provide direction to numerous primary sources of law covering the same topic. Each of the footnotes located under the topic will direct the researcher to cases in various districts and jurisdictions covering this area of the law. The cases cited in the footnotes are references to primary sources of law.

Guide to American Law

West publishes the "World Book" A-to-Z encyclopedia of the law, *Guide to American Law.* Written for lawyers and nonlawyers alike, the 12-volume set covers each legal subject in an easy-to-read style, with formal legal citations. Unique among legal encyclopedias, *Guide to American Law* contains biographies of famous people in the law, articles about famous cases and movements, and articles about governmental bodies and other legal organizations. If, for example, you want to find out when the American Bar Association was founded, you could find the answer in *Guide to American Law.* If you have no idea where to start when researching a new topic, use this underrated general legal encyclopedia.

Corpus Juris Secundum

West's original encyclopedia for lawyers and legal researchers was *Corpus Juris* (C.J.), first published in 1936. Famous because a volume of the set sat on Perry Mason's desk in the opening of the classic television program, the title means "the body of the law."

In the late 1950s, West began publishing a modern version of the set, *Corpus Juris Secundum* (C.J.S.), the title meaning "the body of the law, second." Containing over 100 thick bound volumes, C.J.S. attempts to cover "the body" of U.S. law from its inception. The coverage includes federal law and, insofar as it can be stated generally, state law. Following West's philosophy of comprehensive law publishing, the text is supported by footnotes that purportedly include citations to every reported case on the point covered. (See Figure 9.1.) However, since 1961, C.J.S. has also included cross-references to West topic and key numbers for each encyclopedia topic, so additional cases can be found using the West digests. C.J.S. is supplemented by replacement volumes as needed and annual cumulative pocket parts.

As an A-to-Z encyclopedia, C.J.S. can be entered by finding the volume with the appropriate topic, reviewing the topic outline at the beginning of the topic, and then locating the desired section by its section number. The most common method of entry into C.J.S., however, is through an index. There are both a general index for the set and "volume" indexes for each topic, which are found in the last volume of the set containing that topic. Since the volume indexes are usually

FIGURE 9.1
Excerpt from **Corpus Juris Secundum**

Source: Corpus Juris Secundum, Volume 80. Reprinted by permission of Thomson/West.

Fines.

A sheriff has been held not to be entitled to a commission on fines collected,[8] but he has also been held to be entitled to such a commission.[9] The money does not have to actually pass through the sheriffs hands for the sheriff to be entitled to a commission.[10]

Automobile license fee or tax.

Under a statute allowing a sheriff a fee for collecting an automobile license fee or tax, a sheriff has been held entitled to the entire fee whether the license is for a year, half-year, or quarter-year, but not to the entire fee for each installment paid on one license.[11]

c. *Services in Criminal Proceedings*

§ 490   Generally

A sheriff or constable is entitled to compensation only for such services, in criminal proceedings, as the statutes provide compensation for.

Research References
West's Key Number Digest, Sheriffs and Constables ⌐ 35, 36

A sheriff or constable is entitled to compensation for such,[1] and only such, services in criminal proceedings as the statutes provide compensation for.[2]

A statutory provision pertaining to fees that a sheriff may collect in connection with services performed in civil matters does not authorize a commissioner's court to set fees in criminal matters.[3]

§ 491   Making of arrests, or execution of arrest warrants

The making of arrests or the execution of warrants therefor, is a service for which sheriffs and constables ordinarily are allowed compensation.

Research References
West's Key Number Digest, Sheriffs and Constables ⌐ 37

The making of arrests or the execution of warrants therefor, is a service for which sheriffs and constables ordinarily are allowed compensation.[1] If a warrant of arrest in a criminal action is regular and valid on its face, the sheriff or constable may collect his fees from the county for serving it[2] or for the execution of a warrant of arrest with respect to a person already under arrest.[3]

Where a sheriff arrests a person against whom he holds several warrants, he is entitled to but a single fee and not to a fee for each warrant.[4]

§ 492   Prisoners

Sheriffs and constables usually are en-

[8]S.C.—State v. Sheriff of Charleston Dist., 12 S.C.L. 419, 1. McCord 419, 1821 WL 997 (Const. Ct. App. 1821).

Commissions held to belong to county and not to sheriff

Ark.—Baker v. State, to Use of Independence County, 210 Ark. 690, 197 S.W.2d 759 (1946).

[9]Fla.—Hanchey v. State ex rel. Roberts, 52 So. 2d 429 (Fla. 1951).

[10]Fla.—Hanchey v. State ex rel. Roberts, 52 So. 2d 429 (Fla. 1951).

[11]Ark.—Albright v. State ex rel. Attorney General, 188 Ark. 879, 68 S.W. 2d 90 (1934).

[Section 490]

[1]Fla.—Gray v. Leon County, 96 Fla. 476, 118 So. 305 (1928).

Services outside county in felony cases

Ga.—Floyd County v. Johnson, 80 Ga. App. 785, 57 S.E.2d 502 (1950).

[2]Fla.—Bradford v. Stoutamire, 38 So. 2d 684 (Fla. 1948).

Mo.—Dunklin County v. Donaldson, 164 S.W.2d 367 (Mo. 1942).

[3]Tex.—Camacho v. Samaniego, 831 S.W.2d 804 (Tex. 1992), reh'g of cause overruled, (June 17, 1992).

[Section 491]

[1]Ala.—State, for Use and Ben. of Morgan County v. Norwood, 248 Ala. 128, 26 So. 2d 577 (1946).

Fla.—State v. Faulk, 102 Fla. 886, 136 So. 601 (1931).

Statute held unconstitutional as depriving sheriff of fee for arrest

Ky.—Webster County v. Overby, 240 Ky. 461, 42 S.W.2d 707 (1931).

[2]Fla.—Osceola County v. State ex rel. Newton, 115 Fla. 5, 155 So. 119 (1934).

[3]N.Y.—Village of Solvay v. Town of Geddes, 247 A.D. 89, 286 N.Y.S. 925 (4th Dep't 1936).

[4]Ga.—Sikes v. Charlton County, 103 Ga. App. 251, 119 S.E.2d 59 (1961).

much more detailed than the general index, you should typically use the volume index if you know the topic you want to search. The primary difference between C.J.S. and *American Jurisprudence 2d* is that C.J.S. provides more exhaustive coverage of case law. *American Jurisprudence 2d* has greater coverage of statutory law.

American Jurisprudence 2d

LCP's original encyclopedia for lawyers and legal researchers was *Ruling Case Law,* started in 1914. In 1936, using *American Law Reports* (A.L.R.) annotations as a major resource, LCP began *American Jurisprudence* (Am. Jur.), the title meaning "all the law of America." Described as "[a] thoroughly modern statement of the American law in concise quotable text" [22 A.B.A. J. 363 (1936)], Am. Jur. was conceived as LCP's analytical source to the law in breadth, complementing A.L.R., its analytical source to the law in depth.

A bit of legal research humor was immortalized when volume 16 of Am. Jur. was shipped in November 1938. Indicating the topics covered in the volume, the spine proclaimed "Death to Diplomatic Officers." A whimsical advertisement in the *American Bar Association Journal* mused "Were we thinking of Munich? No—Only of every-day law." [25 A.B.A. J. 263 (1939).]

Planned by LCP editor Alfred W. Gans, who had worked on Am. Jur. from its inception, the modern *American Jurisprudence 2d* (Am. Jur. 2d) was begun in 1962. Containing over 80 volumes, Am. Jur. 2d, like C.J.S., covers federal law and, insofar as it can be stated generally, state law. (See Figure 9.2.) However, following LCP's philosophy of selective law publishing, the text is supported by footnotes that purportedly include citations to only selected leading or landmark cases on the point covered. Footnotes are also made to statutory sources and to A.L.R. annotations. Topics also begin with cross-references to other units of the Total Client Service Library. Am. Jur. 2d, like C.J.S., is supplemented by replacement volumes as needed and annual cumulative pocket parts, except for the federal tax volumes, which are prepared annually by the Research Institute of America (RIA).

FIGURE 9.2

Excerpt from **American Jurisprudence 2d**

Source: American Jurisprudence, 2nd edition, Volume 70. Reprinted by permission of Thomson/West.

§ 84

ficial bond.[1]

However, the liability of the surety is not so clear when the officer makes an arrest unlawfully, without a warrant, or under a void warrant. According to one view, if an unlawful arrest is made under such circumstances, the act of the officer is a personal act or trespass for which the sureties are not liable.[2]

The more liberal cases, while holding that there is no liability upon the surety for acts done neither by virtue of nor under color of the office,[3] declare that where an officer acts in excess of his or her authority in making an arrest without a warrant, it is done under color of office and his or her sureties are liable therefor.[4] Statutes which impose upon sureties liability for acts of an officer done under color of office bind them for an illegal arrest without warrant.[5]

§ 85 Tort by deputy in making arrest

Research References
West's Key Number Digest, Sheriffs and Constables ☞157(4)
Whiteman, Richardson v. McGriff—Eliminating preseizure conduct of a law enforcement officer from review under constitutional and tort law, 61 Md. L. Rev. 1074 (2002)

According to the facts involved, including the terms of the bond and the provisions of applicable statutes, the courts, in some cases, have found that a sheriff, marshal, or constable is liable on his or her bond for a deputy's tort in making an arrest.[1]

A court may require that the acts of the deputy complained of be an official act directly connected with the doing of an official act and constituting a part thereof to hold the sureties on the sheriff's bond liable.[2] In other cases, however, the sureties on the sheriff's bond have been absolved from liability for torts of a deputy committed in making an arrest.[3]

§ 86 Injury to property

Research References
West's Key Number Digest, Sheriffs and Constables ☞ 157(4)

[Section 84]
[1]State v. Cunningham, 113 W. Va. 244, 167 S.E. 595 (1933).
As to liability of sureties for injury or death caused in making or attempting to make an arrest, see § 88.
[2]People v. Beach, 49 Colo. 516, 113 P. 513 (1911); Taylor v. Shields, 183 Ky. 669, 210 S.W. 168, 3 A.L.R. 1619 (1919).
[3]§ 67.
[4]State ex rel. Harbin v. Dunn, 39 Tenn. App. 190, 282 S.W.2d 203 (1943).
As to liability of sureties on the officer's bond for assaults, personal injuries, or death caused by him in making or attempting to make arrests, see § 88.

[5]State ex rel. Harbin v. Dunn, 39 Tenn. App. 190, 282 S.W.2d 203 (1943).
[Section 85]
[1]West v. Cabell, 153 U.S. 78, 14 S. Ct. 752, 38 L. Ed. 643 (1894); State ex rel. Coffelt v. Hartford Acc. & Indem. Co., 44 Tenn. App. 405, 314 S.W.2d 161 (1958).
As to liability of sheriff for acts of his or her subordinate, generally, see §§ 54 to 60.
[2]People v. Beach, 49 Colo. 516, 113 P. 513 (1911).
[3]Commonwealth v. Hurt, 23 Ky. L. Rptr. 1171, 64 S.W. 911 (Ky. 1901).

RESEARCH THIS

Locate both C.J.S. and Am. Jur. 2d. Look up the issue of excessive force used by a police officer at the time of an arrest. Answer the following question. When does excessive force by a police officer during an arrest rise to the level of a federal crime? Look in the headnotes of each encyclopedia and provide one case law cite from C.J.S. and one statutory cite from Am. Jur. 2d. that deal with the same legal issue.

As an A-to-Z encyclopedia, Am. Jur. 2d can be entered by finding the volume with the appropriate topic, reviewing the topic outline at the beginning of that topic, and then locating the desired section by its section number. The most common method of entry into Am. Jur. 2d, however, is through an index. There are both a general index for the set and "volume" indexes for each topic, which are found in the last volume of the set containing that topic. Again, since the volume indexes are usually much more detailed than the general index, you should generally use the volume index if you know the topic you want to search.

Am. Jur. 2d includes a separate volume entitled *Table of Statutes and Rules Cited,* which allows a researcher of a federal statute or rule to find the Am. Jur. 2d topic and section number, if any, in which it is cited. The Am. Jur. 2d *New Topic Service,* as its name implies, contains new topics not yet incorporated into the main volumes. The one-volume Am. Jur. 2d *Desk Book,* created as a marketing tool, is a general legal almanac. Other than a list of Am. Jur. 2d topics, the *Desk Book* contains an odd collection of information, including historical documents, ethical codes, bar admission standards, uniform laws, financial tables, reporter abbreviations, and Latin phrases.

LCP also sells a separate student textbook, *Summary of American Law,* which is keyed to, and summarizes, Am. Jur. 2d. The first edition was prepared in 1947 (for Am. Jur.) by LCP editor Robert T. Kimbrough, with later editions by George L. Clark (1974) and Martin Weinstein (1988).

In the mid-1980s, LCP set out to modernize Am. Jur. 2d and its state encyclopedias. The editors of new and revised topics were encouraged to cite more modern cases in the supporting footnotes. However, to cut costs, LCP instructed some of its editors *not* to take the time to update material used from earlier versions. Thus, even in new and revised topics, some footnotes cite old cases.

Another aspect of LCP's modernization can be gleaned from an October 1987 advertising mailer:

> *The contemporary topics in Ohio Jur 3d are grouped together under "problem areas." This eliminates searching through several volumes for one answer. For example, "Creditors' Rights and Remedies" gathers information from the areas of attachments, garnishment, civil arrest, fraudulent conveyances, and insolvency. And related matters are brought to your attention automatically. It's an approach designed for the practitioner and not the professor.*

State Encyclopedias

In states with a sufficient customer base to make publication of an encyclopedia feasible, there are state encyclopedias. West publishes encyclopedia sets in the style of C.J.S. for Illinois, Maryland, and Michigan. LCP publishes encyclopedia sets in the style of Am. Jur. 2d for California, Florida, New York, Ohio, and Texas. Although a state encyclopedia can be quite specific as to the law of a given topic, you should remember that as an encyclopedia, it

Eye on Ethics

Remember, as a paralegal doing legal research, it may be necessary to use legal encyclopedias to assist in the understanding of legal issues and concepts. However, they are not primary sources and should not be cited or quoted.

RESEARCH THIS

Research the same "excessive force" issue in the state encyclopedias for Maryland and California. Identify one primary source from each of the encyclopedias covering the elevation of excessive force by a police officer to a crime.

is a summary secondary source of the law. As such, it should never be cited as if it were a primary authority.

LAW OUTLINES

outline
The skeleton of a legal argument, advancing from the general to the specific; a preliminary step in writing that provides a framework fot the assignment.

While an encyclopedia is a narrative summary, an **outline** is a summary showing the pattern of subordination of one thought to another. Most law schools use the casebook method. Under this method, law students read cases and are encouraged to prepare for exams by outlining what they have learned. Commercially prepared law outlines are frowned upon and carry about as much weight as Cliff's Notes do with the typical high-school English teacher. Because of this attitude, you should never cite a commercial law outline as either primary or secondary authority.

Nevertheless, commercial law outlines, like legal encyclopedias, summarize the law and cite cases and other legal materials. Many law students find through the grapevine they can learn the fundamentals of the law effectively by reading and studying commercial law outlines. They're the books that everyone knows about, buys, and uses, but nobody talks about.

One publisher of a complete series of law outlines is Emanuel Law Outlines, Inc., founded by a *cum laude* graduate of Harvard Law School, Steven L. Emanuel. Emanuel law outlines feature an easy, read-like-a-book writing style, concise summaries of significant cases, and numerous examples, all set in large, easy-to-read type. In the 1988–1989 academic year, Emanuel sold nearly 100,000 law outlines. Emanuel also sells the *Smith's Review Series,* formerly published by West.

canned brief
Preanalyzed summary or abstract of a legal case.

dictionary
A book containing words usually arranged alphabetically with information about their forms, pronunciation, function etymologies, meanings, and syntactical and idiomatic uses.

There are many other sets of commercial law outlines. They include *Gilbert Law Summaries, Legalines, Ryan Law Capsules, Sum & Substance,* and West's *Black Letter Series.* There are also guides to law school casebooks known as **canned briefs,** since each major case is preanalyzed ("canned") for the reader. The major canned-brief series are *Casenote Legal Briefs* and *Cambridge Law Study Aids.*

Law outlines and canned briefs are often sold in law school bookstores and are generally available by mail from the Chicago Law Book Company of Chicago, Illinois, The Law Annex at Harvard Book Stores, Inc., of Cambridge, Massachusetts, and the Law Distributors of Gardena, California.

DICTIONARIES

etymology
The history of a linguistic form shown by tracing its development and relationship.

A **dictionary** is a book containing an alphabetical list of words, along with information about each word, usually including its spelling, pronunciation, **etymology** (word origin), **definitions** (meanings), forms, and uses. A **law dictionary** is a book containing a list of words unique to the legal profession, words often used by the legal profession (e.g., Latin phrases), and ordinary words with a legal meaning.

definitions
A statement of the meaning of a word or word groups.

The two leading law dictionaries are published by the two largest law publishers: *Black's Law Dictionary* by West and *Ballentine's Law Dictionary* by LCP. Both dictionaries were originally prepared over 90 years ago: *Black's* in 1891 and *Ballentine's* in 1916.

law dictionary
A book containing definitions of legal words and phrases.

Because of their age and dated word lists, *Black's* and *Ballentine's* have become the objects of increasing derision within the legal profession. In 1985, Robert D. White took aim at *Black's Law Dictionary* with a satirical book entitled *White's Law Dictionary* (NY: Warner Books, Inc., 1985). The cover of *White's Law Dictionary* defines *Black's Law Dictionary* as "an overlarge medieval legal lexicon. Preeminent in the field, until superseded by this book." As White explains:

Lawyers say words are their stock in trade. If so, they are burdened by an excess of inventory. Consider a volume which by default has held primacy among legal lexicons since its original publication in 1891: Black's Law Dictionary. *The preface to* Black's *states that the latest edition includes 10,000 entries. Let's examine some of those 10,000.*

A random perusal turns up zemindar. *You think, "Wow, I really didn't know that one. Good thing I have* Black's." *Its definition? "In Hindu Law, Landkeeper." You sigh a breath of relief; thank God your ignorance of zemindars didn't come up in public. Flipping back to the beginning, you see*

- A *The first letter in the English and most other alphabets derived from the Roman or Latin alphabet, which was one of several ancient Italian alphabets derived from the Greek, which was an adaptation of the Phoenician.*
- *Amazing. Just the other day you were wondering if that wasn't adapted from the Phoenician.*
- *Come on, Mr. Black, what gives?*
- *Do we really need a sixty-seven-word definition of "wrongful act," including a citation to a decision of the Illinois Court of Appeals? You couldn't leave it at "something one shouldn't do?"*
- *How about "Apt Fit; suitable; appropriate"? Do I see a little padding to get the total up to 10,000?*
- *And "Cerebellum Lower portion of brain below back of cerebrum concerned with muscular coordination and body equilibrium"—aren't we poaching a wee bit on another profession's turf?*

White could have just as easily attacked *Ballentine's Law Dictionary.* Among its 30,000 terms is *zingara,* meaning "[a]ny female in a band of gypsies." It also defines the letter *A,* gives a 350-word definition for *accident,* and defines words such as *weather* and *umbilical cord.*

The problem with both *Black's* and *Ballentine's,* and virtually all other law dictionaries, is that they are not citation-based. A **citation-based** dictionary, the standard among general dictionaries, is created by collecting a fair sample of actual uses of each word in context (**citations**), allowing the editor of the dictionary to authoritatively determine whether the word is current or archaic, and its "correct" spelling, etymology, meaning, and usage. The current law dictionaries simply do not include etymologies or citation-based authoritative definitions, and archaic words are rarely identified or eliminated.

Law dictionaries are substandard because of economics. The legal market has not been deemed large enough for a private publisher to profitably commit the resources necessary to create a citation-based law dictionary, although both West and LCP have the resources to do so. In 1989, the University of Texas School of Law and the Oxford University Press announced their plan to produce a citation-based law dictionary entitled the *Oxford Law Dictionary,* but the project has been abandoned.

citation-based
A dictionary that refers to legal authorities.

citations
Information about a legal source directing you to the volume and page in which the legal source appears.

Black's Law Dictionary

Despite its limitations, *Black's Law Dictionary* remains the most cited, most respected, and best-selling dictionary for the legal profession. It was originally prepared in 1891 (as *A Dictionary of the Law*) by Henry Campbell Black, the author of an obscure series of law treatises. Since then, *Black's* has been published in seven editions, dated 1910, 1933, 1951, 1957, 1968, 1979, and 1990. After Black's death, revisions were made by the publisher's editorial staff.

The major features of *Black's* include pronunciations for selected entries, selected citations to cases, a table of abbreviations, the Constitution of the United States, a time chart of the U.S. Supreme Court, an organizational chart of the U.S. government, and a table of British regnal years.

Black's is available in its standard edition (the basic hardcover version), a deluxe edition (a more expensive version with a fancy cover and thumb-hole tabs), and an abridged edition (a shorter, cheaper softcover version). *Black's* is also available on the Westlaw (DI database) computer-assisted legal research system.

West also publishes a set of word-books combining elements of the National Reporter System and West's digest system: *Words and Phrases.* When a case opinion appears to judicially define a word or phrase, a headnote is drawn from the definition. These headnotes are collected in the manner of a digest, under the appropriate words and phrases listed from A to Z. *Words and Phrases* allows you to look up a word or phrase and to read digest paragraphs summarizing judicial definitions of that word or phrase. (See Figure 9.3.) The set is supplemented by annual cumulative pocket parts. Modern volumes of the National Reporter System also include a "Words and Phrases" section derived from the cases in those volumes.

Ballentine's Law Dictionary

Despite its limitations, *Ballentine's Law Dictionary* continues to be a major dictionary for the legal profession. Originally prepared in 1916 by James A. Ballentine, Assistant Professor of Law at the University of California and Dean of the San Francisco Law School, *Ballentine's* has had five printings and three editions: 1916 and 1923—first edition, 1930 and 1948—second edition, and 1969—third edition. The third edition was edited by LCP editor William S. Anderson.

The major features of *Ballentine's* include pronunciations for selected entries, selected citations to cases, and selected citations to *United States Supreme Court Reports, Lawyers' Edition* (L. Ed.), A.L.R., and Am. Jur.

Gifis's Law Dictionary

The most practical, readable, and useful law dictionary currently published is Gifis's *Law Dictionary*, published by Barron's Educational Series, Inc. Originally prepared in 1975 by Steven H. Gifis, Associate Professor of Law at the Rutgers School of Law, Gifis's *Law Dictionary* is now in its fifth edition, published in 2003.

The major feature of this law dictionary is Gifis's careful selection of entries to include modern legal words and ancient legal words still in use, and to exclude archaic legal words. Other features include the cross-references of entries with their use in other definitions, pronunciations

FIGURE 9.3
Excerpt from **Words and Phrases**

Source: Words and Phrases, Volume 32. Reprinted by permission of Thomson/West.

POLICE JURIES

Corp. v. City of Shreveport, 397 F.3d 297.—Counties 24; Mun Corp 65.

C.C.A.5 (La.) 1938. In Louisiana, the "police juries" are the governing bodies of the "parishes", which are political subdivisions of the state, comparable to counties in other states.—National Liberty Ins. Co. of America v. Police Jury of Natchitoches Parish, 96 F.2d 261.—Counties 1, 38.

La. 1935. "Police juries" are political corporations whose powers are specially defined by Legislature, and they can legally exercise no other powers than those delegated to them. Act No. 22 of 1934, 3d Ex.Sess.; LSA-Const.1921, art. 2, §§ 1, 2.—State ex rel. Porterie v. Smith, 166 So. 72, 184 La. 263.—Counties 47.

La. 1935. "Police juries" are political corporations to which state has delegated limited portion of its governmental or police powers. —State ex rel. Porterie v. Smith, 162 So. 413, 182 La. 662.—Counties 38, 47.

La.App. 2 Cir. 1939. "Police juries" are political corporations to which the state has delegated a limited portion of its governmental or police powers, and their rights and powers are defined by Legislature and exist only to extent delegated to juries by positive legislation. LSA-R.S. 33:1236.—Stoker v. Police Jury of Sabine Parish, 190 So. 192.—Counties 38.

POLICE JURY

La. 1923. The name "police jury" implies a body or jury for exercise of limited portion of governmental or police power, which, under uniform jurisprudence, exists to extent only that it is delegated by positive legislation.—Union Sulphur Co. v. Parish of Calcasieu, 96 So. 787, 153 La. S57.—Counties 47.

La.App. 2 Cir. 1989. "Police jury" is parish governing body that exercises legislative and executive functions as a political subdivision created by and subject to state legislative authority.—McIntosh v. Madison Parish Police Jury, 554 So.2d 227.—Counties 38.

POLICE JUSTICE

N.Y.A.D. 2 Dept. 1945. City judge under charter of city of Peekskill is not a "police justice" within scope of code section prohibiting reduction in salary by city council of a police justice, and council could properly reduce salary of city judge. Code Cr.Proc. § 78; Laws 1938, c. 194.—Gambino v. City of Peekskill, 55 N.Y.S.2d 107, 269 A.D. 781, affirmed 64 N.E.2d 273, 295 N.Y. 552.—Judges 22(7).

POLICE JUSTICE PRO TEMPORE

Miss. 1975. A "justice of the peace", as a judge, would not be required to go out of city or to a hospital in order to recuse himself to be "absent" within statute which provides that "In any municipality where any police justice is appointed, the governing authority shall have the power and authority to elect a "police justice pro tempore", who shall have the same powers and shall perform all duties of the police justice in the absence of such police justice."Code 1972, § 21-23-9).—Raper v. State, 317 So.2d 709.—J P 20.

POLICE MAGISTRATE

N.D. 1896. A "police magistrate" is a magistrate charged exclusively with

FIGURE 9.3
(*continued*)

the duties incident to the common-law office of conservator or justice of the peace, and the prefix "police" serves merely to distinguish them from justices having also civil jurisdiction. A police magistrate is an inferior judicial magistrate, whose jurisdiction, in the absence of constitutional or statutory extensions, is confined to criminal cases arising under the ordinances and regulations of a municipality, and in such sense the word is used in Const. § 113, declaring that the legislative assembly shall provide by law for the election of police magistrates in cities.—McDermont v. Dinnie, 69 N.W. 294, 6 N.D. 278.

POLICEMAN

Ariz. 1979. Although an off-duty or "at-rest" "policeman" was required to respond with police action to any criminal activity coming to his attention and was instructed to carry a concealed handgun, injuries sustained by off-duty city police officer when he was demonstrating gun's safety device to his wife did not "arise out of" officer's employment within meaning of Workmen's Compensation Statute; officer took it on himself to demonstrate safety mechanism in response to spouse's inquiry and no benefit inured by such action to his employer. A.R.S. § 23–1021[A].—Peetz v. Industrial Commission, 604 P.2d 255, 124 Ariz. 324.—Work Comp 706.

Conn.App. 2000. Security officer of the state military department, who derived his police powers from statute providing that Commissioner of Public Safety may appoint persons nominated by administrative authority of any state buildings or lands to act as special policeman in such buildings and upon such lands, was not "policeman" within meaning of policeman exception to the "coming and going rule," and as such, officer was not entitled to workers' compensation benefits for injuries sustained in vehicular accident that occurred while he was traveling to work. C.G.SA. § 31–275(l)(A).—Diluciano v. State of Conn. Military Dept., A.2d 1019, 60 Conn. App. 707, certification denied 767 A.2d 98, 255 Conn. 926.—Work Comp 726.

D.C.Mun.App. 1960. A defendant was neither a "policeman" nor a "law enforcement officer" so as to be exempt from the statute against carrying a pistol without a license, where defendant was a special policeman appointed by the Commissioners and he was not "on actual duty in the area" of the place where he was arrested nor was he "traveling without deviation immediately before and immediately after the period of actual duty between such places and his residence" within the Commissioner's regulation authorizing the carrying of firearms by special policemen under such circumstances. D.C.Code 1951, §§ 4–115, 22–3204, 22–3205—McKenzie v. U.S., 158 A.2d 912.—Weap 11(1).

for selected entries, selected citations to cases, the Constitution of the United States, the ABA Model Code of Professional Responsibility, and the ABA Model Rules of Professional Conduct. Perhaps most important, this law dictionary is reasonably priced.

Other Dictionaries

thesauri
Books of words and their synonyms.

Many other law dictionaries have been published. They include West's *Bouvier's Law Dictionary* (1914); Datinder S. Sodhi's *The Attorney's Pocket Dictionary* (1981), published by Law and Business Publications Inc.; William Statsky's *Legal Thesaurus/Dictionary* (1985), published by West; and Wesley Gilmer, Jr.'s *The Law Dictionary* (1986), published by Anderson Publishing Co.

directory
An alphabetical or classified list, especially of names and addresses.

There are also legal **thesauri** (books of words and their synonyms and near synonyms). These include *Cochran's Law Lexicon* (1973), Burton's *Legal Thesaurus* (2001), and Statsky's *Legal Thesaurus/Dictionary* (1985).

DIRECTORIES

legal directory
A list or guide typically of law firms, lawyers, or courts and their jurisdictions.

A **directory** is a list of names and certain other information, such as addresses, telephone numbers, and the like. A **legal directory** is a guide to lawyers, law firms, and/or governmental agencies.

Legal directories are often used to find and select lawyers admitted to practice in another state or in another jurisdiction. This is necessary because no lawyer is admitted to practice in every state, or can practice in every jurisdiction, and clients may have legal problems that extend into

RESEARCH THIS

Research the terms "vicarious liability" and "respondeat superior" in Gifis's *Law Dictionary*.	Identify by their definitions how these two terms may be related.

other states and jurisdictions. Legal directories are also used to find correct addresses for, and certain information about, other lawyers. Moreover, legal directories are effective job-hunting tools, particularly if you are seeking a position in another state.

Martindale-Hubbell Law Directory

The long-established leading national law directory is the *Martindale-Hubbell Law Directory,* published annually by the Martindale-Hubbell division of Reed Publishing (USA) Inc. The directory is a multivolume set, arranged in alphabetical order by state. Since 1990, *Martindale-Hubbell* is also available for purchase on CD-ROM. It is also available on the LexisNexis computer-assisted legal research system.

Each volume of *Martindale-Hubbell* has two parts. The first part, containing relatively few pages, purports to list all the lawyers in a given state, arranged alphabetically by city of practice, and then by last name and first name. The information provided in this part includes birth date, bar admission date, college attended, and law school attended. Where *Martindale-Hubbell* has received confidential recommendations, a lawyer may be given a rating, the highest being *av,* meaning *a,* very high legal ability; and *v,* very high faithful adherence to ethical standards. Lawyers are listed in the first part at no cost.

The second part, containing most of the pages, consists of paid advertisements. Arranged by city of practice, then by sole practitioner or law firm, the information provided in this part includes addresses, telephone and fax numbers, areas of practice, biographies, and representative clients.

Martindale-Hubbell also includes, in separate volumes, "Law Digests" that summarize the laws of the various states, the laws of many foreign countries (including Canada and Canadian provinces), and other useful information (e.g., summaries of U.S. copyright, patent, and trademark laws). The state law digests, written by law firms in the respective states, are excellent starting points for researching the law in each state.

Other National Directories

There are several other national directories of lawyers, and two have unique formats. Marquis Who's Who, Macmillan Directory Division, publishes *Who's Who in American Law.* The 14th edition was published in 2005. As its preface states, *Who's Who in American Law* "provides biographical information on approximately 27,600 lawyers and professions in law-related areas, including, among others, judges, legal educators, law librarians, legal historians, and social scientists."

West is developing, and has online, *West's Legal Directory.* Part of the Westlaw computer-assisted legal research system, *West's Legal Directory* is an online database (WLD). For each attorney, there is a basic attorney profile (including address and telephone number, bar admissions, and areas of practice) and a professional profile (including birth date, education, representative clients, and foreign language ability).

State, Local, and Specialized Directories

Legal directories for several states and regions are published by the Legal Directories Publishing Company, Inc., of Dallas, Texas. The directories include alphabetical lists of attorneys statewide, an alphabetical list of law firms statewide, and an attorney list by county and city.

Local legal directories are also published by local bar associations and other publishers. In Ohio, for example, Anderson Publishing Company publishes the multivolume *Profiles of Ohio Lawyers.*

There are countless specialized directories, ranging from the *Congressional Directory* to the Association of American Law Schools' *Directory of Law Teachers* (for law school teachers). Some are available on the Lexis and Westlaw computer-assisted legal research systems.

CYBER TRIP

Martindale-Hubbell is now available on the Internet at www. martindale.com. Find a local law firm and look up their rating.

A Day in the Life

Can a police officer be charged with a federal crime for the use of excessive force during an arrest? Use *American Jurisprudence 2d* to look up the terms "police" and "excessive force." You will see that a police officer can be charged with a federal crime for the use of excessive force during the arrest of a suspect. After the beating of Rodney King in Los Angeles, some of the police officers involved in his arrest were charged with a federal crime for using excessive force. In this case, the officers were charged with violating Rodney King's civil rights—a federal crime.

Summary

It has always been the dream of legal researchers to be able to read a text statement of the law that brings it all together. Written for both lawyers and nonlawyers alike, West publishes the easy-to-read A-to-Z encyclopedia of the law, *Guide to American Law.* West's current encyclopedia for lawyers and legal researchers is *Corpus Juris Secundum* (C.J.S.), the title meaning "the body of the law, second." Following West's philosophy of "comprehensive" law publishing, the text in C.J.S. is supported by footnotes that purportedly include citations to every reported case on the point covered. C.J.S. also includes cross-references to West topic and key numbers. The most common entry into C.J.S. is through the general index or a volume index. LCP's current encyclopedia for lawyers and legal researchers is *American Jurisprudence 2d* (Am. Jur. 2d), the title meaning "all the law of America, second." Am. Jur. 2d, like C.J.S., covers federal law and, insofar as it can be stated generally, state law. Following LCP's philosophy of "selective" law publishing, the Am. Jur. 2d text is supported by footnotes that purportedly include citations to only selected leading or landmark cases on the point covered, and to A.L.R. annotations. The most common entry into Am. Jur. 2d is through the general index or a volume index. Am. Jur. 2d includes *Table of Statutes and Rules Cited, New Topic Service,* and a desk book. LCP also sells a separate student textbook, *Summary of American Law,* which is keyed to, and summarizes, Am. Jur. 2d. Some states have a state encyclopedia.

Although they should never be cited as either primary or secondary authority, many law students find that they can effectively learn the fundamentals of the law by reading and studying commercial law outlines, including Emanuel law outlines, *Gilbert Law Summaries, Legalines, Ryan Law Capsules, Sum & Substance,* and West's *Black Letter Series.*

The two leading law dictionaries are *Black's Law Dictionary* and *Ballentine's Law Dictionary.* Because of their dated word lists, both are being increasingly derided within the legal profession. The problem with both *Black's* and *Ballentine's,* and virtually all other law dictionaries, is that they are not citation-based. Despite its limitations, *Black's* remains the most cited, most respected, and best-selling dictionary for the legal profession. West's *Words and Phrases* allows you to read digest paragraphs summarizing judicial definitions of particular words or phrases. Despite its drawbacks, *Ballentine's Law Dictionary* also continues to be a major dictionary for the legal profession. The most practical, readable, and useful law dictionary currently published is the *Law Dictionary* (second edition) by Steven H. Gifis. It excludes archaic legal words and is reasonably priced.

Legal directories are often used to find and select lawyers admitted to practice in another state or in another jurisdiction, and to find correct addresses for, and certain information about, other lawyers. They are also effective job-hunting tools. The long-established leading national law directory is the *Martindale-Hubbell Law Directory.* Lawyers are listed in the first part at no cost, whereas the second part contains paid advertisements. Marquis Who's Who publishes *Who's Who in American Law,* and West is developing, and has online, *West's Legal Directory,* a legal database. Legal directories for several states and regions are published by the Legal Directories Publishing Company, Inc.

Key Terms

canned briefs   133
citation-based   134
citations   134
definitions   133
dictionary   133
directory   136

etymology   133
law dictionary   133
legal directory   136
legal encyclopedia   128
outline   133
thesauri   136

Review Questions

1. Where would you begin research about a legal topic if you had no idea what it was about (e.g., Admiralty)?
2. What is West's national encyclopedia?
3. What is LCP's national encyclopedia?
4. Is there a legal encyclopedia for your state?
5. Why should you never cite a commercial law outline?
6. What quality do virtually all law dictionaries lack?
7. Why would you cite a definition from *Black's Law Dictionary* in a brief?
8. Why would you cite a definition from *Ballentine's Law Dictionary* in a brief?
9. Why would a student want to buy Gifis's *Law Dictionary*?
10. What is the leading long-established national legal directory?

Exercises

1. Use the CJS to look up whether or not a police officer can conduct a search of a motor vehicle during a routine vehicle stop. Find the volume index for the topic and provide the location of the full cite.
2. Using either *Black's Law Dictionary* or *Ballentine's Law Dictionary,* define the following terms:
   arbitrage
   res ipsa loquitur
   prima facia
3. Research the law firm of Baum Hedlund online at www.martindale.com. Where are they located? What type of law do they practice? List five of their past clients.

Vocabulary Builders

Find and circle the following terms in the subsequent word search puzzle. The terms may appear up, down, sideways, or diagonal, and forward or backward, ignoring any spaces in phrases.

F	Z	A	B	D	Q	R	A	I	D	J	A	L	P	W	O	X	H	H	B	B	W	Q	U	S	B
A	E	I	B	P	R	N	I	C	Z	B	V	Y	H	U	S	Y	D	I	C	T	P	B	A	A	E
L	E	E	Y	C	Y	D	D	O	B	Q	R	D	S	A	N	M	V	I	D	S	Q	I	L	M	P
E	I	O	J	U	C	I	E	T	X	E	K	I	M	W	E	A	D	I	C	T	I	L	S	Z	A
N	H	U	K	T	Y	Q	P	F	S	C	I	C	Q	E	R	K	L	I	U	Y	E	N	B	C	V
C	S	T	D	H	C	F	O	D	V	Y	F	T	N	T	Q	A	X	F	D	N	K	H	J	N	M
Y	M	D	S	B	B	N	L	C	E	C	D	I	G	V	D	G	U	E	T	X	D	I	C	T	I
C	U	I	L	W	A	S	C	U	I	L	L	O	E	C	C	Y	C	I	K	L	O	P	E	D	E
L	D	R	Q	C	L	K	Y	O	T	T	S	N	J	M	I	U	N	O	U	T	L	K	J	D	A
B	N	B	Z	Y	L	U	C	E	U	P	C	A	O	R	P	E	J	U	R	O	S	T	G	V	B
S	U	A	B	C	E	T	N	O	A	E	B	R	H	D	S	K	L	O	P	Y	M	S	C	E	I
K	C	L	P	D	I	R	E	C	T	O	R	Y	A	O	U	E	D	J	E	H	N	R	A	G	J
P	E	L	P	N	N	Y	F	B	D	A	S	J	J	T	B	E	K	L	O	S	F	K	R	D	K
R	S	R	O	E	E	M	F	N	I	D	D	E	C	O	N	C	Y	C	L	O	P	E	A	D	I
O	O	Z	A	R	X	N	S	Y	R	J	D	I	R	E	C	Y	M	H	E	I	I	G	O	I	A
C	O	R	P	U	S	J	U	R	I	S	S	E	C	U	N	D	U	M	A	K	L	P	G	F	V

BALLENTINES, CORPUS JURIS SECUNDUM, DICTIONARY, DIRECTORY, ENCYCLOPEDIA, and **OUTLINE.**

Chapter 10

Secondary Sources: Specialized

CHAPTER OBJECTIVES

After reading this chapter, you should be able to:

- Recognize the differences between textbooks and treatises.

- Define "hornbook" and how it is used.

- Understand how to use a "restatement."

- Compare and contrast legal forms, as well as pleading and practice forms.

- Identify and use national legal form sets.

- Identify and use national pleading and practice form sets.

- Recognize trial and practice books.

- Explain how the "law review" is used.

- Recognize and list key national legal magazines.

- Identify and list key national legal newspapers.

Secondary sources are not limited to encyclopedias and dictionaries. A great many other secondary sources are available to the legal researcher so they can better understand legal issues. Again, secondary sources simply point the researcher to the appropriate primary sources and should be neither cited nor quoted.

TEXTBOOKS AND TREATISES

textbook
A book used in the study of a subject.

treatise
A scholarly study of one area of the law.

A **textbook** contains the principles of a given subject making it useful in the study of that subject. Most nonfiction books contain at least some of the principles of a given subject, and may be loosely termed textbooks.

A **treatise** is a systematic scholarly discussion, or "treatment," of the principles of a given subject; it is especially useful in the study of that subject. Since most legal textbooks are written in a systematic form by legal professionals for legal professionals, they are generally known as treatises. Legal treatises contain references to case opinions, statutes, and other primary and secondary sources of the law. They may be critical (suggesting what the law should be), interpretative (explaining the law as it is), or expository (enumerating the sources of the law), or a combination of each type.

Thousands of legal textbooks and treatises exist, covering virtually every legal subject. Textbooks and treatises may be published in single volumes or multivolume sets, and may be published either in bound volumes or as a loose-leaf service. They include the features of an

Case Fact Pattern

Someone tells you they heard a woman won a sexual harassment case against an employer because she overheard two people talking graphically about a sexually suggestive *Seinfeld* episode by the water cooler. You wonder if this could be true. Which resources provide insight into trends in workplace sexual harassment law?

ordinary book, such as a table of contents, the main body in chapters, and an index. Textbooks and treatises also include "legal" features, such as a table of cases cited, organization by section number, and pocket parts or other supplementation. Textbooks and treatises usually cover a subject in more detail than an encyclopedia, outline, periodical, or other secondary source. Treatises may be a single volume or a multivolume set. They generally contain numerous references to primary authorities on the topic.

In most law libraries, textbooks and treatises are shelved together according to the Library of Congress Classification. (See Figure 10.1.) Because there are so many different textbooks and treatises, you have to check what is available in your local law library.

Although there is no formal classification of textbooks and treatises beyond the Library of Congress Classification system, textbooks and treatises may be grouped by their purpose for publication.

Many textbooks and treatises are written for practicing lawyers and paralegals. Examples include *Legal Ethics and Professional Responsibility* (Thomson Delmar Learning, 1994) by Jonathan S. Lynton and Terri Mick Lyndall; *An Introduction to Bankruptcy Law, 4th ed.* (Thomson Delmar Learning, 2004) by Martin A. Frey, Sidney K. Swinson, and Phyllis Hurley Frey; and *Business Law* (Barrons, 2004) by Robert W. Emerson.

Some textbooks and treatises are written for scholarly purposes, such as *The Legal and Regulatory Environment of Business* (McGraw-Hill, 2005) by O. Lee Reed, and *The Language of the Law* (Brown and Co., 2001) by David Mellinkoff.

Most textbooks and treatises, however, are written for educational purposes. Along with casebooks, and continuing legal education seminar outlines, examples include *Business Law: With UCC Applications, 9th ed.* (McGraw-Hill, 1996) by Gordon W. Brown, Edward E. Byers, and Mary Ann Lawlor; *Fundamentals of Criminal Advocacy* (LCP, 1974) by F. Lee Bailey and Henry B. Rothblatt; and *Business Law* (McGraw-Hill, 1993) by Peter J. Shedd and Robert N. Corley.

hornbooks
Scholarly texts; a series of textbooks which review various fields of law in summary narrative form, as opposed to casebooks which are designed as primary teaching tools and include many reprints of court opinions.

Hornbooks and Nutshells

Named after teaching tablets with handles used from the late 1400s to the middle 1700s (i.e., a sheet of paper protected by a sheet of translucent horn), **hornbooks** are today a series of one-volume, student-oriented treatises published by Thomson/West. Hornbooks generally cover basic

FIGURE 10.1
Example of a Treatise Shelf Directory

KE 426 to KF 320

Law of Canada (KE)

Legal Research

Legal Writing

Legal Education

Legal Profession

legal subjects, such as criminal law, evidence, and property. (See Figure 10.2.) The authors are generally law professors renowned as experts in their field.

Among hornbooks, the most famous and influential was probably William L. Prosser's *Handbook of the Law of Torts*. Often cited in briefs and court opinions, Prosser's text trained a generation of lawyers in the law of torts, to the point that a lawyer's "innate" ability to find a legal theory under which to sue is a national stereotype. Charles T. McCormick's *Law of Evidence, 2nd ed.* (1972) was another leading hornbook. *Corbin on Contracts* (1952) also deserves special mention. Many people believe that the character Professor Kingsfield in the movie and television series *The Paper Chase* was based on its author, Yale Law School professor Arthur Linton Corbin.

Thomson/West's hornbooks are true treatises, and expensive. Realizing that there is a market for a wider range of less expensive textbooks than the hornbook series, Thomson/West also publishes an "accurate, brief, convenient" series of paperback textbooks "priced for student

FIGURE 10.2

Excerpt from a

Hornbook

Source: Handbook of Torts, Prosser 2d. Reprinted by permission of Thomson/West.

CHAPTER 12

VICARIOUS LIABILITY

62. Nature of Liability.
63. Servants.
64. Independent Contractors.
65. Joint Enterprise.
66. Other Applications.

NATURE OF LIABILITY

62. Vicarious liability is the responsibility of one person, without any wrongful conduct of his own, for the tort of another. Its modern justification is a policy which places such responsibility upon the party best able to bear and distribute the risk.

Vicarious liability is the responsibility of A for the tort of B committed against C, where A himself has had no part in the tortious conduct. Since A has been free from any negligence or any wrongful intent, it is a form of strict liability. Its foundation, however, is still a tort on the part of B, and its effect is to make A liable to the same extent as B.[1] The most familiar illustration, of course, is the liability of a master for the torts of his servant in the course of his employment.

The idea of vicarious liability was common enough in primitive law. Not only the torts of servants and slaves, or even wives, but those of inanimate objects, were charged against their owner. The movement of the early English law was away from such strict responsibility, until by the sixteenth century it was considered that the master should not be liable for his servant's torts unless he had commanded the particular act.[2] But soon after 1700 this rule was found to be far too narrow to fit the expanding complications of commerce and industry, and the courts began to revert to something like the earlier rule, under the fiction of a command to the servant "implied" from the employment.[3]

A multitude of very ingenious reasons have been offered for the vicarious liability of a master:[4] he has a fictitious . . .

---

1. Thus the defenses of contributory negligence and assumption of risk are open to A as well as B; and a judgment for B in an action brought against him by 0 is res judicata as to A's vicarious liability to 0. See McGinnis v. Chicago, R. I. & P. R. Co., 1906, 200 Mo. 347, 98 S.W. 590, 9 L.R.A.,N.S., 880, 9 Ann. Cas, 656, 118 Am.St.Rep. 661; Doremus v. Root, 1901,23 Wash. 710,63 P. 572,54 L.R.A. 649; Bradley v. Rosenthal, 1908, 154 Cal. 420, 97 P. 875, 129 Am. St.Rep. 171; Pangburn v. Buick Co., 1914, 211 N.Y. 228, 105 N.E. 423. See Note, 1926, 12 Corn.L.Q. 92.
One important distinction is that many courts refuse to hold the principal vicariously liable for punitive damages. See Raines v. Schultz, 1888, 50 N.J.L. 481, 14 A. 488; Craven v. Bloomingdale, 1902, 171 N.Y. 439, 64 N.D. 169; Lake Shore & M. S. R. Co. v. Prentice, 1893, 147 U.S. 101, 13 S.Ct. 261, 37 L.Ed. 97. But even here some courts have held a corporate employer liable. Goddard v. Grand Trunk R. Co., 1869,

57 Me. 202, 2 Am.Rep. 39; Hayes v. Southern R. Co., 1906, 141 N.C. 195, 53 S.E. 847; Beauchamp v. Winnsboro Granite Corp., 1920, 113 S.C. 522, 101 S.E. 856. See McCormick, Damages, 1935, 180.
Another distinction Is that the master does not necessarily have the benefit of immunity from suit, as where the servant is a husband and the plaintiff is his wife. See infra, p. 678; Hughes and Hudson, The Nature of a Master's Liability in the Law of Tort, 1953, 31 Can.Bar Rev. 18.

2. Wigmore, Responsibility for Tortious Acts: Its History, 1894, 7 Harv.L.Rev. 315, 383, 441; Holdsworth, History of English Law, 4th Ed. 1935, vol. 3, 382–387, vol. 8, 472–482; Baty, Vicarious Liability, 1916, ch. 1.

3. 1 Bl.Comm 49 9; Hern v. Nichols, 1708, 1 Salk. 289; Brucker v. Fromont, 1796, 6 Term Rep. 659.

4. See Baty, Vicarious Liability 1916, ch. 8; Smith, Frolic and Detour, 1923, 23 Col.L.Rev. 444, 454;

Eye on Ethics

When using secondary sources of law it is important to ensure they are up-to-date. Always check the copyright of the books and determine if it has been supplemented with more recent information. Remember, these sources are not primary sources and should not be cited or quoted.

nutshells
A paperback series of the law; condensed versions of hornbooks.

budgets" known as **nutshells.** Named after the student's perpetual dream of putting an entire subject "in a nutshell" (like one's cranium), a nutshell, focusing on essentials and citing less law, costs about half of what a hornbook costs. Nutshells cover both basic subjects (e.g., criminal law, evidence, and property) and esoteric subjects (e.g., injunctions, insurance, and military law). Nutshells and hornbooks are typically used by law school students to master basic concepts of law. They are not to be cited or quoted and are only used to understand concepts of law.

A list of Thomson/West hornbooks and nutshells is printed on the pages preceding the title page of any nutshell.

Using a Treatise

Most treatises contain an index at the back of the book that will enable the researcher to locate their research topic. Make sure that the copyright date of the treatise is checked to ensure that the information is current. There could also be a pocket part supplement that provides an update to the treatise and that should be checked as well. The steps to utilizing a treatise are

- Identify the legal topic
- Check the index at the back of the book to locate the topic
- Check the copyright date on the treatise
- Determine if the treatise has been updated or supplemented

Restatements

In 1923, a group of judges, lawyers, and law professors founded the American Law Institute (ALI), an organization dedicated to the simplification of the common law. This was to be achieved by preparing a clear and systematic exposition of the common law as if it were a codified statutory code, known as a **restatement,** prepared by expert "reporters." From 1923 to 1944, restatements were adopted and published for the laws of agencies, contracts, property, torts, and several other subjects, but they never became authorities on a par with the decisions of the courts as originally intended. They have been frequently cited as persuasive authority, however, and since 1952, a second series of restatements has been adopted and published.

restatement
A recitation of the common law in a particular legal subject; a series of volumes authored by the American Law Institute that tell what the law in a general area is, how it is changing, and what direction the authors think this change is headed in.

The current set of restatements may be determined from the latest ALI *Annual Report.* Each restatement has an index, and the First Series has its own index. In the Second Series, the "Reporter's Notes" after each section contains case citations. There may also be references to Thomson/West's digest system and annotations to the *American Law Reports* (A.L.R.). The *Restatement in the Courts* collects summaries of cases citing a restatement.

Sample of Thomson/West Hornbooks and Nutshells

The restatements are organized by legal topic such as the *Restatement of Torts* and the *Restatement of the Law of Contracts.* The information in the restatements often resembles code sections, but

RESEARCH THIS!

Locate William L. Prosser's *Handbook of the Law of Torts.* Look in the index at the back of the book and locate the phrase *"res ipsa loquitur."* Go to the section that talks about this topic and define what the phrase means. Locate a primary authority that can be cited using this concept.

Eye on Ethics

Remember that if a case is found in the annotations of a uniform law and it does not come from your state, it can only be used as persuasive authority.

RESEARCH THIS!

Check to see if your state has adopted the Uniform Commercial Code, and if so, what it is referred to in your state.

they are not. The restatements are only secondary sources and are not primary authority. Once the legal topic has been identified, the restatement provides the legal points that are essential to the topic. Comments and examples often follow the elements. It is important to remember that the law discussed in the restatements may or may not follow the particular state law that the researcher is concerned with. However, the restatements can be helpful when state law is unclear or ambiguous and may provide guidance.

Uniform Laws

uniform laws
Similar laws that are enacted by the legislatures of different states; intended to create uniformity in the law.

Some uniformity has been achieved in state statutory law through the work of the National Conference of Commissioners on Uniform State Laws, created in 1912. Following up on a recommendation by the American Bar Association, each state and the District of Columbia have appointed commissioners who meet once a year to review drafts of proposed **uniform laws.** If the commissioners find that a proposed uniform law is desirable and practical, they promote its passage by their state legislature. Approved uniform laws are published in the commissioners' annual handbook and in Thomson/West's *Uniform Laws Annotated, Master Edition.*

For example, ALI worked with the National Conference of Commissioners on Uniform State Laws to draft and promote the most pervasive uniform law to be substantially enacted in all 50 states and the District of Columbia: the Uniform Commercial Code (U.C.C.). As a result, the state laws of sales, negotiable instruments, and secured transactions are almost identical throughout the country.

Uniform laws are not the laws in any state unless they have been enacted by that state's legislature. When researching statutory law, it is important to refer to the governing state law and not to the uniform law. If a state has enacted the uniform law, it is important to check the annotations in the uniform law to find case law that controls the particular factual situation at hand.

FORM BOOKS

form books
Publications that contain complete or partial sample documents, often with sample factual situations and various alternative methods of stating that legal document.

Lawyers and paralegals use **form books,** collections of sample legal documents used by other lawyers and paralegals to help them prepare documents for clients. Most form books also include checklists, and case, statute, and other cross-references, which are very helpful in preparing legal documents. However, while form books are excellent sources of ideas for how to handle a legal matter, you should *never* blindly follow a form. The law must always be individualized for the client. Most legal professionals agree with the statement: "I never saw a form that didn't need to be fixed." Remember, the forms in these books are just samples and may or may not conform to the law in the state that has jurisdiction over the legal issue. Various types of form books can be found on both Westlaw and LexisNexis and incorporate all areas of the law and many jurisdictions.

legal forms
Forms that can be used as sample documents, as well as blank forms that are utilized by the court system during the course of an adjudication of an issue through the court system.

Legal Forms

Samples of legally effective documents—such as contracts, deeds, and wills—are known as **legal forms.** Several legal form books are available, some devoted to legal forms in general and others devoted to a single subject or jurisdiction.

One leading general legal form set is *American Jurisprudence Legal Forms 2d,* published by Lawyers Cooperative Publishing (LCP). Covering over 100 topics, the set is a collection of forms actually used in practice. (See Figure 10.3.) Cross-referenced with LCP's Total Client Service Library, the appropriate form can be found using the set's index volumes.

Thomson/West also publishes an excellent general legal form set: *West's Legal Forms, 2d.* The set is divided into 11 topical units authored by experienced experts. In a guide to the set, Thomson/West lists the following features: "expert authors; summary of contents for each volume; detailed table of contents; general background information; text analysis of subject matter; forms for information gathering; drafting checklists; basic and comprehensive forms; alternative provisions; comments to specific forms; tax considerations; federal laws; references to model acts and uniform laws; library references (including Key Numbers and C.J.S.); automation of form drafting; 'plain language' forms; indexes and tables; and updating."

Matthew Bender & Company, Inc. (MB), also publishes an excellent general legal form set: *Current Legal Forms with Tax Analysis,* originally prepared by Jacob Rabkin and Mark H. Johnson.

FIGURE 10.3
Excerpt from
American Jurisprudence Legal Forms 2d

Source: American Jurisprudence Legal Forms, 2nd edition. Reprinted by permission of Thomson/West.

Requisites, validity and enforceability of releases. Am. Jur. 2d, Release §§ 3 et seq.
Interpretation, operation and effect of releases. Am. Jur. 2d, Release §§ 28 et seq.
West's Digest References
Release ☞34, 35

§ 223:54   Release of claims based on automobile accident— With dismissal of pending legal action

Release

Release given on _____ *[date]*, by _____, of _____ *[address]*, _____ *[city]*, _____ County, _____ *[state]* ("releasor"), to _____ , of _____ *[address]*, _____ *[city]*, _____ County, - _____ *[state]* ("releasee").

STIPULATIONS

A. Releasor suffered property damage, personal injuries and other losses as a result of an automobile collision that occurred on _____ *[date]*, at _____ *[specific location]*, involving releasor's automobile, driven by releasor at the time of the accident, and an automobile driven by releasee.

B. Releasor asserts that the collision was caused by the negligence of releasee. Based on such assertion, releasor commenced an action for property damages and personal injuries in the _____ *[specify court]*, Civil Case No. _____ entitled _____ v. _____. Damages of $ _____ as alleged in releasor's _____ *[complaint or petition or declaration]* in that action are being sought in such litigation.

SECTION ONE
RELEASE OF ALL CLAIMS

Releasor understands that _____ *[he or she]* may have suffered injuries that are unknown to _____ *[him or her]* at the present time and that unknown complications may arise in the future from injuries of which _____ *[he or she]* is at present unaware. Releasor acknowledges that the possibility of such unknown injuries and complications was discussed in the course of negotiations leading to agreement on the terms of this release, and the sum to be paid by releasee was determined with due regard for such possibility.

With such knowledge, and in consideration of $ _____, receipt of which is acknowledged, releasor elects to and does assume all risks for claims previously or later arising, known or unknown, including, but not limited to, claims for property damage, direct or indirect medical expense, pain and suffering, disability, and loss of income, based on the automobile accident described in this release. Releasor, for _____ *[himself or herself]* and for _____ *[his or her]* heirs, legal representatives and assigns, knowingly releases and forever discharges releasee and *[his or her]* heirs and legal representatives from all liability with respect to such matters and from all claims and causes of action based in any manner on the accident.

SECTION TWO
COMPROMISE OF DISPUTED CLAIM

RESEARCH THIS!

Locate the appropriate volume of Matthew Bender's *Pleading and Practice* for California. You may be able to locate it at your law library or on-line on LexisNexis. Locate a sample complaint for a personal injury action. List some possible causes of action that are appropriate for the form.

The major feature of "Rabkin and Johnson" is its emphasis on the tax aspects of legal transactions represented by the legal forms involved.

Along with other national legal form books, there are also legal form books covering particular states. MB is the leader, publishing a "Transaction Guide" for each of several different states and regions.

The competition in form books can be intense. In Ohio, for example, there are four general legal form sets to choose from: Anderson Publishing Company's *Couse's Ohio Form Book;* Banks-Baldwin Law Publishing Company's *Baldwin's Ohio Legal Forms;* MB's *Ohio Transaction Guide—Legal Forms;* and LCP's *Ohio Forms: Legal and Business.*

Also, many court systems have legal forms on their Web sites. These are the forms that are usually used in the course of court business. Oftentimes, they can be filled out online using one of many platforms such as Adobe Acrobat and printed right off the computer. The then completed and printed legal form can be filed in the courthouse. By utilizing the legal forms from the pertinent court Web site, the paralegal can ensure that the most current and appropriate legal forms for that court are being filed.

Pleading and Practice Forms

pleading and practice forms
Form books containing forms for use in connection with litigation.

Samples of documents used in actually litigating a case—such as complaints, answers, replies, interrogatories, motions, and judgments—are known as **pleading and practice forms.** Again, there are several pleading and practice form books; some are devoted to pleading and practice forms in general, while others are devoted to a single subject or jurisdiction. These books can be especially helpful for legal researchers and paralegals that are tasked with the creation and preparation of various pleadings for filing with the court. The forms in these books provide a skeletal format and typically point out the most pertinent areas of the law that need to be covered in a particular pleading. They can assist the legal professional in formulating a working draft of a particular pleading.

One leading set of general pleading and practice forms is LCP's *American Jurisprudence Pleading and Practice Forms Revised.* LCP also publishes an excellent pair of guides to federal pleading and practice (including practice before federal administrative agencies): a textbook set, *Federal Procedure, Lawyers' Edition,* and a form book set, *Federal Procedural Forms, Lawyers' Edition.* The pair anchor what LCP advertised in 1991 as its federal "family," including *United States Supreme Court Reports, Lawyers' Edition, Second Series* (L. Ed. 2d), A.L.R. Fed., *United States Code Service* (U.S.C.S.), and several other federal law publications. These sets can be entered through the general index for each set.

There are several other guides to federal procedure. Thomson/West publishes *West's Federal Practice Manual* and *West's Federal Forms.* MB publishes *Moore's Federal Practice* and *Bender's Federal Practice Forms.* MB also publishes *Bender's Forms of Discovery* and several state pleading and practice form books.

Again, the competition in form books can be intense. In Ohio, for example, there are three general pleading and practice form sets to choose from: Anderson Publishing Company's *Anderson's Ohio Civil Practice with Forms,* Banks-Baldwin Law Publishing Company's *Baldwin's Ohio Civil Practice,* and MB's *Ohio Forms of Pleading and Practice.*

Trial and Practice Books

trial and practice books
Books for use in federal and state legal practice; these often contain discussions of an area of law and provide forms needed for practice in that legal area.

Books that guide a lawyer or a paralegal through the proof of contentions at trial, often with samples of litigation aids and trial testimony, are known as **trial and practice books.** LCP publishes two unique trial and practice sets: *American Jurisprudence Proof of Facts 2d* and *American Jurisprudence Trials. American Jurisprudence Proof of Facts 2d* includes checklists

FIGURE 10.4

Excerpt from American Jurisprudence Proof of Facts 2d

Source: Lawyers Cooperative Publishing. Reprinted by Permission of Thomson/West.

II. ELEMENTS OF DAMAGES

§ 27. Checklist—Elements of damages

Testimony about the following elements of damages should be elicited, when applicable, from the plaintiff and her witnesses in an action to recover damages for injuries suffered as a result of a rape or sexual assault:

Damages recoverable by or on behalf of injured person—
- ☐ Impairments and complications associated with emotional problems arising from sexual assault
- ☐ Necessary and reasonable medical expenses
  - —Actual past expenses for physician, hospital, nursing, and laboratory fees; medicines; prosthetic devices; etc. [12 ALR3d 1347]
  - —Anticipated future expenses [69 ALR2d 1261]
- ☐ Loss of past and future earnings [15 POF2d 311]
  - —Actual loss of wages or salary
  - —Loss of existing vocational skill
  - —Loss of capacity to earn increased wages [18 ALR3d 88]
  - —Loss of profits or net income by person engaged in business [45 ALR3d 345]
- ☐ Cost of hiring substitute or assistant [37 ALR2d 364]
- ☐ Cost of hiring home-care attendants for cooking, cleaning, and the like [15 POF2d 311, §§ 18–29]
- ☐ Cost of occupational therapy or training
- ☐ Pain and suffering from physical injuries [23 POF2d 1; 8 POF3d 91]
- ☐ Pain and suffering reasonably likely to occur in the future [18 ALR3d 10]
- ☐ Mental anguish
  - —Fright and shock
  - —Anxiety, depression, and other mental suffering or illness [29 POF 529; 30 POF 1; 29 POF2d 571]
  - —Anxiety as to future disease or condition [50 ALR4th 13]
  - —Physical injuries caused by mental anguish
- ☐ Harm from loss of sleep [28 POF 1]
- ☐ Sexual dysfunction [13 ALR4th 183]
- ☐ Past and future impairment of ability to enjoy life [24 POF 171; 34 ALR4th 293]

Damages recoverable by dependents of injured person—
- ☐ Loss of consortium [30 POF 73; 27 POF2d 393]

for the proof of crucial facts in depositions and trials, and sample questions and answers to use in doing so. (See Figure 10.4.) *American Jurisprudence Trials,* after six volumes of general trial practice advice, is a collection of advice on how to try over 200 different kinds of cases, from airplane crashes to exploding gas tanks, from lawyers who have taken such cases to court. Each of these trial and practice guides has a general index for the set.

Trial and practice books blur into textbooks and treatises. There are several excellent guides to trial practice. For example, MB publishes the *Art of Advocacy* series, including *Preparation of the Case, Discovery, Settlement, Jury Selection, Opening Statement, Documentary Evidence, Direct Examination, Cross-Examination of Medical Experts, Cross-Examination of Non-Medical Experts, Summation,* and *Appeals.* LCP publishes the *Federal Trial Handbook 2d,* by Robert S. Hunter, and a series of state trial handbooks. An excellent state trial handbook, *Trial Handbook for Ohio Lawyers, Second Edition,* was put together for LCP by former Judge Richard M. Markus.

Again, it is important to remember that all of these books are secondary sources of law and while they can assist in locating primary sources, these texts themselves cannot be cited as primary authority.

PERIODICALS

periodical
Legal material published at regular intervals; includes magazines, journals, and law reviews.

A **periodical** is a work that is published at regular intervals. Whereas reporters are published at regular intervals because cases occur chronologically, periodicals are published at regular intervals by the publisher's design. A.L.R. qualifies as a periodical, since the reported cases are not always reported in chronological order.

In the same way that ordinary periodicals are excellent sources of market information, recent scholarship, and current events, legal periodicals are excellent sources of information about the legal market, legal scholarship, and legal events. Specialty periodicals are also available to help keep the specialists up-to-date in their areas of specialty. Periodicals are also useful for historical research—to find out what people knew and what people were thinking at any given time. Because periodicals are published with relative frequency, they usually deal with current legal topics and can be a good source of information for relevant current information or legal trends.

Most of the periodicals in the following discussion are available on either or both the LexisNexis and Westlaw computer-assisted legal research systems.

Guide to Using Periodicals

The only practical way to find an article in a periodical that is no longer current is through an index. Two principal general legal periodical indexes are available.

The *Index to Legal Periodicals* covers the period from 1908 to the present, the *Index to Legal Periodicals* is published monthly (except September) and includes articles in over 500 periodicals deemed to have permanent reference value. The index is primarily by subject, with secondary indexing by author. The *Index to Legal Periodicals* is also available in many law libraries on the Wilsondisc CD-ROM system, and on the LexisNexis (LAWREF; LGLIND and LEXREF; LGLIND files) and Westlaw (LRI database) computer-assisted legal research systems.

In 1980, the Information Access Corporation began to put out two indexes published with the assistance of an Advisory Committee of the American Association of Law Libraries: *Current Law Index* and *Legal Resource Index*. The *Current Law Index* indexes over 700 permanent legal periodicals by author, title, and other indexes. The *Legal Resource Index* is the computerized and microfilmed version of the *Current Law Index.* In addition to the coverage of the *Current Law Index,* the *Legal Resource Index* covers legal newspapers and other similar sources. The *Legal Resource Index* is also available in many law libraries as the LegalTrac database on the InfoTrac CD-ROM system, and on the LexisNexis (LAWREF; LGLIND and LEXREF; LGLIND files), Westlaw (LRI database), and DIALOG computer-assisted legal research systems.

As stated above, the indexes are primarily organized by subject, and then author. You may use the following techniques for locating an article:

- Subject—Think of a word that describes the subject matter of your issue. The subject/author index will point you to articles about the subject.

- Author—If you know the name of the author that you wish to research, you may look up articles by that author in the subject/author index.

- Table of Cases—If you know the name of the case that you want to review, you may look up articles that talk about this case. Sometimes you may have to research it by either the plaintiff's or defendant's name.

- Table of Statutes—Articles concerning a statute can be located using the Table of Statutes in the index.

- Book Review—The Book Review index contains a list of articles that speak about a certain book. You may locate the book by searching its title in the Book Review Index.

Numerous specialized legal periodical indexes exist. Check with your local law library to see what they have available. These indexes enable researchers to locate information by subject matter or by author. When using periodicals, it is important to check the current status of the law being researched.

law reviews
Periodicals edited by the top students at each law school, featuring scholarly articles by leading authorities and notes on various topics written by the law students themselves.

Law Reviews

A scholarly periodical published by a law school is known as a **law review.** Law reviews generally contain articles written by law professors, prominent practitioners, or outstanding students (known as comments), and short book, case, or subject reviews (known as notes).

A quality law review article, as an excellent critical commentary, may be treated by a court as persuasive authority. Because it may lead to the development of a new field of law or turn an

CYBER TRIP

Some law reviews can be accessed online through www.jmls.edu./law/journals.html.

law journal
A type of legal periodical that focuses on current events or trends in the law.

bar journal
A legal periodical that is published by a local or national bar association.

newsletter
A small newspaper containing news or information of interest chiefly to a specialized group.

established field of law in a new direction, it may have a significant and substantial effect on the law. Some lawyers, however, believe that most law review articles are nothing but academic drivel.

Virtually every law school publishes a law review. Most cover the law in general, but some stress the law of the state where the school is located.

Some law schools publish more than one review. One covers the law in general and the rest cover a specialized subject, such as environmental law or international law.

Law reviews are usually edited by law students as an academic exercise. Students research topics and check the work of outside authors and each other. Because the students invited to work on a law review usually have high grade point averages or demonstrated writing ability, serving on a law review is usually considered an honor.

Law Journals

A **law journal** is a legal periodical emphasizing current events; if published by a bar association, it is usually known as a **bar journal.** Law journals are legal magazines, supported in part by advertising that gives the readers market information. These journals keep legal professionals informed about current legal events and trends.

The leading national legal magazine is the American Bar Association's *ABA Journal* (A.B.A. J.). Self-described as "the lawyer's magazine" and "an independent, thoughtful, and inquiring observer of the law and the legal profession," A.B.A. J. is a monthly that is "edited for members of the American Bar Association." Along with the feature articles, A.B.A. J. regularly includes a message from the ABA president, letters, news, the Supreme Court Report, trends in the law, books, classified advertising, and legal "war" stories. (See Figure 10.5.)

Specialty sections of the American Bar Association also publish journals. For example, the section on Business Law publishes *The Business Lawyer* quarterly and *The Business Lawyer Update* bi-monthly; the section on General Practice publishes *The Compleat Lawyer* quarterly; and the section on Law Practice Management publishes *Legal Economics* eight times a year.

Most state bar associations also publish journals. The Ohio State Bar Association, for example, publishes the weekly *Ohio State Bar Association Report* containing legislative reports, classified advertising, court rule changes, and official advance sheets. It also publishes *Ohio Lawyer,* a monthly journal with articles.

Many large county and city bar associations also publish journals. Local journals usually emphasize local activities, court decisions, and current events.

There are hundreds of journals covering specialized subjects, published by a variety of organizations. Examples include the *Catholic Lawyer,* the *Practical Lawyer,* and the *Practical Tax Lawyer.* Two journals cover the subject of legal research: *Law Library Journal* and *Legal Reference Services Quarterly.*

Newsletters

As they come down in scale and scope, legal journals blur into **newsletters.** Some formal governmental publications are published in newsletter form. The Internal Revenue Service (IRS), for example, publishes a weekly *Internal Revenue Bulletin* (I.R.B.), which is compiled yearly in their *Cumulative Bulletin* (C.B.). The IRS's district directors publish *Tax Practitioner Newsletter,* which is distributed to tax practitioners in their districts. State newsletters are also published, such as *The Ohio State Tax Report,* published by the Ohio Department of Taxation, and the *State Public Defender Report,* published by the Ohio Public Defender.

Countless newsletters are published by private publishers. For example, Boardroom Reports, Inc., publishes the monthly *Tax HOTline,* featuring inside information from tax lawyers, accountants, and former IRS agents.

Newspapers

The national weekly legal newspapers are the *National Law Journal* and the *Legal Times* (formerly the *Legal Times of Washington*). *The American Lawyer* is a national monthly newspaper.

In major metropolitan areas, there are local legal newspapers. Examples include the *Los Angeles Daily Journal* and the *New York Law Journal.*

FIGURE 10.5
Excerpt from the **ABA** *Journal*

PICKET FENCING

Laws Blunting Church's Protests Worry First Amendment Experts

MOLLY McDONOUGH

ON ANY OTHER DAY, A CLERGY-man known as the "biker bishop" and his pack of some 200 leather-clad, American-flag-carrying motorcycle riders might have been the object of media attention as they gathered for a soldier's funeral.

But on a sunny April 19, reporters and photographers in South Holland, Ill., in Chicago's south suburbs, were congregating down the street, barely within earshot of the biker crowd.

There, on a usually quiet neighborhood corner, with Peace Christian Reformed Church as an unintentional but ironic backdrop, a small church group from Kansas shouted chants and shook signs summing up their "protest ministry." The words, "God Hates Fags," "Semper Fi Semper Fag" and "Priests Rape Boys," were emblazoned onto brightly colored placards. They were held by young boys and an elderly woman. Margie Phelps, the wife of the protest ministry's founder, Fred Phelps. Leading the protest was the couple's daughter, Shirley Phelps-Roper, who also is the ministry's lawyer.

"You turn this nation into fags, our soldiers are coming home in body bags," shouted Phelps-Roper, who wore a blue T-shirt extolling the group's Web site. A full-size American flag was tucked into her pants.

Phelps-Roper drove from Topeka, Kan., home of the family's Westboro Baptist Church, to protest at the funeral of Lance Cpl. Philip J. Martini, who died April 8 in combat operations in Al Anbar Province, Iraq.

The Westboro group had been protesting in similar fashion for more than 15 years, preaching that homosexuality is an abomination and bad things are happening—tsunamis, terrorist attacks and other tragedies—because God is punishing America, Canada and the world.

The message had received little attention until the 60 protesters, almost exclusively members of the Phelpses' extended family, began showing up in small groups to protest at soldiers' funerals in June 2005.

Lawmakers have responded with dozens of proposed statutes—dubbed Let Them Rest in Peace bills—that limit funeral protests, mainly by keeping protesters at least 200 feet from a funeral and restricting activity to at least 30 minutes before or an hour after a funeral. As of June 5, 10 states had passed such legislation. And on Memorial Day, President Bush signed into law the Respect for America's Fallen Heroes Act, which limits protests related to veterans buried on federal property.

Bishop James Alan Wilkowski of the Evangelical Catholic Church, who is known as the "biker bishop" because of his penchant for motor-cycles, supports the legislation, especially if part of the goal is to encourage responsible free speech.

"Funerals are not supposed to be public," says Wilkowski, who recalls that Westboro protesters picketed a funeral of a veteran who died of AIDS, threw rocks and cursed at the man's grieving mother.

SHAKY GROUND IN KENTUCKY?

CONSIDERING THE INFLAMMATORY style of the Westboro crowd, the bills aren't a surprising political reaction. But many constitutional law experts worry that the new measures are threatening the right of Americans to peaceably protest in public places. At the very least, they argue, the laws are on shaky constitutional ground.

If the legislation is narrowly drafted and enhances disturbing-the-peace statutes, then states may have little to worry about, experts say. But if the laws are drafted more broadly and aren't viewpoint-neutral, there will likely be successful challenges.

Phelps-Roper says that after the legis-

A Day in the Life

In order to obtain current information on the status of sexual harassment litigation in the workplace, a legal researcher could look to legal periodicals such as law review articles and journals. Many human-resource organizations publish newsletters containing articles by experts in the area about legal issues.

Summary

The principles of a given legal subject can be found in a textbook or a treatise. There are thousands of legal textbooks and treatises, and they cover virtually every legal subject. They may be published in either single volumes or multivolume sets. Textbooks and treatises usually include the features of an ordinary book (e.g., a table of contents, the main body in chapters, and an index) and legal features (e.g., a table of cases cited, organization by section number, and pocket parts or other supplementation). In most law libraries, textbooks and treatises are shelved together according to the Library of Congress Classification system. Hornbooks are a series of one-volume, student-oriented treatises. Nutshells focus on essentials and cite less law. Restatements restate the common law as if it were a statutory code.

Lawyers and paralegals use form books—collections of sample legal documents used by other lawyers and paralegals—to help them prepare documents for clients. Most form books also include checklists, and case, statute, and other cross-references that are very helpful in the preparation of legal documents. Samples of legally effective documents, such as contracts, deeds, and wills, are known as legal forms. There are several legal form books, some devoted to legal forms in general, and others devoted to a single subject or jurisdiction. National general legal form sets include *American Jurisprudence Legal Forms 2d* and *West's Legal Forms, 2d*. Samples of documents used in actually litigating a case—such as complaints, answers, replies, interrogatories, motions, and judgments—are known as pleading and practice forms. There are several guides to federal procedure. Books that guide a lawyer or paralegal through the proof of contentions at trial, often with samples of litigation aids and trial testimony, are known as trial and practice books.

A periodical is a work published at regular intervals. Legal periodicals are excellent sources of information about the legal market, legal scholarship, and legal events. A scholarly periodical published by a law school is known as a law review. A quality law review article may be treated by a court as persuasive authority. Virtually every law school publishes a law review. A law journal is a legal periodical emphasizing current events; if published by a bar association, it is usually known as a bar journal. The leading national legal magazine is the American Bar Association's *ABA Journal* (A.B.A. J.). Specialty sections of the American Bar Association also publish journals, as do most state bar associations. Some formal governmental publications are published in newsletter form. Countless newsletters are published by private publishers. The national legal weekly newspapers are the *National Law Journal* and the *Legal Times*. The only practical way to find an article in a periodical that is no longer current is through an index. The two principal general legal periodical indexes are the *Index to Legal Periodicals,* published by the H. W. Wilson Company, which is also available on the Wilsondisc CD-ROM system, and the *Current Law Index/Legal Resource Index,* published by the Information Access Corporation, which is also available as the LegalTrac database on the InfoTrac CD-ROM system.

Key Terms

bar journal   149
form books   144
hornbooks   141
law journal   149
law review   148
legal forms   144
newsletter   149
nutshells   143

periodical   147
pleading and practice forms   146
restatement   143
textbook   140
treatise   140
trial and practice books   146
uniform laws   144

Review Questions

1. When does a textbook become a treatise?
2. What is a hornbook?
3. What is a restatement?
4. What is the difference between a legal form and a pleading and practice form?
5. Where can you find legal forms?
6. Where can you find pleading and practice forms?
7. Who uses *American Jurisprudence Trials*?
8. How important are law reviews?
9. What is the leading national legal magazine?
10. What is the *National Law Journal*?

Exercises

1. Read through a chapter of a Thomson/West hornbook. Was the subject of the chapter explained to your satisfaction? Would you ever use a hornbook as a case finder?
2. Imagine that you are drafting the articles of incorporation for a nonprofit corporation, and use the form books available to you. Which form books were most helpful? Would your answer be different if you were drafting a purchase agreement for the sale of a business?
3. Examine the law review of the law school closest to your home. How practical are the articles? Read through an article. Did you learn anything you couldn't have found out yourself?

Vocabulary Builders

Find and circle the following terms in the subsequent word search puzzle. The terms may appear up, down, sideways, or diagonal, and forward or backward, ignoring any spaces in phrases.

P	Z	A	B	D	Q	R	T	R	E	A	T	I	S	E	O	X	H	H	B	B	W	Q	U	S	H
R	E	I	B	P	R	N	I	C	Z	B	V	Y	H	U	S	Y	D	I	C	T	P	B	A	A	E
A	E	E	Y	C	Y	D	D	O	B	Q	R	D	S	A	N	W	V	I	D	S	Q	I	L	M	P
C	I	O	J	U	C	I	E	T	X	E	K	I	M	W	E	A	D	I	C	T	I	L	S	Z	A
T	H	U	K	T	Y	Q	P	F	S	C	I	C	Q	I	R	K	L	I	U	Y	E	N	B	C	V
I	S	T	D	N	C	F	O	D	V	Y	F	T	V	T	Q	A	X	F	D	N	K	H	J	N	M
C	M	D	S	E	B	N	L	C	E	C	D	E	G	V	D	G	U	E	T	X	D	I	C	T	L
E	U	I	L	M	A	S	C	U	I	L	R	O	E	C	C	Y	C	I	K	L	O	P	E	A	E
B	D	R	Q	E	L	K	Y	O	T	W	S	N	J	M	I	U	N	O	U	T	L	K	C	D	K
O	N	B	Z	T	L	U	C	E	A	P	C	A	O	R	P	E	J	U	R	O	S	I	G	V	O
O	U	A	B	A	E	T	N	L	A	E	B	R	H	D	S	K	L	O	P	Y	D	S	C	E	O
K	C	L	P	T	I	R	E	C	T	O	R	Y	A	O	U	E	D	J	E	O	N	R	A	G	B
S	E	L	P	S	N	Y	F	B	D	A	S	J	J	T	B	E	K	L	I	S	F	K	R	D	N
R	S	R	O	E	E	M	F	N	I	D	D	E	C	O	N	C	Y	R	L	O	P	E	A	D	R
O	O	Z	A	R	X	N	S	Y	R	J	D	I	R	E	C	Y	E	H	E	I	I	G	O	I	O
L	E	G	A	L	F	O	R	M	S	S	S	E	C	U	N	P	U	M	A	K	L	P	G	F	H

HORNBOOK, LAW REVIEW, LEGAL FORMS, PERIODICAL, PRACTICE BOOKS, RESTATEMENT, and **TREATISE.**

Chapter 11

A Uniform System of Citation

CHAPTER OBJECTIVES

After reading this chapter, you should be able to:

- Recognize the importance of *The Bluebook: A Uniform System of Citation.*

- Identify and use *The Bluebook: A Uniform System of Citation.*

- Identify other systems of citation.

- Properly cite case names.

- Properly cite case reporters.

- Properly cite deciding courts.

- Properly cite decision dates.

- Properly cite statutes.

- Properly cite constitutions, court rules, and administrative regulations.

- Properly cite books and periodicals.

Legal writing is very much like writing a term paper or any other type of research paper. All research sources need to be cited properly. In term papers and book reports, proper citations are found in footnotes and bibliographies. In legal writing, there is a unique set of citation rules. Legal writing must have very specific citation information such as (1) where the legal authority can be located, (2) whether the authority is mandatory or persuasive, and (3) the writer's intent in using the citation. The basic purpose of a legal citation is to allow the reader to locate a cited source accurately and efficiently.

CITATION STYLE

cite
To read or refer to legal authorities, in an argument to a court or elsewhere, in support of propositions of law sought to be established.

No matter how well you perform legal research, if you cannot communicate your results to others, most of your time and effort will be wasted. It is not enough that you have found cases like yours (or other law) that are favorable to your position. You must be able to communicate that fact to the decision maker involved. In court, the judge will want you to prove your case, if only to make it easier for him or her to decide in your favor. Thus, the judge will expect you to **cite** the law that supports your case. With your cites (i.e., your references to legal authority) in hand, the judge can compare the originals of what you've found with what, if anything, your opponent has found, and then make a decision.

Case Fact Pattern

The law director, impressed with the breadth and depth of the legal research you did on public religious displays, wants you to write a legal memorandum by the end of the week.

You must cite all legal authority in proper citation form for use in a future pleading.

citation style
The manner in which a reference to legal authorities is communicated or abbreviated to the reader.

As a matter of style, if you always cite legal materials in full (e.g., the annotation "Standing to sue for copyright infringement under 17 U.S.C.S. § 501(b)," by Edward A. Nolfi, J.D., found on page 509 of volume 82 of *American Law Reports, Federal,* published by the Lawyers Co-operative Publishing Company of Rochester, New York, in 1987), your reader would soon become overwhelmed by the citations, and the law for which you cite the legal materials will be obscured. For brevity and clarity, it is much more efficient to cite legal materials in an abbreviated form (e.g., Edward A. Nolfi, Annotation, *Standing to sue for copyright infringement under 17 U.S.C.S. § 501(b),* 82 A.L.R. Fed. 509 (1987) or simply 82 ALR Fed. 509), and that is the custom.

The only question is **citation style:** how legal materials should be abbreviated to avoid reader confusion. Without a uniform system of citation style, there might be confusion if the same or different abbreviations are used for the same or different publications covering the same or different law. For example, "M.C.A." might indicate the Annotated Code of Maryland, Mississippi, or Montana.

The question of citation style has never been answered comprehensively and authoritatively by the command of a sovereign, probably because of the complexity of the task. For the most part, there is no citation style required by law. Instead, there is a widely followed system developed by the editors of the East Coast Ivy League law school law reviews, and other systems developed by major law publishers.

The Bluebook: A Uniform System of Citation

One leading system of citation style is *The Bluebook: A Uniform System of Citation, 18th ed.* (2005), compiled by the editors of the Columbia Law Review, the Harvard Law Review, the University of Pennsylvania Law Review, and The Yale Law Journal, and published by the Harvard Law Review Association. A spiral-bound book with a blue cover, *The Bluebook: A Uniform System of Citation* is often referred to as *The Bluebook,* and the citation style it suggests is often referred to as **Bluebook style.** Some people incorrectly refer to the book as the "Harvard Blue Book" or the "Harvard Citator" but, as the editors explain on page vii, the book is titled *The Bluebook* and subtitled *A Uniform System of Citation.*

The Bluebook
Widely used legal citation resource, published by the Harvard Law Review Association, that is regularly revised and updated.

The Bluebook expresses an appropriate citation style for law review articles and other legal writing, including appellate briefs. As the back cover indicates, *The Bluebook* consists of an introduction, practitioners' notes, general rules of citation style, specialized rules, tables and abbreviations, and an index. For the most part, *The Bluebook* is a reference book, not a textbook.

Bluebook style
The type styles used in citations found in academic legal articles (always footnoted) as well as those citations found within some court documents.

The Bluebook rules, full of exceptions and inexplicable conventions, display some favoritism toward particular publishers and publications. These rules have long been criticized as being complex, complicated, confusing, and vague, but they do reflect the tremendous variety of legal sources available in the United States and around the world. However, the most recent edition of *The Bluebook* has sought to make it easier to use. *The Bluebook* has sought to organize its format in a more easily understood manner. For example, *The Bluebook* has added a feature known as the "Bluepages." The Bluepages is an easy to use and understand how-to guide for everyday citations. The goal of the Bluepages is to provide for the needs of the first-year law student, law clerks, paralegals, and other legal professionals. The Bluepages is perhaps the first place to begin when locating the manner in which to cite a certain resource using *The Bluebook.*

Located after the Bluepages are the "white pages." The white pages provide the legal writer with the comprehensive rules of citation and style. The first section looks at rules 1 through 9

RESEARCH THIS!

Review the citations that are listed below. Using your *Bluebook,* tell what is wrong with each of the citations.

Title 15, U.S.C.A. Section 212
Eighth Amendment to the Constitution of the United States

USA v. Daniel Wright, 118 Federal Supplement (Second Series) 423, decided in District Court in Washington D.C.

which establish the general standards of citation and style for all forms of legal writing. The second section deals with rules 10 through 21 and are the rules of citation for specific kinds of authorities such as cases, statutes, books, periodicals, and foreign and international materials. The final section is comprised of the tables that provide examples of how to abbreviate properly specific cited authorities.

For the most part, there is no law requiring Bluebook style. In fact, as we shall see in the final section of this chapter, there are some laws that direct you not to follow Bluebook style. While Bluebook style is the customary standard for briefs, law review articles, and other legal writings, if there is no requirement to the contrary (e.g., an instructor's requirement or a court rule) and you're not preparing the final draft of a legal writing, it is not absolutely necessary to use Bluebook style. Nevertheless, it is good practice, both literally and figuratively, to use Bluebook style whenever possible.

The *ALWD* Citation Manual

ALWD
A legal citation resource, published by the Association of Legal Writing Directors, that contains local and state sources that may not be found in *The Bluebook.*

The other leading system of legal citation and style is the *ALWD Citation Manual, 2d ed.* (2003). This manual is gaining in acceptance and popularity. The *ALWD* was written to provide one system for legal citations for all documents, as opposed to *The Bluebook,* which distinguishes law journals and law reviews from other types of legal documents. The Association of Legal Writing Directors got together approximately 150 legal writing professionals from around 200 schools to create a comprehensive citation manual that would provide the ease of one system of citations for all legal documents, with the goal of replacing *The Bluebook.* The *ALWD* has now been accepted as the standard citation manual by professors at over 90 law schools.

The goal of the *ALWD* is to reflect high-usage citations. It also provides online updates to the manual so current information is always available to the legal writer. At this point, either system of legal citation is acceptable. Pick the system that is clear, concise, and easily understood by you and be consistent with that style throughout your legal document.

Other Systems of Citation

Many people wonder why all law books do not use the same citation style. Because no comprehensive citation style is required by law, major publishers have adopted their own citation style for competitive reasons.

At Thomson/West, for example, National Reporter System volumes suggest a citation style for the reported cases in the running head. These cites do not give parallel cites to non-West reporters. Moreover, citations in *Corpus Juris Secundum* (C.J.S.) do not include dates. Therefore, to formally cite a case found in C.J.S., you must refer to the West reporter for the date of the case. In other words, once you have located the information in C.J.S., you must still check the appropriate West reporter to obtain the official citation.

Lawyers Cooperative Publishing (LCP) also leaves dates out of its encyclopedia *American Jurisprudence 2d,* which frequently cites *American Law Reports* (A.L.R.). LCP claims this is done to save space, even though its cites often contain long strings of parallel citations. LCP's modern citation style (e.g., Miller v Robinson (1966) 241 Md 335, 216 A2d 743, 17 ALR3d 1425) minimizes the number of periods and spaces in the citation in order to save memory space in the company's computers, and thereby save money. Underscoring and italics are avoided to save production costs.

RESEARCH THIS!

Look up the leading case for the nativity scene scenario that was given to you in the case fact pattern at the beginning of this chapter and determine how to cite it in a legal memorandum to the firm using the *ALWD*.

Eye on Ethics

Remember to check for specific citation manuals in your state that supersede *The Bluebook* or the *ALWD*. Make sure you know the style manual your law firm prefers to use.

Shepard's/McGraw-Hill, Inc. has developed and maintained its own system of citation and symbols in order to pack into each column and each page of its *Shepard's Citations* as much information as possible.

In addition, many states have their own citation and style manuals that take precedence over either *The Bluebook* or the *ALWD*. *The Bluebook* provides a table in the rear of the book that gives a list of these types of specialized style manuals. States such as California, Illinois, and New York are states that have specialized manuals.

Unfortunately, under the circumstances, many legal researchers follow the citation style of the material they happen to be using and attempt to convert it into Bluebook style when they prepare their final draft.

TECHNICAL RULES

While Bluebook or ALWD style is not required by law, they are the styles a legal researcher must know. Most courts do not explicitly require it, but the majority of judges expect a legal professional's briefs and other legal writings to substantially conform to Bluebook style and now the ALWD style. It is a badge of competence. The judge will be impressed if, based on the style used in the brief, the author was once a member of a law review, or could have been.

This "badge-of-competence" attitude is pervasive in the legal profession. Most legal research and writing instructors require Bluebook or ALWD style to be followed in all academic work. It is appropriate and commendable, but some have taken this attitude too far. They *define* sound legal research by its legal citation style. Sound research is proved by citing sound authority. If you cite poor authority properly, all you prove is that you can properly cite unsound research.

The following discussion covers the basic elements of Bluebook style for the simplest and most common citations. It is designed to be easily recalled so that in a pinch, you can quickly and confidently prepare briefs that substantially conform to Bluebook style. To strictly follow Bluebook style, however, carefully study *The Bluebook* or a *Bluebook* guide.

Citing Cases

Case citations usually have six components:

- The name of the case
- The official reporter, if required
- An unofficial reporter, if required
- The court, if its identity is not known clearly by the name of the official reporter
- The date of the decision
- The subsequent history, if any

FIGURE 11.1
Citing a Case

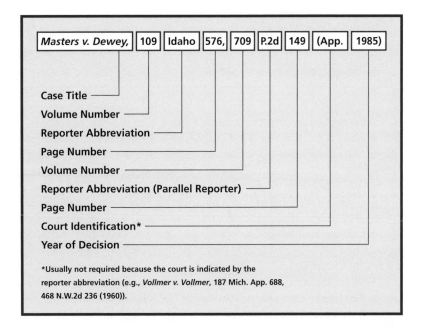

Cases are usually cited by an underscored abbreviated case title, volume-reporter-page citations, court identification (if necessary), and year of decision. (See Figure 11.1 and *Bluebook* Rule 10.)

Case titles are abbreviated versions of the full name of the case, usually the last name of the first named plaintiff, followed by a space, the letter *v* and a period, a space, then the last name of the first named defendant, all underscored. Thus, Robert Smith suing John Doe, Jane Doe, and Richard Roe, comes out "*Smith v. Doe.*" Use appropriate abbreviations (see *Bluebook* Table T.6), but spell out all essential terms of a name or title (e.g., *"Red Lion Broadcasting Co. v. FCC"*) and eliminate redundant abbreviations (e.g., omit *Inc.* from *ABC Co., Inc.*). *State, People,* or *Commonwealth* is sufficient to identify a state in a case from that state's state courts. These names are only used in the actual state where the case was adjudicated. Outside the state of adjudication, the name of the state is necessary. For the federal government, use *United States.* If the cite is used in a formally printed publication, put the case title in italics instead of underscoring it.

Separate the case title from the reporter citations with a comma and a space. What follows is the volume number of the official reporter (if any), a space, the proper abbreviation of the official reporter, a space, and the page number of the first page of the case report in the official reporter (e.g., *New York Times Co. v. Sullivan,* 376 U.S. 254). If the volume number or page number is currently unknown, insert an underscore blank in place of the unknown number (e.g., _____ U.S. _____).

For example, most case citations follow this basic format:				
Name	Volume	Reporter	Page	Year
Miranda v. Arizona	384	U.S.	436	(1966)

Except when citing an officially reported U.S. Supreme Court case in a formal brief (strict Bluebook style requires you to cite only to U.S., but a researcher may appreciate having the parallel cites), follow the official cite of the case (if any) with the appropriate unofficial cite(s) (if any). That is, follow the official cite (if any) with a comma, a space, the volume number of the unofficial reporter, a space, the proper abbreviation of the unofficial reporter, a space, and the page number of the first page in the unofficial reporter, continuing likewise until all unofficial cites are listed (e.g., *New York Times Co. v. Sullivan,* 376 U.S. 254, 84 S. Ct. 710, 11 L. Ed. 2d 686) (strict Bluebook style: *New York Times Co. v. Sullivan,* 376 U.S. 254).

> For the *Miranda* example, the parallel citation would appear as follows:
>
> Parallel Citation
>
> *Miranda v. Arizona,* 384 U.S. 436,   86 S. Ct. 1602, 16 L. Ed. 2d 694 (1966)

After the last reporter citation, put a space, then the year of decision in parentheses (e.g., *New York Times Co. v. Sullivan,* 376 U.S. 254, 84 S. Ct. 710, 11 L. Ed. 2d 686 (1964)) (strict Bluebook style: *New York Times Co. v. Sullivan,* 376 U.S. 254 (1964)). If the citation is to a reporter that covers only one court, or if the particular court can be identified or presumed from the reporters cited (e.g., *Ricketts v. Scothorn,* 59 Neb. 51, 77 N.W. 365 (1898)), the case citation is complete.

However, if the citation is to a reporter that covers more than one court (such as a regional or intermediate appellate court reporter), you should indicate in an appropriate abbreviated form, within the parentheses and before the date, the particular court being cited (e.g., *Mitchell v. C.C. Sanitation Co.,* 430 S.W.2d 933 (Tex. Civ. App. 1968) or *McCormick & Co. v. Childers,* 468 F.2d 757 (4th Cir. 1972)).

With regard to the use of spaces in case names, reporter abbreviations, and court identification, note that single-letter abbreviations (and "2d"-like abbreviations) are not spaced (e.g., N.E.2d), except next to multiletter abbreviations (e.g., F. Supp.), which have a space before and after the multiletter abbreviation (e.g., Cir. Ct. App.).

Citing Statutes

Statutes are usually cited by title number, code abbreviation, section number, and year of publication (See Figure 11.2 and *Bluebook* Rule 12.) Statutes may also be cited by a "statutes at large" reference.

Statutes may be cited to either official or unofficial codes. A proper citation to a federal statute can be as simple as "42 U.S.C. § 1983 (1982)." The essential cite consists of the title number, space, code abbreviation, space, section symbol (i.e., §) or "sec.," space, and section number. After a space, the year of publication is added in parentheses to identify the proper version of the statute. If the statute is in a supplement, that should be indicated within the parentheses and before the date (e.g., 5 U.S.C.A. § 654 (West Supp. 1979)). If desired, the popular name of the statute can be given before the code reference (e.g., National Environmental Policy Act of 1969, § 102, 42 U.S.C. § 4332 (1982)). If necessary, a federal statute may also be cited to the session law (e.g., National Environmental Policy Act of 1969, Pub. L. No. 91-190, 83 Stat. 852 (1970)).

> To make it clearer, look at the following example:
>
> | Name | Number | Code | Section | Date |
> | --- | --- | --- | --- | --- |
> | National Environmental Protection Act | 42 | U.S.C. | 4332 | 1982 |

FIGURE 11.2
Citing a Statute

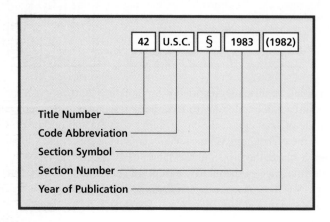

State statutes are usually cited to state codes, beginning with the state code abbreviation, the combination title and section number, and year of publication (e.g., Colo. Rev. Stat. § 24–3–204 (1973)).

Citing Other Primary Sources

Constitutions are cited by sovereign abbreviation, space, "Const." and space, followed by the subdivision cited (e.g., U.S. Const. art. I, sec. 7, para. 2, cl. IV). Use "amend." to cite an amendment (e.g., U.S. Const. amend. IV). (See *Bluebook* Rule 11.)

Court rules are cited by the proper abbreviation for the rules, space, and rule number (e.g., Fed. R. Civ. P. 60(b)). (See *Bluebook* Rule 12.8.3.)

Administrative regulations are usually cited like a statute to the appropriate administrative code (e.g., 45 C.F.R. § 405 (1978)). If a federal administrative regulation is not in C.F.R., cite to the *Federal Register* (e.g., 48 Fed. Reg. 760 (1983)). A federal executive order is cited by "Exec. Order No." and space, order number, comma, space, and a cite to its location in C.F.R., or else in the *Federal Register* (e.g., Exec. Order No. 13,902, 3 C.F.R. 205 (1979)). (See *Bluebook* Rule 14.)

Citing Secondary Sources

Although primary authority is preferred over secondary authority, secondary authority may be cited. Annotations in *American Law Reports* (A.L.R.) are cited by the author's full name, comma, space, "Annotation" and comma, space, the title of the annotation (underscored or in italics), comma, space, volume number, space, proper annotation series abbreviation, space, page number (of the annotation, not the reported case), space, and year of publication in parentheses (e.g., Colleen R. Courtade, Annotation, *Application of Functionality Doctrine Under § 43(a) of Lanham Act (15 U.S.C.S. § 1125(a),* 78 A.L.R. Fed. 712 (1986)). (See *Bluebook* Rule 16.5.5.)

Legal encyclopedias are cited by volume number, space, proper abbreviation, space, topic title (underscored or in italics), space, section symbol and section number, space, and year of publication in parentheses (e.g., 21 Am. Jur. 2d *Bailments* § 3 (1975)). (See *Bluebook* Rule 15.7.)

Textbooks, treatises, and other nonfiction books are cited by volume number (if more than one), author, comma, space, title of the book (underscored or in italics), space, section and/or page (or paragraph) number (if necessary), space, and in parentheses the edition (if more than one; "2d" or whatever, space, "ed." and space) and year of publication (e.g., William L. Prosser, *Law of Torts* § 122 (4th ed. 1972)). (See *Bluebook* Rule 15.) A reasonable alternative (not Bluebook style) to emphasize the publisher is the generally accepted citation style: author, comma, title, edition, and, in parentheses, city of publication, colon, publisher, space, and year of publication, followed by any page references (e.g., Legal citation is also discussed in Frank S. Gordon, Thomas M. S. Hemnes, and Charles E. Weinstein, *The Legal Word Book,* 2nd ed. (Boston: Houghton Mifflin Co., 1982), pp. 149–168).

Consecutively paginated legal periodicals are cited author, comma, space, title of the article (underscored or in italics), comma, space, volume number (or if none, year of publication), space, proper periodical abbreviation, space, first page number of the issue, comma, space, page numbers of the cited material, space, and in parentheses the year of publication (unless used as volume number) (e.g., Patricia J. Williams, *Alchemical Notes: Reconstructed Ideals From Deconstructed Rights,* 22 Harv. C.R.-C.L. Rev. 401, 407 (1987)). (See *Bluebook* Rule 16.2.)

Nonconsecutively paginated legal periodicals are cited author, comma, space, title of the article (underscored or in italics), comma, space, proper periodical abbreviation, comma, space, date of issue, comma, space, "at" and space, first page number of the issue, comma, space, page numbers of the cited material (e.g., Barbara Ward, *Progress for a Small Planet,* Harv. Bus. Rev., Sept.-Oct. 1979, at 89, 90). (See *Bluebook* Rule 16.3.)

CYBER TRIP

With the advent of the Internet, many Web sites are available that provide assistance with citations online. For example, Cornell University has a guide entitled *"Introduction to Basic Legal Citation"* at www.law.cornell.edu/citation.

CITATION REQUIREMENTS

Before citing material in a brief, you should check the applicable court rules and statutes for any matters of citation style required by law. As *The Bluebook* advises: "The practitioner should also be aware that many courts have their own rules of citation that may differ in some respects from *The Bluebook* (p. 11)."

A Day in the Life

Many law firms ask paralegals to research issues that are relevant to their clients' cases and to write legal memorandums summarizing the issues of law. In those legal memorandums, it is important to cite legal authorities in proper citation format for the courts of that jurisdiction. The citations used in the legal memorandum are often used by the attorney preparing pleadings in the case. The attorney counts on the paralegal to provide proper citation format and style so that he or she does not have to spend time in that area. It is one of the important tasks assigned to paralegals in the field.

For example, a lawyer or paralegal preparing a brief for the Ohio Court of Appeals for the First Judicial District (Hamilton County, including Cincinnati), should refer to Local Rule 6, which addresses the "Form and Content of Appellate Briefs." Part D (1) provides

> *a. All citations to reported Ohio cases in briefs or memoranda shall recite the date, volume, and page of the official Ohio report and the parallel citation, where the same exists, to the Northeastern Reporter, e.g., W.T. Grant Co. v. Lindley (1977), 50 Ohio St.2d 7, 361 N.E.2d 454; State v. Durham (1976), 49 Ohio App.2d 231, 360 N.E.2d 743; State v. Gastown, Inc. (1975), 40 Ohio Misc. 29, 360 N.E.2d 970.*
> *b. All citations to the United States Supreme Court cases in briefs or memoranda shall cite the date, volume, and page of the official report and parallel citation to the Supreme Court Reporter, e.g. Jones v. United States (1960), 362 U.S. 257, 80 S.Ct. 725.*

Citing the date first and giving a citation to an unofficial U.S. Supreme Court reporter are not Bluebook style, but they are part of the style required in briefs filed with the Ohio Court of Appeals for the First Judicial District.

The Ohio Supreme Court also follows the "date-up-front" convention since its court rule examples follow that style, but there is no rule that explicitly requires this. The Ohio Supreme Court also prefers the "R.C." abbreviation for citations to the Ohio Revised Code, as explicitly permitted by the Ohio General Assembly in R.C. 1.01.

In the state of Michigan, the *Michigan Uniform System of Citation* "provides a comprehensive scheme for citation of authority in documents filed with, or issued by, Michigan courts."

Again, check the applicable court rules and statutes for special citation requirements, if any, before you submit your brief.

Electronic Sources

With the advent of the Internet, legal citations have taken on a whole new context. They need to be cited to the specific Web page visited. For example, if you want to reference the study done by the American Bar Association regarding bar admission rates from the years 1963 to 2005, you would provide the following citation that references the Web site, along with the date it was visited:

http://www.abanet.org/legaled/statistics/le_bastats.html (last visited Oct. 18, 2005).

Summary

In court, the judge expects you to cite the law that supports your case. For brevity and clarity, legal materials are cited in an abbreviated form. The leading system of citation style is *The Bluebook: A Uniform System of Citation, 18th edition* (2005). It is also known simply as *The Bluebook,* and the citation style it suggests is known as Bluebook style. No law requires Bluebook style—nevertheless, it is good practice to use Bluebook style unless there is a requirement to the contrary. Because there is no comprehensive citation style required by law, major law publishers have adopted their own style for competitive reasons. The other leading system of legal citation and style is the *ALWD Citation Manual, 2d ed.* (2003). This manual is gaining in acceptance and popularity. The *ALWD* was written to provide one system for legal citations for all documents, as opposed to *The Bluebook,* which distinguishes law journals and law reviews from other types of legal documents. The Association of Legal Writing Directors got together approximately

150 legal writing professionals from around 200 schools to create a comprehensive citation manual that would provide the ease of one system of citations for all legal documents, with the goal of replacing *The Bluebook*. The *ALWD* has now been accepted as the standard citation manual by professors at over 90 law schools.

Although most courts do not explicitly require it, the majority of judges and legal research and writing instructors expect a legal professional's briefs and other writings to substantially conform to Bluebook style. Cases are usually cited by an underscored abbreviated case title, volume-reporter-page citations, court identification (if necessary), and year of decision. If the cite is being used in a formally printed publication, put the case title in italics instead of underscoring it. Statutes are usually cited by title number, code abbreviation, section number, and year of publication. Constitutions are cited by sovereign abbreviation, space, "Const." and space, followed by the subdivision cited. Court rules are cited by the proper abbreviation for the rules, space, and rule number. Administrative regulations are usually cited like a statute to the appropriate administrative code. A.L.R. annotations are cited by the author's full name, comma, space, "Annotation" and comma, space, the title of the annotation (underscored or in italics), comma, space, volume number, space, proper annotation series abbreviation, space, page number (of the annotation, not reported case), space, and year of publication in parentheses. Legal encyclopedias are cited by volume number, space, proper abbreviation, space, topic title (underscored or in italics), space, section symbol and section number, space, and year of publication in parentheses. Textbooks, treatises, and other nonfiction books are cited by volume number (if more than one), author, comma, space, title of the book (underscored or in italics), space, section and/or page (or paragraph) number (if necessary), space, and in parentheses the edition (if more than one; "2d" or whatever, space, "ed." and space) and year of publication. Consecutively paginated legal periodicals are cited author, comma, space, title of the article (underscored or in italics), comma, space, volume number (or if none, year of publication), space, proper periodical abbreviation, space, first page number of the issue, comma, space, page numbers of the cited material, space, and in parentheses the year of publication (unless used as a volume number). Legal periodicals that are not consecutively paginated are cited author, comma, space, title of the article (underscored or in italics), comma, space, proper periodical abbreviation, comma, space, date of issue, comma, space, "at" and space, first page number of the issue, comma, space, and the page numbers of the cited material.

Before citing any material in a brief, check the applicable court rules and statutes for any matters of citation style required by law.

Key Terms

The Bluebook   154
ALWD   155
Bluebook style   154

citation style   154
cite   153

Review Questions

1. Why does the legal profession need a uniform system of citation style?

2. What are the two primary guides to legal citation systems?

3. Why do legal publishers use different citation styles?

4. If there is more than one plaintiff or defendant, how do you abbreviate the case name?

5. Why do you need to know which reporters are official and which are unofficial?

6. In a case citation, what is put in the parentheses before the year of decision?

7. Is it true that if the year in a case citation is the year of decision, then the year in a statute citation is the year of enactment?

8. How are federal statutes and state statutes cited?

9. How are constitutions, court rules, and administrative regulations cited?

10. What information do you need to cite a law treatise?

Exercises

1. You need to cite the First Amendment of the U.S. Constitution in your legal memorandum. Check either *The Bluebook* or the *ALWD* and properly cite the amendment.

2. You wish to cite the case of *Mariner Financial Group, Inc. v. Bossley* (which is a Texas case). Look in one of the two main style guides to properly cite the case, including any parallel cites.

3. Check the applicable court rules and statutes in your state for matters of citation style required by law.

Vocabulary Builders

Find and circle the following terms in the subsequent word search puzzle. The terms may appear up, down, sideways, or diagonal, and forward or backward, ignoring any spaces in phrases.

P	Z	A	B	D	Q	R	T	R	E	A	S	D	R	A	P	E	H	S	B	B	W	Q	U	S	H
R	E	I	B	P	R	N	H	C	I	T	A	T	I	O	N	S	T	Y	L	E	P	B	A	A	E
N	E	E	Y	C	Y	S	E	S	A	C	G	N	I	T	I	C	V	E	D	S	Q	I	L	M	P
O	I	O	J	U	C	I	B	T	X	E	K	I	M	W	I	A	D	P	C	T	I	L	S	Z	A
I	H	U	K	T	Y	Q	L	F	S	C	I	C	Q	T	R	K	L	A	U	Y	E	N	B	C	V
T	S	T	D	N	C	F	U	D	V	Y	F	T	E	T	Q	A	X	R	D	N	K	H	J	N	M
I	A	S	E	H	I	S	E	O	R	Y	D	D	G	V	D	G	U	D	T	X	D	I	C	T	L
D	U	I	L	M	A	S	B	U	I	L	C	O	E	C	C	Y	C	I	K	E	O	P	E	A	E
E	D	R	Q	W	L	K	O	O	T	A	S	N	J	M	I	U	N	Z	U	T	T	K	C	D	K
E	N	B	Z	A	L	U	O	E	S	P	C	A	O	R	P	E	J	E	R	O	S	I	G	V	O
T	U	A	B	L	E	T	K	E	A	E	B	R	H	D	S	K	L	O	P	Y	D	S	C	E	O
U	C	L	P	D	I	R	E	C	T	O	R	Y	A	O	U	E	D	J	E	O	N	R	A	G	B
T	E	L	P	O	N	Y	F	B	D	A	S	J	J	T	B	E	K	L	I	S	F	K	R	D	N
A	S	R	O	O	E	M	F	N	I	D	D	E	C	O	N	C	Y	R	L	O	P	E	A	D	R
T	O	Z	A	G	X	N	S	Y	R	J	D	I	R	E	C	Y	E	H	E	I	I	G	O	I	O
S	E	G	A	L	W	D	R	M	S	S	S	E	C	U	N	P	U	M	A	K	L	P	G	F	H

ALWD,* CITATION STYLE, CITE,** and ***THE BLUEBOOK.

Chapter 12

Shepard's Citations and Other Citators

CHAPTER OBJECTIVES

After reading this chapter, you should be able to:

- Find parallel citations using *Shepard's Citations.*

- Find the appropriate volumes and pamphlets of *Shepard's Citations* for a particular search.

- Use *Shepard's Citations* as a case reviewer.

- Use *Shepard's Citations* as a case finder.

- Find parallel citations using cross-reference books.

- Identify the origins and use of Auto-Cite.

- Identify the origins and use of KeyCite.

good law
Law that is still in effect or valid and can be cited as authority.

The law is constantly changing and it is important to be certain the law cited in legal documentation is **good law.** The use of special materials is required in determining good law. This chapter will review some of the special materials available to the researcher to check for good law.

SHEPARD'S CITATIONS

The purpose of legal research is to find a case like yours where the person like you won. Of course, your best "case" could turn out to be a statute, regulation, or other primary law, or a secondary source. Cite your "case" to the judge in the style, argue simple justice ("persons in like circumstances should be treated alike"), and you cannot lose. Or can you?

It is important to realize that there are two powerful forces at work: human nature and time. Acting alone or in concert, these forces can deceive any legal researcher, no matter how experienced.

There is no perfect law book. It is human nature to seize on the first thing that meets one's expectations, even though it may not be the truth. It takes a lot of mental work to be objective, much more than most people imagine. A lot of people are "checkmated" while they dream of checkmating their opponent.

A law book editor, working in a competitive environment under time pressure and other stresses, may unwittingly cut corners. The editor may seize on and write, or be instructed to seize on and write, something not 100-percent accurate. A legal researcher, also working in a competitive environment under time pressure and other stresses, may also unwittingly cut corners. The

Case Fact Pattern

While you were researching the topic of public religious displays, you found the case of *Allegheny County v. ACLU,* 492 U.S. 573 (1989). It is possible a newer case has been decided on this issue. You do not want to miss any important cases that could have been decided more recently.

researcher, eager to find a case like his where the person like him won, may seize on and cite an inaccurate statement without checking it out. As a result, the legal researcher can lose the case to a more careful and objective opponent.

Even if the law book editor and the legal researcher have been careful, honest, humble, and objective, the case can still be lost because of the march of time. The law is always changing. Using a recently published law book, the legal researcher finds a case like the legal researcher's, where the person like the legal researcher won, and argues it to the court. His opponent rises and agrees that the case cited is like the case at bar, but notes that the legal researcher's case was reversed on appeal, and so the person like the opponent ultimately won. The court agrees, and finds for the opponent. The legal researcher has experienced the greatest embarrassment in advocacy: *unwittingly arguing the opponent's case.*

bad law
Law that has been overruled and is no longer considered as precedent.

A legal researcher can lose by unwittingly citing and arguing **bad law:** overruled (or otherwise discredited) precedent. Bad law is precedent without authority. Precedent can lose its value in a number of ways. A precedent may be overruled by a higher court (or by a statute). A court may overrule its own precedent. Or a precedent may be left alone to die, whether distinguished away by other courts, overwhelmed by contrary precedent, or simply forgotten. Courts have the power to declare precedents out-of-date, and they frequently do. It is the insidious power of the march of time.

In 1873, an Illinois law book salesman, Frank Shepard, gave some thought to the nature of law books and precedent, and how the value of a precedent is altered over time by later case precedent. Although he was not a lawyer, Shepard observed that some lawyers made notes in the margins of their law books when they became aware of later cases that altered the presidential value of a reported case. Shepard realized that the idea was sound, but that no practicing lawyer would have the time to keep such a system up-to-date. There were thousands of cases published each year in a variety of reporters and keeping up with it all would be a full-time job. Shepard decided that he would provide the service, and he founded his own company to do so.

Shepard started small. He began to read all the reports of the Illinois courts. He carefully noted every time an earlier case was cited by a later case. He printed his notes for each case on gummed slips and sold them to lawyers, instructing them to paste them in the margins of their reports at the cited case. It was a hit. Shepard expanded into other states, hired several assistants, and changed the format of the service to book form. *Shepard's Citations* quickly became a standard legal research tool.

citators
A set of books which provide, through letter-form abbreviations or words, the subsequent judicial history and interpretation of reported decisions.

After Shepard died in 1900, his business was incorporated and transferred to New York City. In 1947, the company was moved to Colorado Springs, Colorado, and, in 1966, it was acquired by and became a division of McGraw-Hill, Inc. In 1997, Reed Elsevier, Inc. acquired *Shepard's* from McGraw-Hill. LexisNexis is now the exclusive publisher of *Shepard's.*

cited case
To read or refer to a particular case.

Shepard's leads a group of books and other media that list citations, which are known as **citators.** In listing parallel cites, citators list cites to a target case, known as the **cited case.** In

Eye on Ethics

Remember that it is important to know the most relevant precedent or "good law" with regard to the legal issue you are researching.

citing cases
Cases that all refer or reference a particular case.

listing cites of cases that make reference to a target case, citators list referring cases, known as **citing cases.**

Shepard's is a book of tables uniquely listing all the citing cases for a cited case. Under each cited case (volume number and reporter noted in the running head; page number noted in boldface between dashes in the tables), the cites of the citing cases are listed by volume number, *Shepard's* reporter abbreviation, and page number. (See Figures 12.1 and 12.2.) In the first listing for the cited case, parallel citations are listed in parentheses immediately following the page number heading. Note that *Shepard's* cryptic reporter abbreviations are not Bluebook style, and so they should not be used in formal legal writing.

FIGURE 12.1

Example of a *Shepard's Citations* Page

Source: Shepard's Federal Citations. Reprinted by permission of LexisNexis.

Federal Cases			
379	**381**	**382**	**388**
cc) 122US71	112US92	cc) 122US40	109US90
cc) 123US267	28LE632	cc) 122US71	27LE867
cc) 124US694	5SC69	cc) 123US267	3SC61
cc) 30LE1064	Cir. 2	cc) 124US694	Cir. 8
cc) 30LE1074	61F416	cc) 30LE1064	142F386
cc) 31LE160	Cir. 9	cc) 30LE1074	**389**
cc) 31LE557	78F459	cc) 31LE160	54 AR 258n
cc) 7SC1073	83F104	cc) 31LE557	**391**
cc) 7SC1090	30OAG205	cc) 7SC1073	113US752
cc) 8SC101	Ind	cc) 7SC1090	28LE1135
cc) 8SC676	42InA596	cc) 8SC101	5SC768
cc) 7F477	85NE37	cc) 8SC676	**392**
cc) 8F269	Kan	cc) 7F477	a) 104US192
cc) 11F591	80Kan688	cc) 8F269	a) 26LE707
cc) 12F871	103P113	cc) 11F591	Cir. 2
cc) 15F109	Mich	cc) 12F871	73F456
cc) 16F387	99Mch222	cc) 15F109	98F543
cc) 19F420	201Mch472	cc) 16F387	Calif
145US293	58NW63	cc) 19F420	98Cal206
36LE709	167NW892	**384**	33P60
12SC912	Mont	Cir. 2	Iowa
Cir. 6	7Mt427	2F97	119Ia126
95F506	16Mt481	42F688	93NW72
380	16P572	88F303	ND
cc) 122US40	41P272	Cir. 5	26ND275
cc) 122US71	Nebr	130F43	144NW98
cc) 123US267	106Neb853	Cir. 7	**393**
cc) 124US694	184NW927	63F631	Cir. 1
cc) 30LE1064	NJ	54 AR 109n	8FS302
cc) 30LE1074	68NJL93	54 AR 122n	Cir. 2
cc) 31LE160	52At295	**385**	11F2d785
cc) 31LE557	ND	Cir. 2	1926MC352
cc) 7SC1073	23ND86	86F693	1934MC1009
cc) 7SC1090	134NW774	**387**	NY
cc) 8SC101	Okla	Cir. 2	130NYM574
cc) 8SC676	31Ok1115	19F800	224NYS425
cc) 7F477	120P560	Cir. 9	59 AR1355n
cc) 8F269	45SW138	102F926	**395**
cc) 11F591	Pa	67 AR 472n	Cir. 2
cc) 12F871	109PaS351		
cc) 15F109	167At512		
cc) 16F387	Tex		
cc) 19F420	121Tex113		

FIGURE 12.1
(*continued*)

12F71
87F197
  Cir. 6
9F29

397

84US197
262US122
21LE607
67LE902
43SC507
  Cir. 2
173F429
  Cir. 6
47F883
  Cir. 9
73F247
225F177
  CtCl
8CCL173
1923MC556
1940MC245
11OAG437
  Calif
14C2d626
96P2d945
  Nev
23Nev317
46P806
  NC
227NC80
128NCA399
40SE696
496SE815
  Wis
128Wis499
108NW607

398

  Cir. 1
122F825
214F167
  Cir. 2
39F333
46F408
59F482
86F694
135F134
  Cir. 5
403FS394
  Cir. 9
633F2d1306

401

  Cir. 2
5F108
86F694
  Cir. 5
403FS394
  Cir. 9
633F2d1306

402

74US457
19LE198
  Cir. 7
60FS102

404

s) 70US37
s) 18LE50

405

r) 76US203
r) 19LE638
  Cir. 9
109F2d312

407

1997MC1384

408

  N Y
2NYS622

409

a) 59US63
a) 15LE267
58US156
105US634
157US401
279US570
15LE70
26LE1195
39LE749
73LE850
15SC663
49SC422
  Cir. 1
119F750
  Cir. 2
7F680
35F769
24F2d312
25F2d650
  Cir. 4
48F582
89F2d544
  Cir. 5
13F400
  Cir. 6
30F133
110F457
  Cir. 7
69F1013
  Cir. 9
57F2d90
1928MC452
1928MC1012
1929MC836
1932MC668
1937MC649

410

  Cir. 2
35F844
82F478
  Cir. 3
216F240
  Cir. 5
31F847
  Cir. 9
202F29
94LE233n

411

94LE233n

412

47US421
61US322
12LE498
15LE921
  Cir. 2
150FS2d479
186FS2d234
  Ill
15IlA21

414

15USApx56
4LE299
  Cir. 2
269F840
  Cir. 6
75F327
  CtCl
22CCL461
1940MC707
6OAG646
  Haw
30Haw897
  Ind
167Ind557
78NE183
  Iowa
1921a86
182NW230
  Miss
211So2d825
78Corl 105

419

146PaL200

420

  Cir. 2
7F116

421

  Cir. 2
86F694

422

a) 104US185
a) 26LE716
  Cir. 9
60FS388
1945MC1326

423

  Cir. 5
21F2d239
  Cir. 9
172F997
657F2d1016
271FS438
441FS269
1927MC1351
1941MC893
1967MC2668
  NY
261NYAD594
26NYS2d728
  Ore
803P2d1216

428

95US76
24LE376
  Cir. 2
2F369
296F151
  Cir. 6
14F538
1924MC491
80 AR392n

429

  Cir. 2
86F686
158F695
  NJ
38At639

430

  Cir. 2
86F686

431

  Cir. 2
324F2d366
10 AR279n

432

  Cir. 1
28F303
  Cir. 2
29F237
44F819
324F2d366
  Cir. 4

FIGURE 12.1
(*continued*)

29F275	9F673	**470**	**486**
75F107	Cir. 9		
Cir. 6	83F217	370US501	Cir. 7
36F116	141F275	8LE654	357FS213
54F282	Cir. DC	82SC1444	Cir. 9
Cir. 8	175F3d160	Cir. 9	5F2d524
54F465	336ADC6	262F1007	1925MC876
Cir. 9	Ark	Cir. DC	Tex
29F70	72Ark179	113F2d739	157SW297
59F966	78SW773		29A²803n
93F898	Ind	**472**	
13LE1051n	171Ind670		**487**
	87NE106	Cir. 6	
432a	Me	12F275	Cir. 1
	87Me483		15F607
Cir. 2	32At1017	**475**	Cir. 6
324F2d366	Va		30F257
	152Va515	Cir. 6	
433	147SE245	22F643	**488**
	103 AR776n	NY	
28 A³1145n		INY158	a) 101US693
	445	96NYAD769	a) 25LE1005
434		146NYM576	
	Cir. 6	134NE201	**490**
Ark	17F5	261NYS682	
110Ark14	6OAG237	151NYS2d372	Cir. 2
160SW870	100 AR539n	463NYS2d448	9F382
	15A³538n	101CR990	24F554
438	15A³550n	66A²792n	Cir. 6
	66A⁴306n		5F722
a) 94US164		**477**	5F725
a) 24LE97	**446**		
		Cir. 8	**491**
442	Cir. 9	70F2d582	
	236F799		Cir. 2
Cir. 5	Cir. DC	**479**	48F697
70F885	182F2d969		
		Cir. 5	**493**
443	**449**	488F2d883	
		Cir. 6	Cir. 1
s) 2US382	Cir. 9	36F781	181F709
s) 1LE425	71F319	Cir. 10	
	84F365	2F749	**494**
444	162F258	NY	
		38NYAD514	Mo
21US397		56NYS518	150Mo414
49US611	**457**	97 AR352n	51SW745
122US266	Cir. 2		
255US79	9F546	**480**	**495**
266US516			
490US834	**465**	1997MC1384	354US32
5LE645			1LE1171
12LE1219	Cir. 2	**481**	77SC1238
30LE1178	13F2d543		Cir. 1
65LE515	Cir. 6	Cir. 8	251F764
69LE416	241F415	94F1014	
104LE903	Cir. 9		**496**
7SC1182	180F140	**484**	
41SC252			Cir. 2
45SC147	**469**	Cir. 1	12F718
109SC2224		75F429	22F826
Cir. 1	Cir. 4	Cir. 9	238F94
60F426	22F2d54	79F106	Cir. 6
118F3d53	10LE1304n	93F687	256F947
Cir. 2	40 AR612n	1938MC728	Cir. 9
167F961		Mass	102F333
279F690		157Mas157	
Cir. 5		31NE754	**497**
			Minn

FIGURE 12.1
(*continued*)

83Min514	63F2d729	69F791	116F95
86NW776	240F2d713	1955MC538	117F796
90 AR431n	127FS933	Ore	159F244
90 AR433n	Cir. 5	129Ore310	256F593
100 AR 1354n	104F583	275P18	Cir. 6
160 AR 1424n	Cir. 6	132AR22n	117F882
	25FS971	132AR54n	Mass
☐ 498	83FS395	132AR87n	139Mas170
	Cir. 7		29NE379
289US505	74F2d515	☐ 499	
77LE1349	Cir. 8		☐ 500
53SC731	IF214	Cir. 1	
Cir. 2	Cir. 9	199F339	Cir. 5
10F2d938	22F2d63	Cir. 2	35F543
2FRD234	Cir. 10	12F261	
Cir. 3	33F355	16FS513	☐ 501
264F585		Cir. 3	15USApx24

FIGURE 12.2
Excerpt from
Shepard's Citations
Abbreviations

Source: Shepard's Federal
Citations. Reprinted by permission of LexisNexis.

REPORTER ABBREVIATIONS

A2d–Atlantic Reporter, Second Series
AB–American Bankruptcy Reports
AbD–Abbott's Court of Appeals Deci-
    sions (N.Y.)
ABn–American Bankruptcy Reports,
    New Series
AC–American Annotated Cases
AD–American Decisions
ADC–Appeal Cases, District of Columbia
    Reports
Add–Addison's Reports (Pa.)
AiK–Aiken's Reports (Vt.)
AkA–Arkansas Appellate Reports
A^2–American Law Reports, Second Series
A^3–American Law Reports, Third Series
A^4–American Law Reports, Fourth Series
A^5–American Law Reports, Fifth Series
Ala–Alabama Supreme Court Reports
AlA–Alabama Appellate Court Reports
AlF–Alaska Federal Reports
Alk–Alaska Reports
Allen–Allen's Reports (Mass.)
AR–American Law Reports
ARF–American Law Reports, Federal
AN–Abbott's New Cases (N.Y.)
AnC–New York Annotated Cases
AntNP–Anthon's Nisi Prius Cases (N.Y.)
AOA–Anderson's Ohio Appellate
    Unreported Decisions
AR–American Reports
Ark–Arkansas Reports
AS–American State Reports
At–Atlantic Reporter
AVD–Abstracted Valuation Decisions
Az–Arizona Reports
AzA–Arizona Court of Appeals Reports
Bar–Barbour's Supreme Court Reports
    (N.Y.)

BCh–Barbour's Chancery Reports (N.Y.)
Bin–Binney's Reports (Pa.)
Black–Blackford's Reports (Ind.)
Bland–Bland's Chancery Reports (Md.)
Bos–Bosworth's Reports (N.Y.)
Boy–Boyce's Reports (Del.)
Bradb–Bradbury's Pleading & Practice
    Reports (N.Y.)
Bradf–Bradford's Surrogate's Court
    Reports (N.Y.)
Bray–Brayton's Reports (Vt.)
Breese–Breese's Reports (Ill.)
Breese App–Breese Appendix
BRW–Bankruptcy Reporter (West)
BTA–United States Board of Tax Appeals
    Reports
Bur–Burnett's Reports (Wis.)
C2d–California Supreme Court Reports,
    Second Series
C3d–California Supreme Court Reports,
    Third Series
C3dS–California Supreme Court Reports,
    Third Series (Special Tribunal Supple-
    ment)
C4th–California Supreme Court Reports,
    Fourth Series
CA–Court of Customs Appeals Reports;
    Court of Customs and Patent Appeals
    Reports (Customs)
CA2d–California Appellate Reports,
    Second Series
CA2S–California Appellate Reports,
    Second Series Supplement
CA3d–California Appellate Reports,
    Third Series
CA3S–California Appellate Reports,
    Third Series Supplement
CA4th–California Appellate Reports,

FIGURE 12.2
(*continued*)

Fourth Series	CCPA–Court of Customs & Patent
CA4S–California Appellate Reports,	Appeals Reports (Patents)
Fourth Series Supplement	CD–Decisions of the Commissioner of
CaA–California Appellate Reports	Patents
Cai–Caines' Reports (N.Y.)	Chand–Chandler's Reports (Wis.)
CaiCs–Caines' Cases (N.Y.)	ChipD–D. Chipman's Reports (Vt.)
Cal–California Supreme Court Reports	ChipN–N. Chipman's Reports (Vt.)
CaL–California Law Review	ChS–Chancery Sentinel (N.Y.)
CaR–California Reporter	ChS(2)–Chancery Sentinel, No. 2 (N.Y.)
CaR2d–California Reporter, Second	Cir–Connecticut Circuit Court Reports
Series	CIT–United States Court of International
CaU–California Unreported Cases	Trade (Bound Volumes)
CCA–Court of Customs and Patent	CLA–University of California at Los
Appeals Reports (Customs)	Angeles Law Review
CCL–Court of Claims Reports (U.S.)	CLQ–Cornell Law Quarterly

shepardize
Using *Shepard's* verification and updating system for cases, statutes, and other legal resources.

When legal researchers **shepardize** a case, they review all the citing cases for a cited case to make sure the cited case is not bad law or to help find other cases like the cited case. Similarly, when legal researchers shepardize a brief or other legal writing, they review all the cases cited in the brief or other legal writing to make sure the brief or other legal writing does not cite bad law or help find other cases like the case cited to use in a reply or a revision.

There are *Shepard's* sets covering virtually every set of court reports published in the United States, including every major unit of the National Reporter System. Note, however, that a *Shepard's* covering a particular state's reporters lists only citing cases from that state, or cases originating in the federal courts in that state.

For the U.S. Supreme Court, for example, Shepard's/LexisNexis, publishes the *Shepard's United States Citations* (Case Edition) set. Inside are tables for the three major Supreme Court reporters—one for cites to *United States Reports* (U.S.), one for cites to *United States Supreme Court Reports, Lawyers' Edition* (L. Ed.), and *Lawyers' Edition, Second Series* (L. Ed. 2d), and one for cites to *Supreme Court Reporter* (S. Ct.)—running through several bound volumes and pamphlets covering different periods of time.

For example, you wanted to see the complete list of cites made to 450 U.S. 24. To limit the number of volumes and pamphlets you have to look through to make the complete list of cites for a cited case, Shepard's/LexisNexis, periodically publishes comprehensive bound volumes and pamphlets. The last major comprehensive bound volume was published in 2003, covering 450 U.S. was published in 1984, covering cites to 409–458 U.S. (and parallel cites) from the date of the cited case to 2003. The next comprehensive volume where 450 U.S. might be located is in a "Supplement," that was published recently in 2006. Shepard's citators are typically updated by supplements. The hardbound versions are becoming obsolete as LexisNexis provides greater flexibility with searching Shepard's online.

Because some people find the comprehensive volume and pamphlet system confusing, and because the volumes and pamphlets can be easily misshelved by the uninformed, Shepard's/ LexisNexis, publishes a list entitled "What Your Library Should Contain" on the cover of each pamphlet. (See Figure 12.3.) It is a good practice to consult this list, as necessary, before you begin to shepardize a case.

Using *Shepard's* Citators

The main reason for using *Shephard's* is to check to see if an authority is still good law. However, *Shephard's* provides much more information such as parallel cites, cites to the same case that might have been published in other court opinions, cites to all cases that discuss the authority, descriptions of how other cases have handled the authority, and cites to secondary sources.

Shepard's citators are organized in a manner similar to case reporters. Cases are organized numerically by volume and then by the page number of the case. In this way, *Shepard's* provides an easy way for researchers to look up a particular case.

FIGURE 12.3
Shepard's **Cover Listing "What Your Library Should Contain"**

Source: Shepard's Federal Citations. Reprinted by permission of LexisNexis.

| VOL. 105 | JUNE 15, 2006 | No. 12 |

SHEPARD'S
UNITED STATES
CITATIONS

UNITED STATES SUPREME COURT REPORTS, LAWYERS' EDITION

Express Update

IMPORTANT NOTICE

The 2004–2006 Bound Supplement for *Shepard's United States Citations, United States Supreme Court Reports, Lawyers' Edition* will be published in June.

WHAT YOUR LIBRARY SHOULD CONTAIN

BEFORE the 2004–2006 HARDBOUND SUPPLEMENT is SHELVED RETAIN THE FOLLOWING:

2004 Bound Edition, Volumes 2.1–2.11 and 4*

Supplemented with:
 –December 1, 2005 Gold Annual Cumulative Supplement
  Vol. 104, No. 23, Lawyers' Edition, (Parts 1 & 2)
 –June 1, 2006 Red Cumulative Supplement
  Vol. 105, No. 11, Lawyers' Edition
 –June 15, 2006, Blue Express Update
  Vol. 105, No. 12, Lawyers' Edition

AFTER the 2004–2006 HARDBOUND SUPPLEMENT is SHELVED RETAIN THE FOLLOWING:

2004 Bound Edition, Volumes 2.1–2.11 and 4*
2004-2006 Bound Supplement, Volume 2.12

Supplemented with:
 –June 1, 2006 Red Cumulative Supplement
  Vol. 105, No. 11, Lawyers' Edition
 –June 15, 2006, Blue Express Update
  Vol. 105, No. 12, Lawyers' Edition

Once you locate your case in one of the citators, you need to analyze the case information. This information can tell you if the case was overruled in a subsequent case, criticized, approved, questioned or cited in the dissent of a subsequent case. This case information could be very important on how you intend to use the case in your legal documentation.

Frank Shepard conceived of his book as a case reviewer. He listed all the citing cases for a cited case, so a legal researcher could make sure the cited case was not bad law (i.e., make sure it was "still" good law and to what extent). Over time, Shepard and his successors developed a system of analysis abbreviations, listed in the front of each volume, to add to the bare list of citing cases, to help the legal researcher quickly review the cited case, and to do so in a refined way. (See Figure 12.4.)

Shepard and his successors noted that there are two general types of citing cases. Often, the "citing" case is really a later history of the cited case itself; the same case on appeal or remand.

FIGURE 12.4
Excerpt from
***Shepard's* History**
and Treatment
Abbreviations

Source: Shepard's Federal Citations. Reprinted by permission of LexisNexis.

HISTORY AND TREATMENT ABBREVIATIONS

Abbreviations have been assigned, where applicable, to each citing case to indicate the effect the citing case had on the case you are Sheppardizing. The resulting "history" (affirmed, reversed, modified, etc.) or "treatment" (followed, criticized, explained, etc.) of the case you are Sheppardizing is indicated by abbreviations preceding the citing case reference. For example, the reference "f434F2d872" means that there is language on page 872 of volume 434 of the *Federal Reporter*, Second Series, that indicates the court is "following" the case you are Sheppardizing. Instances in which the citing reference occurs in a dissenting opinion are indicated in the same manner. The abbreviations used to reflect both history and treatment are as follows.

History of Case

a	(affirmed)	The decision in the case you are Sheppardizing was affirmed or adhered to on appeal.
cc	(connected case)	Identifies a different case from the case you are Sheppardizing, but one arising out of the same subject matter or in some manner intimately connected therewith.
D	(dismissed)	An appeal from the case you are Sheppardizing was dismissed.
m	(modified)	The decision in the case you are Sheppardizing was changed in some way.
p	(parallel)	The citing case is substantially alike or on all fours, either in law or facts, with the case you are Sheppardizing.
r	(reversed)	The decision in the case you are Sheppardizing was reversed on appeal.
s	(same case)	The case you are Sheppardizing involves the same litigation as the citing case, although at a different stage in the proceedings.
S	(superseded)	The citing case decision has been substituted for the decision in the case you are Sheppardizing.
US cert den		Certiorari was denied by the U.S. Supreme Court.
US cert dis		Certiorari was dismissed by the U.S. Supreme Court.
US cert gran		Certiorari was granted by the U.S. Supreme Court.
US reh den		Rehearing was denied by the U.S. Supreme Court.
US reh dis		Rehearing was dismissed by the U.S. Supreme Court.
v	(vacated)	The decision in the case you are Sheppardizing has been vacated.

Treatment of Case

c	(criticized)	The citing case disagrees with the reasoning/decision of the case you are Sheppardizing.
d	(distinguished)	The citing case is different either in law or fact, for reasons given, from the case you are Sheppardizing.
e	(explained)	The case you are Sheppardizing is interpreted in some significant way. Not merely a restatement of facts.
Ex	(Examiner's decision)	The case you are Sheppardizing was cited in an Administrative Agency Examiner's Decision.
f	(followed)	The citing case refers to the case you are Sheppardizing as controlling authority.
h	(harmonized)	An apparent inconsistency between the citing case and the case you are Sheppardizing is explained and shown not to exist.
j	(dissenting opinion)	The case is cited in a dissenting opinion.
L	(limited)	The citing case refuses to extend the holding of the case you are Sheppardizing beyond the precise issues involved.
o	(overruled)	The ruling in the case you are Sheppardizing is expressly overruled.
q	(questioned)	The citing case questions the continuing validity or precedential value of the case you are Sheppardizing.

RESEARCH THIS!

Shepardize the famous case of *Miranda v. Arizona* in the appropriate *Shepard's* citator.

Look at the subsequent history of the case and become familiar with the abbreviations.

"History of Case" abbreviations—such as *a* for "same case affirmed on appeal," *m* for "same case modified on appeal," and *r* for "same case reversed on appeal"—have been added as appropriate to the citing references for the cited case.

Most often, the citing case is a true citing case—that is, another case citing the cited case, perhaps as precedent. "Treatment of Case" abbreviations—such as *c* for the "decision or reasoning in cited case criticized," *d* for the citing case that "distinguished" itself from the cited case, and *f* for the citing case that "followed" the cited case as "controlling"—have been added as appropriate to the citing references for the cited case.

Although the analysis abbreviations help you to quickly review a cited case, remember they are not perfect, and can't be, because there is no perfect law book. Analysis abbreviations are generally added only when they are supported by the express language of the citing case. If a citing case implicitly criticizes the cited case, no analysis abbreviation appears to indicate that. Since the analysis is a literal one-time judgment expressed in summary form, you should always read the relevant cases. Moreover, *Shepard's* cannot be used in any direct way to determine if a case precedent has been overruled by statute.

One weakness inherent in *Shepard's* results from the fact that the cited case may deal with several points of law. In a citing case, it is not always clear which point of the law (if any) is referred to by the cited case or to which point of law the analysis abbreviation applies. To address this problem, modern *Shepard's* citing references include, to the extent possible, a superior figure (an "exponent") to the left of the page number. The superior figure indicates the headnote or syllabus paragraph of the *cited case* that states the point of law about which the *citing case* referred in to the cited case.

In reviewing a case with *Shepard's,* remember that *Shepard's* lists only all citing cases for a cited case. Two case opinions can discuss the same point of law, but nothing requires the judge drafting the later opinion to cite the earlier case. The judge may not even be aware of the earlier case. Moreover, a case precedent can be "followed" or "overruled"—indirectly—by a nonciting case. *Shepard's* relies heavily on these abbreviations to relay information concerning a case. At the beginning of each *Shepard's* volume, there is a table of abbreviations that will enable you to properly decipher the information provided on the case in the citator.

The main points to remember when shepardizing a case are:

- Note the citation that is being checked.
- Locate all relevant *Shepard's* volumes as well as any supplements, and so on.
- Check "What Your Library Should Contain" on the cover of the supplement.
- Locate the first appearance of the case in *Shepard's.*
- Check your case in all supplements and advance sheets.
- Interpret and analyze your findings.
- Review the abbreviations to make sure you understand all of the information.
- Repeat the process with all parallel cites.
- Check the Daily Update Service.

Shepard's Statutory Citators

statute edition
Volumes of *Shepard's* that cite cases to a particular statute.

Although *Shepard's* was originally designed to list all the citing cases for a cited case, Shepard's/ LexisNexis has added to the concept. As the title page of each *Shepard's* volume indicates for the cited cases in the volume, *Shepard's* may also list other citing legal materials, such as A.L.R. annotations and law reviews, for a cited case. A **statute edition** lists all the citing cases for a particular statute or ordinance. *Shepard's United States Citations* (Statute Edition), for example, lists all the citing cases for a particular section of the *United States Code*. Constitutions, treatises, court rules, selected administrative decisions, and patents listed by patent number, copyrights listed by title of the copyrighted work, and trademarks listed alphabetically can also be shepardized.

Shepard's/LexisNexis also publishes other publications and subject-specific *Shepard's*. Publication examples include *Code of Federal Regulations* (Citations), *Law Review Citations, Professional Responsibility Citations* (covering the American Bar Association *Code of Professional Responsibility* and *Code of Judicial Conduct*), and *Restatement Citations*. Subject examples include *Bankruptcy Citations, Federal Labor Law Citations, Federal Tax Citations, Military Justice Citations,* and *Uniform Commercial Code Citations*.

Using *Shepard's* as a Case Finder

Although *Shepard's* was designed as a case reviewer, it is frequently used as an imperfect case finder to help find other cases like the cited case. *Shepard's* lists all the citing cases for a case. There may be hundreds of cases that have cited a given cited case. Note, however, that the court deciding the citing case may cite the cited case for a number of reasons. Sometimes there's a legal significance; sometimes it's a coincidence. *Shepard's* perpetuates all citations of legal authority: the great, the good, the bad, and the ugly.

You can assume that 50 percent of the citing cases listed in *Shepard's* for a cited case like yours are also cases like yours. If you have found a case that you know is exactly like, or similar to, your case, you can shepardize it, and check out each case listed as a citing case. About 50 percent of the time—more if you're lucky, less if you're not—the citing case will be like yours. Because *Shepard's* systematically lists all the citing cases for a cited case, no editorial judgment is involved. You can often find cases like yours using *Shepard's* that didn't make it into an annotation, digest, encyclopedia, or other law book, because they didn't have to meet stricter editorial standards.

Unlike a case citing another case, when a case cites a statute it is highly probable that the statute is important to the case. You can assume that 75 percent of the citing cases listed in *Shepard's* statute edition for a cited statute like your case are also cases like yours. Because *Shepard's* statute edition systematically lists all the citing cases for a cited statute or ordinance, no editorial judgment is involved. You can often find cases like yours using *Shepard's* statute edition that didn't make it into an annotated code or other law book, because they didn't have to meet stricter editorial standards.

Again, *Shepard's* is an imperfect case finder. You have to consider your chances of success. *Shepard's* may list hundreds of citing cases for a cited case like yours, and about 50 percent will *not* be cases like yours. In a given case, using *Shepard's* as a case finder may not be worth the time and effort involved.

Shepard's on LexisNexis

Many authorities can be electronically shepardized, including statutes, cases, and administrative materials. The electronic version contains the same type of information as the print version with a few differences. *Shepard's* on Lexis is constantly updated; it also allows the researcher to view the complete *Shepard's* entry or a more restricted entry with less information to wade through. The electronic version will not automatically show the researcher headnote references, however. If you need to see them, they are available using one of the program's many options.

Another advantage to the electronic version of *Shepard's* is that it is linked with other services within LexisNexis, and when researching on Lexis, a notation will tell you every time you retrieve a case using Lexis whether or not *Shepard's* contains an entry for it and what kind of treatment that case has received. These helpful notations are called Shepard's Signals. They also appear at the start of the *Shepard's* entry for the case.

It is important, however, not to rely exclusively on Shepard's Signals to determine if a case is good or bad law. A case with a negative signal may no longer be good law for one of its points but may still be good on other points. Being too quick to dismiss a case because of a negative Shepard's Signal could cause you to miss a case which is ultimately essential to the issue you are researching.

OTHER CITATORS

case history
The history of how a case has been handled in subsequent cases.

While *Shepard's Citations* uniquely lists all the citing cases for a cited case, there are other useful citators that simply list parallel citations for a cited case and/or list all the cites to a single case as it has made its way through the court system. The path a legal controversy has taken through the court system is known as its **case history.**

KeyCite on Westlaw

KeyCite was originally called Insta-Cite and was introduced in 1983. It was West's Westlaw response to Auto-Cite on LexisNexis. Compared with Auto-Cite's history dating back to the 1800s, West created KeyCite from scratch, for purely competitive reasons. KeyCite is nearly identical to Lexis' electronic *Shepard's.*

KeyCite has three main features: case history, parallel citations, and citation verification. KeyCite's case history is case history: the ability to determine whether a case has become bad law as a result of its own history in the courts. KeyCite's parallel citations emphasize parallel citations to units of the National Reporter System. KeyCite's citation verification is simply case information (title, year of decision, etc.).

KeyCite entries start with the full citation of the case, statute, or administrative material, and the relevant complete direct history. After the direct history, the negative and/or indirect history is implicated. If a case has received negative indirect history, this is indicated by stars. The star categories show you how much discussion concerning the original case you will be able to find within the citing case. One star means it has been mentioned. Two stars mean it was cited. Three stars indicate it was discussed, and four stars mean it was thoroughly examined.

Besides case history, KeyCite also has research references to the original case. The KeyCite entry, called KC Citing Ref, has the citations to a case. Negative cases are always listed first. They are followed by positive cases and then by secondary sources.

Like *Shepard's* on Lexis, KeyCite is also linked with Westlaw's databases and has a notation system similar to that of Shepard's Signals. KeyCite uses status flags to give you some idea about how KeyCite treats a case. A red flag means the case is no longer good law for at least one of its points. A yellow flag means a case has some negative history, but has not yet been reversed or overruled. A blue "H" means the case has some history but that history is not known to be negative, and a green "C" means that the case, while having citing references, has no direct or negative indirect history.

CYBER TRIP

KeyCite is available online at www.west-group.com/keycite/.

Shepard's on LexisNexis or KeyCite on Westlaw

Selected *Shepard's Citations* are available on LexisNexis (SHEP command), and the very similar KeyCite system is available on Westlaw. The principal advantage of using *Shepard's* or KeyCite online is that the bound volume and pamphlet lists of citing cases are automatically merged for each cited case. In addition, analysis abbreviations are spelled out in *Shepard's* online, and you can quickly retrieve a citing case from the computer-assisted legal research system.

Auto-Cite

The first commercial computer case history citator was Auto-Cite, introduced directly to the public by the Lawyers Co-operative Publishing Co. (LCP) in 1982. Its origins date back to the preparation of *Lawyers' Reports Annotated* (L.R.A.) from 1888–1918, and include a citation service once offered by the company at no charge.

In 1913, LCP began "The Co-op. Citation Bureau" to help promote L.R.A. A legal researcher could send a case cite to LCP, and LCP would return, at no charge, by mail or "telegraph collect" (1) the citations to "All the cases which have ever cited that case," (2) where, if at all, the case was reported in a "leading selected case series" (such as LCP's L.R.A.), and (3) where, if at all, the case was cited in an L.R.A. annotation, insofar as all of the preceding had already been found by LCP editors in preparing L.R.A. and other texts. The "Citation Bureau" was based on a card file of approximately 1.4 million cards on which LCP editors had checked and noted the histories of cases before citing them in L.R.A.

The free "Citation Bureau" faded out of existence, but as L.R.A. became A.L.R., LCP editors continued to keep case history file cards. Of course, until 1977, LCP never saw the need to publish the cards, because A.L.R. theoretically contained all its case analysis. Theoretically, A.L.R. readers did not need *Shepard's,* because A.L.R. editors picked up the value of case precedents reading all the on-point cases in the course of preparing annotations. Instead of a few analysis abbreviations, A.L.R. provided a detailed narrative analytical treatment of all the case law on the point annotated, with complete case summaries set out for all relevant cites.

By 1977, LCP was looking for a way to get into "electronic publishing." The pages of LCP's books were then being composed by computer, and the company had begun to look into computerizing other aspects of the manufacturing process. One aspect was editorial "testing." A clerical staff assisted LCP editors in checking the validity of cases cited in LCP publications using the LCP's case history collection. LCP decided to computerize its "testing" department. The new computer system was known as Auto-Cite (Automated Citation Testing Service).

In 1977, LCP entered into talks with Mead Data Central, publisher of the LexisNexis computer-assisted legal research system. On January 22, 1979, the companies signed a royalty agreement whereby LCP's Auto-Cite system would be provided to LexisNexis subscribers. LexisNexis had already demonstrated that information could be economically entered into a computer database, and with the development of personal computers, acoustic couplers (a device in which a telephone receiver can be inserted), and modems, customers could be linked to an electronic publisher over telephone lines.

By 1982, LCP had collected nearly four million case histories. LCP decided to once again provide "testing" services not only to its own editors and LexisNexis subscribers, but to its own customers as well, this time for a fee.

Auto-Cite allows the user to make an electronic citation search. Enter a cite by volume, reporter abbreviation, and page, and Auto-Cite displays the full citation to the case, including title, court (if necessary), date, parallel cites, references in A.L.R. annotations, and case history citations, all in an easy-to-read "sentence."

Auto-Cite is *not,* however, the same as *Shepard's. Shepard's* has all the citing cases for a cited case, and so is useful in both case review and case finding. *Shepard's* covers both the history and the treatment of a cited case. Auto-Cite covers only the history of the cited case and leaves case reviewing and case finding to A.L.R. In 1997, Lexis acquired *Shepard's.*

Differences Between Auto-Cite and *Shepard's*

When using *Shepard's,* you may restrict your search by negative or positive analysis, by jurisdiction, by custom analysis, by headnotes, or by date. *Shepard's* uses a Focus Search on the citing references and will find all citing references to your case. It includes all Auto-Cite information, including the prior and subsequent appellate history.

Using Auto-Cite limits a search to the following information: prior and subsequent appellate history and citing references that negatively affect the validity of your case. Because *Shepard's* includes the Auto-Cite data for case law, you do not generally need to use Auto-Cite too unless you want to include all available indirect history information.

LexisNexis or Westlaw as a Citator

LexisNexis or Westlaw can be used as a citator by using the cited case's cite as a word search for citing cases. Once the cite is typed into the database, both search services will provide a history of the treatment of the case just as a citatory does. The same information can be obtained using the online versions as using the hardbound citators.

PARALLEL CITES

It is necessary to find the appropriate parallel cites to a case, if any, to properly cite the case in Bluebook style. There are often more practical reasons for finding a parallel cite. Law libraries, particularly law firm libraries, do not always contain the same sets of books. As a result, you must be able to find and use alternative sources. For example, in the early stages of your research, you may have only the cite to a case in a state reporter, but need to find the case in the West regional reporter, or you may have only the cite to the case in the West regional reporter, but need to find the case in a state reporter.

A Day in the Life

Shepardize the *Allegheny* case when doing your legal memorandum. It is also important to shepardize all parallel citations, as well as state cases, to determine if your legal matter has been handled in a local court and to find the most recent determination *and* interpretation of the law.

Until computers were commonly used in legal research (see Auto-Cite and Insta-Cite discussed earlier), the most common way to get back and forth between state reporters and the National Reporter System was to use West's *National Reporter Blue Book* (not to be confused with *The Bluebook: A Uniform System of Citation*) and the appropriate West's state "Blue and White Book."

The *National Reporter Blue Book,* as its name suggests, is a blue book. Its tables list state citations for each state and give for each the parallel citations in the National Reporter System. The state "Blue and White Book" (e.g., *Ohio Blue and White*), as its name suggests, is a blue and white book. The blue pages repeat the parallel citation information found in the *National Reporter Blue Book* for that state. The white pages have tables that list the National Reporter citations for the state and give for each the parallel citations in the state reporters.

Besides *Shepard's,* other historic methods of finding parallel cites included searching tables of cases in volumes and digests, checking for cross-reference tables in volumes, thumbing through running heads, and other trickery. These methods then became overshadowed by two computer case history citators: Auto-Cite and Insta-Cite.

Summary

It takes a lot of mental work to be objective. Because of human nature, a legal researcher may seize on and cite an inaccurate statement without checking it out. Due to the march of time, a legal researcher can also suffer the greatest embarrassment in advocacy: unwittingly arguing the opponent's case. Bad law is precedent without authority. Starting in 1873, Frank Shepard provided a service of systematically noting every time an earlier case was cited by a later case. *Shepard's Citations* quickly became a standard legal research tool, leading a group of books and other media known as citators. In listing parallel cites, citators list cites to a target case, known as the *cited case.* In listing cites of cases that refer to a target case, citators list referring cases, known as *citing cases. Shepard's* is a book of tables uniquely listing all the citing cases for a cited case. When legal researchers shepardize a case, they review all the citing cases for a cited case to make sure the cited case is not bad law or to help find other cases like the cited case. There are *Shepard's* sets covering virtually every set of court reports published in the United States, including every major unit of the National Reporter System. A statute edition lists all the citing cases for a particular statute or ordinance. A legal researcher using *Shepard's* can review all the citing cases for a cited case. With help from analysis abbreviations for case history and treatment, the legal researcher can determine whether the cited case is bad law. A legal researcher can also use *Shepard's* as an imperfect case finder to uncover other cases like the cited case. Selected *Shepard's Citations* are available on the LexisNexis and Westlaw computer-assisted legal research services.

Until Auto-Cite and KeyCite were developed, the most common way to get back and forth between state reporters and the National Reporter System was to use West's *National Reporter Blue Book* and the appropriate West's state "Blue and White Book." The first commercial computer case history citator was Auto-Cite, introduced directly to the public by LCP in 1982. Auto-Cite allows the user to make an electronic citation search. Enter a cite by volume, reporter abbreviation, and page, and Auto-Cite displays the full citation to the case, including title, court (if necessary), date, parallel cites, references in A.L.R. annotations, and case history citations, all in an easy-to-read "sentence." Auto-Cite has three main features: citation verification, parallel case referencing, and A.L.R. referencing. Other than a check of citation information, the citation verification of Auto-Cite extends only to a determination of whether a case has become bad law as a result of its own history in the courts (e.g., reversed by a higher court). Since April 1, 1991, Auto-Cite has been available only on the LexisNexis computer-assisted legal research system. LexisNexis subscribers can purchase CheckCite software to automatically use *Shepard's* to check citations in a word-processing document on their personal computer. KeyCite was West's Westlaw response to Auto-Cite on LexisNexis. Similar to Auto-Cite, KeyCite has three main features: case history, parallel citations, and citation verification. KeyCite's citation verification is simply case information. In addition, LexisNexis or Westlaw can be used as a citator by using the cited case cite itself as a word search for citing cases.

Key Terms

bad law   164
case history   174
citators   164
cited case   164

citing cases   165
good law   163
shepardize   169
statute edition   173

Review Questions

1. Why is it hard for human beings to be objective while performing legal research?
2. Why should you hesitate to cite a case you found in a 20-year-old law book?
3. What is the greatest embarrassment in advocacy?
4. Where are parallel citations located in *Shepard's*?
5. What important feature of *Shepard's* do you find on the cover of its pamphlets?
6. How would you use *Shepard's* analysis abbreviations?
7. Why is *Shepard's* an "imperfect" case finder?
8. Can statutes be shepardized?
9. What are the main features of Auto-Cite?
10. What are the main features of KeyCite?

Exercises

1. Locate the *Shepard's* sets in your local law library. Referring to the "What Your Library Should Contain" information on the covers of the pamphlets, determine if all the pamphlets have been properly shelved. Have superseded volumes and pamphlets been properly removed?
2. Shepardize the case of *Robinson v. Shell Oil* Company, 519 U.S. 337. Describe the process you used to shepardize the case and give all of the history and parallel citations for the case.
3. Shepardize the statute of 18 U.S.C.S. §242. Give an explanation of what the statute is and how it is handled in the citators.

Vocabulary Builders

Find and circle the following terms in the subsequent word search puzzle. The terms may appear up, down, sideways, or diagonal, and forward or backward, ignoring any spaces in phrases.

P	Z	A	B	D	Q	R	T	R	E	A	S	D	R	A	P	E	H	S	B	B	W	Q	U	S	H
R	E	I	B	P	R	N	I	C	Z	B	V	Y	H	U	S	Y	D	H	C	T	P	B	A	A	E
N	E	E	Y	C	Y	S	E	S	A	C	G	N	I	T	I	C	V	E	D	S	Q	I	L	M	P
O	I	O	J	U	C	I	E	T	X	E	K	I	M	W	I	A	D	P	C	T	I	L	S	Z	A
I	H	U	K	T	Y	Q	P	F	S	C	I	C	Q	T	R	K	L	A	U	Y	E	N	B	C	V
T	S	T	D	N	C	F	O	D	V	Y	F	T	E	T	Q	A	X	R	D	N	K	H	J	N	M
I	A	S	E	H	I	S	T	O	R	Y	D	D	G	V	D	G	U	D	T	X	D	I	C	T	L
D	U	I	L	M	A	S	C	U	I	L	C	O	E	C	C	Y	C	I	K	L	O	P	E	A	E
E	D	R	Q	W	L	K	Y	O	T	A	S	N	J	M	I	U	N	Z	U	T	L	K	C	D	K
E	N	B	Z	A	L	U	C	E	S	P	C	A	O	R	P	E	J	E	R	O	S	I	G	V	O
T	U	A	B	L	E	T	N	E	A	E	B	R	H	D	S	K	L	O	P	Y	D	S	C	E	O
U	C	L	P	D	I	R	E	C	T	O	R	Y	A	O	U	E	D	J	E	O	N	R	A	G	B
T	E	L	P	O	N	Y	F	B	D	A	S	J	J	T	B	E	K	L	I	S	F	K	R	D	N
A	S	R	O	O	E	M	F	N	I	D	D	E	C	O	N	C	Y	R	L	O	P	E	A	D	R
T	O	Z	A	G	X	N	S	Y	R	J	D	I	R	E	C	Y	E	H	E	I	I	G	O	I	O
S	E	G	A	L	F	O	R	M	S	S	S	E	C	U	N	P	U	M	A	K	L	P	G	F	H

CITED CASE, CITING CASES, GOOD LAW, SHEPARDIZE, and **STATUTE EDITION.**

Chapter 13

Computerized Legal Research

CHAPTER OBJECTIVES

After reading this chapter, you should be able to:

- Understand the use of microforms in legal research.

- Understand the use of floppy disks and CD-ROMs in legal research.

- Understand the use of video and sound recordings in legal research.

- Use the Westlaw and LexisNexis Web sites as resources.

- Understand strategies for conducting legal research on the Internet.

Due to rapidly changing technology, many methods for conducting legal research are now available to the researcher. While it is important to understand how to use the various "old-school" legal resources available, because of cost, lack of space, and expense, most law firms today are using virtual libraries as opposed to actual books. Therefore, it is important for the legal researcher to be familiar with those elements that constitute a virtual library.

MICROFORMS

Computer-modem technology is not the only way that technology has been used to aid in the search of legal materials. When law books began to overflow their shelves, lawyers, librarians, and other law office managers began to explore ways of solving the problem. Firms renting space by the foot in expensive downtown office buildings were particularly interested in cutting overhead by reducing the amount of space taken up by their books. In addition, many libraries were running out of shelf room as the number of published volumes grew.

microform
A record of images in a reduced format on film.

To respond to these concerns, many libraries and publishers began to utilize **microforms.** Microforms are images that are recorded in a greatly reduced form on rolls or sheets of film. They are usually viewed on a device that looks like a computer screen, which is attached to a printer so material can be printed from the film.

Microforms are a common repository of the briefs and records of federal and state appellate courts, as well as governmental documents and records. More than half of the documents published by the Government Printing Office are available in microform. Check with your local law library to find out which microforms are available there.

microfilm
A film bearing a photographic record on a reduced scale.

Microforms are typically of three types: microfilm, microfiche and ultrafiche. **Microfilm** is reels or cassettes of film that contain miniature pictures of printed pages. The film comes in two sizes: 16 and 35 millimeters. Microfilm is not usually used for legal information. However, the legal researcher may encounter microfilm when dealing with governmental records, bank

Case Fact Pattern

Recently, with the demise of companies such as Enron and Arthur Anderson, Congress enacted the Sarbanes-Oxley Act of 2002. Your firm is handling a large corporate client that is thinking about taking the company public. The attorney assigned to service this client has asked you to research the requirements of corporate executives under Sarbanes-Oxley and the trends in the industry regarding executive compliance under this Act.

records, and other documentation that are nonlegal in nature. Some public libraries will record old books and journals on microfilm, which is read on a microfilm reader that usually has printer capabilities as well. Adequate microform readers have since been developed, but they remain bulky and inconvenient. Space is a more important consideration than ever, but microforms are not frequently used outside of library research.

microfiche
A sheet of microfilm containing rows of images that are recorded pages of printed matter.

Microfiche are another type of microform that the researcher may encounter. They are thin transparent sheets that can hold approximately 400 pages of images, which are usually arranged in a grid pattern. Microfiche are not usually used for legal documents; however, a researcher may run into this type of microform at a library, which may use microfiche to record their card catalogs. In addition, Lexis publishes the *Congressional Bills, Resolutions & Laws on Microfiche*. This publication is used to compile legislative history and provides a method for the researcher to obtain copies of bills and their amendments. The *Federal Register* and the *Code of Federal Regulations* are also available on microfiche. Microfiche are viewed on a reader. The microfiche sheet is placed into the reader and viewed on a screen.

ultrafiche
Sheets of microfiche that can hold up to 1,800 images per sheet.

Ultrafiche is like microfiche, except that it can hold many more images than microfiche. A sheet of ultrafiche can contain up to 1,800 pages of text on one sheet. Viewing ultrafiche is done in the same manner that one would view microfiche—on a reader—and the sheets are the same size as those of microfiche. The researcher could encounter ultrafiche when looking at some of the West publications, which includes as "Ultra Fiche Edition" of the National Reporter System.

SOUND RECORDINGS AND VIDEOS

The legal researcher may encounter sound recordings when utilizing CD-ROMs used to record seminars, continuing education programs, and other secondary sources of information. Video-tapes are sometimes used by firms to videotape deposition testimony, make presentations to clients, and to provide basic information to clients regarding trial processes and deposition procedures. Videotapes are a convenient method of conveying basic information.

Recent uses of videotapes can be seen in trial evidence and testimony. The beating of Rodney King in Los Angeles was caught on videotape and played not only in the media but at the trial of the officers who faced charges for violating Mr. King's civil rights. Sound recordings were also used during the murder trial of Scott Peterson who was accused of killing his wife and unborn child. The police worked with Mr. Peterson's then girlfriend, Amber Frey, to record telephone conversations between her and Mr. Peterson that were later used at trial to convict him of the murders.

CD-ROM

CD-ROM
Compact disks with read-only memory that can store over 200,000 pages of text.

A **CD-ROM** can contain over 200,000 pages of text on one disc. Because of this, many legal publishers now produce numerous books and treatises on CD-ROMs, thus saving space for their customers. If the materials need to be updated, the publisher simply provides updated materials on CD-ROM, or replacement CDs are available with the updated information. CDs can be used with laptop computers and enable the legal researcher to continue their work while traveling or from the comfort of their home.

Many volumes of text are available on CD-ROM. For example, in 1988, West began publishing "CD-ROM Libraries," including *Bankruptcy Library, Delaware Corporation Law Library, Federal Civil Practice Library, Government Contracts Library,* and the *Federal Tax*

Library, this last entry containing the Bureau of National Affairs's (BNA) *Tax Management* portfolios. In 1990, Martindale-Hubbell announced the *Martindale-Hubbell Law Directory on CD-ROM.* The Michie Company published *New Mexico Statutes Annotated* on CD-ROM, and in 1991, it released the *Code of Virginia* on CD-ROM. In 1991, Matthew Bender & Co. Inc. announced the publication of its "Search Master" compact disk libraries, including *Collier Bankruptcy, Intellectual Property, Business Law, Federal Practice, Tax, Personal Injury, California Practice,* and *Texas Practice.* Check with your legal librarian about which volumes are available on CD-ROM.

COMPUTER-ASSISTED LEGAL RESEARCH

Computerized research has become a critical part of legal research due to its speed, the quantity of material that can be searched at one time, and the efficiency and variety of resources available to the researcher.

Two major computer-assisted research services are used by many legal professionals: Lexis-Nexis and Westlaw. Both systems are adequate to conduct legal research, and which system to use is a matter of personal preference. Both services have thousands of **databases** available to the researcher. These databases include cases, statutes, constitutions, administrative regulations, and other legal authorities and references a researcher may need.

database
A collection of information used in computer systems to provide access to related fields of interest.

Both LexisNexis and Westlaw add materials and update their databases continually. These services can be accessed through the Internet. The services are fee-based, meaning a fee is charged for each minute spent online. The researcher needs to be cognizant of the cost a research project may incur while using these databases. Many clients may not want to spend money for such research. When using these types of services, it behooves the researcher to be as efficient as possible with their search in order to keep costs down. Some law firms and lawyers have negotiated contracts with these services to pay a flat monthly fee so as to conduct computer-assisted legal research without worry of costs.

LexisNexis

LexisNexis was the first computerized legal research service, and its database contains over three billion documents. The LexisNexis database is organized into topics called "libraries." For example, the library entitled "GENFED" refers to documents that relate to general federal issues. Within each library are files. For instance, in the "GENFED" library you will find files for the United State Supreme Court cases, the *Federal Register,* and the CFR.

LexisNexis also provides current resources to the researcher. During the O.J. Simpson trial, the daily court proceedings were posted on LexisNexis as they were produced, thus enabling a researcher to obtain access to the legal documentation as fast as possible. Public records, court filings, and real estate records can also be accessed using LexisNexis. If the researcher wants to know if a particular plaintiff or defendant has been involved in prior litigation, they can search the court filings by the party's name and locate any past cases that may have been filed in a particular court involving that party.

LexisNexis is a subscription service, meaning that in order to access it, the researcher must pay a fee. LexisNexis can be accessed via the Internet by going to http://www.lexis.com. LexisNexis also enables the researcher to type in a client number associated with a particular case, allowing the researcher to keep track of the computerized legal research charges associated with the client's specific case. On the home page of the LexisNexis screen, the researcher can do the following:

- The Search icon enables the researcher to review sources like federal and state authorities, public records, and other secondary sources of information.
- The Search Advisor icon enables the researcher to review an area of the law and locate cases by legal issue or topic.
- The Get Document icon allows the researcher to obtain a document quickly when the researcher knows the case citation, statute, or regulation.
- The Check Citation icon does just as its name implies—it enables the researcher to shepardize primary authorities.

RESEARCH THIS!

Visit the Web site for both LexisNexis (http://www.lexis.com) and Westlaw (http://www.westlaw.com) and summarize their features.

Many other documents and business records are available through the LexisNexis company and can be used online.

Westlaw

Westlaw is very similar to LexisNexis in the materials available to the researcher, how they are organized, and the search method available. Westlaw is also a subscription service, so fees are associated with its use. It is composed of approximately 15,000 databases, over 6,000 news and business publications, and more than a billion public records, all of which are available to the researcher. The databases contained in Westlaw are arranged in files similar to that used by LexisNexis. For example, the database entitled Federal Materials contains federal case and statute materials. Like LexisNexis, the researcher can use the Find Document icon to quickly obtain a document if the citation to the case, statute, or regulation is already known. Westlaw can be found on the Internet at http://www.westlaw.com. The one feature Westlaw uses that LexisNexis does not is the key number system. Because Westlaw is a part of the Thomson/West publishing empire, it provides the key number system as a way of navigating through documentation, just as the key numbering system is used to navigate through its hardcover publications.

Internet

Numerous legal resources are available to the researcher via the Internet. Many of the sources can be accessed for free, while some are available for a fee. Such Internet material can be had 24 hours a day, seven days a week for the convenience of the researcher. Besides providing access to public documentation, the Internet also offers access to sample briefs, memorandum, and other documents of interest to the researcher. In addition to legal resources, the Internet provides access to nonlegal documentation and information to assist the researcher. Internet research should be used to complement other research techniques employed, such as traditional legal research and computer-assisted legal research services.

CYBER TRIP

The Internet offers numerous Web sites containing legal information useful for researchers. The following lists some of those available:

- www.findlaw.com
- www.hg .org
- www.law.emory.edu
- www.jmls.edy/cyber/index
- www.patents.com
- www.legalcounsel.com/resource.htm
- www.ncsc.dni.us/courts/sitets/lawsites
- www.ncsc.dni.us/court/sites/libs.htm
- www.abanet.org
- www.lcweb.loc.gov/homepage/lchp.html
- www.uspto.gov
- www.whitehouse.gov
- www.senate.gov
- www.house.gov

- www.un.org
- www.fedworld.gov
- www.uscourts.gov
- www.ucab.uscourts.gov
- www.martindale.com
- www.law.com
- www.law.cornell.edu
- www.lawguru.com
- www ll.georgetown.edu
- www.washlaw.edu
- www.ilrg.com
- www.catalaw.com
- http://megalaw.com

Eye on Ethics

While the Internet is a terrific research tool, remember that just about anyone can post just about anything to the Internet. As such, the source of some information may be suspect. Always try to verify your Internet research through reliable sources. Failure to do so could lead you to cite information that is incorrect, inaccurate, or libelous.

SEARCH METHODS

No matter what material you are searching through, the search method used for that material is very similar. Some of the main methods for conducting computer-assisted legal research are described next.

Full-Text Searching

One of the advantages of computer-assisted legal research is that it will allow you to search the entire text of a document to find information you are looking for. In other words, the researcher is not searching an index, but rather the document itself. In a full-text search, the researcher tells the computer which words or combination of words to look for in a document and the full-text search locates those words in the document and identifies them. Two ways are typically employed to conduct a search: Boolean and Natural Language.

Boolean

connector
Words such as "and" or "or" used in a search to demonstrate the relationship between key words or terms.

query
A string of key terms or words used in a computer search.

Boolean is a special type of logic used in computer searches that employs symbols, word phrases, and numbers rather than plain English in order to conduct a search. The searches are conducted by using words called **connectors.** The most commonly used connectors are the words "and" and "or." When performing a Boolean search, you must first formulate a **query** composed of possible words contained in a case under the topic you are searching. For instance, if you were searching for a case dealing with police brutality, you would type the word "police" and join it with the word "and" and then the word "brutality." This type of query would instruct the computer to search for documents containing both the words "police" and "brutality." "And" and "or" are not the only connectors that can be used. When using LexisNexis or Westlaw, you can construct a query that will look for certain words in the same sentence, in the same paragraph, or within a certain number of words from each other. For example, you might type "police within five words of brutality." This search would search the text for every instance that the word "police" shows up within five words of "brutality."

Boolean searches also enable the researcher to search for variations of words without typing in each and every variation of that word. You can do this with two particular characters: "*" and "!". The asterisk is known as a universal character and can be used in place of a character in a word. This tells the computer to look for variations of that word as well. For example, if the researcher types the word "m*n", the computer will search for both the words "man" and "men." The exclamation mark is known as a root extender and is used at the end of the word to enable the researcher to hunt for variations of the word that end differently. For instance, if you type in the word "anal!", the computer will search for words such as "analysis," "analyze," and "analyst."

Natural Language or Plain English

Boolean search techniques can be awkward and difficult for researchers unaccustomed to them. Therefore, LexisNexis, Westlaw, and the Internet allow the researcher to search in natural language or plain English as well. Natural language searches enable the researcher to forget about connectors and simply type a search query in plain English. The computer then locates documents containing the words in the natural language search. Natural language searches are particularly helpful when the researcher is looking for broad concepts.

Before You Search

Before beginning your research, it's important you be prepared, especially if you are searching on a fee-based service. Performing the following steps can help you prepare for your search.

- It is critical to make sure you completely understand your research assignment. It could be a waste of time and money should you spend hours researching the wrong topic.
- Review all the facts of the assignment before beginning your research.
- Identify all key facts and legal issues. Create the vocabulary lists that were suggested previously.
- Consider variations of the words and terms you wish to search.
- Look at the relationship between words, and try searches using these relationships.
- Develop search queries in advance.
- Determine the relevant legal resources that might be the best sources for information prior to beginning your search.

If you prepare your research assignment in advance, your search will be conducted more efficiently and effectively.

A Day in the Life

Recently, there has been an influx of regulations for corporate officers as a result of Enron. Conduct a search on the Internet regarding the Sarbane-Oxley requirements for corporate executives. You will find that, in the wake of Enron, one of the requirements now is that corporate executives must sign-off and certify the company's financial statements.

Summary

Computer-modem technology is not the only way that technology has been used to aid in the search of legal materials. When law books began to overflow their shelves, lawyers, librarians, and other law office managers began to explore ways to solve the problem. Firms renting space by the foot in expensive downtown office buildings were particularly interested in cutting overhead by reducing the amount of space taken up by their books. In addition, many libraries were running out of shelf space as the number of published volumes grew. To respond to these concerns, many libraries and publishers began to utilize microforms. Microforms are images recorded in greatly reduced form on rolls or sheets of film. Microforms are usually viewed on a device that looks like a computer screen, which is attached to a printer so material can be printed from the film.

A CD-ROM can contain over 200,000 pages of text on one disc. Because of this, many legal publishers now produce numerous books and treatises on CD-ROMs, thus saving space for their customers. If the materials need to be updated, the publisher simply provides updated materials on CD-ROM, or replacement CDs are available with the updated information. CDs can be used with laptop computers and enable the legal researcher to continue their work while traveling or from the comfort of their home.

LexisNexis was the first computerized legal research service, and its database contains over three billion documents. The LexisNexis database is organized into topics called "libraries." For example, the library entitled "GENFED" refers to documents that relate to general federal issues. Within each library are files. For instance, in the "GENFED" library you will find files for the United State Supreme Court cases, the *Federal Register,* and the CFR.

Westlaw is very similar to LexisNexis in the materials offered to the researcher, how they are organized, and the search method available. Westlaw is also a subscription service and there are fees associated with its use. It is composed of approximately 15,000 databases, over 6,000 news and business publications, and more than a billion public records, all of which are available to the researcher. The databases contained in Westlaw are arranged in files similar to those used by LexisNexis.

One of the advantages of computer-assisted legal research is that it allows you to search the entire text of a document to find information you are looking for. In other words, the researcher is not searching an index, but rather searching the document itself. In a full-text search, the researcher tells the computer which words, or combination of words, to look for in a document, and the full-text search will locate those words in the document and identify them.

Boolean is a special type of logic used in computer searches that uses symbols, word phrases, and numbers rather than plain English to conduct the search. The searches are conducted by using words called connectors. The most commonly used connectors are the words "and" and "or." When using a Boolean search, you must first formulate a query composed of words you believe might be contained in a case concerning the topic you are searching.

Boolean search techniques can be awkward and difficult for researchers unaccustomed to them. Therefore, LexisNexis, Westlaw, and the Internet allow the searcher to use natural language or plain English. Natural language searches enable the researcher to forget about connectors and simply type a search query in plain English. The computer then locates documents containing the words in the natural language search. Natural language searches are particularly helpful when the researcher is looking for broad concepts.

Key Terms

CD-ROM   180
connectors   183
database   181
microfiche   180

microfilm   179
microform   179
query   183
ultrafiche   180

Review Questions

1. What is computer-assisted legal research?
2. How much data can be held on a CD-ROM?
3. Where might you encounter data on a microfiche?
4. What types of materials can be found on LexisNexis?
5. What types of materials can be found on Westlaw?
6. What is the difference between LexisNexis and Westlaw?
7. What is a connector?
8. What is a Boolean search?
9. What is a natural language search?
10. When would it be best to use the Internet to conduct a search?

Exercises

1. Visit Web sites for LexisNexis, Westlaw, and www.findlaw.com. Look at the materials and describe the similarities and differences between them.
2. Go to www.uscourts.gov and find the information related to the United States Bankruptcy Courts. What is the difference between Chapter 7 and Chapter 13 bankruptcy?
3. Go to www.law.cornell.edu and find the Uniform Commercial Code. Describe what the Uniform Commercial Code covers.

Vocabulary Builders

Find and circle the following in the subsequent word search puzzle. The terms may appear up, down, sideways, or diagonal, and forward or backward, ignoring any spaces in phrases.

P	Z	A	B	D	Q	R	T	R	E	A	T	I	S	E	O	X	H	H	B	B	W	Q	U	S	H
R	E	I	B	P	R	N	I	C	Z	B	V	Y	H	U	S	Y	D	I	C	T	P	B	A	A	E
A	E	E	Y	C	Y	D	D	O	B	Q	R	D	S	L	N	W	V	I	D	S	Q	I	L	M	P
C	I	O	J	U	C	I	E	T	X	E	A	I	M	T	E	A	D	I	C	T	I	L	S	Z	A
T	H	U	K	T	Y	Q	P	F	S	T	I	C	Q	R	R	K	L	I	U	Y	E	N	B	C	V
I	S	T	D	N	C	F	O	D	A	Y	F	T	V	A	Q	A	X	F	D	N	K	H	J	N	M
C	M	D	S	E	B	N	L	B	E	C	D	E	G	F	D	G	U	E	T	X	D	I	C	T	I
E	U	I	L	M	A	S	A	U	I	L	R	O	E	I	C	Y	C	M	K	L	O	P	E	A	C
B	D	R	Q	E	L	S	Y	O	T	W	S	N	J	C	I	U	N	L	U	T	L	K	C	D	R
O	N	B	Z	U	E	U	C	E	A	P	C	A	O	H	P	E	J	I	R	O	S	I	G	V	O
O	U	A	B	A	E	T	N	L	A	E	B	R	H	E	S	K	L	F	P	Y	D	S	C	E	F
K	C	L	P	T	I	R	E	C	T	O	R	Y	A	O	U	E	D	O	E	O	N	R	A	G	I
S	E	L	P	S	N	Y	Y	B	D	A	S	J	J	T	B	E	K	R	I	S	F	K	R	D	C
R	S	R	O	E	E	M	F	N	I	D	D	E	C	O	N	N	E	C	T	O	R	S	A	D	H
O	O	Z	A	R	X	N	S	Y	R	J	D	I	R	E	C	Y	E	I	E	I	I	G	O	I	E
M	I	C	R	O	F	O	R	M	S	S	S	E	C	U	N	P	U	M	A	K	L	P	G	F	H

CONNECTORS, DATABASE, MICROFICHE, MICROFILM, MICROFORM, QUERY, and **ULTRAFICHE.**

Appendix

THE CONSTITUTION OF THE UNITED STATES: A TRANSCRIPTION

We the People of the United States, in Order to form a more perfect Union, establish Justice, insure domestic Tranquility, provide for the common defence, promote the general Welfare, and secure the Blessings of Liberty to ourselves and our Posterity, do ordain and establish this Constitution for the United States of America.

ARTICLE. I.

Section. 1.

All legislative Powers herein granted shall be vested in a Congress of the United States, which shall consist of a Senate and House of Representatives.

Section. 2.

The House of Representatives shall be composed of Members chosen every second Year by the People of the several States, and the Electors in each State shall have the Qualifications requisite for Electors of the most numerous Branch of the State Legislature.

No Person shall be a Representative who shall not have attained to the Age of twenty five Years, and been seven Years a Citizen of the United States, and who shall not, when elected, be an Inhabitant of that State in which he shall be chosen.

Representatives and direct Taxes shall be apportioned among the several States which may be included within this Union, according to their respective Numbers, which shall be determined by adding to the whole Number of free Persons, including those bound to Service for a Term of Years, and excluding Indians not taxed, three fifths of all other Persons. The actual Enumeration shall be made within three Years after the first Meeting of the Congress of the United States, and within every subsequent Term of ten Years, in such Manner as they shall by Law direct. The Number of Representatives shall not exceed one for every thirty Thousand, but each State shall have at Least one Representative; and until such enumeration shall be made, the State of New Hampshire shall be entitled to chuse three, Massachusetts eight, Rhode Island and Providence Plantations one, Connecticut five, New-York six, New Jersey four, Pennsylvania eight, Delaware one, Maryland six, Virginia ten, North Carolina five, South Carolina five, and Georgia three.

When vacancies happen in the Representation from any State, the Executive Authority thereof shall issue Writs of Election to fill such Vacancies.

The House of Representatives shall chuse their Speaker and other Officers; and shall have the sole Power of Impeachment.

Section. 3.

The Senate of the United States shall be composed of two Senators from each State, chosen by the Legislature thereof for six Years; and each Senator shall have one Vote.

Immediately after they shall be assembled in Consequence of the first Election, they shall be divided as equally as may be into three Classes. The Seats of the Senators of the first Class shall be vacated at the Expiration of the second Year, of the second Class at the Expiration of the fourth Year, and of the third Class at the Expiration of the sixth Year, so that one third may be chosen every second Year; and if Vacancies happen by Resignation, or otherwise, during the Recess of the Legislature of any State, the Executive thereof may make temporary Appointments until the next Meeting of the Legislature, which shall then fill such Vacancies.

No Person shall be a Senator who shall not have attained to the Age of thirty Years, and been nine Years a Citizen of the United States, and who shall not, when elected, be an Inhabitant of that State for which he shall be chosen.

The Vice President of the United States shall be President of the Senate, but shall have no Vote, unless they be equally divided.

The Senate shall chuse their other Officers, and also a President pro tempore, in the Absence of the Vice President, or when he shall exercise the Office of President of the United States.

The Senate shall have the sole Power to try all Impeachments. When sitting for that Purpose, they shall be on Oath or Affirmation. When the President of the United States is tried, the Chief Justice shall preside: And no Person shall be convicted without the Concurrence of two thirds of the Members present.

Judgment in Cases of Impeachment shall not extend further than to removal from Office, and disqualification to hold and enjoy any Office of honor, Trust or Profit under the United States: but the Party convicted shall nevertheless be liable and subject to Indictment, Trial, Judgment and Punishment, according to Law.

Section. 4.

The Times, Places and Manner of holding Elections for Senators and Representatives, shall be prescribed in each State by the Legislature thereof; but the Congress may at any time by Law make or alter such Regulations, except as to the Places of chusing Senators.

The Congress shall assemble at least once in every Year, and such Meeting shall be on the first Monday in December, unless they shall by Law appoint a different Day.

Section. 5.

Each House shall be the Judge of the Elections, Returns and Qualifications of its own Members, and a Majority of each shall constitute a Quorum to do Business; but a smaller Number may adjourn from day to day, and may be authorized to compel the Attendance of absent Members, in such Manner, and under such Penalties as each House may provide.

Each House may determine the Rules of its Proceedings, punish its Members for disorderly Behaviour, and, with the Concurrence of two thirds, expel a Member.

Each House shall keep a Journal of its Proceedings, and from time to time publish the same, excepting such Parts as may in their Judgment require Secrecy; and the Yeas and Nays of the Members of either House on any question shall, at the Desire of one fifth of those Present, be entered on the Journal.

Neither House, during the Session of Congress, shall, without the Consent of the other, adjourn for more than three days, nor to any other Place than that in which the two Houses shall be sitting.

Section. 6.

The Senators and Representatives shall receive a Compensation for their Services, to be ascertained by Law, and paid out of the Treasury of the United States. They shall in all Cases, except Treason, Felony and Breach of the Peace, be privileged from Arrest during their Attendance at the Session of their respective Houses, and in going to and returning from the same; and for any Speech or Debate in either House, they shall not be questioned in any other Place.

No Senator or Representative shall, during the Time for which he was elected, be appointed to any civil Office under the Authority of the United States, which shall have been created, or the Emoluments whereof shall have been encreased during such time; and no Person holding any Office under the United States, shall be a Member of either House during his Continuance in Office.

Section. 7.

All Bills for raising Revenue shall originate in the House of Representatives; but the Senate may propose or concur with Amendments as on other Bills.

Every Bill which shall have passed the House of Representatives and the Senate, shall, before it become a Law, be presented to the President of the United States: If he approve he shall sign it, but if not he shall return it, with his Objections to that House in which it shall have originated, who shall enter the Objections at large on their Journal, and proceed to reconsider it. If after such

Reconsideration two thirds of that House shall agree to pass the Bill, it shall be sent, together with the Objections, to the other House, by which it shall likewise be reconsidered, and if approved by two thirds of that House, it shall become a Law. But in all such Cases the Votes of both Houses shall be determined by yeas and Nays, and the Names of the Persons voting for and against the Bill shall be entered on the Journal of each House respectively. If any Bill shall not be returned by the President within ten Days (Sundays excepted) after it shall have been presented to him, the Same shall be a Law, in like Manner as if he had signed it, unless the Congress by their Adjournment prevent its Return, in which Case it shall not be a Law.

Every Order, Resolution, or Vote to which the Concurrence of the Senate and House of Representatives may be necessary (except on a question of Adjournment) shall be presented to the President of the United States; and before the Same shall take Effect, shall be approved by him, or being disapproved by him, shall be repassed by two thirds of the Senate and House of Representatives, according to the Rules and Limitations prescribed in the Case of a Bill.

Section. 8.

The Congress shall have Power To lay and collect Taxes, Duties, Imposts and Excises, to pay the Debts and provide for the common Defence and general Welfare of the United States; but all Duties, Imposts and Excises shall be uniform throughout the United States;

To borrow Money on the credit of the United States;

To regulate Commerce with foreign Nations, and among the several States, and with the Indian Tribes;

To establish an uniform Rule of Naturalization, and uniform Laws on the subject of Bankruptcies throughout the United States;

To coin Money, regulate the Value thereof, and of foreign Coin, and fix the Standard of Weights and Measures;

To provide for the Punishment of counterfeiting the Securities and current Coin of the United States;

To establish Post Offices and post Roads;

To promote the Progress of Science and useful Arts, by securing for limited Times to Authors and Inventors the exclusive Right to their respective Writings and Discoveries;

To constitute Tribunals inferior to the supreme Court;

To define and punish Piracies and Felonies committed on the high Seas, and Offences against the Law of Nations;

To declare War, grant Letters of Marque and Reprisal, and make Rules concerning Captures on Land and Water;

To raise and support Armies, but no Appropriation of Money to that Use shall be for a longer Term than two Years;

To provide and maintain a Navy;

To make Rules for the Government and Regulation of the land and naval Forces;

To provide for calling forth the Militia to execute the Laws of the Union, suppress Insurrections and repel Invasions;

To provide for organizing, arming, and disciplining, the Militia, and for governing such Part of them as may be employed in the Service of the United States, reserving to the States respectively, the Appointment of the Officers, and the Authority of training the Militia according to the discipline prescribed by Congress;

To exercise exclusive Legislation in all Cases whatsoever, over such District (not exceeding ten Miles square) as may, by Cession of particular States, and the Acceptance of Congress, become the Seat of the Government of the United States, and to exercise like Authority over all Places purchased by the Consent of the Legislature of the State in which the Same shall be, for the Erection of Forts, Magazines, Arsenals, dock-Yards, and other needful Buildings;–And

To make all Laws which shall be necessary and proper for carrying into Execution the foregoing Powers, and all other Powers vested by this Constitution in the Government of the United States, or in any Department or Officer thereof.

Section. 9.

The Migration or Importation of such Persons as any of the States now existing shall think proper to admit, shall not be prohibited by the Congress prior to the Year one thousand eight hundred and eight, but a Tax or duty may be imposed on such Importation, not exceeding ten dollars for each Person.

The Privilege of the Writ of Habeas Corpus shall not be suspended, unless when in Cases of Rebellion or Invasion the public Safety may require it.

No Bill of Attainder or ex post facto Law shall be passed.

No Capitation, or other direct, Tax shall be laid, unless in Proportion to the Census or enumeration herein before directed to be taken.

No Tax or Duty shall be laid on Articles exported from any State.

No Preference shall be given by any Regulation of Commerce or Revenue to the Ports of one State over those of another; nor shall Vessels bound to, or from, one State, be obliged to enter, clear, or pay Duties in another.

No Money shall be drawn from the Treasury, but in Consequence of Appropriations made by Law; and a regular Statement and Account of the Receipts and Expenditures of all public Money shall be published from time to time.

No Title of Nobility shall be granted by the United States: And no Person holding any Office of Profit or Trust under them, shall, without the Consent of the Congress, accept of any present, Emolument, Office, or Title, of any kind whatever, from any King, Prince, or foreign State.

Section. 10.

No State shall enter into any Treaty, Alliance, or Confederation; grant Letters of Marque and Reprisal; coin Money; emit Bills of Credit; make any Thing but gold and silver Coin a Tender in Payment of Debts; pass any Bill of Attainder, ex post facto Law, or Law impairing the Obligation of Contracts, or grant any Title of Nobility.

No State shall, without the Consent of the Congress, lay any Imposts or Duties on Imports or Exports, except what may be absolutely necessary for executing it's inspection Laws: and the net Produce of all Duties and Imposts, laid by any State on Imports or Exports, shall be for the Use of the Treasury of the United States; and all such Laws shall be subject to the Revision and Controul of the Congress.

No State shall, without the Consent of Congress, lay any Duty of Tonnage, keep Troops, or Ships of War in time of Peace, enter into any Agreement or Compact with another State, or with a foreign Power, or engage in War, unless actually invaded, or in such imminent Danger as will not admit of delay.

ARTICLE. II.

Section. 1.

The executive Power shall be vested in a President of the United States of America. He shall hold his Office during the Term of four Years, and, together with the Vice President, chosen for the same Term, be elected, as follows:

Each State shall appoint, in such Manner as the Legislature thereof may direct, a Number of Electors, equal to the whole Number of Senators and Representatives to which the State may be entitled in the Congress: but no Senator or Representative, or Person holding an Office of Trust or Profit under the United States, shall be appointed an Elector.

The Electors shall meet in their respective States, and vote by Ballot for two Persons, of whom one at least shall not be an Inhabitant of the same State with themselves. And they shall make a List of all the Persons voted for, and of the Number of Votes for each; which List they shall sign and certify, and transmit sealed to the Seat of the Government of the United States, directed to the President of the Senate. The President of the Senate shall, in the Presence of the Senate and House of Representatives, open all the Certificates, and the Votes shall then be counted. The Person having the greatest Number of Votes shall be the President, if such Number be a Majority of the whole Number of Electors appointed; and if there be more than one who have such Majority, and have an equal Number of Votes, then the House of Representatives shall immediately chuse by Ballot one of them for President; and if no Person have a Majority, then from the five highest on the List the said House shall in like Manner chuse the President. But in chusing the President, the Votes shall be taken by States, the Representation from each State having one Vote; A quorum for this purpose shall consist of a Member or Members from two thirds of the States, and a Majority of all the States shall be necessary to a Choice. In every Case, after the Choice of the President, the Person having the greatest Number of Votes of the Electors shall be the Vice President. But if there should remain two or more who have equal Votes, the Senate shall chuse from them by Ballot the Vice President.

The Congress may determine the Time of chusing the Electors, and the Day on which they shall give their Votes; which Day shall be the same throughout the United States.

No Person except a natural born Citizen, or a Citizen of the United States, at the time of the Adoption of this Constitution, shall be eligible to the Office of President; neither shall any Person be eligible to that Office who shall not have attained to the Age of thirty five Years, and been fourteen Years a Resident within the United States.

In Case of the Removal of the President from Office, or of his Death, Resignation, or Inability to discharge the Powers and Duties of the said Office, the Same shall devolve on the Vice President, and the Congress may by Law provide for the Case of Removal, Death, Resignation or Inability, both of the President and Vice President, declaring what Officer shall then act as President, and such Officer shall act accordingly, until the Disability be removed, or a President shall be elected.

The President shall, at stated Times, receive for his Services, a Compensation, which shall neither be increased nor diminished during the Period for which he shall have been elected, and he shall not receive within that Period any other Emolument from the United States, or any of them.

Before he enter on the Execution of his Office, he shall take the following Oath or Affirmation:–"I do solemnly swear (or affirm) that I will faithfully execute the Office of President of the United States, and will to the best of my Ability, preserve, protect and defend the Constitution of the United States."

Section. 2.

The President shall be Commander in Chief of the Army and Navy of the United States, and of the Militia of the several States, when called into the actual Service of the United States; he may require the Opinion, in writing, of the principal Officer in each of the executive Departments, upon any Subject relating to the Duties of their respective Offices, and he shall have Power to grant Reprieves and Pardons for Offences against the United States, except in Cases of Impeachment.

He shall have Power, by and with the Advice and Consent of the Senate, to make Treaties, provided two thirds of the Senators present concur; and he shall nominate, and by and with the Advice and Consent of the Senate, shall appoint Ambassadors, other public Ministers and Consuls, Judges of the supreme Court, and all other Officers of the United States, whose Appointments are not herein otherwise provided for, and which shall be established by Law: but the Congress may by Law vest the Appointment of such inferior Officers, as they think proper, in the President alone, in the Courts of Law, or in the Heads of Departments.

The President shall have Power to fill up all Vacancies that may happen during the Recess of the Senate, by granting Commissions which shall expire at the End of their next Session.

Section. 3.

He shall from time to time give to the Congress Information of the State of the Union, and recommend to their Consideration such Measures as he shall judge necessary and expedient; he may, on extraordinary Occasions, convene both Houses, or either of them, and in Case of Disagreement between them, with Respect to the Time of Adjournment, he may adjourn them to such Time as he shall think proper; he shall receive Ambassadors and other public Ministers; he shall take Care that the Laws be faithfully executed, and shall Commission all the Officers of the United States.

Section. 4.

The President, Vice President and all Civil Officers of the United States, shall be removed from Office on Impeachment for, and Conviction of, Treason, Bribery, or other high Crimes and Misdemeanors.

ARTICLE. III.

Section. 1.

The judicial Power of the United States shall be vested in one supreme Court, and in such inferior Courts as the Congress may from time to time ordain and establish. The Judges, both of the supreme and inferior Courts, shall hold their Offices during good Behaviour, and shall, at stated Times, receive for their Services a Compensation, which shall not be diminished during their Continuance in Office.

Section. 2.

The judicial Power shall extend to all Cases, in Law and Equity, arising under this Constitution, the Laws of the United States, and Treaties made, or which shall be made, under their Authority;–to all Cases affecting Ambassadors, other public Ministers and Consuls;–to all Cases of admiralty and maritime Jurisdiction;–to Controversies to which the United States shall be a Party;–to Controversies between two or more States;– between a State and Citizens of another State;–between Citizens of different States;–between Citizens of the same State claiming Lands under Grants of different States, and between a State, or the Citizens thereof, and foreign States, Citizens or Subjects.

In all Cases affecting Ambassadors, other public Ministers and Consuls, and those in which a State shall be Party, the supreme Court shall have original Jurisdiction. In all the other Cases before mentioned, the supreme Court shall have appellate Jurisdiction, both as to Law and Fact, with such Exceptions, and under such Regulations as the Congress shall make.

The Trial of all Crimes, except in Cases of Impeachment, shall be by Jury; and such Trial shall be held in the State where the said Crimes shall have been committed; but when not committed within any State, the Trial shall be at such Place or Places as the Congress may by Law have directed.

Section. 3.

Treason against the United States, shall consist only in levying War against them, or in adhering to their Enemies, giving them Aid and Comfort. No Person shall be convicted of Treason unless on the Testimony of two Witnesses to the same overt Act, or on Confession in open Court.

The Congress shall have Power to declare the Punishment of Treason, but no Attainder of Treason shall work Corruption of Blood, or Forfeiture except during the Life of the Person attainted.

ARTICLE. IV.

Section. 1.

Full Faith and Credit shall be given in each State to the public Acts, Records, and judicial Proceedings of every other State. And the Congress may by general Laws prescribe the Manner in which such Acts, Records and Proceedings shall be proved, and the Effect thereof.

Section. 2.

The Citizens of each State shall be entitled to all Privileges and Immunities of Citizens in the several States.

A Person charged in any State with Treason, Felony, or other Crime, who shall flee from Justice, and be found in another State, shall on Demand of the executive Authority of the State from which he fled, be delivered up, to be removed to the State having Jurisdiction of the Crime.

No Person held to Service or Labour in one State, under the Laws thereof, escaping into another, shall, in Consequence of any Law or Regulation therein, be discharged from such Service or Labour, but shall be delivered up on Claim of the Party to whom such Service or Labour may be due.

Section. 3.

New States may be admitted by the Congress into this Union; but no new State shall be formed or erected within the Jurisdiction of any other State; nor any State be formed by the Junction of two or more States, or Parts of States, without the Consent of the Legislatures of the States concerned as well as of the Congress.

The Congress shall have Power to dispose of and make all needful Rules and Regulations respecting the Territory or other Property belonging to the United States; and nothing in this Constitution shall be so construed as to Prejudice any Claims of the United States, or of any particular State.

Section. 4.

The United States shall guarantee to every State in this Union a Republican Form of Government, and shall protect each of them against Invasion; and on Application of the Legislature, or of the Executive (when the Legislature cannot be convened), against domestic Violence.

ARTICLE. V.

The Congress, whenever two thirds of both Houses shall deem it necessary, shall propose Amendments to this Constitution, or, on the Application of the Legislatures of two thirds of the several States, shall call a Convention for proposing Amendments, which, in either Case, shall be valid to all Intents and Purposes, as Part of this Constitution, when ratified by the Legislatures of three fourths of the several States, or by Conventions in three fourths thereof, as the one or the other Mode of Ratification may be proposed by the Congress; Provided that no Amendment which may be made prior to the Year One thousand eight hundred and eight shall in any Manner affect the first and fourth Clauses in the Ninth Section of the first Article; and that no State, without its Consent, shall be deprived of its equal Suffrage in the Senate.

ARTICLE. VI.

All Debts contracted and Engagements entered into, before the Adoption of this Constitution, shall be as valid against the United States under this Constitution, as under the Confederation.

This Constitution, and the Laws of the United States which shall be made in Pursuance thereof; and all Treaties made, or which shall be made, under the Authority of the United States, shall be the supreme Law of the Land; and the Judges in every State shall be bound thereby, any Thing in the Constitution or Laws of any State to the Contrary notwithstanding.

The Senators and Representatives before mentioned, and the Members of the several State Legislatures, and all executive and judicial Officers, both of the United States and of the several States, shall be bound by Oath or Affirmation, to support this Constitution; but no religious Test shall ever be required as a Qualification to any Office or public Trust under the United States.

ARTICLE. VII.

The Ratification of the Conventions of nine States, shall be sufficient for the Establishment of this Constitution between the States so ratifying the Same.

The Word, "the," being interlined between the seventh and eighth Lines of the first Page, the Word "Thirty" being partly written on an Erazure in the fifteenth Line of the first Page, The Words "is tried" being interlined between the thirty second and thirty third Lines of the first Page and the Word "the" being interlined between the forty third and forty fourth Lines of the second Page.

Attest William Jackson Secretary

Done in Convention by the Unanimous Consent of the States present the Seventeenth Day of September in the Year of our Lord one thousand seven hundred and Eighty seven and of the Independence of the United States of America the Twelfth In witness whereof We have hereunto subscribed our Names.

THE BILL OF RIGHTS: A TRANSCRIPTION

Note: The following text is a transcription of the first ten amendments to the Constitution in their original form. These amendments were ratified December 15, 1791, and form what is known as the "Bill of Rights."

AMENDMENT I [1791]

Congress shall make no law respecting an establishment of religion, or prohibiting the free exercise thereof; or abridging the freedom of speech, or of the press; or the right of the people peaceably to assemble, and to petition the Government for a redress of grievances.

AMENDMENT II [1791]

A well regulated Militia, being necessary to the security of a free State, the right of the people to keep and bear Arms, shall not be infringed.

AMENDMENT III [1791]

No Soldier shall, in time of peace be quartered in any house, without the consent of the Owner, nor in time of war, but in a manner to be prescribed by law.

AMENDMENT IV [1791]

The right of the people to be secure in their persons, houses, papers, and effects, against unreasonable searches and seizures, shall not be violated, and no Warrants shall issue, but upon probable cause, supported by Oath or affirmation, and particularly describing the place to be searched, and the persons or things to be seized.

AMENDMENT V [1791]

No person shall be held to answer for a capital, or otherwise infamous crime, unless on a presentment or indictment of a Grand Jury, except in cases arising in the land or naval forces, or in the Militia, when in actual service in time of War or public danger; nor shall any person be subject for the same offence to be twice put in jeopardy of life or limb; nor shall be compelled in any criminal case to be a witness against himself, nor be deprived of life, liberty, or property, without due process of law; nor shall private property be taken for public use, without just compensation.

AMENDMENT VI [1791]

In all criminal prosecutions, the accused shall enjoy the right to a speedy and public trial, by an impartial jury of the State and district wherein the crime shall have been committed, which district shall have been previously ascertained by law, and to be informed of the nature and cause of the accusation; to be confronted with the witnesses against him; to have compulsory process for obtaining witnesses in his favor, and to have the Assistance of Counsel for his defence.

AMENDMENT VII [1791]

In Suits at common law, where the value in controversy shall exceed twenty dollars, the right of trial by jury shall be preserved, and no fact tried by a jury, shall be otherwise re-examined in any Court of the United States, than according to the rules of the common law.

AMENDMENT VIII [1791]

Excessive bail shall not be required, nor excessive fines imposed, nor cruel and unusual punishments inflicted.

AMENDMENT IX [1791]

The enumeration in the Constitution, of certain rights, shall not be construed to deny or disparage others retained by the people.

AMENDMENT X [1791]

The powers not delegated to the United States by the Constitution, nor prohibited by it to the States, are reserved to the States respectively, or to the people.

Note: The capitalization and punctuation in this version is from the enrolled original of the Joint Resolution of Congress proposing the Bill of Rights, which is on permanent display in the Rotunda of the National Archives Building, Washington, D.C.

THE CONSTITUTION: AMENDMENTS 11–27

Constitutional Amendments 1–10 make up what is known as the Bill of Rights. Amendments 11–27 are listed next.

AMENDMENT XI [1795]

Note: Article III, section 2, of the Constitution was modified by Amendment 11.

The Judicial power of the United States shall not be construed to extend to any suit in law or equity, commenced or prosecuted against one of the United States by Citizens of another State, or by Citizens or Subjects of any Foreign State.

AMENDMENT XII [1804]

The Electors shall meet in their respective states and vote by ballot for President and Vice-President, one of whom, at least, shall not be an inhabitant of the same state with themselves; they shall name in their ballots the person voted for as President, and in distinct ballots the person voted for as Vice-President, and they shall make distinct lists of all persons voted for as President, and of all persons voted for as Vice-President, and of the number of votes for each, which lists they shall sign and certify, and transmit sealed to the seat of the government of the United States, directed to the President of the Senate; – the President of the Senate shall, in the presence of the Senate and House of Representatives, open all the certificates and the votes shall then be counted; – The person having the greatest number of votes for President, shall be the President, if such number be a majority of the whole number of Electors appointed; and if no person have such majority, then from the persons having the highest numbers not exceeding three on the list of those voted for as President, the House of Representatives shall choose immediately, by ballot, the President. But in choosing the President, the votes shall be taken by states, the representation from each state having one vote; a quorum for this purpose shall consist of a member or members from two-thirds of the states, and a majority of all the states shall be necessary to a choice. [And if the House of Representatives shall not choose a President whenever the right of choice shall devolve upon them, before the fourth day of March next following, then the Vice-President shall act as President, as in case of the death or other constitutional disability of the President. –]* The person having the greatest number of votes as Vice-President, shall be the Vice-President, if such number be a majority of the whole number of Electors appointed, and if no person have a majority, then from the two highest numbers on the list, the Senate shall choose the Vice-President; a quorum for the purpose shall consist of two-thirds of the whole number of Senators, and a majority of the whole number shall be necessary to a choice. But no person constitutionally ineligible to the office of President shall be eligible to that of Vice-President of the United States.

AMENDMENT XIII [1865]

Section 1. Neither slavery nor involuntary servitude, except as a punishment for crime whereof the party shall have been duly convicted, shall exist within the United States, or any place subject to their jurisdiction.

Section 2. Congress shall have power to enforce this article by appropriate legislation.

AMENDMENT XIV [1868]

Section 1. All persons born or naturalized in the United States, and subject to the jurisdiction thereof, are citizens of the United States and of the State wherein they reside. No State shall make or enforce any law which shall abridge the privileges or immunities of citizens of the United States; nor shall any State deprive any person of life, liberty, or property, without due process of law; nor deny to any person within its jurisdiction the equal protection of the laws.

Section 2. Representatives shall be apportioned among the several States according to their respective numbers, counting the whole number of persons in each State, excluding Indians not taxed. But when the right to vote at any election for the choice of electors for President and Vice-President of the United States, Representatives in Congress, the Executive and Judicial officers of a State, or the members of the Legislature thereof, is denied to any of the male inhabitants of such State, being twenty-one years of age,* and citizens of the United States, or in any way abridged, except for participation in rebellion, or other crime, the basis of representation therein shall be reduced in the proportion which the number of such male citizens shall bear to the whole number of male citizens twenty-one years of age in such State.

Section 3. No person shall be a Senator or Representative in Congress, or elector of President and Vice-President, or hold any office, civil or military, under the United States, or under any State, who, having previously taken an oath, as a member of Congress, or as an officer of the United States, or as a member of any State legislature, or as an executive or judicial officer of any State, to support the Constitution of the United States, shall have engaged in insurrection or rebellion against the same, or given aid or comfort to the enemies thereof. But Congress may by a vote of two-thirds of each House, remove such disability.

Section 4. The validity of the public debt of the United States, authorized by law, including debts incurred for payment of pensions and bounties for services in suppressing insurrection or rebellion, shall not be questioned. But neither the United States nor any State shall assume or pay any debt or obligation incurred in aid of insurrection or rebellion against the United States, or any claim for the loss or emancipation of any slave; but all such debts, obligations and claims shall be held illegal and void.

Section 5. The Congress shall have the power to enforce, by appropriate legislation, the provisions of this article.

AMENDMENT XV [1870]

Section 1. The right of citizens of the United States to vote shall not be denied or abridged by the United States or by any State on account of race, color, or previous condition of servitude.

Section 2. The Congress shall have the power to enforce this article by appropriate legislation.

AMENDMENT XVI [1913]

The Congress shall have power to lay and collect taxes on incomes, from whatever source derived, without apportionment among the several States, and without regard to any census or enumeration.

AMENDMENT XVII [1913]

The Senate of the United States shall be composed of two Senators from each State, elected by the people thereof, for six years; and each Senator shall have one vote. The electors in each State shall have the qualifications requisite for electors of the most numerous branch of the State legislatures.

When vacancies happen in the representation of any State in the Senate, the executive authority of such State shall issue writs of election to fill such vacancies: *Provided,* That the legislature of any State may empower the executive thereof to make temporary appointments until the people fill the vacancies by election as the legislature may direct.

This amendment shall not be so construed as to affect the election or term of any Senator chosen before it becomes valid as part of the Constitution.

AMENDMENT XVIII [1919]

[Repealed by Amendment 21]

Section 1. After one year from the ratification of this article the manufacture, sale, or transportation of intoxicating liquors within, the importation thereof into, or the exportation thereof from the United States and all territory subject to the jurisdiction thereof for beverage purposes is hereby prohibited.

Section 2. The Congress and the several States shall have concurrent power to enforce this article by appropriate legislation.

Section 3. This article shall be inoperative unless it shall have been ratified as an amendment to the Constitution by the legislatures of the several States, as provided in the Constitution, within seven years from the date of the submission hereof to the States by the Congress.

AMENDMENT XIX [1920]

The right of citizens of the United States to vote shall not be denied or abridged by the United States or by any State on account of sex.

Congress shall have power to enforce this article by appropriate legislation.

AMENDMENT XX [1933]

Section 1. The terms of the President and the Vice President shall end at noon on the 20th day of January, and the terms of Senators and Representatives at noon on the 3d day of January, of the years in which such terms would have ended if this article had not been ratified; and the terms of their successors shall then begin.

Section 2. The Congress shall assemble at least once in every year, and such meeting shall begin at noon on the 3d day of January, unless they shall by law appoint a different day.

Section 3. If, at the time fixed for the beginning of the term of the President, the President elect shall have died, the Vice President elect shall become President. If a President shall not have been chosen before the time fixed for the beginning of his term, or if the President elect shall have failed to qualify, then the Vice President elect shall act as President until a President shall have qualified; and the Congress may by law provide for the case wherein neither a President elect nor a Vice President shall have qualified, declaring who shall then act as President, or the manner in which one who is to act shall be selected, and such person shall act accordingly until a President or Vice President shall have qualified.

Section 4. The Congress may by law provide for the case of the death of any of the persons from whom the House of Representatives may choose a President whenever the right of choice shall have devolved upon them, and for the case of the death of any of the persons from whom the Senate may choose a Vice President whenever the right of choice shall have devolved upon them.

Section 5. Sections 1 and 2 shall take effect on the 15th day of October following the ratification of this article.

Section 6. This article shall be inoperative unless it shall have been ratified as an amendment to the Constitution by the legislatures of three-fourths of the several States within seven years from the date of its submission.

AMENDMENT XXI [1933]

Section 1. The eighteenth article of amendment to the Constitution of the United States is hereby repealed.

Section 2. The transportation or importation into any State, Territory, or Possession of the United States for delivery or use therein of intoxicating liquors, in violation of the laws thereof, is hereby prohibited.

Section 3. This article shall be inoperative unless it shall have been ratified as an amendment to the Constitution by conventions in the several States, as provided in the Constitution, within seven years from the date of the submission hereof to the States by the Congress.

AMENDMENT XXII [1951]

Section 1. No person shall be elected to the office of the President more than twice, and no person who has held the office of President, or acted as President, for more than two years of a term to which some other person was elected President shall be elected to the office of President more than once. But this Article shall not apply to any person holding the office of President when this Article was proposed by Congress, and shall not prevent any person who may be holding the office of President, or acting as President, during the term within which this Article becomes operative from holding the office of President or acting as President during the remainder of such term.

Section 2. This article shall be inoperative unless it shall have been ratified as an amendment to the Constitution by the legislatures of three-fourths of the several States within seven years from the date of its submission to the States by the Congress.

AMENDMENT XXIII [1961]

Section 1. The District constituting the seat of Government of the United States shall appoint in such manner as Congress may direct:

A number of electors of President and Vice President equal to the whole number of Senators and Representatives in Congress to which the District would be entitled if it were a State, but in no event more than the least populous State; they shall be in addition to those appointed by the States, but they shall be considered, for the purposes of the election of President and Vice President, to be electors appointed by a State; and they shall meet in the District and perform such duties as provided by the twelfth article of amendment.

Section 2. The Congress shall have power to enforce this article by appropriate legislation.

AMENDMENT XXIV [1964]

Section 1. The right of citizens of the United States to vote in any primary or other election for President or Vice President, for electors for President or Vice President, or for Senator or Representative in Congress, shall not be denied or abridged by the United States or any State by reason of failure to pay poll tax or other tax.

Section 2. The Congress shall have power to enforce this article by appropriate legislation.

AMENDMENT XXV [1967]

Section 1. In case of the removal of the President from office or of his death or resignation, the Vice President shall become President.

Section 2. Whenever there is a vacancy in the office of the Vice President, the President shall nominate a Vice President who shall take office upon confirmation by a majority vote of both Houses of Congress.

Section 3. Whenever the President transmits to the President pro tempore of the Senate and the Speaker of the House of Representatives his written declaration that he is unable to discharge the powers and duties of his office, and until he transmits to them a written declaration to the contrary, such powers and duties shall be discharged by the Vice President as Acting President.

Section 4. Whenever the Vice President and a majority of either the principal officers of the executive departments or of such other body as Congress may by law provide, transmit to the President pro tempore of the Senate and the Speaker of the House of Representatives their written declaration that the President is unable to discharge the powers and duties of his office, the Vice President shall immediately assume the powers and duties of the office as Acting President.

Thereafter, when the President transmits to the President pro tempore of the Senate and the Speaker of the House of Representatives his written declaration that no inability exists, he shall resume the powers and duties of his office unless the Vice President and a majority of either the principal officers of the executive department or of such other body as Congress may by law provide, transmit within four days to the President pro tempore of the Senate and the Speaker of the House of Representatives their written declaration that the President is unable to discharge the powers and duties of his office. Thereupon Congress shall decide the issue, assembling within forty-eight hours for that purpose if not in session. If the Congress, within twenty-one days after receipt of the latter written declaration, or, if Congress is not in session, within twenty-one days after Congress is required to assemble, determines by two-thirds vote of both Houses that the President is unable to discharge the powers and duties of his office, the Vice President shall continue to discharge the same as Acting President; otherwise, the President shall resume the powers and duties of his office.

AMENDMENT XXVI [1971]

Section 1. The right of citizens of the United States, who are eighteen years of age or older, to vote shall not be denied or abridged by the United States or by any State on account of age.
Section 2. The Congress shall have power to enforce this article by appropriate legislation.

AMENDMENT XXVII [1992]

No law, varying the compensation for the services of the Senators and Representatives, shall take effect, until an election of representatives shall have intervened.The Constitution of the United States: A Transcription

Glossary

A

act a bill considered and passed by one house of the Congress of the United States of America.

adjudication an awarding by judicial decision.

administrative agency a governmental body charged with administering and implementing particular legislation.

administrative codes processes and guidelines established under the particular administrative section that describe acceptable conduct for persons and situations under the control of the respective agency.

administrative decision the issuing of an order or determination by the administrative law judge adjudicating the issues at the hearing and explaining his or her reasoning behind the determination.

administrative law judge one who presides at an administrative hearing; with the power to administer oaths, take testimony, rule on questions of evidence, regulate the course of the proceedings, and make agency determinations of fact.

administrative order administrative acts having the force of law that are designed to clarify or implement a law or policy.

advance sheets softcover pamphlets containing the most recent cases.

affirm disposition in which the appellate court agrees with the trial court.

ALWD a legal citation resource, published by the Association of Legal Writing Directors, that contains local and state sources that may not be found in *The Bluebook*.

analogy an inference that if two or more things agree in some respects, they will probably agree in others.

annotate to note or mark up.

annotated code a code that provides, in addition to the text of the codified statutes, such information as cases that have construed the statute, law review articles that have discussed it, the procedural history of the statute, cross-references to superceded codifications, cross-references to related statutes, and other information.

annotated constitution a version of a constitution containing case summaries of how the courts have interpreted it.

annotation an in-depth analysis of a specific and important legal issue raised in the accompanying decision, together with an extensive survey of the way the issue is treated in various jurisdictions.

appellant the party filing the appeal.

appellee the prevailing party who will respond to the appellant's argument.

attorney general the chief law officer of the sovereign, who represents the sovereign in legal matters generally and gives advice and opinions to the heads of the government as requested.

B

bad law law that has been overruled and is no longer considered as precedent.

bar journal a legal periodical that is published by a local or national bar association.

bill a proposed permanent law.

Bill of Rights set forth the fundamental individual rights government and law function to preserve and protect; the first ten amendments to the Constitution of the United States.

binding authority another term for mandatory authority.

The Bluebook widely used legal citation resource, published by the Harvard Law Review Association, that is regularly revised and updated.

Bluebook style the type styles used in citations found in academic legal articles (always footnoted) as well as those citations found within some court documents.

brief a formal written argument presented to the court.

C

canned brief a preanalyzed summary or abstract of a legal case.

case at bar the actual lawsuit being heard in the court or that is at issue.

case history the history of how a case has been handled in subsequent cases.

case in point an example that is used to justify similar occurrences at a later time.

case law published court opinions of federal and state appellate courts; judge-created law in deciding cases, set forth in court opinions.

case of first impression a case in which no previous court decision with similar facts or legal issue has arisen before.

casebook a law school textbook containing a series of selected cases on each topic to be covered.

casenotes case summaries in the United States Code Service (U.S.C.S.).

cases a general term for actions, causes, suits, or controversies, at law or in equity, that are contested before a court of law.

CD-ROM compact disks with read-only memory that can store over 200,000 pages of text.

charter the documents that form a government. The fundamental law of a local government.

chronologically in a sequence arranged according to time.

citation or cite information about a legal source directing you to the volume and page in which the legal source appears.

citation style the manner in which a reference to legal authorities is communicated or abbreviated to the reader.

citation-based a dictionary that refers to legal authorities.

citations information about a legal source directing you to the volume and page in which the legal source appears.

citators a set of books which provide, through letter-form abbreviations or words, the subsequent judicial history and interpretation of reported decisions.

cite to read or refer to legal authorities, in an argument to a court or elsewhere, in support of propositions of law sought to be established.

cited case to read or refer to a particular case.

citing cases cases that all refer or reference a particular case.

code set of volumes that group statutes by subject matter and is well indexed in order to make the statutes more accessible for research purposes.

codification the process of collecting the permanent public statutes topically, adding amendments, and deleting expired, repealed, or superseded statutes.

common law judge-made law; the ruling in a judicial opinion.

concurrent resolution a proposed administrative (not legislative) statement of Congress.

concurring opinion an opinion in which a judge who agrees with the ultimate results wishes to apply different reasoning from that in the majority decision.

Congress a two-year period in which the legislature of the United States meets.

connector words such as "and" or "or" used in a search to demonstrate the relationship between key words or terms.

considered *dicta* opinions of a judge that do not embody the resolution or determination of the specific case before the court, but that may tend to show how a court may decide a case in the future if the facts were a bit different than the facts being heard in the case at bar.

constitution the written fundamental law of a sovereign, such as the Constitution of the United States.

constitutional law based on federal constitution and arising from interpretations of the intent and scope of constitutional provisions.

cross-references in an index, references to other entries.

D

database a collection of information used in computer systems to provide access to related fields of interest.

decision the formal written resolution of a case; it explains the legal and factual issues that were presented, the resolution of the case, and the law that was used in reaching the ruling.

decree to determine or order judicially.

defendant the party against whom a lawsuit is brought.

definitions a statement of the meaning of a word or word groups.

dicta statements made by the court in a case that is beyond what is necessary to reach the final decision.

dictionary a book containing words usually arranged alphabetically with information about their forms, pronunciation, function etymologies, meanings, and syntactical and idiomatic uses.

dictum the singular form of *dicta*.

digest a collection of all the headnotes from an associated series of volumes, arranged alphabetically by topic and by key number or summary of testimony with indexed references of a deposition.

digests or digest paragraphs a collection of all the head notes from an associated series of volumes, arranged alphabetically by volume or by key number or summary of testimony with indexed references of a deposition.

directory an alphabetical or classified list, especially of names and addresses.

dissenting opinion opinion in which a judge disagrees with the results reached by the majority; an opinion outlining the reasons for the dissent, which often critiques the majority and any concurring opinions.

docket number the number assigned to a case for its own administrative purposes.

E

enabling act a statute creating and/or empowering a local government or agency.

enactment the legislative process that results in the making of a statute.

engrossed bill the final, officially signed copy of an act.

enrolled bill a final, officially signed copy of a parchment of a bill that has passed both houses of the Congress of the United States of America.

entries in an index, words or phrases used to note key concepts, words, and phrases in the text indexed.

etymology the history of a linguistic form shown by tracing its development and relationship.

ex post facto literally "after the fact," referring to an act or fact occurring after some previous act of fact, and relating thereto.

executive the branch of government that enforces the law.

executive agreement a President's agreement with a foreign country that is not nation-binding.

executive department the branch of government charged with carrying out the laws enacted by the legislature.

executive order order issued by the U.S. president having the force of law but without going through the typical process for enacting legislation.

F

FAQ an acronym for "frequently asked question."

federalism balanced system of national and state government in the U.S. Constitution; the federal government has jurisdiction over all matters related equally to all citizens of all states, and the state governments have specific authority in matters affecting only the citizens of the respective state entity.

form books publications that contain complete or partial sample documents, often with sample factual situations and various alternative methods of stating that legal document.

G

good law law that is still in effect or valid and that can be cited as authority.

H

headnotes a key-numbered paragraph; an editorial feature in unofficial reporters that summarizes a single legal point in the court opinion.

holding that aspect of a court opinion which directly affects the outcome of the case.

hornbooks scholarly texts; a series of textbooks which review various fields of law in summary narrative form, as opposed to casebooks which are designed as primary teaching tools and include many reprints of court opinions.

I

in point relevant or pertinent.

international law the rules governing sovereign countries by their consent. The law of nations.

J

joint resolution a proposed temporary (time-oriented) law.

judgment the court's final decision regarding the rights and claims of the parties.

judicial belonging to the office of a judge as a judicial authority.

judicial review the doctrine that the clauses of the Constitution like statutes, are subject to interpretation by the courts, and, in particular, by the U.S. Supreme Court.

jump cite or pinpoint cite the page reference in a citation that directs the reader to the cited material in the case.

jur table the "Jurisdictional Table of Cases, Laws, and Rules" or the "Table of Jurisdictions Represented" in an A.L.R. annotation.

jurisdiction the power or authority of the court to hear a particular classification of case.

jurisprudence the science of law—namely, that science which has as its function the ascertainment of the principles on which legal rules are based, so as not only to classify those rules in their proper order, and to show the relation in which they stand to one another, but also to settle the manner in which new or doubtful cases should be brought under the appropriate rules.

justices a title given to judges, particularly those of the U.S. Supreme Court and state supreme courts, as well as to judges of appellate courts.

K

key number system a detailed system of classification that currently divides the law into more than 400 separate categories or topics..

L

landmark case a decision of the Supreme Court that significantly changes existing law.

law a set of rules and principles that govern any society.

law dictionary a book containing definitions of legal words and phrases.

law journal a type of legal periodical that focuses on current events or trends in the law.

law reviews periodicals edited by the top students at each law school, featuring scholarly articles by leading authorities and notes on various topics written by the law students themselves.

lawyer a legal expert.

leading case a case opinion laying out all the precedent on an issue, and decided favorably.

legal directory a list or guide typically of law firms, lawyers, or courts and their jurisdictions.

legal encyclopedia a multivolume compilation that provides in-depth coverage of every area of the law.

legal forms forms that can be used as sample documents as well as blank forms that are utilized by the court system during the course of an adjudication of an issue through the court system.

legal issue the point in dispute between two or more parties in a lawsuit.

legislative the branch of government that makes law.

legislative department the department of government whose appropriate function is the making or enactment of laws, as distinguished from the judicial department which interprets and applies the laws, and the executive department, which carries them into execution and effect.

legislative history the transcripts of the legislative debates leading up to the passage of the bill that became the law or statute.

local case the most recent case from the local jurisdiction, decided favorably.

loose-leaf service a service that publishes recently decided court decisions in loose-leaf binders, such as U.S. Law Week; provides for information to be easily updated. The loose pages are used to replace the existing pages in the notebook to ensure that the most current information is available.

M

majority opinion an opinion where more than half of the justices agree with the decision. This opinion is precedent.

mandatory authority authority that is binding upon the court considering the issue—a statute or regulation from the relevant jurisdiction that applies directly.

memorandum of law analysis and application of existing law setting forth the basics for filing a motion.

memorandum opinion a court's decision that gives the ruling, but no opinion.

microfiche a sheet of microfilm containing rows of images portraying pages of printed matter.

microfilm a film bearing a photographic record on a reduced scale.

microform a record of images in a reduced format on film.

N

newsletter a small newspaper containing news or information of interest chiefly to a specialized group.

nutshells a paperback series of the law; condensed versions of hornbooks.

O

obiter dicta an opinion voiced by a judge that has only incidental bearing on the case in question and is therefore not binding.

official reports the publication of cumulated court decisions of state or federal courts in advance sheets and bound volumes as provided by statutory authority.

on point a statute or case is "on point" if it has a direct application to the facts of a case currently before a tribunal for determination.

opinion a formal statement by a court or other adjudicative body of the legal reasons and principles for the conclusions of the court.

order the rule of law or the specific authoritative directive from the court.

ordinance a legislative act of a local government.

outline the skeleton of a legal argument, advancing from the general to the specific; a preliminary step in writing that provides a framework for the assignment.

P

parallel citation or parallel cite a citation of a case text found in two or more reporters.

per curiam a phrase used to distinguish an opinion of the whole court from an opinion written by any one judge.

periodical legal material published at regular intervals; includes magazines, journals, and law reviews.

persuasive authority a source of law or legal authority that is not binding on the court in deciding a case but may be used by the court for guidance.

petitioner name designation of a party filing an appeal.

plaintiff the party initiating the legal action.

plaintiff in error another name for the appellant in some states.

pleading and practice forms form books containing forms for use in connection with litigation.

plurality opinion a plurality opinion is the opinion from a group of justices, often in an appellate court, in which no single opinion received the support of a majority of the court. The final decision is determined by the opinion which received support from a mere plurality of the court. That is, the plurality opinion did not receive the support of half the justices, but received more support than any other opinion.

pocket veto the untimely nonreturn of a bill presented to the President, with the result that a return thereafter cannot be overridden because the houses of Congress have adjourned.

positive law a codified law passed as a statute. The law actually enacted.

practice pointers the part of an A.L.R. annotation that contains "useful hints" on how to handle a case involving the topic or point annotated.

preamble the introductory statement of legal intent, such as the "We the People" portion of the Constitution of the United States.

precedent the holding of past court decisions that are followed in future judicial cases where similar facts and legal issues are present.

prima facie accepted on its face, but not indisputable.

primary authority a primary source of law in the state or federal system that can be found in statutes, constitutions, rules of procedure, codes, and case law; the most fundamental place in which law is established.

private law a law that applies only to an individual or to a few individuals.

proclamation the act of publicly proclaiming or publishing; a formal declaration; an avowal; a public announcement giving notice of a governmental act that has been done or is to be done.

promulgated made official and public.

public law a law that applies to everyone.

Q

query a string of key terms or words used in a computer search.

R

references in an index, page numbers indicating the location in the text at which key concepts, words, or phrases appear.

regulate to direct by rule or restriction; to subject to governing principles or laws.

regulation a rule or order having force of law issued by executive authority of government.

related matters when LCP published A.L.R., the part of an A.L.R. annotation that listed similar, related annotations, along with a token sample of law review articles and treatises on the point annotated.

remand disposition in which the appellate court sends the case back to the lower court.

reporter hardbound volumes containing judicial decisions.

reports books and electronic files that collect the opinions written by judges.

respondent name designation of the party responding to an appeal.

restatement a recitation of the common law in a particular legal subject; a series of volumes authored by the American Law Institute that tell what the law in a general area is, how it is changing, and what direction the authors think this change is headed in.

reversal the act or instance of changing or setting aside a lower court's decision by a higher court.

reverse disposition in which the appellate court disagrees with the trial court.

rulemaking the power to prescribe rules of procedure to be followed under the topics and issues directed by a certain administrative agency.

S

scheme or Schematic Article Outline the detailed logical section-numbered outline of an A.L.R. annotation.

scope the part of an A.L.R. annotation that states the purported contents of the annotation.

secondary authority authority that analyzes the law, such as a treatise, encyclopedia, or law review article.

sections the subdivisions of statutes under each title of a code.

separation of powers a form of checks and balances to ensure that one branch does not become dominant.

session the sitting of a court, legislature, council, commission, and so on for the transaction of its proper business.

session law a bill or a joint resolution that has become law during a particular session of the legislature; the second format in which new statutes appear as a compilation of the slip laws.

setout the paragraph sketch of a case in an A.L.R. annotation.

shepardize using *Shepard's* verification and updating system for cases, statutes, and other legal resources.

simple resolution a proposed administrative (not legislative) statement of one house of Congress.

slip law a copy of a particular law passed during a session of the legislature; the first format in which a newly signed statute appears.

slip opinion the first format in which a judicial opinion appears.

sovereign a person, body, or state in which independent and supreme authority is vested.

stare decisis decisions from a court with substantially the same set of facts should be followed by that court and all lower courts under it.

statute edition volumes of *Shepard's* that cite cases to a particular statute.

statutes a formal written enactment of a legislative body, whether federal, state, city, or county.

statutory law derived from the Constitution in statutes enacted by the legislative branch of state or federal government.

strategy a method for making, doing, or accomplishing something.

superseding annotation an annotation that replaces another annotation.

supplementing annotation an annotation that provides additional cases on a topic or point already annotated.

syllabus a short paragraph summary in the official reporter identifying issue, procedural history, and ruling of the court.

synopsis a short paragraph summary prepared by the publisher in unofficial reporters that identifies the issue, the procedural history, and the ruling of the court in the instant case.

T

table of authorities section of the appellate brief that identifies cases, statutes, constitutional provisions, and all other primary and secondary authorities contained within the brief.

TAPP Rule the rule of thumb that legal researchers should be able to find the law they are looking for by looking up terms representing the thing, act, person, or place involved in the case.

taxonomy an organization of classifications from general to specific.

TCSL Box when LCP published A.L.R., the part of an A.L.R. annotation that listed cross-references to other units of LCP's Total Client Service Library.

textbook a book used in the study of a subject.

thesauri books of words and their synonyms.

titles the major topical divisions of a code, such as the 50 topical divisions of the United States Code.

topically by subject or by topic.

topics the major divisions in a subject outline.

Total Client Service Library LCP's marketing slogan for its national law book sets, which were thoroughly cross-referenced with each other.

treaties compacts made between two or more independent nations with a view toward the public welfare.

treatise a scholarly study of one area of the law.

treaty a nation-binding agreement with a foreign country.

trial and practice books books for use in federal and state legal practice; these often contain discussions of an area of law and provide forms needed for practice in that legal area.

U

ultrafiche sheets of microfiche that can hold up to 1,800 images per sheet.

unconstitutional not in accord with the principles set forth in the constitution of a nation or state.

uniform laws similar laws that are enacted by the legislatures of different states; intended to create uniformity in the law.

U.S. Constitution the fundamental law of the United States of America, which became the law of the land in March of 1789.

V

vacate disposition in which the appellate court voids the decision of the lower court.

veto to return to the Congress a bill without the President's signature that had been presented to the President by Congress, with the result that the bill does not become law, unless the President's return is overridden by a two-thirds vote of each house.

W

writ of certiorari granting of petition, by the U.S. Supreme Court, to review a case; request for appeal where the Court has the discretion to grant or deny it.

Index